FAITH AND
FREEDOM

PUBLISHED TO COMMEMORATE
THE ONE HUNDREDTH ANNIVERSARY
OF THE FOUNDING OF
THE EPISCOPAL THEOLOGICAL SCHOOL

FAITH AND FREEDOM

A Study of
Theological Education
and the Episcopal
Theological School

GEORGE L. BLACKMAN

The Seabury Press

New York

With gratitude and affection
this book is dedicated to
ESTHER LITTLE
and the
DEAN and FACULTY
of
THE EPISCOPAL THEOLOGICAL SCHOOL
who in the year 1948
through
THE FRANCIS LITTLE MEMORIAL FELLOWSHIP
sent a young church historian
to the University of Cambridge
to study under
NORMAN SYKES
at Emmanuel College

Preface

IN THE AUTUMN of 1964 the trustees, dean, and faculty of the Episcopal Theological School commissioned me to write a new history of the School which was to be ready in time to be published as part of the celebration of the School's one hundredth anniversary in 1967. The trustees kindly arranged to provide me with assistance in the parish three days a week throughout most of 1965 and the first quarter of 1966, thereby giving me time to conduct the required research and finish the major portion of the manuscript. They also gave me access to all material in the school archives and *carte blanche* as to what form the history was to take. Only one suggestion was made. Twenty-odd years before, the then Professor of Church History, the late James A. Muller, had been commissioned in similar fashion to write a "full and complete" history of the School for the seventy-fifth anniversary in 1942; and his account, when published a year later, carried the narrative through the successive deanships of Stone, Gray, Lawrence, Hodges, Washburn, and Dunn to the year 1943, with charm, accuracy, and remarkably skillful comprehensiveness. To attempt to duplicate it so soon again would have been both unnecessary and presumptuous. To write a sequel covering the later 1940's, 1950's, and 1960's, furthermore, seemed inadvisable. Those years were still too close, emotionally as well as chronologically, to permit the judicious assessment necessary if such a sequel was to be more than merely a bald chronicle. Instead, therefore, it was suggested that I should make it my task to attempt to set the School in historical perspective within the period which saw its foundation and subsequent development. What actually had determined the peculiarities of its administrative structure: its lay board of trustees, its independence of espiscopal or diocesan control? What distinctive features, if any, had characterized its spirit or been manifest in either the form or content of the instruction carried on within its walls? It had once been said, a touch sardonically (possibly after a more than usually euphoric alumni banquet), that the School's friends seemed to ascribe to it "every virtue except humility," while others accused it of "every vice except cowardice." Every family, including a school, may be forgiven its moments of self-congratulation—especially at anniversaries—but it makes a difference whether such moments spring from genuine insight or, instead, simply reflect a very limited experience of what other families are like. Had the School, when compared with other theological seminaries, really been *quite* so extraordinary as both enthusiastic admirers and equally enthusiastic detractors had at various times asserted? The suggestion that I concern myself with searching for answers to such questions as these was a suggestion only, not a command; but the ensuing months of reading repeatedly underlined its wisdom and attractiveness. This book is the result.

To my regret, one tempting avenue of research proved to be a blind alley. At the outset it seemed obvious that one way of determining the nature of the School's influence over the years would be to scrutinize the list of alumni carefully to see if any distinctive, developing pattern became apparent which was not duplicated elsewhere (like, for example, the influence of Virginia in the mission field). The School had published full class lists and an alumni directory annually in its catalogue until recent years, although it possessed no card file containing the complete *curriculum vitae* of each alumnus. Using successive catalogues, I promptly set out to make such a file; and when it became clear (as it did very rapidly) that if I continued the task until it was finished, I should have no time to write the book, Mrs. Gabriel Farrell volunteered to complete the file for me. Her detective's eyes soon discerned disconcerting inconsistencies in the record. Dates and entries conflicted with those listed in contemporaneous editions of *Stowe*. The listing of names was unexpectedly capricious. For many years, as it began to appear, it had been the custom of the editors to include in the class list and directory only the names of alumni, living or dead, who had pursued the active ministry throughout their careers. Names of alumni who, for whatever reason, left the ministry were expunged from both class list and directory (sometimes, it should be noted in fairness, at the request of the man himself). In subsequent editions of these latter-day diptychs, such alumni continued to "have no memorial," and were indeed "as though they had never been." Obviously no very accurate "pattern" could be safely deduced from a record which so dulcetly marked "only the sunlit hours." Nor could the corrected and amplified file be completed in time for information garnered from it to be included in this book.

The other historical material which I consulted virtually dictated the present arrangement of the book. The men who established the Episcopal Theological School had been strongly influenced by what they had learned, both through hearsay and from personal experience, about the troubled infancy of earlier theological seminaries—information not readily accessible to the modern reader, at least within the covers of a single volume. Part I, therefore, must trace the history of formal theological education in the Episcopal Church from 1804 to 1870, paying special attention to the three seminaries which had most vitally affected the shaping of the School: Virginia, Bexley Hall, and General. The peculiarities of structure and policy which had been deliberately introduced in the hope of preserving the School from the misadventures which had befallen its predecessors had shown such vitality that some had even persisted to the present day. Part II, therefore, must examine the School's original constitution and organization, relating them to what had gone before as well as to what was to come. The professors at the School had for many years enjoyed a freedom without parallel in other Episcopal seminaries of the day; and they had used that freedom boldly, constantly revising reading lists, reshaping the curriculum to meet changing needs, welcoming new disciplines—higher criticism, comparative religions, science, sociology, economics, psychology— as legitimate aids in the preparation of men for the Christian ministry. In a day, furthermore, when in many parts of the Church the presentation of the Christian faith was still shadowed by a Calvinistic emphasis on God's transcendence and on the gulf which separated him from the world which he had brought into being, the teaching at the School, while neither infected with a shallow optimism nor bemused by pantheism, emphasized the reality of God's indwelling Presence at work within his Creation. That is the theme of Part III, and from it comes the title of the book. Running through the whole is a subsidiary theme, the problems universally shared and the solutions universally tried among the various seminaries— problems so persistent, and solutions so repetitive, that I once thought of entitling the book, in deliberate echo of Dr. Allen, "The Continuity of Theological Education."

Where source material at my disposal permitted, I have sought to trace the development of the teaching at the School right up to the present; but only the first professors, who established the pattern, have received extensive treatment. To subject their successors to equally detailed examination would necessarily have involved a certain amount of repetition and greatly increased the book's length. References to persons still living or to those who have died within recent years have been kept to a minimum. Where modern professors introduced something new or exemplified traits which had also characterized their predecessors, I have noted the fact, but little more. Most of the present members of the faculty are simply listed in the footnotes. Conscious of my admiration for the men who taught me at the School in my own student days, an admiration which time has not dimmed, and hearing older alumni frequently express a similar debt to men like Angus Dun, Thayer Addison, and Norman Nash, I was tempted more than once to alter my design; but a careful reading of other histories always dissuaded me in the end. In parish histories the final chapters dealing with the incumbent and his most immediate predecessors may be the ones to which people turn first when the book is published, but they are also the very ones from which interest and value leach away most rapidly. Reading them after the passage of years, one can almost see the historian being elbowed aside, as it were, by the toastmaster. My old friends and sometime colleagues deserve a more enduring record than that.

It is a great pleasure to express my gratitude to the many people who sped the writing and publication of the book. Dean Hodges's daughter, Miss Elizabeth Hodges, the School Librarian, was indefatigable in tracking down material for me. So were Miss Beatrice Hamilton, Administrative Assistant to the Dean; Mr. Charles E. Norton, the Bursar; and Miss Gladys McCafferty, Librarian at the Diocesan House. Dr. Frank H. Stubbings, Vice-Master and Librarian of Emmanuel College, Cambridge, England, kindly admitted me to the eighteenth-century collection there to identify and hunt out early editions of books mentioned in the bishops' Course of Study of 1804. The Reverend Eugene Van Ness Goetchius and the Very Reverend Charles H. Buck, Jr., read the manuscript and the proof. Miss Martha Jane Aldridge prepared the Index. Mr. Arthur R. Buckley and his assistants at The Seabury Press gave sensitive editorial advice, and were unfailingly tactful and patient with a fledgling author.

Within the parish, the corporation and vestry of the Church of Our Saviour warmly encouraged me in my task. They would wish to join with me in expressing my thanks to the Reverend Francis Caswell, Headmaster Emeritus of the Dexter School, who as Vicar carried on a wise and friendly ministry during the months when the Rector was closeted with typewriter and manuscript; and they would also join me in expressing gratitude to my wife, who, as unofficial parish secretary in the same harried period, kept the parish wheel smoothly turning. Nor should those who enjoy these pages be unaware of the debt they owe members of the parish who, in moments of personal distress, chose to keep their suffering to themselves rather than impede the Rector in his work of authorship. By their self-sacrifice they contributed materially to its completion.

Finally, I should like to thank the present trustees, dean, and faculty of the Episcopal Theological School for giving me the privilege of becoming better acquainted with the men, both within the Episcopal Church and beyond, who in the last century furthered the development of formal theological education in this country. Research for this book has given me a deeper respect for the accomplishments of the nineteenth century and a more modest opinion of the twentieth than I had possessed before. Perhaps the readers of the book will come to share them.

GEORGE L. BLACKMAN

Brookline, Massachusetts
January, 1967

Contents

Part I

MODELS AND PRECEDENTS

1

The Beginning of Formal Theological Education in the Episcopal Church

FOR SOME FIFTEEN years after the close of the American Revolution, the Episcopal Church was too preoccupied with mere survival to worry much about proper standards either of recruitment or of training for the ministry. *Change and decay in all around I see* has been a theme congenial to gloomy men of God all the way from Noah to the leader of yesterday's conference bemoaning the obsolescence of the parish; but for American Episcopalians between 1785 and 1800 it was a statement of fact. The fervor of Dissenting Enthusiasts threatened to melt the Church away on one side. Deists and Rationalists threatened to freeze it out on the other. In Boston a number of Congregationalists from the North End, with an eye to the social prestige that went with ownership of a burial vault in King's Chapel, bought up the rights to the pews (and vaults beneath) abandoned by exiled Tories, then voted King's Chapel out of the Episcopal Church altogether, turning it Unitarian. In Virginia the Baptists led a coalition of interests in a prolonged legislative struggle to deprive the Episcopal Church of the property with which it had been endowed in the pre-Revolutionary

days of its establishment; and the longer the struggle en-
dured, the more clearly it promised eventual victory to
the Baptists. Even within its own borders the Church
was only uneasily at peace. Sometime Patriots and erst-
while Loyalists eyed one another with suspicion, and on
occasion (as in the persons of Bishops Provoost and Seabury) treated one another with studied rudeness.

It is not surprising, therefore, that for some years any
young man optimistic enough about the Church's future
to volunteer for the ministry at all was received with enthusiasm rather than with caution. There is no evidence
that the examinations prior to ordination ever acquired
quite the breathtaking simplicity of the Hebrew oral
examination for the A.B. degree at Oxford once wit-
nessed by Bishop White, in which the two candidates had
been asked one question apiece: the first, to give the English for *gabbatha;* the second, to give the Hebrew for "O
God, my God, why hast thou forsaken me?";[1] nonetheless
it was generally conceded that the times demanded (as
Bishop White put it) "a ministry, accommodated in some
instances rather to the necessities of congregations than
to what it were wished to be considered as a standard of
sufficiency."[2] This was the more readily accepted because, as the bishop was to complain when efforts to raise
the standard were ultimately made—and resisted, "there
are always some who, laying due stress on the religious
qualifications called for by the ministry, and being lauda-
bly desirous of fencing the sanctity of its character in this

[1] Bird Wilson, *Memoir of the Life of the Right Reverend William White, D.D., Bishop of the Protestant Episcopal Church in the State of Pennsylvania,* p. 39.

[2] Daniel Dana, Jr. (ed.), *Proceedings relating to the Organization of the General Theological Seminary of the Protestant Episcopal Church in the United States of America from its Inception to its final Estab-lishment in the City of New York, together with the regular Proceedings of the Board of Trustees from its Commencement, A.D. 1821 until 1838, Proceedings,* I, p. 9, *et seq.* (Hereafter cited as *Proceedings.*) Letter of Bishop White to the Rev. D. Nathaniel Bowen, D.D., of Philadelphia, July 13, 1817.

respect, entertain the opinion that it requires but a slender furniture of intellectual information." [3]

Weaknesses of Private Tutoring

Yet while laymen might be willing to have their parsons' minds as sparsely furnished as their rectories, the clergy were not so complaisant. With their fellows in other denominations they shared a common dissatisfaction with the conventional pattern of theological training. The pursuit of a course of reading in the local parson's library under his direction for a period of two or three years had one obvious merit: it was cheap. Its weakness was equally obvious; for the extensiveness or comprehensiveness of the reading course would clearly be determined almost entirely by the size of the parson's purse and the vagaries of his personal taste. [4]

Bishop White felt that his own preparation for the ministry had suffered in this respect. He had enjoyed the unusual fortune of studying under two divines, not one; but the first was too deeply immersed in the mystical writings of William Law to be easily intelligible, and the second swung from a passion for the German mystics to a bald Calvinism and back again, ending up a follower of Baron Swedenborg. [5] Neither divine wished him to read any book that expressed a point of view in opposition to his own. The result was a "singularity" in his theological education which the bishop deprecated; and when it came his turn to prepare ordinands he bent over backwards to

---

[3] *Proceedings*, I, p. 7.

[4] For the Episcopal analysis of the inadequacies of private theological education, see the report of the Rev. Dr. Gadsden of South Carolina to the General Convention of 1821. *Proceedings*, I, p. 97. A similar view, this time from a Congregationalist, is to be found in the *History of the Andover Theological Seminary*, written by the seminary's first Abbot Professor of Christian Theology, the Rev. Leonard Woods, D.D., pp. 18-19.

[5] Wilson, *Memoir*, pp. 27-30.

suggest books on every conceivable side of a question for their reading.[6]

Such exemplary moderation, however, had its drawbacks too, as the bishop's students discovered. Like most busy clergymen, Bishop White found it difficult to give much time to recitations. Many of his students were in the habit of visiting him in his study as infrequently as once a month while under his tutelage, and were subjected to no examination of any description except the one immediately before their ordination.[7] It was not enough. One admiring but discerning pupil, the Rev. Samuel Turner, later commented:

If the plan of stated recitations had been pursued with some regularity, my studies would, no doubt, have been more thorough and my knowledge more accurate. As it was, I read a great deal, but studied and thought little. To use common language, I crammed so fully that I had neither opportunity nor ability to digest anything intellectually. Consequently, my conceptions of theology as a system were vague and undefined, and my acquaintance with the several departments of divinity loose and imperfect.

    . . . At one period of the course I got together all the commentators I could procure, had them opened and arranged on a large table, and read one after the other with persevering industry until I became tired and bewildered. The result was a confused jumble of information, often inconsistent, sometimes positively contradictory; and vague, indefinite, unsatisfactory notions of meaning. I learned by experience that no clear perception of the oracles of God was attainable in this way. I was incompetent to form a judgment respecting the truth among diversified and opposing expositions, and the views of one respectable commentator were received as sufficiently satisfactory until the conflicting views of the next in order suggested difficulties that weakened or destroyed the

---

[6] *Autobiography of the Rev. Samuel H. Turner, D.D., Late Professor of Biblical Learning and the Interpretation of Scripture in the General Theological Seminary of the Protestant Episcopal Church in the United States of America,* p. 23. (Hereafter cited as Turner, *Autobiography.*)

[7] Turner, *Autobiography,* p. 22.

impressions which had been made by the former. To which I add that in many cases none of them gave satisfactory expositions. With the principles of sound criticism and interpretation I had no acquaintance. The idea of settling the true text of the Bible by referring to written authorities of manuscripts, versions, and quotations, a thousand years or more older than the invention of printing, had never occurred to me.[8]

Samuel Turner was one of the most distinguished scholars in the Church of his day, and, as professor in the General Theological Seminary, intimately connected with theological education most of his life. If he found his training bewildering, it is safe to assume that many of his colleagues would have confessed themselves utterly lost. So might the Ethiopian eunuch have lifted up his voice had his call for help in interpreting Isaiah been answered not just by Philip but by "above five hundred of the brethren at once." A familiar note in the professor's plaint, even after more than a century of experiment with different methods of theological education, suggests that the problem is perhaps less susceptible of solution by the juggling of curricula and changes in teaching methods than Dr. Turner hoped; but when dissatisfaction is widespread almost any change has the appearance of improvement—for the moment. So it was in the 1800's.

The Bishops' Course of Study of 1804

The obvious first step in improving the quality of theological preparation was to set a standard by publishing a suggested course of study that would have the Church's authority behind it. The General Convention proposed this in 1801, and the House of Bishops duly established such a course at the General Convention of 1804.

The student who followed the plan prescribed was directed to begin his studies with reading on the evidences

---

[8] *Ibid.,* pp. 27-28.

of the truth of Christianity as revealed in history and the natural order. At the head of the list was the classic apologetical manual written by the Dutch jurist and theologian Hugo Grotius in the first half of the seventeenth century: *De veritate religionis christianae*. An English translation by Simon Patrick, one of the founders of the Society for Promoting Christian Knowledge, had been published in 1680; but an edition more likely to be available to American readers was the 1711 translation by John Clarke, D.D., which had been frequently reprinted. Also recommended were six other books: *The Certainty and Reasonableness of Christianity*, by Robert Jenkin (pub. 1715); the *View of the Evidences of Christianity*, by Archdeacon Paley (1743-1805); the *Method with the Jews and Deists*, written by the Nonjuror Charles Leslie (1650-1722); the *Origines Sacrae* of Bishop Stillingfleet (1635-1699); the famous *Analogy* of Bishop Butler (1692-1752); and the *View of the Principal Deistical Writers*, written by the Nonconformist divine Dr. John Leland (1691-1766). In addition, the student was advised to familiarize himself with the works of the Deists themselves.

That completed, the next step was the study of the Scriptures with the aid of approved commentaries. For the Old Testament, the student was referred to the series begun by Simon Patrick (1626-1707) and continued with the publication between 1714 and 1725 of a commentary on the Prophets written by William Lowth, D.D. (1660-1732). For the New Testament, there was more of a choice. The student could use the annotated paraphrase written by that gentlest of the Laudians, Henry Hammond (1605-1660), or the commentary written by one of Jonathan Edwards's most articulate English opponents, Daniel Whitby (1638-1726), or (with an allowance for the taint of Nonconformity in his point of view) the commentary by Whitby's admirer and Isaac Watts's protégé: *The Family Expositor* of Dr. Philip Doddridge

(1702-1751). For more detailed study of the "design" of
the various books, the bishops recommended *The Canon
of Scripture,* by the French critic, the Oratorian Richard
Simon (1638-1712), along with *The Sacred Interpreter,*
by Jeremy Collier (1650-1726), the *Key to the Old Testament,* by Robert Gray (1762-1834), the Bampton Lecturer for 1796, and the *Key to the New Testament,* by
Thomas Percy (1729-1811), better known to a later generation as the editor of "Percy's Reliques." Where the
student might be expected to bog down—as in the study
of Leviticus or the more esoteric passages of the Prophets
—he was urged to consult the simplified schematization
worked out by Bishop Thomas Kidder (1633-1703) in his
commentary on the Pentateuch (pub. 1694), or Bishop
Thomas Newton's ingenious *Dissertation on the Prophe-
cies, which have been remarkably fulfilled, and are at this
time being fulfilled* (first pub. 1754). For the intertesta-
mental period, *The Old and New Testament Connected
in the History of the Jews,* by the Orientalist Humphrey
Prideaux (1648-1724), was suggested, along with the sequel
by Samuel Shuckford (1694-1754), in which the "connection" was extended clear back to the Creation. In further-
ing his study of the New Testament, the student was told
to read a harmony of the Gospels, choosing between one
published in 1756 by a Scot, James MacKnight (1721-
1800), and one published in 1778 by William Newcome
(1729-1800), the future Archbishop of Armagh, in which
the inclusion of some textual readings of LeClerc and
Wetstein would put the student in touch with the fruits
of Continental scholarship. (A harmony in English, based
on Newcome, had been published in 1802.) And before
beginning a detailed study of the Gospels, he was to read
the *Introductory Dissertations on the New Testament,*
by Hume's shrewd adversary Dr. George Campbell (1719-
1796), the Aberdonian divine. On the resurrection, he was
to study either Gilbert West's *Observations on the Resur-*

rection (pub. 1747) or Bishop Sherlock's *Trial of the Witnesses* (pub. 1729)—both of which were detailed vindications of the credibility of the resurrection narratives (the latter in the manner of a lawyer pleading a case in court).

Church history was the next field of study. Here the student was advised to read Eusebius and the Apostolic Fathers, using, if necessary, the translation prepared by Archbishop Wake (1657-1737), and *The Lives of the Apostles* and *Lives of the Fathers,* by the learned William Cave (1637-1713). Then he was to examine two important subjects of controversy: the divinity of Christ, and episcopacy. For the first he was to resort to the apologetical writings of Bishop Bull (1634-1710), Bishop Horsley (1733-1806), and Charles Leslie. For the second he was to read Hooker's *Ecclesiastical Polity,* the *Discourse of Church Government* written by Archbishop Potter (1674?-1747) while chaplain to Tenison, and the *Guide to the Church,* a scheme for reunion put forward by the Archdeacon of Salisbury, Charles Daubeny (1745-1827). He was also to consult the *Enquiry into the Constitution, Discipline, Unity and Worship of the Primitive Church,* published in 1691 by Peter King (1669-1734), the future Lord Chancellor, together with a corrective for King's congregationalist analysis, the *Original Draught of the Primitive Church,* by the Nonjuror William Sclater (published in 1717, and thereafter frequently reprinted in conjunction with the *Enquiry* in subsequent editions). The basic history text was the *Ecclesiastical History* of Johann Lorenz von Mosheim (1693-1755), onetime chancellor of the University of Göttingen—a work that had won the praise of Gibbon. This was to be supplemented by the epitomes of mediaeval writers contained in the twenty-volume ecclesiastical history of the French historian Claude Fleury (1640-1723). For the great controversy over papal supremacy the student was referred to Chillingworth's *Religion of Protestants a Safe Way to Salva-*

tion (frequently reprinted since its first appearance in 1638), the mastery *Treatise of the Pope's Supremacy* by Isaac Barrow (1630-1677), and the *History of the Council of Trent* by Paul V's determined opponent, the Venetian Professor of Philosophy Paolo Sarpi (1552-1623). At length, approaching nearer home, he was to read Jeremy Collier's *History of the Church of England* (pub. 1708-1714), referring to Hooker and the "London cases" for a clearer understanding of the dispute with the Puritans.

Only when his studies of scripture and church history had been completed was the student to begin the systematic study of theology (or "Divinity," as it was then called). Two basic texts were recommended: the *Exposition of the Creed* by Bishop Pearson (1612-1686), and the *Exposition of the Thirty-Nine Articles* by Bishop Burnet (1643-1715). Following these the student was to turn to a "larger system," the *Complete Body of Divinity in Five Parts from the Best Ancient and Modern Writers,* compiled in 1729 by Thomas Stackhouse (1677-1752). He was also referred to two more contemporary works: a manual for ordination that was to go through twelve editions by 1818, the *Elements of Christian Theology,* by George Pretyman Tomline, Bishop of Lincoln (1750-1827); and *The Scholar Armed against the Errors of the Time,* a collection of tracts "on the principles and evidences of Christianity, the constitution of the Church, and the Authority of Civil Government" published in 1795. The latter consisted principally of treatises by Charles Leslie (including his *Method,* which had already been cited once in the bishops' list), Bishop Horne of Norwich (1730-1792), and some letters written by William Law to Bishop Hoadly at the time of the Bangorian controversy (1717-18). It was intended to provide its readers with a defense against the attacks of Thomas Paine, Voltaire, and "novels . . . written to insinuate under that disguise the errors of heresy and infidelity: as people, if they were to poison children, would mix arsenic with their sugar plums." [9]

In liturgics the student was referred to Charles Wheatly's *The Church of England Man's Companion, or a Rational Illustration of the Harmony . . . and Usefulness of the Book of Common Prayer* (pub. 1710), or to an edition of the English Book of Common Prayer, with preface and notes by the Hebraist, lawyer, and King's printer John Reeves, which had been published in 1801.

On the "duties of the pastoral office" Chrysostom on *The Priesthood* was suggested, along with Bishop Burnet's *Discourse on Pastoral Care,* and the *Parochialia* of Thomas Wilson (1663-1755), the exemplary Bishop of Sodor and Man. For training in homiletics the student was urged to read the sermons of a number of eighteenth century bishops—Zachary Pearce, George Horne, Beilby Porteus, and Samuel Seabury—together with the tracts of Bishop Gibson (1669-1748), the *Companion to the Festivals and Fasts of the Church Year,* by Robert Nelson (1656-1715); Jeremy Taylor's classic *Holy Living* and *Holy Dying;* the *Life of God in the Soul of Man,* by the Scottish Episcopalian Henry Scougal (1650-1678); and the *Discourses on Death, Judgment, a Future State,* and *on Providence,* by the famous English preacher William Sherlock (1641-1707). The student was to use the standard work on *Ecclesiastical Law* published in 1760 by Richard Burn, chancellor of the Diocese of Carlisle, as the basis for his study of polity and canon law, consulting as well appropriate passages in the writings—some apologetical, some historical—of Daubeny, Prideaux, Clarke, Cudworth (1617-1688), Echard (1670?-1730), and Archbishops Tillotson (1630-1694) and Secker (1693-1768).

The bishops were aware that the amount of reading prescribed in the list was too much for most students to manage in the time available. Their purpose was to suggest an ideal, and possibly—as is customary among com-

---

[9] *The Scholar Armed against the Errors of the Time,* I, p. ii.

pilers of book lists—to provide a number of choices to
choose from should some of the titles prove difficult to
find. As a minimum, they were agreed to require familiarity only with Paley, Hooker, Mosheim, Stackhouse, and
Reeves (hardly a demanding list), while strongly implying
that where Scripture was concerned the student would do
well to cut no corners if he wished to meet the requirements.

It is generally supposed that Bishop White drew up the
course of study, just as he was the author of other papers
published by the House of Bishops in that period. The
task was one for which he was eminently suited by his
experience in training ordinands, his wide reading, his
acquaintance among English divines, and his habit of
browsing in Philadelphia bookshops. He knew what ordinands ought to read and what was available. And certainly the tactful inclusion of Bishop Seabury's sermons
among those recommended, coupled with the omission of
any reference to his own, seems a characteristic touch. But
whether the list was entirely White's composition or not, it
was a notably solid achievement. There was nothing eccentric or novel about it. Biographical or publication
dates have been appended to show how few of the books
recommended were really new; many of them in 1804
might have been called venerable. A survey of the letters, memoirs, and biographies of English clerics, both
Anglican and Nonconformist, indicates that a large number of the titles must already have been considered staple
fare for divinity students for well over half a century,
while the casual way in which both titles and authors are
mentioned in the text of the course of study itself suggests that they were expected to be equally familiar to the
American clergy who would henceforth be using the
course as a guide. Most of the books had gone through
several printings by 1804, and fresh editions were to continue to appear on both sides of the Atlantic for another

fifty years. In fact the course was to stand the test of time with a strength that seems remarkable today, when text-books in high favor in one decade are so frequently dis-carded with contumely in the next. When one of the first of domestic (as opposed to missionary) English the-ological training colleges was founded at Chichester in 1839, its reading list closely resembled the one published thirty-five years before by the American bishops. In the late 1860's some of the books were still required reading at Virginia, General, and the Episcopal Theological School; and although most of them were dropped in the course of the next twenty years (at least at ETS), a num-ber remained on the list at General as late as 1892. The bishops themselves made no material alterations in the list whatever until 1889.

Apart from a few obvious classics, however, few of the books would be of interest now to any save antiquaries; and many of the authors have dwindled to dry little en-tries in the *Dictionary of National Biography*. Where an eighteenth-century library with a pronounced ecclesiasti-cal flavor has survived intact—as at Emmanuel College, Cambridge—the volumes are still readily available; but with few exceptions they have disappeared from the shelves of American theological school libraries. The sec-ond half of the nineteenth century either turned atten-tion away from the questions answered with such pains-taking ingenuity in the sermons, tracts, and treatises rec-ommended in 1804, or else led men to formulate them in very different terms. The eminently practical compendia of "ancient and modern writers"—like that of Stackhouse —were displaced by such far more complete collections as the Library of Ante-Nicene and Nicene Fathers or the publications of the Parker Society. Between 1850 and 1890 German textbooks in theology, history, and biblical criticism supplanted their English predecessors. Only in the Library of Anglo-Catholic Theology were these Anglican divines to renew their youth; and even there the interest of the editors waned rapidly with the dawn of the Augustan Age.

Nonetheless, despite their antique appearance, these largely forgotten books occasionally sound an oddly contemporary note. Their authors, so many of whom were English bishops, may have affected a prose style that had all the majesty and aplomb that we associate with Gibbon; but they saw themselves not as serenely pompous prelates but rather as conscientious guardians of a demoralized remnant hard beset on every side by an aggressively unbelieving world. Long before Matthew Arnold, their ears had already picked up the Tide of Faith's "long, withdrawing roar." Consequently they were tireless in diagnosis and debate, but had—as Dr. Turner discovered to his disappointment—less heart for straightforward exposition or positive and constructive thought. In that they closely resemble some of the most "modern" of their twentieth-century successors.

Establishing a "General Seminary"

With the approved course of study in hand, the next step in the improvement of theological education was clearly to set up a seminary with a full-time faculty, where formal instruction in accordance with the prescribed curriculum could be given. It was a step on which all were agreed; but a decade and a half was to pass before it was actually taken.

Before that, the bishops tried to form tutoring schools of a sort, taking their candidates to live with them in their episcopal residences, giving them opportunities for some supervised pastoral work as well as for reading. The expedient had a long tradition behind it. St. Augustine had used it with success in turbulent Hippo; and it had been commended to the equally storm-tossed Elizabethan bishops in the abortive *Reformatio Legum Ecclesiasticarum*.

In early-nineteenth-century America it had very practical attractions. It kept candidates at home, safe from the blandishments of other dioceses (a point on which western bishops were always sensitive). It kept instruction firmly in the bishop's hands (a prospect that appealed strongly to Bishop Hobart). It made for a placidly monochromatic establishment, ecclesiastically speaking, in which the dissension that sometimes set one diocese against another and ruffled the waters at meetings of the General Convention might well be avoided (a possibility that delighted Bishop White). Nor did such a prospect appeal to bishops alone. In several of the dioceses laymen and parsons banded together to organize societies whose purpose was to foster theological education by supplementing the stipend of a talented teacher so that he could spend more time in teaching and less in parish work, and by paying part of the expenses of the men who studied under him. It was from such a society in Virginia that the seminary in Alexandria stemmed. In fact there was really only one objection to the attractive scheme of multiplying diocesan seminaries in this fashion, but that one proved decisive. It was money.

In the 1800's a capital fund of $100,000 was generally considered the minimum required to establish a theological school on a sound financial footing. Almost precisely that sum started Andover on its way in 1808. But Andover owed its origin in large part to the rage provoked among New England Congregationalists by Harvard's appointment of a Unitarian as Hollis Professor of Divinity. Partisan controversy had not yet raised the temperatures of Episcopalians to anything like such a pitch of feverish generosity. It was thought that possibly all the dioceses acting together might manage to raise $60,000 to found (precariously) one centrally located seminary that could serve the general Church; but for every diocese that wanted one to launch a fund drive for $100,000 to establish a seminary of its own was out of the question. In the entire Church there were only 75 candidates to be "parcelled out." An official proposal was made by the South Carolina delegation at the General Convention of 1814; and although Bishop Hobart was cool and Bishop White jittery, the General Convention of 1817 decisively approved the foundation of such a general theological seminary in New York, appointing a committee to put its decision into effect. The committee took two years to do so; but at length in 1819 the two first professors of the new school, the Rev. Samuel Jarvis and the Rev. Samuel Turner, began holding classes in what was little more than a vestibule off the gallery in St. Paul's Church. The Church's program of formal theological training was underway.

The first year, however, was anything but encouraging. Not that the students were lacking in spirit. One was George Washington Doane, future Bishop of New Jersey, who was to become one of the most adroit ecclesiastical wire-pullers of his time; another was Manton Eastburn, future Bishop of Massachusetts, who was not. Nor was the diminutive faculty undistinguished. Jarvis was known to have strong convictions about the necessity of a demanding academic preparation for the ministry; and Turner had already earned a reputation as a teacher in Philadelphia. But Bishop Hobart virtually ignored the seminary's existence, and the rest of his diocese discreetly followed his example. There was no official opening ceremony. Neither of the professors was invited to give the formal inaugural lecture customary in that day. Almost no one took any notice of them at all.[10] Professor Turner in time became rather short with New York friends who, meeting him in the street that winter, expressed voluble surprise and asked why he wasn't home in Philadelphia where he belonged.[11] Professor Jarvis had nursed doubts about the

[10] Turner, *Autobiography,* p. 84.
[11] *Ibid.,* p. 86.

project from the first (partly, perhaps, because Boston friends had been constantly pressing him to move there, even promising to build a new church for him if he would come[12]); and when the school's finance committee cut his salary from $3,000 to $2,500, his doubts crystallized. He resigned and went to Boston to become the first rector of St. Paul's Church.

To add to the demoralization, in the first months of its existence the school was forced to change its location twice. It was pushed out of St. Paul's by the cold (there was no stove) and out of St. John's by the sexton (there was a stove, but he cut off the fuel supply). By the end of the winter it had been reduced to meeting in the rooms of a seminary for young ladies run by one of the theological students.

It is not entirely surprising, therefore, that when the school's Board of Directors met in June, 1820, to review the seminary's first dismal months, it voted to desert New York altogether and move to New Haven. As one of the members later recalled the arguments in favor of the decision,

. . . the attention of the General Convention was directed to Connecticut by motives of economy, by the habits of order, industry, and good morals, by which the people of New England are characterized, by the belief that a favorable charter could be obtained in that state . . . and finally by the circumstance that the Bishop of Connecticut was unincumbered with a parochial charge, and therefore, could bestow on the Seminary a more than ordinary degree of fostering care. . . . New Haven was selected chiefly because it was the seat of one of the first colleges of our country.[13]

In fact, the board estimated that the operating expenses of the seminary would be only half what they had

---

[12] *Ibid.*, p. 90.
[13] *Proceedings*, I, p. 104.

been in New York. This was an important consideration as financial support for the venture, while broad in base, had been skimpy at best. Far too much of it had come in in the canny form of pledges that were not to be paid until the entire capital of $60,000 had been raised.

At the same time the directors were confident that New Haven would provide the students with the desired polish even more satisfactorily than New York. "It is," they pointed out, "equally removed from the expensive extravagances of a large city, and the vulgar manners of an obscure village." [14]

Accordingly, on September 13, 1820, the seminary reopened in New Haven. Professor Turner signalized the official beginning of its second academic year with a discourse which was to set the tone for the term, expatiating on the need for a ministry that was at once pious and learned, versed in the twin disciplines of biblical criticism (to which he appended theology) and ecclesiastical history (to which pastoral skill, apologetics, and polity were related). The professor's own passion for textual criticism was indirectly revealed when he confessed that it was unwise to encourage the student to enter too deeply into such investigations as "the probability must be acknowledged, that, occasionally, a fondness for critical disquisition might so predominate in the mind, as to produce a distaste for parochial duties." [15] This distaste he hastened to reprove, firmly stating that preparation for pastoral duties was "the ultimate object of the study of theology in this institution." He ended with a peroration in which echoes still lingered of the defensive and apologetical note struck in so many of the texts recommended by the bish-

---

[14] *Ibid.,* p. 36.
[15] A précis of the sermon is contained in Turner, *Autobiography,* pp. 101-102. The following quotations are taken from the text of the printed version of the sermon: *Introductory Discourse Delivered at New Haven at the Opening of the Theological Seminary of the Protestant Episcopal Church, September 13, 1820*

ops in 1804, affirming that the seminary's design was to
"so train the pious youth . . . that, being well grounded
in the faith he professes to teach, he may be able to repel
the attacks of the infidel, to remove the doubts of the
wavering, and to give instruction to the ignorant. In a
word, that being furnished with all necessary armour,
intellectual and spiritual, he may be able to defend the
citadel of God."

The first term was to run from the first Thursday in
September to the second Thursday in December. The
students then dispersed to the schools where most of them
had to earn a living as teachers, to work until the second
Thursday in March, when they reassembled in New
Haven for the second term that ran until the last Thursday in June. Reflecting either Bishop White's fear of needless controversy or, possibly, one year's experience of having Doane and Eastburn together in the same class, a rule
was made that students would be liable for dismissal who
"persist in the promulgation of opinions tending to disturb the harmony of the Protestant Episcopal Church." [16]
The rule setting forth a second ground of expulsion, however, can hardly be blamed on Eastburn at any rate: "gross
levity."

The General Theological Seminary

A year later, probably to everyone's surprise, the seminary
was back in New York. (It no doubt came as a relief to
Professor Turner, who had discovered that Connecticut
churches were even colder than New York ones.)[17] In
March, 1821, Jacob Sherred of that city, a vestryman of
Trinity Church, died leaving to a "theological seminary
in New York" an estate estimated at $60,000. To this the

---

[16] *Proceedings*, I, p. 40. The rule was inserted when it was proposed to
throw the seminary open to students from other denominations. The
proposal was subsequently withdrawn. Turner, *Autobiography*, p. 99.
[17] Turner, *Autobiography*, p. 105.

New Haven seminary had a claim as it had been operating in New York at the time the will had been originally drawn. On the other hand, Bishop Hobart had taken immediate advantage of its move to Connecticut to set about organizing the diocesan seminary he had wanted all along; and by the time Mr. Sherred died, the bishop's seminary had been about to open. At the regular session of the diocesan convention shortly thereafter he was able to present the opinions of several lawyers asserting that the new seminary had a stronger claim to the Sherred legacy than did the old.[18] The happiest solution to this conflict of claims was obviously to resolve the dispute by combining the seminaries, an expedient which Bishop Hobart himself had the Solomonic wisdom to suggest; and this was at length effected, after much working out of complicated bylaws, at a special meeting of the General Convention held at the beginning of November.

As might have been expected with a seminary that was to satisfy both a forceful diocesan and the Church at large, the organization of the governing board was a ponderous work of legal ingenuity. The trustees of the new combined school were to be the bishops—all of them—together with clerical and lay trustees nominated by each of the several dioceses and elected by the General Convention in the following proportions: one for each diocese, and one additional trustee for every eight clergymen and for every $2,000 contributed up to $10,000, and thereafter one for every $10,000 contributed. This enormous board was to meet once or twice a year, as well as at the time of meetings of the General Convention, to which it was to submit a report. The rest of the time its duties were delegated, so far as administration went, to an executive board made up principally of New Yorkers. Although reminiscent of *Alice in Wonderland* ("all have won, and

---

[18] *Proceedings,* I, pp. 54-59.

all shall have prizes"), it worked reasonably well in placid times; but in times of controversy (and the nineteenth century was unfortunately to produce plenty of these), it proved exasperatingly pompous and cumbersome.

The two faculties were united in a fashion that was much to Bishop Hobart's credit. The chair of Systematic Divinity, which the bishop had originally marked out for himself, he yielded to the Rev. Bird Wilson of the New Haven establishment. This was a notable gesture of friendship; for Wilson, a former lawyer, while he shared with Hobart a common admiration and affection for their old master, Bishop White (Wilson was to write a memoir of the bishop after his death), shared little else. Hobart could have little sympathy with the Philadelphian's middle-of-the-road theological opinions. Another concession was to make the Rev. Samuel Turner (whose theology was equally uncongenial to the bishop) the professor of biblical learning and the interpretation of scripture. This post had originally been intended for Clement Moore, the Hebraist, son of Bishop Moore, who had generously presented the seminary with sixty-two lots of potentially valuable land near his home on the city's edge. He was appointed professor of Hebrew instead. Hobart himself became professor of pastoral theology and pulpit eloquence; Benjamin Onderdonk, professor of church history and polity; Gulian Verplanck, a New York lawyer and seminary trustee, professor of the evidences of revealed religion; and the Rev. Henry J. Feltus, librarian. Wilson and Turner were the only full-time teachers. They were each paid $1,500 a year;[19] Moore received $750, and Feltus $150. The rest provided their services *gratis*. The professors in their various departments were to use only textbooks recommended in the bishops' course of study or

---

[19] Low funds sometimes forced the trustees to reduce these salaries, as in 1828 when one was cut to $1,250, the other to $1,000. *Proceedings*, I, p. 292.

others which the faculty had approved as a whole. There
was no provision for a dean or other administrative head.
The Bishop of New York (successively Hobart and Onderdonk) presided over faculty meetings.

The reorganized seminary—now for the first time officially christened the "General Theological Seminary"—
opened once more on March 11, 1822, with a service in
Trinity Church, New York. This time the keynote address was given by Bishop Hobart. It bore his characteristic touch. In New Haven Professor Turner had emphasized that ministers must be pious and learned. In
New York Bishop Hobart added that they must also be
orthodox and practical. On the latter he laid particular
stress:

Practical must the minister be in the judicious application of
his talents and knowledge to the discharge of his *parochial*
duties—in establishing the religious principles of the young,
by catechetical lecturing and instruction—in dispensing to the
sick and the afflicted the warnings and the consolations with
which his Master has charged him—in removing the doubts of
the wavering, answering the cavils of the sceptical, correcting
the errors of the uninformed or the perverse, admonishing the
careless and the secure, guarding the weak, and fortifying the
timid—and in administering to the edification and the comfort
of all, according to their respective circumstances, by pastoral
and friendly conversation.

Learning and orthodoxy may enable him with whom the
charge of the sacred oracles is committed, to prove their divine
origin, to illustrate and to explain their meaning, to unfold
their hidden beauties, to exhibit, and to maintain, and to vin-
dicate their doctrines against all the objections with which
they may be assailed by the pride and power of human talent,
or the corrupt passions of the human heart. And happy the
Church whose endowments, while they furnish the means of
thus providing learned and orthodox champions of the Christian faith, afford to them the leisure uninterruptedly and
solely to devote themselves to the task of defending its momen-

tous truths. But it is only under ministers thus *practical* that learning, and orthodoxy, and piety will be instrumental in enlarging the fold of Christ, and in bringing the flock committed to the Christian pastor to that "ripeness and perfectness of age in Christ, so that there be no place left among them for error in religion or for viciousness of life." And it can scarcely be necessary to mention, that in the peculiar circumstances of our own country, where an enterprising population advances into the uncultivated wilds far beyond the provisions that exist for their religious instruction, a practical ministry must appear of peculiar and indispensable importance.[20]

In 1823 the first class graduated. In 1824 it was decided to move the seminary yet again, but this time only uptown to the suburban lots that Dr. Moore had given it. In 1825 the cornerstone of the first seminary building was laid by Bishop White.[21] When it was finished, Professor Turner moved into one wing; and the remainder was divided up into classrooms, a library (which also served for a chapel), and rooms for students. Although there was to be talk of other moves now and again in later years as the surrounding fields and apple orchards were replaced by row houses and paved streets, the seminary was there to stay.

In the same period two other seminaries in the United States found homes that were to be permanent. Virginia had begun classes in Alexandria in 1823 under the direction of the Rev. Reuel Keith; and in 1827 moved some three miles out of the town to the hill sloping down to the Potomac where it stands today. In Ohio Bishop Chase had started a seminary at his farm in Worthington in 1825; and in 1828 moved it to its permanent location on the hill which he had named Gambier in honor of the most generous benefactor of the infant institution. With

---

[20] John Henry Hobart, *An Introductory Address on the Occasion of the Opening of the General Theological Seminary*, New York, 1822.
[21] *Proceedings*, I, p. 227*ff.*

Virginia and Kenyon (or, more accurately, that part of Kenyon which was later to be renamed Bexley Hall) set each on its hill, and General settled in its hollow, theological education for Episcopalians in the United States may be said to have reached "the end of its beginning."

¤ 2

Virginia: Evangelical Eden,

ALTHOUGH they had been launched with general approval, the seminaries were to enjoy a somewhat tenuous, not to say precarious, existence for another fifty years. More than once strenuous efforts were required just to keep them afloat. Sometimes it was family rows that set them rocking, like the ecclesiastical or administrative quarrels that seriously damaged General and almost destroyed Kenyon. Sometimes they were shaken by more general calamity: financial panic or war. Between 1861 and 1865, for example, Kenyon lost one of the most effective of its early presidents, a casualty of the war, and saw its student body shrink to half its size. General, already darkly suspected of cherishing an indiscreet *tendre* for the Pope, fell under suspicion of entertaining an even more indiscreet sympathy for Jefferson Davis.[1] And Virginia was forced to close its doors and abandon its Hill altogether until war

---

[1] Professor Mahan's resignation in 1864 to accept the rectorship of St. Paul's, Baltimore, was said to have been motivated partly by his Southern sympathies. W. F. Brand, *Life of William Rollinson Whittingham*, Vol. II, p. 51. At a meeting of the trustees October 26, 1864, notice was given of a motion to require a "loyalty oath"—to the U.S.A. and to the Episcopal Church—at the seminary. *Proceedings*, III (1855-65), p. 650.

was over. All three seminaries, furthermore, found that erecting the buildings they needed, paying teachers, and meeting other expenses subjected their resources to constant and debilitating strain. Attempts to increase their funds were both ingenious and unremitting; but what they brought in was all too quickly swallowed up by new needs or fresh catastrophes.

Budgets and Bank Accounts

The most successful of the three in balancing its budget was Virginia, although its initial endowment was scanty. This is principally because it had from the beginning the help of an active Education Society which enjoyed increasingly widespread support, at first within the state itself, and then all along the Atlantic seaboard as the seminary attracted the affections and loyalty of eastern Evangelicals to whom General's Tractarian atmosphere was distasteful. Encouraged assiduously by Bishop Meade, many Virginia Episcopalians made subscriptions of anything from five dollars to two hundred dollars apiece to support the society's work.[2] These were duly collected by authorized agents and turned in to the society after the deduction of personal expenses. (One agent cannily began his collecting within walking distance of the seminary, bought a horse with the first receipts, and then—having thus provided himself with transportation—proceeded to cover the rest of the state.) Even the women were organized. In January, 1824, a "Sewing Society of the Protestant Episcopal Church in Baltimore" was formed, its members sending the profits gained from the sale of their handiwork to swell the society's funds;[3] and by 1832

---

[2] Two early lists of subscribers taken from Diocesan Convention Journals are printed in the Centennial *History of the Theological Seminary in Virginia and Its Historical Background,* edited by W. A. R. Goodwin, D.D., II, pp. 222-231. (Hereafter cited as *Virginia Seminary.*)

[3] *Virginia Seminary,* I, p. 143.

twenty-seven auxiliaries on the same pattern had been organized, some as far away as Brooklyn, New York, and Beaufort, South Carolina.[4] The contributions from all these sources enabled the society to function for years as virtually the seminary's commissariat and treasury department. It helped to cover the cost of the students' board, bought firewood, coal, milk, and brooms, whitewashed and repaired the buildings, built houses for the professors as the faculty expanded, and paid the janitor, the matron, the servants, and, either in whole or in part, even the professors themselves.[5] The responsibility for these budgetary decisions was vested in a large board of officers that included a president (usually the bishop), four vice-presidents, a secretary and treasurer, and fifteen clerical and fifteen lay managers. The seminary professors always served on the Board of Managers; and so did several of the clergymen or laymen who served as well on the seminary's Board of Trustees. But the managers were not limited to men near at hand. Some came from Philadelphia, New York, Providence, and even as far north as Pittsfield, Massachusetts.[6]

With the society assuming so much of the financial burden, the seminary trustees themselves were free to put a little money aside each year to build up their own invested funds. These totalled $11,000 in 1829, $20,000 in 1840. In the mid-1850's there was a capital funds drive handsomely supported by Philadelphians and New Yorkers; and by 1860 the endowment was close to $100,000. But then came the war. The seminary's funds were all in Virginia banks; and, along with other Confederate investments, they simply melted away. By the war's end nothing was left. The seminary buildings had been preserved,

---

[4] *Ibid.*

[5] *Ibid.*, p. 145.

[6] Transcript of Minutes of the Education Society 1818-42. *Virginia Seminary*, II, Appendix.

thanks to being used as a military hospital by the Union forces; but they had been roughly treated. All the furnishings had been either stolen or destroyed except for the seminary library, which had been carefully packed away. Only the happy discovery of the unpaid portion of a legacy lying in a Baltimore bank where it had been frozen in 1861 made it possible to reopen the seminary on the Hill in 1865.

Thereafter energetic attempts were made to improve the seminary's financial position. In these, for the first time, the faculty played a more conspicuous part than the trustees. Particularly active was one of the two professors surviving from prewar days, Dr. William Sparrow, who was appointed dean in 1868. Fund-raising had hitherto been exclusively the responsibility of the trustees; but it was at their urging that Dr. Sparrow became what he called "beggar-general for the Institution," [7] and a shrewd move it proved. The trustees' links were all with the Diocese of Virginia—and Virginian pockets were empty. Dr. Sparrow, on the other hand, was a Massachusetts man by birth, an Irishman by descent and education, an Ohioan by adoption, and enjoyed a national reputation in Evangelical circles. In the North he could rely for help on friends like Heman Dyer, an associate from Ohio days who had entrée to the offices of J. P. Morgan and of Jay Cooke, the Civil War financier. He could also appeal to the sympathies of former pupils—Edwin M. Stanton, the Secretary of War (another link with the years in Ohio), Henry Codman Potter and Phillips Brooks. Dr. Sparrow was a shy man; but so prestigious an array of associations gave him a *charisma* that was virtually irresistible. When the trustees, only twelve years after the war (and two years after Dr. Sparrow's death), could report that the endow-

---

[7] Cornelius Walker, *The Life and Correspondence of Rev. William Sparrow, D.D.* Sparrow to the Rev. John Hubbard, Nov. 27, 1865, p. 270.

ment had grown to nearly $200,000, they knew that they had him to thank for a large part of it.

Grace Under Pressure

During all these years the relationship between trustees and faculty continued unruffled. One sign of this is the faculty's willingness to continue with the uncongenial task of fund-raising even after the financial strain had eased. Another is the infrequency of new faculty appointments. Between 1842 and 1866 no appointments were made at all. When men joined the faculty on the Hill, they tended to stay there until they died or retired. Dr. Packard was an active presence on the Hill as successively professor, dean, and professor emeritus for sixty-six years—a reign even longer than Queen Victoria's. Dr. Sparrow taught at the seminary for thirty-three years, and refused repeated invitations elsewhere, including one to Trinity Church, Boston, at nearly three times his seminary salary. Dr. Walker taught at Virginia for thirty-two years; Dr. Keith for twenty-one, Dr. May for nineteen. Not until 1898 did a professor resign because he was not in entire sympathy with seminary policies, and then only after more than a decade of teaching on the Hill.

In this respect Virginia was unusually fortunate, and possibly unique. What is even more remarkable, its freedom from friction does not appear to have been due to any striking originality in organization or administration; for in both spheres the seminary was relatively conventional. Minute-books are notoriously impassive guides to the past; nonetheless, those at Virginia suggest that there were on the Hill the same seeds of potential discord that germinated so fruitfully at General and at Kenyon, had anyone wished to cultivate them.

One possible source of trouble was the bishop. The Bishop of Virginia was *ex officio* president of the Board of Trustees, and in the early years presided at faculty meetings whenever he was present, just as Bishop Hobart did in New York. Bishop Meade served as professor of pastoral theology during his episcopate, spending a fortnight at the seminary every spring to deliver his lectures and appearing at other times to lead prayer meetings. Bishop Johns, his successor, did the same; taught homiletics for a period as well; and found the location so convenient that after relinquishing the presidency of William and Mary in 1854, he built a house for himself on the Seminary Hill and lived there until his death in 1876 (save for the years of enforced exile during the war). Both men had strong characters. Bishop Meade, in particular, as one of the seminary's founders had a paternal sense of personal concern for its welfare so uninhibited that when, one day, he suddenly took a dislike to the wooden crosses with which the architect had ornamented the pew-ends in the chapel built in 1840, he summarily had them sawn off and thrown out without a moment's hesitation.[8]

Just as likely a source of friction was the Board of Trustees. At Virginia the trustees met only once or twice a year; but they interfered with enthusiasm in the most minute details of seminary administration, and at the same time persisted in conducting their own meetings in an atmosphere of the most splendid isolation. They did not consult the faculty officially in any way. The professors submitted reports to the board's annual meeting in writing, and had to wait weeks, or even months, to receive a letter from the secretary telling them what action, if any, had been taken.[9] Sometimes they did not hear at all. This could be inconvenient because the trustees reserved to themselves the approval of all textbooks used in the seminary, and prescribed details of classroom work in a

[8] T. J. Packard, ed., *Recollections of a Long Life by Joseph Packard, D.D. 1812-1902*, p. 134.

[9] *Virginia Seminary*, I, p. 623.

fashion that a modern faculty would find intolerable. As late as 1875, hearing that one of the professors (himself a former trustee) had brought into his class a textbook which had not received the prior approval of the board, the trustees resolved "that in case of any proposed change in the textbook or course of study in the Seminary, the proposal for such change be made at one annual meeting of the Board of Trustees to be acted upon at the next annual meeting, except there should be an unanimous vote of the quorum of the Board to take action at the time when the proposal was first made." [10] The Holy Office could not have acted with more exemplary caution. A year later the board resolved that the "Professor of Systematic Divinity be requested to require his students to commit to memory the Thirty-nine articles of Religion, and also the proof texts in Knapp's *Theology,* and that the other Professors be requested to require their students to commit portions of the Gospel and Epistles to memory." [11] In 1878 the board instructed the secretary to confer with the professor of Hebrew and apologetics, the venerable Dr. McElhinney, to find out why he was not teaching the first and second books of Hooker's *Ecclesiastical Polity.*[12]

Yet the faculty submitted to these attentions with equanimity, and usually with amiability as well. They were more amused than annoyed by Bishop Meade's outburst of iconoclasm. Putting it down to the weakness for overemphasis that periodically overcomes "strong" men, they keenly enjoyed the happy coincidence whereby on the following Sunday—with the scent of freshly sawn wood still in the air—the Psalm appointed for the day was found to contain the verse: *But now they break down all the carved work thereof with axes and hammers.* The

---

[10] *Ibid.,* p. 252.
[11] *Ibid.*
[12] *Ibid.,* p. 253.

older professors were no more put out by the trustees' fussing about the curriculum in the 1870's. (Possibly they saw in it merely the reassertion of a responsibility which the trustees had regularly exercised in earlier years when they were expected to be present at the annual examinations and set the standard of academic requirements themselves.) The younger professors were less happy about it, but contented themselves with making quietly invidious comparisons between the observation of personal courtesies by parish vestries (all laymen) and by boards of seminary trustees (dominated by clergy)—to the detriment of the latter. Dr. McElhinney, when asked about the omission of Hooker in his class, simply replied sweetly that "he did not teach these two books because they were being taught by Professor Nelson."

The professors were, by all accounts, blessed with unusual sweetness of temper, and much of the credit for the atmosphere of patience and understanding clearly belongs to them. But not all. "The voice of free grace" was not a favorite hymn in Virginia conventions for nothing. Bishop Johns had a personal charm that sweetened even the pointed criticisms with which he dissected the students' sermons in his preaching class; and he was so free of self-assertion that—almost alone among his episcopal contemporaries—he gave orders that none of his manuscripts should be published after his death, so that no "Letters and Papers" biography of him was ever written. Bishop Meade was more intimidating. He had a somewhat Roman manner (the only "Roman" thing about him, as his friend, Bishop Clark, used to say with a chuckle),[13] and his sense of duty inspired friends and enemies alike with awe. But he also had unusual powers of self-restraint. His position as Bishop of Virginia and leader of the Evangelicals inevitably compelled him to

---

[13] T. M. Clark, *Reminiscences*, p. 125.

play a prominent part in the ecclesiastical controversies and episcopal trials that troubled his day, and he was as quick as any of his colleagues to rush home afterwards and write down a detailed explanation of his conduct in case questions were raised later. But there the resemblance ended. His colleagues also rushed into print; Bishop Meade rarely did. And as he grew older, he mellowed. In letters to the students at the seminary in the 1850's, he was unpretentious, frank, patiently reasonable, with a touching air of quiet respect for their integrity as future ministers of the Gospel. Their replies showed that they regarded him with affection, and were not in the least put off by his antique manner.[14] Of these same years the story used to be told of a Virginia lady who, speaking of the bishop to a clergyman friend, said, "When he comes to our house, he loves to have my sister or myself stand behind his chair and comb his beautiful white hair. He thanks us so affectionately, and says it soothes him and cures his headache. Don't you think," she went on, "that the Bishop is just the dearest, sweetest, old man in the world?" "Yes, my dear," her friend replied, with becoming judiciousness, "I think so, on the whole; though it does make some difference whether you happen to be combing his head or he is combing yours."[15] Apparently Bishop Meade combed few heads on the Hill.

As for the trustees, it is important to remember that even while officially maintaining their distance from the faculty, many of them sat side by side with the professors for years as fellow-members of the Education Society's Board of Managers, and that in this way they were administering together a large portion of the seminary's financial affairs at least. Out of the association strong

---

[14] John Johns, D.D., *A Memoir of the Life of the Right Rev. William Meade, D.D., Bishop of the Protestant Episcopal Church in the Diocese of Virginia*, pp. 242-247.

[15] *Virginia Seminary*, I, p. 100.

friendships grew, like that between Dr. Sparrow and the trustees' treasurer, Cassius Lee. This dual administration was Virginia's one unusual feature, and its importance in keeping the seminary on an even keel should not be underestimated. When, in the closing years of the century, the trustees took over more and more of the society's role in seminary affairs, while preserving all their old isolation (and, despite the faculty's successful fund-raising efforts, keeping salaries at the level fixed in 1865), the relationship between the two bodies promptly became infused with a warmth that was due more to frustration than to friendship.[16]

A less important factor, though not entirely negligible, was the theological point of view which in these years united all concerned with the seminary. Bishops, trustees, Education Society managers, professors, and students were all fervent Evangelicals, usually with a strong admixture of Calvinism. Bishop Meade and Dr. Sparrow were so mildly influenced by the Calvinistic outlook that their friends thought they should more properly be called Arminians; but the same could not be said of the others. Dr. Reuel Keith, who taught at the seminary from its beginning, was once asked, after he had given the Calvinistic point of view on some theological issue in class, when he would give the "other side of the question." "There is no other," was his reply,[17] and his colleagues, Dr. Lippitt and Dr. Packard, as well as a successor, Dr. May, would no doubt have said the same. After Dr. Sparrow came to Virginia from Kenyon in 1841, one of the first things he did was to go to hear Dr. Keith preach in Alexandria, and he reported at once to a friend in Gambier, "He is a very holy man, and very solemn in the pulpit. I suspect he brings the strong meat of Calvinism,

---

[16] *Virginia Seminary,* I, p. 255.
[17] Packard, *Recollections,* p. 95.

in huge joints and sirloins, on the table. It is not with him, as at Gambier, employed as sugar, to sweeten the tea." [18] Dr. Sparrow obviously thought so massive a diet of Calvinistic protein a bit indigestible for his taste, and it proved rather too much for the preacher as well. Dr. Keith had lost his wife in 1840, and being prone to periodic fits of melancholia, he was plunged by her death into a severe depression during which he came to despair —like not a few Calvinists before him—of his own salvation. He died in 1842 still convinced that he was a lost soul, but retaining a certain grim logic to the end. One of the seminary students who had a spotty complexion and was of weedy build came to see him where he sat hunched in a chair in his study, and in an effort to cheer him up said, "Why, Doctor, you don't look very badly, you don't look worse than I do." One flashing glance from Dr. Keith's black eyes was enough: "You are looking very badly, Sir," was all he said.[19]

The "Andover" of the South

The professors, until 1866, were all from the North; and two of them, Keith and Packard, had been trained at Andover, the famous seminary which had owed its inception to Harvard's lapse into Unitarianism in 1808. Andover had also trained one of the early trustees, Dr. Dana, the rector of Christ Church, Alexandria. Indeed, the influence of the New England seminary on the development of Virginia was so strong that in certain distinctive features it must have served as a model. No other explanation adequately accounts for the pronounced resemblance between the two.

There was, first of all, the emphasis on foreign missions. Andover had been the first of the American theo-

---

[18] Walker, *Sparrow*, p. 103. Sparrow to M. T. C. Wing, April 19, 1841.
[19] Packard, *Recollections*, p. 97.

logical schools to stress the Church's responsibility for carrying the Gospel "into all the world," and it did not remain satisfied simply with talking about it from the pulpit and in the classroom. In the first fifty years of its history, one hundred and thirty-five Andover men went as missionaries overseas. Virginia did the same. And for years every Episcopal missionary who left the United States to minister in Turkey or Liberia or China or Japan was a Virginia man. Three Virginia women—daughters of seminary professors—went too. It is a record of consistent concern that no other Episcopal seminary has ever equaled.

There was, as well, the ingenious adaptation of the midweek prayer meeting (so staple a part of the religious practice of nineteenth-century Evangelicals, whether Congregationalists or Episcopalians), on which the religious life of both institutions came before long to focus. Andover had the daily services of prayer, morning and evening, which were customary in all educational establishments, not just seminaries; and on Sundays there were services in which the students and faculty at both the seminary and Phillips Andover Academy could join. But life did not center there. Rather was its center to be found in the Wednesday Evening Conference, a weekly prayer meeting for students and faculty instituted early in the seminary's history by two of the first professors, Leonard Woods and Moses Stuart. On these occasions, as Woods described it in his memoir, the professors "from the fulness of our hearts spoke to our pupils on the great principles of our holy religion, both doctrinal, experimental, and practical." [20] Sometimes the professors spoke one after another without interruption; sometimes they answered questions from the students. What mattered was that the meetings should be friendly, informal, and really interesting. The subjects were carefully tailored to the

---

[20] Woods, *Andover Theological Seminary*, p. 164.

natural concerns of men who were studying theology in order to prepare themselves for ministering to a Christian congregation: prayer, religious reading, the proper care of health, Christian love, the mingled difficulties and joys of the parochial ministry, pastoral problems, the care and feeding of revivals, methods of study, death, grief, ministering to the sick, the religious training of children, and the like.[21] On each of these topics the students had the advantage of hearing what each professor might have to contribute out of his own store of learning and experience, not just from the acknowledged specialist as would more often be the case today when few of the subjects have escaped being tidied away into academic departments. It is not surprising that they deeply appreciated the meetings, or that Stuart in his closing years as he looked back on his teaching career was fond of observing that "if there is any part of our duty as Professors which we can remember with pleasure on a dying bed, it is what we did in the Wednesday evening Conference." [22]

At Virginia, students and professors met on Thursdays instead of Wednesdays, and the occasion was called a Faculty Meeting, not a conference; but the meetings were almost exactly like those at Andover in form, and occupied the same high place of affection and inspiration in popular memory. The Virginia men heard the professors talk informally about the ministry in their own studies, for faculty homes on the Hill were always as open to students at Virginia as they were at Andover. They could also hear them preach in more formal ecclesiastical surroundings. There was the Chapel where, after the establishment of the High School next door to the seminary on the Hill in 1840 produced a new congregation of boarders and staff families, the professors took turns filling the

___

[21] *Ibid.*, pp. 165-166.
[22] *Ibid.*, p. 167.

pulpit. There were also the mission stations in the countryside around Alexandria, ministered to most of the time by the students themselves to gain experience,[23] but visited by the professors for baptisms, burials, and celebrations of Communion. Opinions of the professors' homiletical performances naturally varied ("pitches the fodder too high in the rack for me" [24] was the pungent criticism of Dr. Sparrow's style—a failing not uncommon in preachers who spend their days chiefly in academic circles), but on one thing all agreed: at Faculty Meetings the professors were at their best. There, as was said by Dr. Packard of his dear friend, Dr. May, their tongues "dropped manna." [25]

Even in the classroom the students came to recognize an "Andover" touch. Dr. Keith used Knapp's *Theology* in his classes, and Dr. Sparrow continued to use it when he took Keith's place. Knapp had been translated into English by Leonard Woods. The interest shown by both Woods and Stuart in the works of the German biblical scholars and theologians led Keith to perfect his own command of the language in order to translate Hengstenberg's Christology. An Alexandria friend was willing to publish the book when Keith had completed it; but the actual printing had to be done at Andover, nonetheless. Dr. Packard saw it safely through the press there just before travelling south to join the faculty at Virginia in 1836.[26] Some twenty years later the teaching at Virginia still had so noticeably an Andover flavor that Phillips Brooks and a friend, in a moment of depression at Alexandria, considered transferring to the New England semi-

---

[23] This experience was not 100% effective. One of the graduates of Virginia was so nervous at his first baptism that he dropped the baby into the font. Packard, *Recollections,* p. 328.

[24] *Ibid.,* p. 170.

[25] *Ibid.,* p. 177.

[26] *Ibid.,* p. 94.

nary where they could "get the same theology first-hand" —and be nearer home as well.[27]

In one area, however, the two seminaries remained dissimilar. At Andover classroom instruction, whether in the elementary form of recitations or in the more advanced form of something very like a modern seminar, had by statute to be accompanied by a number of public lectures.[28] Both Woods and Stuart allowed the students to interrupt the lectures with questions,[29] and Stuart's lectures appear to have been shaped in part by the students' response—as lectures in a modern theological school would be.[30] Nonetheless, the lectures were much more formal, by and large, than those that modern students attend. They were virtually "set pieces"—platform performances that were intended to be equally impressive for scholarship and rhetoric. And once a lecture was composed to the satisfaction of its author, he might well deliver it unaltered year after year. Students at Andover noticed that the paper on which Leonard Woods's lectures were written grew crisp and yellow as time went by; but that was the only change.[31] When Woods printed his lectures near the end of his career, students who had heard him deliver them years before instantly recognized the text.[32]

Lectures of the type required at Andover were too grandiose for Virginia. Of that the professors had no doubts. Bishop Meade could lecture on pastoral theology and publish his lectures towards the end of his career in conventional pattern because, as bishop, it would have been impractical for him to do anything else. The resi-

[27] R. W. Albright, *Focus on Infinity, A Life of Phillips Brooks*, p. 38. Many of the commentaries used in the Biblical classes were by Moses Stuart. *Virginia Seminary*, I, p. 192.
[28] Woods, *Andover Theological Seminary*, p. 234.
[29] *Ibid.*, p. 160.
[30] Packard, *Recollections*, p. 61.
[31] *Ibid.*, p. 54.
[32] *Ibid.*

dent professors, however, stuck to recitations. In his classes
Dr. Sparrow used to assign various students the task of
writing brief essays on whichever textbook chapter was to
be discussed on a given day, and have the essays read
aloud at the beginning of the class as a springboard for
recitation by the other students. When the subject was
Butler's *Analogy* in the first year, or the Thirty-nine Articles in the third year, he resorted to an even older teaching method, one used by the Congregationalist divine,
Dr. Bellamy, in his own "School of the Prophets" in the
mid-eighteenth century,[33] and adapted by his better-known
disciples, Smalley and Emmons. Using the *Analogy* or the
Articles as a basic text, he drew up a series of questions to
which were appended brief quotations from scholarly
works that would not be available to Virginia students
and suggestions for special reading.[34] It was the task of
each student to write out his own answers to the various
questions; and class time was spent in hearing the answers
read, criticizing them, and then assisting the students to
recast them in different form until an answer was achieved
that satisfied both the student and Dr. Sparrow himself.
The purpose was apologetical rather than simply exposi-
tory—the aim, with regard to the Articles, being quite
as much to enable the students to refute the interpretations imposed on the Articles by the Tractarians as to
teach the students what the Articles actually said.[35] As a
method of instruction it may not have been very exciting;
but it made intellectual demands on the students—com-
pelling each one to wrestle with the material and think
his own way through to a conclusion—which many modern lecture courses do not.

One subject taught at Andover did not appear in the

---

[33] Woods, *Andover Theological Seminary*, p. 19, *et seq.*

[34] *Virginia Seminary*, I, p. 191; Walker, *Sparrow*, pp. 391-392.

[35] *Virginia Seminary*, I, p. 191. From manuscript recollections of Dr.
Walker, who was a pupil at the time.

Virginia curriculum at all: church music. The constitution drawn up for the New England seminary in 1807 had
laid down the following as the thirtieth of thirty-four
governing regulations:

Sacred Music, and especially Psalmody, being an important
part of public, social worship; and as it is proper for those,
who are to preside in the assemblies of God's people, to possess
themselves so much skill and taste in this sublime art, as at
least to distinguish between those solemn movements, which
are congenial to pious minds, and those unhallowed, trifling,
medley pieces, which chill devotion; it is expected, that serious
attention will be paid to the culture of a true taste for genuine
Church Music in this Seminary; and that all Students therein,
who have tolerable voices, will be duly instructed in the theory and practice of this celestial art; and whenever it shall be
in the power of either of the said Professors, it shall accordingly be his duty to afford this necessary instruction; and
whenever this shall not be the case, it is expected, that an
Instructor will be procured for this purpose.[36]

This had no counterpart in the regulations at Virginia
for a great many years. Some of the students made their
own private arrangements for instruction in elocution at
the time when Phillips Brooks was studying at the seminary just before the Civil War;[37] but the professors made
no provision for it. In these aspects of public worship,
perhaps, the trustees and faculty felt that professional
training would only inhibit "the voice of free grace."

Dr. Sparrow

During the entire period of his service to the seminary,
Dr. Sparrow was to Virginia what Moses Stuart was to
Andover: the teacher who stood head and shoulders above
his fellows in the estimation of students and colleagues

---

[36] Woods, *Andover Theological Seminary,* p. 243.
[37] Albright, *Focus on Infinity,* p. 49.

alike. Indeed, the warmth with which admiration, un-shadowed by a trace of vanity or envy, was expressed for the two men by those who taught alongside them over the years is a refreshing contrast to the atmosphere more prevalent in modern academic circles, where praise is tempered with such extreme judiciousness that it is vir-tually indistinguishable from blame. Dr. Packard, who succeeded Dr. Sparrow as dean after the latter's death in 1874, said of his onetime colleague:

Dr. Sparrow was a teacher by nature, and education and ex-perience had done much for him. His teacher's chair was to him a very throne from which he ruled the hearts and minds of men. So absorbed would he become in his subject that rarely the bell that rang at the close of the hour was heard by him, and I had to go in and tell him that it had rung, in order to get my class, even fifteen minutes late. . . . When you met him, the charm of his countenance, his ripe scholar-ship, his wide and varied learning, rich with the spoils of ancient and modern times, his sympathetic and loving heart, his countenance lighting up with a beautiful smile, all com-bined to make a deep impression.[38]

At Dr. Packard's request, Phillips Brooks wrote his own tribute to Dr. Sparrow. Men had said of Moses Stuart that he "waked up more minds than any other man";[39] Brooks said very much the same of his onetime teacher:

It is easy to say of men who have not much accurate knowl-edge to impart, that they are men of suggestion and inspira-tion. But with the Doctor clear thought and real learning only made the suggestion and inspiration of his teaching more vivid. I have never looked at Knapp since he taught us out of it; my impression of it is that it is a very dull and dreary book, but it served as a glass for Dr. Sparrow's spirit to shine through, and perhaps from its own insignificance I remember

---

[38] Packard, *Recollections,* pp. 168-169.
[39] *Ibid.,* p. 61.

him in connection with it more than in connection with Butler. His simplicity and ignorance of the world seemed always to let me get directly at the clearness of his abstract thought, and while I have always felt that he had not comprehended the importance of the speculative questions which were just rising in those days, and which have since then occupied men's minds, he unconsciously did much to prepare his students' minds to meet them. His intellectual and spiritual life seem to me, as I look back upon him, to have been mingled in singular harmony and to have made but one nature as they do in few men. The best result of his work in influence on any student's life and ministry must have been to save him from the hardness on the one hand, or the weakness on the other, which purely intellectual or purely spiritual training would have produced. His very presence on the Hill was rich and salutary. He held his opinions and was not held by them. His personality impressed young men who were just at that point of life when a thinker is more to them than the results of thought, because it is of most importance that they should learn to think, and not that they should merely fortify their adherence to their inherited creed.[40]

On a visit to Virginia in 1891, two years before his own death, Brooks was even more explicit in his praise of Dr. Sparrow: "He taught me to think. He taught us that thought was the noblest exercise of man. He taught us that however far thought might travel, it would still find that God was there." [41] In that context the doctor's words, engraved in part on his tombstone and familiar to generations of Virginia men, speak for themselves: "Seek the truth; come whence it may, lead where it will, cost what it may." [42]

The courageous and expansive spirit implicit in Dr. Sparrow's teaching, however, was as unusual at Virginia as it was in any other of the Evangelical circles of his day.

[40] *Ibid.*, pp. 171-172.
[41] *Virginia Seminary*, II, p. 77.
[42] Packard, *Recollections*, p. 169.

Dr. Grammer once wrote of Bishop Whittle, a distinguished Virginia graduate, that "he lived his brave, consistent Christian life under the shadow of a great distrust of progress." [43] It is an expressive phrase, and could have been used of many of the Virginia faculty and all the trustees. "The old is better," [44] was Dr. Packard's characteristic comment. At Virginia's Semi-Centennial in 1873 he said, "We have been suspicious of novelties of fine-spun philosophical speculations. We have held that Christianity, as a documentary religion, was to be *learned* and not improved. We have had too deep convictions of the truth, and loved it too well to be tolerant of error." [45] When a man says that something is "to be *learned,* and not improved," what he generally means is that the way *he* learned it (and is now teaching it) cannot be improved. That is certainly what Professor Packard meant; and in expressing so conservative a conviction he spoke for most of his contemporaries as well.

[43] *Virginia Seminary,* I, p. 633.
[44] *Ibid.,* p. 570.
[45] The full text was printed after the Semi-Centennial. Most of the speech was inserted in Professor Packard's *Recollections,* pp. 310-311, without identifying it.

3

The Tribulations of Gambier

GAMBIER IN OHIO was like Virginia in many ways; in fact the two seminaries were often mentioned in the same breath. Gambier was just as self-consciously orthodox as its sister in Alexandria, just as forthrightly Evangelical, and even more fervent in the warmth of its religious feeling. Like so many communities in the West, it was swept periodically by revivals that filled its halls with enthusiastically praying students and spilled over into corridors and dormitories. In the opinion of both students and professors these revivals were largely responsible for fostering the spirit of mutual friendship and solicitude that was such a feature of the life at Kenyon in the first thirty years of its history.[1] The books studied at Gambier were the same ones that served as textbooks at Virginia; and this is not surprising, for two of the professors who taught at Gambier, Dr. Sparrow and Dr. McElhinney, ultimately moved to Alexandria. Like the Virginia students, the Gambier men gave expression to their evangelistic zeal— and gained practical experience—by ministering in mission stations set in the wild country roundabout. The

---

[1] Heman Dyer, *Records of an Active Life,* pp. 55-56.

only difference was that these were frontier outposts in every sense, ministering to settlers who were as illiterate as the slaves on the Virginia farms (in one congregation of sixty souls, fifty-nine did not possess so much as a Bible between them),[2] but dressed in the picturesque garb—and often engaged in the same roving life—as Cooper's Natty Bumppo.[3]

Yet in one important feature the two seminaries were not a bit alike. Where Virginia went on quietly from year to year, growing slowly but steadily, Gambier staggered from crisis to crisis. It was like a ship that hardly has time to right itself, untangle its rigging, and dry its sails after one storm before another squall comes whistling over the water to lay it over on its side. Financial weakness, peculiarities of the administrative structure, and conflicting personalities were all to blame for this.

Financial Strains

Throughout most of the nineteenth century the financial condition of Gambier was quite sufficiently depressing in itself, without taking other complications into account. Money kept on running out with unnerving regularity. Thanks to Bishop Chase's triumphant tour of England in 1823-24 the college opened with $30,000 behind it, as well as $10,000 more that was contributed from American sources after Chase's return.[4] This was four times as much as Virginia had at its disposal when it began.[5] Yet within five years this was all gone—sunk in land and buildings— and Gambier was $15,000 in debt.[6] Some ten years after that, the debt had soared to nearly $35,000.[7] At one point matters became so desperate that part of the land was

---

[2] Walker, *Sparrow*, p. 43.
[3] Dyer, *Records*, pp. 57-63.
[4] G. F. Smythe, *Kenyon College*, pp. 64-65.
[5] *Virginia Seminary*, I, p. 134.
[6] Smythe, *Kenyon College*, p. 119.
[7] *Ibid.*, p. 147.

seized by the government and sold to pay taxes that were two years in arrears.[8] One of the early financial agents for the seminary was a plausible rascal who produced more trouble than he did money;[9] and, perhaps because of their embarrassing experiences with him, the trustees were inclined thereafter to be so tense in their relationship with his successors that more than one lost heart and resigned.[10] Only the bishops seemed to be able to raise funds with any success. In fact the constant need for more money became such an obsession with Bishop Chase that when the *Episcopal Recorder,* a church periodical of the day, asked each of the bishops what he thought about the eagle lecterns that were just being introduced into churches in the late 1820's despite mutterings of disapproval from conservative-minded parishioners, Chase's spontaneous reply was, "I do not know anything about bronze eagles, but I know about gold eagles and I would like to have some for Kenyon." [11]

Fortunately for Gambier, both Bishop Chase and his successor, Bishop McIlvaine, knew about "gold eagles," and were skilled fowlers when it came to snaring them. Otherwise the seminary would have been as short-lived as many similar educational institutions in the West which eventually withered and died after auspicious beginnings. In England Chase knew precisely the most affecting note to strike—appealing both to his hearers' piety and to a romantic interest in the red men picturesquely prowling the forest aisles that has not dulled even now, over a century later. It was an irresistible combination. When the Dowager Countess of Rosse sent him a gift of £100 which he decided to put toward the building of a suitable chapel at Gambier, his note of thanks was typical of him:

---

[8] *Ibid.,* p. 149.
[9] *Ibid.,* pp. 89-92.
[10] *Ibid.,* pp. 141-142.
[11] Packard, *Recollections,* p. 126.

Though the sum, the use of which I am now considering, may seem small in your ladyship's eyes, yet with *us* it will be great indeed. Methinks I see this lovely spectacle rise to my view, and quickly filled with devout worshippers from "the sons of the soil," all in successful training for future ministers of the blessed gospel of salvation. Amidst our wild woods, where so lately were heard only the war-whoops of the savage and the howling of the forest wolf, will be sung the sweet songs of Zion, mellowed by the controlling organ.[12]

He had a sure sense of what was appropriate. When he turned from addressing a widowed peeress to appeal to the American public, his style at once became less upholstered, and various sizes of type were used to convey a sense of urgency with an inventiveness worthy of Madison Avenue. One of the most famous of his printed brochures was *The Star in the West, or Kenyon College, in the Year of Our Lord, 1828,* sent out almost in desperation after Chase had tried in vain to get Congress to make Kenyon a land-grant college. It ended with this touching request of the reader: "A SMALL SUM ONLY *is asked of* every friend of every name and class. . . . Whoever reads this is, therefore, most respectfully and earnestly entreated *immediately* to enclose ONE DOLLAR, in aid of the present struggles of Kenyon College, in a letter addressed to, P. Chase, P. M. GAMBIER, KNOX CO., OHIO." [13] Even the bishop, whose expectations were nothing if not sanguine, was surprised at the number of readers who took him at his word. Bishop McIlvaine, when it came his turn to send out appeals, used more uniform type—thereby lowering the emotional pitch; but interspersed the text with tasteful engravings of Gambier scenes that endowed the Ohio countryside with the Arcadian quality of a landscape on a contemporary Staffordshire plate. Both men

---

[12] Smythe, *Kenyon College,* Appendix IV.
[13] *Ibid.,* p. 77.

were indefatigable in whirlwind tours where, by a combination of personal calls, distribution of printed appeals, sermons, and addresses, they anticipated many of the devices dear to modern professional fund raisers. Bishop Chase even followed Bishop Meade's example by prevailing upon the ladies in a number of New England towns to organize "Kenyon Circles of Industry" similar to the sewing auxiliaries that contributed to Virginia in the South.[14]

Nothing, however, was enough. Much of the English money had been invested in land with the intention of eventually recovering much more than the original capital sum by selling off the superfluous lots when the value of the land had sufficiently appreciated. Yet even though Bishop McIlvaine managed at various times to bring in over $60,000 in new contributions, the need for cash forced the seminary to begin selling off the land early in its history and consequently at a lower figure than expected. Worse still, local support for the seminary within the diocese itself was very slow in developing. In this sense Ohio was almost a textbook example of the missionary enterprise that depends for its life on help from outside and threatens to collapse the moment it is left on its own. Much of the time the diocese not only contributed nothing whatever to the seminary (while reserving the right to appoint all the trustees), it expected as well that the seminary would be responsible for paying the bishop's salary.[15] Parsimony could hardly be carried further.

As a result, life at Gambier for many years was uncomfortably primitive, and sometimes squalid. Heman Dyer was first attracted to the college by reading of the fantastically low level of student expenses ($70 a year) in Bishop Chase's *Star in the West* appeal; but he soon discovered the cost at which such "unexampled cheapness"

[14] *Ibid.,* p. 65.
[15] *Ibid.,* p. 124.

(Chase's words) had been purchased. When he arrived at Gambier in 1829, after a two-week stagecoach ride over mud holes and corduroy roads from his home in Vermont, he found the professors and students living in log cabins and "slab-houses" and waiting for the permanent buildings to be finished. So sketchy was the construction of these that a student who found one of the upstairs rooms uncomfortably cold on an early spring morning could lie on the floor and stick his legs outdoors through a crack between the boards to warm his feet in the sun.[16] Dyer's own room, when he was eventually assigned one to himself, was at first empty of furniture, light, and bedding. He made a bedstead of sorts for himself out of a freshly-cut slab of oak propped up on two sawhorses; but when his sheets were brought to him after dark, he found that for some reason they had been sewn together in such a way that no matter how he made the bed up, he couldn't get into it. Only when dawn came did he discover why: Mrs. Chase, who acted as matron, had gone to the wrong shelf in the linen room and inadvertently sent up, not sheets at all, but a roller towel. He later discovered that the mistake would have been all too easy to make; for when the real sheets finally arrived, they turned out to be no more than a foot and a half wide—just about the width of a towel.[17]

When Dyer was drafted into teaching by Bishop Chase some time afterward, he still found living conditions no easier. Even in the mid-1850's the professors were paid salaries of no more than $500 to $600, and the salaries were usually in arrears.[18] They had houses to live in; but the roofs often leaked, responsibility for the upkeep rested with the residents, and they were responsible for paying

---

[16] Dyer, *Records*, p. 42.
[17] *Ibid.*, pp. 43-45.
[18] Smythe, *Kenyon College*, p. 153.

the taxes on them as well.[19] The professors did not grumble about the low pay or about having to live under difficult conditions where decisions were almost all made by the bishop, who lived among them; but the strain imposed undoubtedly helped to distort and magnify other troubles when they arose. Anyone who lived in England in the late 1940's when rationing in many forms persisted for years after the war itself had ended, will remember how tempers grew short, and minor differences of opinion between friends would suddenly erupt, to everyone's surprise, into volcanic quarrels.

Administrative Schizophrenia

A more immediate cause of dissension than lack of money was the anomalous composition of Gambier itself. Its English friends had contributed funds to support a theological seminary; and by the terms of its charter a theological seminary was precisely what it was. It was as a possible rival of General in New York, furthermore, that it had provoked the enthusiastic hostility of Bishop Hobart in 1823. From the first, however, the foundation provided for instruction which was by no means limited exclusively to theological subjects. A college course in arts and sciences was offered, as well as a grammar school training; and very shortly the seminary faculty was given authority by the Ohio General Assembly to award suitable degrees under the title of "Kenyon College." [20] This was natural enough in one way; for Bishop Chase had presided over just such an academic potpourri at Worthington in order to make a living.[21] It was also a sensible solution of one problem that troubled every seminary of the period (and not that period alone)—the fact that so few candidates for the ministry were adequately prepared to pursue theo-

---

[19] *Ibid.*
[20] *Ibid.*, p. 44.
[21] *Ibid.*, p. 6. "Moonlighting" is hardly a modern problem.

logical studies in accordance with the provisions laid down by the canons. Partly for that reason Virginia established the High School on the Hill in 1839, followed it with the preparatory department, and considered establishing a college as well.[22] For the same reason General seriously discussed developing a preparatory department of its own in New York, and at various times considered the advisability of drawing closer to Columbia.[23] But the problem was even more pressing in Ohio, where schools were so few and the level of literacy so low that unless teachers were rapidly provided from somewhere, fewer and fewer Ohioans could be expected to attain a level of academic achievement where they could successfully apply to be trained as ministers at all. Chase had no patience, therefore, with any suggestion that a rapid expansion of both the college and school could possibly work to the disadvantage of the seminary, even though, as a result, it soon dwindled to little more than a vestigial appendix, existing still impressively enough on paper, but limited in actuality to two or three men who, either in conjunction with their college course or at its conclusion, were privately preparing for the ministry under the guidance of professors who spent most of their time teaching classes in the college, but who were equally competent to supervise theological studies.[24] As he pointed out to the diocesan convention in 1826:

Much of the field of art and science, is open alike to the physician, civilian and the divine. What one studies the others must not neglect. The knowledge of the language, philosophy and Belles letters [sic], is necessary to all, and in the attainment of this, the ability and number of the professors and teachers, the quality and extent of the libraries and the use

---

[22] *Virginia Seminary*, I, pp. 332-339; II, pp. 413 *et seq.*
[23] *Proceedings*, IV, pp. 284-285, 487, 521.
[24] Smythe, *Kenyon College*, p. 98.

and value of an astronomical and philosophical apparatus may be greatly enlarged, for the benefit of each, by a junction of the funds of both. It was therefore to *promote*, and not to impede the original design of our institution, that I have endeavoured to annex a college of general science to our Seminary, and to open our doors to students designed eventually for all the learned professions.[25]

This was sensible and practical enough. But it produced in time a fateful shift in emphasis of which Chase himself was never clearly aware. The vision with which he had mesmerized Lady Rosse and her friends—"sons of the soil" singing the "sweet songs of Zion" in a monumental Gothick fane set in the wilderness while they prepared to enter the ministry—did not fade. It was, however, elbowed as it were to one side by a still more grandiose vision that embraced, not simply the diocese of Ohio, but the entire Mississippi basin. Within a few years Chase was assuring the convention that the real purpose of Gambier was:

. . . to cherish an institution of Christian education at a rate of unexampled cheapness, bringing science with all its blessings within the reach of thousands and tens of thousands of people, who, by reason of their straightened circumstances must forever remain in comparative ignorance. It is to teach the children of the poor to become *school-masters,* to instruct our common schools throughout the vast valley of the Mississippi. It is to teach the children of the poor to rise by their wisdom and merit into stations hitherto occupied by the rich; to fill our pulpits, to sit in our senate chambers, and on our seats of justice; and to secure in the best possible way the Liberties of our country.[26]

Like all Chase's visions, it turned out, when stripped of the episcopal rhetoric which he considered appropriate for such occasions, to be based on a shrewd, and notably un-

---

[25] *Ibid.*, p. 42.
[26] *Ibid.*, p. 43.

romantic, assessment of what was required. In a letter to his brother, Dudley Chase, senator from Vermont, the bishop wrote frankly that the reason for turning out schoolteachers "drawn from the poorer classes of society" was because such men would be "not above their business." [27]

Chase was entirely right in his conviction that each of the academic departments—college, school, or seminary— would benefit from its association with the other. In this the evidence of the ensuing years bore him out. The college benefited most obviously, perhaps. The staunchly Evangelical tone of the seminary faculty at Gambier first attracted the attention, then won the admiration of Evangelicals in the East (both North and South). Many of them sent their sons to Kenyon as a result.[28] When wealthy Evangelical laymen or parishes gave the money to put up buildings or endow professorial chairs, which they did more often for the seminary than for the college, the close connection between the two institutions made it possible for the college to share in the benefits. In fact, the college depended so much on using seminary funds and staff for its own instruction program that, when there was a thorough administrative reorganization in the 1880's, it insisted that its own president, be he clergyman or layman, ought always to be president of the seminary too.[29] Yet the other departments also benefited. While the grammar school was a notable feeder of the college in the early years, later on it owed its continuation (under a variety of names and forms) principally to the college, both in terms of personnel and financial assistance, even though most of

---

[27] *Ibid.*, p. 44.

[28] Dyer, *Records*, pp. 76-77. Poor men, like Dyer or A. V. G. Allen, who came from hardscrabble farming communities in Vermont, were obviously drawn as well by the low expenses charged to the students. Modest tuition, however, was not a decisive factor with men like Rand, the son of a prominent Boston lawyer, or Wilmer or Minor of Virginia.

[29] Smythe, *Kenyon College*, pp. 223-225.

its students went elsewhere.[30] The seminary, like the grammar school, almost expired several times. The number of theological students would drop off sharply, and sometimes for brief periods there would be none at all. When this happened, there can be little doubt that the arrangement by which the seminary professors taught in the college as well as in the seminary helped to keep the institution afloat where a more isolated seminary would almost certainly have come to grief.[31] Thanks to Chase's foresight, no one at Gambier made the mistake of construing success or failure solely in terms of the prosperity or weakness of any one of the institutions considered all by itself. Together, more than once, they kept one another from falling.

What Chase did not foresee at all, however, was that the expansion of his original conception, which was so happy in other respects, meant the beginning of the end of his own association with Gambier. The juxtaposition of college and school and theological seminary under one administrative head, the bishop, and under one Board of Trustees set the stage for a dispute over the proper limits of the bishop's jurisdiction and the precise character of the authority which it was permissible for him to exercise in the various departments. So heated did it become that Chase resigned in 1831, and the conflict between bishop, trustees, and faculty continued to set Gambier by the ears at intervals for the next sixty years. Although the debate was inevitable in all probability, it would have been less freighted with rancor at the beginning had it not been for Gambier's origin. Gambier had not come into being as a result of the considered demand of the entire Church, as had General. It had not come into being in response to the considered demand of a strong, cohesive diocese, as had Virginia. Like Minerva springing from the head of

[30] *Ibid.*, pp. 219ff.
[31] *Ibid.*, pp. 203, 223.

Jove, it was one man's brain-child; and consequently the rebellion of the child against its creator (for so it seemed to him) was bound to be unusually painful for all concerned. What made it even more unhappy was that Chase's own personality provided the catalyst.

Bishop Chase Strikes His Tent

Philander Chase has unfortunately been ill-served by the illustrators of history books. Most of the pictures of him have been taken from daguerreotypes or ambrotypes, which did not come into use until he was an old man. They show him dressed in rochet and chimere, jaw set, eyes partially hidden behind heavy spectacles, with a little black cap on his head like a judge about to pronounce the death sentence. Perhaps because of some distortion of the lens he looks dwarfed by his robes, a squat figure, bumptious and bad-tempered: Harold Ickes in petticoats. The sight is enough to enlist every sympathy with his opponents at once. But it was not so that his contemporaries saw him. He was well over six feet tall, and big to boot. William Sparrow, who taught both at Gambier and at Virginia, married Chase's sister-in-law; and he vividly remembered that when he first set eyes on his brother-in-law-to-be in the latter's study, he thought him "the most majestic man I had ever seen. He filled the whole door!" [32] Everything about Chase seemed a little larger than life: his stature, his energy, his humor, his imagination. Whether in his accustomed high spirits or in a rage, he expressed himself with a freedom and a booming gusto that still echoes in his letters and in reports of his conversation. He had in ample measure the precious gift of infecting others with his own enthusiasm; and as he was in general a good judge of men, he drew around him by the vigor and charm of his ebullient personality a faculty of real merit, at least one of whose members, William Sparrow, gave up

[32] Walker, *Sparrow,* p. 48.

a better-paying position elsewhere in order to join him. Whatever his other faults, Chase was not the kind of clerical *prima donna* who carefully surrounds himself only with amiable mediocrities so that his own talents may seem the more effulgent. Doubtless his regime at Gambier would have been smoother if he had. A faculty made up of dull and malleable nonentities might have put up with his administrative whimsies and occasional vapors with less demur.

The most salient of Chase's characteristics was his certitude. Immune to doubt, insensitive to fear, he knew what he knew and saw what he saw with complete clarity. This gave him an assurance that verged on the sublime. In consequence, it was with unwearied zest that he daily devised the improvisations whereby, despite the inadequate resources at his disposal, Gambier slowly arose in the wilderness; and in moments of crisis he could imbue others with his intrepidity. Bishop Clark used to tell a delightful tale of Bishop Chase coming one very windy day to the shore of a pond he wanted to cross, and being refused passage by an Indian who was too frightened by the tossing waters to venture out. Chase promptly drew himself up to his full height and roared, "Launch your canoe! *Jehovah jireh!*" It was enough. The impassioned delivery of what he took to be either a curse or a spell convinced the quaking Indian that the bishop was even more dangerous than the waves, and without further protest he paddled him across the pond as fast as he could.[33]

Yet the very force and simplicity of Chase's convictions which served him so well in emergencies became a serious handicap when faculty and students at Gambier began to develop an *esprit de corps* of their own. As the professors gained experience and became accustomed to working together (a process hastened by Chase's frequent absences from Gambier on money-raising expeditions or diocesan

[33] Clark, *Reminiscences*, pp. 174-175.

business), it was inevitable that sooner or later something would come up on which they and the bishop would not see eye to eye. And when that happened, it was bound to be only a matter of time before the disagreement produced an explosion. For, with his almost total insensitivity to the shifting ambiguities of life, Chase was far too sure of what he thought about everything—and thought it far too vehemently—to remain calm when anyone disagreed with him. Differences of opinion baffled as much as they vexed him. Real opposition he found incomprehensible. The least introspective of men, he would have dismissed Cromwell's famous plea to the Scottish General Assembly, "I beseech you in the bowels of Christ, think it possible that you may be mistaken" (had it been suggested that it might apply also to him) as being no less preposterously wide of the mark than the Lord Protector's deplorable prejudice against bishops. The longer opposition persisted, therefore, the more firmly he became convinced that those behind it must be either fools or rogues. Nor did he temper this conviction one jot when his opponents happened to include close relatives and friends of long standing. In his eyes their failure to see things his way simply showed that the relationship had been false all along. As a result Chase strode through life tossing behind him one by one the husks of friendships which he himself proclaimed to be empty or rotten, while those who cared about him looked on in impotent distress.[34] Only very seldom did second thoughts ever lead him to go back and pick them up again. Such traits ensured that a conflict at Gambier would be bitter.

The conflict came in 1830, and sprang from Chase's basic conception of his proper role at Gambier. In his history of Kenyon, G. F. Smythe likened the institution in that period to "some great monastery in the Middle Ages, planted in a remote spot, with its farms, its dairies,

---

[34] Smythe, *Kenyon College*, p. 14.

its mills, its workshops, its guest house, its domestic establishment, its scholars, its laboring brethren, and its auto-
cratic abbot." [35] The analogy is a perceptive one, and
helpful to the modern reader whose mental image of
academic institutions is derived from the behemoths of
our own day. But Chase is unlikely to have seen Gambier
that way. For him its organization was even more directly
familial than that of the mediaeval monastic community.
Gambier was simply an extension of his own household.
Even when the faculty had increased to six, and there
were more than one hundred students on the hill above
the Kokosing, Mrs. Chase continued to supervise all the
housekeeping and cooking. Chase's brother-in-law was
in general charge of the teaching, prominently assisted by
Chase's nephew. Another relative ran the commissary.
And Chase himself, like Pooh-Bah in *The Mikado,* served
as Lord High Everything Else: overseer of farm and dairy,
manager of sawmill and quarry and stagecoach line, chief
logger, chief carpenter, postmaster, and rector of the
local church. What was this but a "School of the Prophets"
—vastly swollen in size, no doubt, but recognizably on
the lines of the parsonage seminaries and tutoring schools
run by men like Bellamy and Emmons and Cotton Mather
Smith in the eighteenth century?

It was with entire confidence, therefore, that Chase interfered in every aspect of the life at Gambier, ordering
this and countermanding that just as it suited him. In
exactly similar fashion another redoubtable parental figure, Clarence Day's father, would think it no less than his
duty to go into the kitchen to sample the soup if he chose
(and suggest improvements to the cook), or climb to the
nursery to see how the nursemaid was training the children (and tell her how she could do it better). The careful legal language of charters and bylaws, with their
distinctions and differentiations of responsibility, meant

---

[35] *Ibid.,* p. 86.

no more to Chase than the chart that modern parents may pin up on the kitchen wall assigning minor housekeeping chores to various children, and serving as a check-off list to encourage the regular washing of faces and brushing of teeth. They were rules that he felt free to make or unmake at his pleasure. When the faculty began holding regular meetings in the winter of 1829-30 during his absence from Gambier, and continued the practice after his return, he was as put out as a modern father might be if his small children got together down in the cellar to decide where the family would spend his vacation while he himself was upstairs reading his newspaper blissfully unawares.[36] Like a father who sometimes overprotects the younger children from being pushed around by the older, furthermore, Chase tended to side with the students whenever they had a falling-out with a member of the faculty; and sometimes rushed in to upbraid an unfortunate teacher in front of his students when the teacher happened to be entirely in the right.[37] Such partiality is unwise in a family; in an academic institution it is disastrous.

The professors liked the Chases, and were perfectly aware that Gambier owed everything to the bishop. They were willing to put up with the frustrating and sometimes unnerving aspects of their life there for his sake, and, when the regular faculty meetings were instituted, were even willing to give him the veto over their proceedings which he insisted upon.[38] But Chase unfortunately was not content with that. Irritated to discover that his position seemed unaccountably more vulnerable to his colleagues than it did to himself, he made the fatal mistake of attempting to strengthen it by claiming the right to impose by episcopal authority what he could not command by the force of his own arguments or the charm of

---

[36] *Ibid.*, p. 101.
[37] *Ibid.*, p. 102.
[38] *Ibid.*, p. 104.

his personality. Pointing to the clause in the charter which placed the institution "under the immediate charge and superintendence of the Bishop of the Diocese, for the time being, as President of the institution," [39] he asserted that he had the right, even the obligation, to rule Gambier as Father in God *de jure divino*. Harking back to a biblical parallel, he said of Kenyon that

like Abraham on the plain of Mamre it hath pitched its tent under the trees of Gambier hill, it hath its flocks and its herds, and its different families of Teachers, Scholars, Mechanics and Labourers; all united under one head, pursuing one common interest and receiving their maintenance and food from one common source, the funds and farms of the College. This Patriarchal establishment must, it is obvious, have a Father and that Father must be clothed with authority to seek and effect the common good. Deprive him of this, and the family must come to ruin.[40]

This claim to exercise prerogative government had been singularly ineffective in subduing dissent when the Stuarts advanced it in England in the seventeenth century; and it was even less successful in Ohio in the nineteenth. It excited at once the American's deep-rooted distrust of *ex officio* authority. In the particular form in which it was raised by Chase, furthermore, it offended the newly developing respect for academic competence and the authority imparted by specialized training which has since become such a staple of American life. It was one thing for a bishop to exercise close personal oversight in the theological seminary. Theology was his field, and he had been trained in it as carefully, presumably, as any other contemporary clergyman. It was quite another thing, however, for him to rule the college in the same way. Secular studies were not his field; and the members of the faculty considered themselves better qualified both

[39] *Ibid.,* p. 98.
[40] *Ibid.,* p. 99.

by training and experience to make judgments concerning them than he. In the opinion of the Gambier faculty, therefore, Chase's episcopal character was merely coincidental; it gave no special *cachet* to his authority as president of Kenyon College. The two offices were distinct even though one man held them both at the same time. Because of their respect for the man himself, the professors were willing to grant him the reality of considerable power; but they yielded it to him as Philander Chase, Gambier's founder, not as Bishop of Ohio.[41] To have done otherwise would virtually have ensured that *Life With Father* would go on at Gambier indefinitely just as long as there was a bishop in the vicinity to fill the title role —an exhausting prospect.

Chase, however, would not compromise. Temperamentally he could not. Circumstances combined to strain his nerves almost to the breaking point in 1830 and 1831, fatally affecting both his temper and his judgment. His self-confidence had been badly shaken by his second failure, after a fatiguing and fruitless winter of lobbying in Washington, to get a bill through Congress granting land to the college. He was in pain much of the time from a stagecoach accident. His agent in England, the egregious George Montgomery West, a malicious windbag straight out of the pages of a Dickens novel, had so damaged Chase's credit in New York by tales of the mismanagement of Gambier funds that the bishop was forced to spend months working on a pamphlet that would prove his own innocence and expose West. Understandably irascible and increasingly arbitrary, Chase became for the moment like those unhappy parishioners, familiar to every pastor, who, frustrated by a life whose harsh conditions they are powerless to change or mitigate, sometimes find an emotional outlet by way of compensation in bitterly criticizing the choice of hymns in the service or the supposed unfriend-

---

[41] *Ibid.*, pp. 106-107.

liness of some luckless usher. On the jurisdictional dispute he vented all the pent-up fury generated by impotent anxiety and disappointment. When the professors refused to give in, he abruptly broke off friendly relations with them and appealed to the trustees. Even his brother-in-law could communicate with him only in writing by way of the local post office, though they were almost next-door neighbors. When the trustees sided with the faculty, he appealed to the diocesan convention; and when the convention decided against him, in great distress of mind he resigned forthwith both as president and as bishop, leaving Gambier permanently two or three days later.[42]

Chase's precipitate resignation and departure shelved the problem of episcopal authority, but only temporarily; it did not solve it. His successor, Charles P. McIlvaine, learned enough about the dispute to wish to move the bishop's residence from Gambier to Cleveland or Cincinnati, leaving Kenyon discreetly to its own devices; but the financial plight of the institution seemed to require the support his presence would provide, and he changed his mind. Within seven years he was at loggerheads with trustees and professors (two of whom, by that time, *were* trustees) over his powers just as Chase had been; and, like Chase, he carried the matter to the diocesan convention when the faculty and board of trustees refused to give way to him. But at that point history ceased to repeat itself. Chase's personality had lost him the first round; McIlvaine's won him the second.

Bishop McIlvaine Quells a Mutiny

Charles McIlvaine was fully as opinionated and domineering as his predecessor, but he had none of Chase's propen-

---

[42] *Ibid.*, p. 108. The convention resolved that "although the Right Rev. Bishop, by the Constitution is ex officio President of the College; yet as President, he cannot invoke his episcopal functions, or any powers or authority other than the customary functions of president and principal professor of a theological and literary seminary, aided by such as the Board of Trustees by law shall confer on him. . . ."

sity to bluster. In appearance he bore a resemblance to George Washington which was so striking that strangers used to stop him in the street to comment on it; and in manner he more than lived up to his looks. This helps to explain why, despite the ecclesiastical eminence which he achieved in later life, his friends felt that he was happiest and most successful at the beginning of his ministry, when he served as chaplain at West Point;[43] for in a community where most of the inhabitants spent a good deal of time standing at attention, McIlvaine's inclination to the statuesque would hardly be noticed, and the genuine warmth and kindness of heart which were natural to him would show through—as indeed they did. The marble manner was more of a handicap to him as rector and as bishop.[44] Yet even at worst it was a misfortune only, not a calamity; and at Gambier in 1838 and 1839 it probably worked to his advantage. In 1831 Chase's hectoring had stimulated opposition; in similar circumstances McIlvaine's chill displeasure alienated, but did not antagonize.

As a result the bishop never lost control of the convention that met in September, 1839, to take up the question at issue between himself and the Gambier faculty and trustees. There was no sign of the organization that had marshaled the convention so smoothly against Chase in 1831 (even to the point of proceeding to elect his successor within only two hours of receiving the discomfited bishop's resignation). Exactly the reverse. At McIlvaine's own suggestion the convention (at which less than half the clergy, and delegates from less than half the parishes were present) authorized him to appoint a committee to discuss and report on what changes, if any, "should be made, and under what securities, in the present relation of Kenyon College to the Episcopate and the Theological Seminary of the Diocese." [45] Blandly appointing men who supported

---

[43] Clark, *Reminiscences*, p. 129.
[44] *Ibid.*
[45] Smythe, *Kenyon College*, p. 129.

his own position, McIlvaine can hardly have been surprised when the committee duly presented a report in
which it recommended three amendments to the constitution shrewdly calculated to defeat, and even disperse,
the bishop's opponents. The first excluded all officers of
either seminary or college from membership on the Board
of Trustees, thereby severely impairing the easy communication and cooperation between the faculty and trustees
that had hitherto successfully thwarted the bishop in his
claims. The second made the bishop "the Prudential
Committee in all secular matters of the institution" [46]
between meetings of the Board of Trustees, thereby restor-
ing all the executive powers ever exercised by Chase. The
third, ignoring the then Kenyon College as if it had never
existed, ordered the trustees, when so instructed by the
convention, to "annex to the Seminary a College with the
necessary preparatory schools," [47] with a separate faculty
and a president who was to be nominated by the bishop.
All three amendments were passed by substantial majorities.

The convention's action left things at Gambier in an
uncomfortably amorphous state. Within less than a year,
however, all ambiguities were dispelled. In 1840 the convention appointed a Board of Trustees composed of men
approved by the bishop; and in August of the same year
the new board adopted a resolution directing that "a
College under the control and direction of the Trustees
of the Theological Seminary of the Protestant Episcopal
Church in the Diocese of Ohio, be established at Gambier
under the name of Kenyon College, and that the buildings
heretofore occupied by an institution of the same name be
henceforth set apart for the uses and purposes of Kenyon
College as now organized." [48] The College is dead! Long

[46] *Ibid.*
[47] *Ibid.*
[48] *Ibid.,* p. 131.

live the College! At a stroke, as it were, the institution to which all but the seminary professors belonged, vanished; and not one of them was rehired to teach in the new one that instantaneously took its place. A smoother method of getting rid of a "difficult" faculty could not have been devised. Such a piece of legal sleight of hand was deft enough to be worthy of a Talleyrand, and it would be highly interesting to know just who was responsible for it; but on that point the record (understandably, perhaps) has remained opaque. The professors had no choice but to shake the Gambier dust from their boots and depart even as Chase had done nine years before. Indeed some, Heman Dyer among them, had sensed what was in the wind, and left Kenyon to take posts elsewhere before the trustees met.[49]

The bishop now reigned supreme, and the "jealous professors" (as he termed them in a private crow of triumph to his mother)[50] could no longer disturb his peace; but his satisfaction—like his "peace"—was to prove disappointingly short-lived. The victory was in reality a Pyrrhic one. McIlvaine had found the old faculty insufferably independent; but its members had at least been intelligent, experienced, and well trained. The new professors, with one exception, were not. They were gratifyingly submissive, as the bishop was determined they should be; but they could not boast one academic degree among them, and at least two were really fit only to be monitors—apprentice teachers.[51] Nor was David Bates Douglass, the new head of the college (Sparrow had discreetly accepted an appointment at Virginia), much better. Significantly, Douglass was an old friend of McIlvaine's from West Point days. An old Army man and engineer, he amply fulfilled every expectation as an uncomplaining sub-

[49] Dyer, *Records*, p. 77.
[50] Smythe, *Kenyon College*, p. 130.
[51] *Ibid.*, p. 132.

ordinate to the bishop and an energetic custodian of buildings and grounds. One of the conspicuous results of his administration was the tidying up at last of the frontier-style squalor which had characterized Kenyon since Chase's time. But in other areas he was less successful. Conscientious, straightforward, but unimaginative, humorless, and military to the core, he was no diplomat. When it came to maintaining discipline, he saw no difference between a civilian college and an army post, running Kenyon rather as if it were "Fort Apache." The students, however, viewed this regimen with none of the appreciative enthusiasm of Rin Tin Tin and Rusty. They came to dislike Douglass heartily; and so did the townspeople and most of his own colleagues. The effect might have been foreseen: with an unpopular president and an ineffective faculty, the enrollment began to drop. Within four years the number of students in the college had shrunk from a high of seventy-seven (just before the administration changed) to forty-three.[52] The grammar school had slipped even more drastically: from one hundred and fifteen students to forty-eight. By 1844 Bishop McIlvaine might well have begun to wonder whether Douglass might eventually be called upon to exercise at Kenyon a talent which had probably not figured largely in his appointment as president—his gift for designing municipal cemeteries.

In February, 1844, McIlvaine intervened to repair the deteriorating situation. His friendship with Douglass had foundered already—shipwrecked on the rock of the bishop's somewhat illogical irritation over the president's failure to produce, as it were, the results expected of a commander in chief while being forced by McIlvaine himself to operate with the restricted powers and initiative of a chief of staff. Summoning the trustees to Gambier, he instructed them to investigate the unsatisfactory condition

---

[52] *Ibid.*, p. 138.

of the college; and they dutifully did so, prowling through the buildings and about the town asking people what they thought about it all, but with never a word to the unsuspecting Douglass. Only when their investigation had been completed did they offer him an opportunity to speak in his own defense. Douglass demanded what amounted to a trial, insisting that real charges must be presented against him before he would reply at all; but this the trustees refused—probably because they had no serious charges to bring. Douglass could hardly be charged with being the wrong man for the job—his actual offense— when he had only come to Gambier reluctantly after fervent and repeated appeals from McIlvaine. So instead they suggested that he resign. Douglass refused. This was a little awkward, but the trustees saw a way out of the impasse. In 1840 they had had to abolish an entire college; in 1844 all they had to do was abolish Douglass. By vote they declared the presidency vacant. Douglass joined the lengthening procession of outcasts from Gambier's unstable Eden, and went off to salve his feelings by designing a cemetery for the city of Albany.

Yet although the Douglass administration had shortcomings, it could boast of one unexpected success: it had convinced McIlvaine that his policy in 1839 and 1840 had been a mistake. The second Bishop of Ohio was of a more reflective disposition than his predecessor, and far readier to admit the possibility of error on his own part. He was also intellectually aware of the virtue of episcopal restraint, even though to practice it was not in the least congenial to his temperament. From the disconcerting experience with Douglass, McIlvaine concluded that his earlier determination to live in another part of the diocese and permit Gambier to function with a minimum of interference from the bishop had been wiser than the course he had actually followed. He was unable to prevail on Sparrow to take up his former post again (Sparrow

could scarcely have left Virginia with decency so soon);
but what he could do, he did. After much casting about,
the trustees finally appointed one of their own number
president in 1845, the Rev. Sherlock Bronson, a graduate
of both college and seminary; but arrangements were
made so that the new president retained his place on the
board as Sparrow had done between 1836 and 1840.[53] A
year later, at McIlvaine's request, the trustees appointed
a committee to assist the bishop in carrying out the duties
assigned him as "prudential committee" in the second
amendment to the constitution made in 1840. Significantly, the men chosen to sit on the committee were Bronson, Professor Wing (the only member of the seminary
faculty left who had served almost since the beginning,
and a great friend of Sparrow's), Professor Denison
(Chase's nephew, who had assisted in running the college
under Sparrow in the old days, and had recently rejoined
the faculty), and a layman from Mount Vernon, Colum-
bus Delano.[54] For all practical purposes this arrangement
meant a return to the form and manner of operation
which had obtained in the college and seminary between
1831 and 1840; for McIlvaine moved to the outskirts of
Cincinnati in the same year that the committee was appointed, and thereafter left it free to act in his stead with
very little interference. He retained in his own hands
only the active direction of the seminary, of which he
continued to be president—an activity, it may be remembered, which had never been involved in the controversy
over the bishop's jurisdiction. The pragmatic solution
seems to have satisfied everyone. McIlvaine was able
henceforth to turn his energies to marshaling the Evangelicals against Tractarianism, a task that increasingly
monopolized his interest. At the college the old relationship of frank communication between faculty and trustees

[53] *Ibid.*, p. 148.
[54] *Ibid.*, p. 145.

was restored, and morale improved. Severe financial squalls set in in 1848, the effects of which, in the form of cheeseparing economies and unpaid salaries, were felt more keenly by the faculty than by anyone else; but although the resulting hardships provoked three professorial resignations before they were over, the administration was strong enough and confident enough to weather the storm. Another attempt to bring Sparrow back as president, this time in 1851, failed due to Mrs. Sparrow's insistence that her husband's health would not stand such a strain;[55] but the appointment of Lorin Andrews in 1853 ushered in a long era of placid growth and even prosperity. Gambier was not to enter another Time of Troubles until open warfare between the Evangelicals and those whom they considered harbingers of either Romanism or Rationalism broke out in both Bexley Hall and Kenyon in the late 1860's and 1870's.

---

[55] Walker, *Sparrow,* p. 189.

✳ 4

The Difficulties of Being General

ONCE SETTLED in New York and secure in Bishop Hobart's favor, with the Sherred bequest behind it, General might have been expected to escape almost entirely the financial hardship that was to be the lot of the other seminaries in varying degree in the years to come. Unlike Virginia or Gambier, it was the responsibility of the entire Church. Unlike them, also, it was strategically located in the Church's strongest diocese, and in a city that was fast becoming the nation's commercial heart. From the beginning, furthermore, resources were placed at its disposal which made the sums with which Virginia and Gambier were launched (to say nothing of Nashotah, founded in 1844) seem modest. By 1862 the seminary's treasurer could report that General had received, since its foundation, the impressive total of $344,791.99 in legacies, cash contributions, and other forms of endowment.[1] Nonetheless, the seminary suffered from financial embarrassments just as acutely as did the others. Very quickly it began dipping into principal to meet annual deficits that rose, with few interludes, from around $1,500 a year in the

---

[1] *Proceedings*, III, p. 607.

early 1830's to $4,000 in the 1840's, and jumped in 1855 to nearly $15,000 a year. By 1864 the entire $344,791.99 had been swallowed up; and all that was left was real estate which, in wartime, had proved impossible to lease or sell, although that part of it that was unencumbered by any lien was estimated to be worth $144,882.80.[2] Had not friends joined with the "Society for Promoting Religion and Learning in the State of New York" to help pay the professors' salaries and buy books for the students, the seminary would have had to close.

Money Troubles

One cause of trouble was the seminary's location. It cost more to build up and maintain an academic institution in New York than it did elsewhere. As early as 1820 the trustees had calculated that the move to New Haven would slice the seminary's operating expenses in half; and in ensuing years the cost of living on the banks of the Hudson instead of the banks of the Potomac or the Kokosing did not decrease. Philander Chase's monumental "Old Kenyon," with its walls of native stone four feet thick was in a category by itself; but Virginia, using wood and brick, was able to put up three substantial buildings for what it cost General to put up one. The East and the West Buildings both exceeded the original estimates of construction expense, and between them ate up $66,000 of the seminary's funds.[3] Nor were they cheap to maintain. The hollow on Clement Moore's Chelsea estate where the buildings stood was so low-lying, and so close to the Hudson, that until the filling-in of the shoreline in the mid-century the ground was regularly flooded one or two inches deep in the winter months—to the point where Professor Turner went to the trouble of having a door cut through the wall separating his attic from the middle

---

[2] *Ibid.*, p. 608.
[3] *Ibid.*, p. 607.

section of the East Building so that he could get across to
meet his classes without having to wade through the
mud outside.[4] Sometimes the winter quagmire was so
deep that only a man on horseback could safely reach
the front door.[5] As the East Building had no cellar, the
omnipresent damp rotted floors and brought down ceil-
ings. Dry rot was a constant threat to any unpainted wood
surface in or outside the building.

In addition, "improvements" had a way of depleting
the seminary treasury. The filling-in of the river lots, the
installation of paved roads, curbs, and efficient sewers
were unavoidable, but extremely expensive, consequences
of the city's encroachment on the peace of the Chelsea apple orchards and fields. If the seminary had refused to take
the steps itself, the Common Council would have taken
them anyway—at even greater expense—and assessed General for the cost.[6] The buildings themselves, furthermore,
had to be altered from time to time, if not in the interests of convenience, then of simple health. The flues, for
example, were adequate for wood-burning fires—the only
method of furnishing heat at the time the East and West
buildings were put up; but when coal replaced wood as
fuel in 1836, their draught proved insufficient. Everyone
was half-poisoned by coal-gas fumes for an entire winter;
and the trustees were forced to adopt the radical expedient
of removing all the wood stoves, installing grates in the
reopened fireplaces, and taking the most inefficient of the
chimneys completely to pieces and rebuilding them.[7]

The improvements to the seminary's real estate, while
a considerable burden on its resources at the time, ultimately brought in more money than they cost. After the
Civil War was over, the sale of some of the lots pulled

[4] Turner, *Autobiography*, p. 123.
[5] *Ibid.*
[6] *Proceedings*, III, p. 609.
[7] *Proceedings*, I, p. 586.

General out its financial hole in the same way that Kenyon
and Bexley Hall had been freed of debt in the 1850's by
the sale of the land around Gambier. But other investments were not equally fruitful. The straits to which the
seminary was reduced in the 1860's, in fact, were due in
large part to the mishandling of the largest legacy to be
left to General during the entire period: the Kohne bequest. Of this fund, $90,000—almost the entire sum—was
loaned to a real estate speculator in 1853 at the height of
a building boom; and when the boom collapsed, the bottom dropped out of the legacy. All the trustees had to
show for their investment, after foreclosing the mortgage,
were a few half-finished, jerry-built houses in Brooklyn;
and although they eventually managed to recover about
half of what they had lost by finishing the houses and
selling them, some $40,000 had gone whistling down the
wind beyond recall.[8]

Besides unlucky investments, the trustees were also
troubled by what they considered inadequate support
from the Church at large. As early as 1828 the General
Convention urged all parishes to set aside one Sunday
offering each year for the benefit of the General Theological Seminary—a foreshadowing of our modern Theological Education Sunday;[9] but except where propinquity
naturally stimulated interest, the response was slim. Over
the years the contributions from New York far exceeded
those from all the other dioceses put together. In forty
years men from Massachusetts managed to send just over
$4,900.[10] Virginia sent a little over $600, although too absorbed in the affairs of its own seminary ever to bother to
nominate the clerical and lay trustees for General to which
the Constitution entitled it.[11] Only $71 came from Rhode

---

[8] *Proceedings*, III, p. 607.
[9] *Proceedings*, I, p. 306.
[10] *Proceedings*, III, p. 530.
[11] *Ibid.*, pp. 530, 717.

Island during the same period, and Vermont and Maine never sent anything at all.[12] In 1850 only one parish in the entire Protestant Episcopal Church sent a contribution to General: the sum of $17.16.[13]

The trustees were convinced that inflated rumors of the seminary's endowed wealth were principally responsible for such apathy—rumors that never took account of the time that often elapsed between official notification and actual receipt of a legacy, or of the erosion worked by the fluctuation of stock values and by the ever-increasing cost of living. The munificent Kohne bequest, for example, fell to the seminary on Mr. Kohne's death in 1829; but his widow's life interest in the estate prevented the seminary from enjoying a penny of the legacy until 1853. Yet even in the dark days of the 1860's, an agent who was engaged to raise funds for General reported to the trustees that many whom he approached asserted, with some heat, that the seminary's endowment had made it far too well off to be asking for still more money from them.[14]

Another reason for lack of interest, the trustees suggested, was the peculiar nature of General itself—part general, part diocesan in character. What belongs to everybody is sometimes the personal concern of nobody, as the custodians of parish houses or municipal parks have long since discovered; and General, by the terms of its constitution, suffered from a similar devolution of individual responsibility. Because it was theoretically the seminary of the entire Church, it did not invite the degree of enthusiastic support from the Diocese of New York which it would have done, in the trustees' opinion, had it been a straightforwardly diocesan seminary on the same footing as the rest. On the other hand, because General's Board of Trustees and working committees were

---

[12] *Ibid.*
[13] *Ibid.*, p. 606.
[14] *Ibid.*, pp. 557-558.

dominated by New Yorkers, with the Bishop of New York serving on the faculty and presiding (at least in the early years) at faculty meetings, the other dioceses could well conclude that a diocesan seminary was, practically speaking, precisely what General was already in all but name, and decide to husband their always meager financial resources for the training of needy candidates for Orders at home. Whenever funds ran low at General, therefore, someone was likely to suggest that the only satisfactory remedy would be to tie it more tightly to the diocese in which it was situated, and sever its connection with the Church at large.[15] The trustees seriously considered it more than once.

Still another explanation for the Church's faltering support may suggest itself to the historian, although it does not appear to have occurred to the trustees: that the trustees themselves were partially at fault. They were apparently as unimaginative in their methods of raising funds as they were unlucky in their management of what funds they had. When it came to asking for money, ardor for the cause could never quite quench an invincible distaste for the task. A reading of the volumes of the *Proceedings* reveals little of the assiduous cultivation of a base of support at the grass roots among parishes and women's groups that so materially benefited Virginia, and none of the abounding fertility of resource that distinguished Bishop Chase and, to a lesser degree, Bishop McIlvaine in procuring aid for hard-pressed Gambier. The periodic resolutions and appeals circulated among the clergy of the Church by the General trustees had nothing in common with a pamphlet like Chase's *Star in the West* but their purpose. Where Chase was eloquent, enthusiastic, personal —and calculatingly pathetic—the trustees were terse, matter of fact, simultaneously apologetic and censorious. The most ambitious of the Board's attempts in this line was the

---

[15] *Ibid.*, p. 717.

Appeal to the Churches published in 1861.[16] It was written in the uneasy style of a company statement that purports to explain to the shareholders why the management has decided not to declare a previously expected dividend, the elaborate courtesy as it were only imperfectly concealing the directors' irritation at being forced by circumstances into making any explanation to the shareholders at all. Nor did it carry much more conviction. The trustees' sense of injury was understandable. They were, after all, in the invidious position of exercising a responsibility delegated to them by the very bodies which, as the trustees saw it, were at the same time lethargically denying them the means with which they could properly fulfill that responsibility. Nonetheless, the effect on their appeal was the reverse of inspiring. Winning people to generosity as Chase did is one thing; shaming them into it as the trustees of General tried to do is another. It is not surprising that the *Proceedings* eventually carried a report that the 1861 appeal, like its starchy predecessors, had brought in less than expected.

How to Lose Friends and Alienate Evangelicals

Obtuse though the trustees were as fund-raisers, however, they were acute enough when it came to identifying a further—and much more serious—cause of the seminary's disappointingly feeble hold on the affections of the general Church, the alienation of the Evangelicals. For beginning in the late 1830's General became associated more and more strongly in peoples' minds with the most vociferous supporters of Tractarianism, giving it a reputation for "unsound teaching" that discouraged contributions (as the trustees frankly acknowledged)[17] and decisively

---

[16] *Ibid.*, pp. 445-448.
[17] *Ibid.*, p. 606.

changed the composition of the student body. For this, Hobart's successor, Bishop Onderdonk of New York, and the students themselves were chiefly responsible.

Benjamin Treadwell Onderdonk was an utterly loyal Episcopalian; but he shared what must have seemed to that generation almost a family failing for overemphasis. Like his brother, he did not know when to stop. He embraced everything that attracted him with a warmly undiscriminating enthusiasm that was as frank as it was unrestrained. This made him an engaging friend, a stimulating teacher, and a sometimes disconcertingly sympathetic pastor; but it played him false with spectacular results after he became bishop. It gave his manners a Regency exuberance that was all too easily misunderstood by a society that was becoming increasingly straitlaced in everything but the design of its furniture; and the same excess of vivacity overheated his public utterances to the point where misinterpretations of another kind unjustly but inevitably damaged not only Onderdonk himself, but also the seminary and the cause he had so much at heart.

The Oxford Tracts naturally contained much that appealed to the followers of Hobart, awaking interest among some of the professors and most of the students at General, who stood in that tradition. But the Evangelicals could hardly be expected to share this sympathy, and when the later tracts gave the Thirty-nine Articles and the doctrine of Justification by Faith—both touchstones of Evangelicalism—a face-lifting that strangely altered their appearance, they triggered every conditioned reflex of revulsion, rage, and dismay. In such circumstances it would have been difficult for anyone in Onderdonk's position to preserve the old atmosphere of mutual confidence which in the late 1820's had encouraged even such ferociously High and Low Church parsons as William Whittingham and Manton Eastburn to join together in a plan of com-

mon study;[18] but Onderdonk did not even try. In 1840
Evangelicals like Dr. Milnor began to express considerable
anxiety as to the implications of the enthusiasm for the
Oxford Tracts expressed at General.[19] Yet in 1841, in his
address to the diocesan convention, Onderdonk blithely
combined fervid praise of the tracts with an excoriation of
Protestantism as "covering with its name every variety
of schism, and every bold and wicked innovation of heresy;
forming an unholy alliance with the veriest infidelity." [20]
Pope Pius V could not have been more savage. In Onderdonk's classroom at General so intemperate a statement
might have been acceptable as a way of shocking apathetic
students into thought; but as part of the diocesan bishop's convention address in a moment of tension for the
Church it was an irresponsible piece of rhetorical self-
indulgence. Repeated lapses of judgment of this kind
stimulated all the Evangelicals' worst fears, with the result that when controversy erupted in 1843 over the ordination of Arthur Carey, a young graduate of General
whose Tractarian sympathies had alienated his rector, it
stirred up an emotional whirlwind. For once, Onderdonk
acted with dignity and studied moderation; but the dam-
age had already been done. The Evangelicals were convinced that General, if it did not harbor actual Roman-
ists, at least was an hospitable haven for "fellow-travelers"
with the bishop's blessing. From the Carey case it was only
a step to the Tudor-style investigation of the seminary by
the bishops in their visitatorial capacity in 1844, and the
presentation of Onderdonk himself for trial in 1845.

The investigation of the seminary was limited to a
cross-questioning of the faculty and an inspection of the
classroom space, chapel, and library.[21] The students were

---

[18] Turner, *Autobiography*, pp. 166-167.
[19] J. S. Stone, *Memoir of the Life of James Milnor*, p. 544.
[20] *Journal of Convention of Diocese of New York*, 1841, pp. 80-81.
[21] Turner, *Autobiography*, pp. 201-202.

left out of the inquiry.[22] The investigation therefore
cleared the professors, but did little to clear the air—for
the reason that the movement towards Rome which the
Evangelicals had thought they would uncover, had never
existed in the faculty at all, but among the students. Early
in 1845, Dr. Sparrow reported that word had reached him
in Virginia of a "regular conspiracy in the General Seminary to Romanize the Church. The students had formed
a society, secret, with the watchword " 'C.U.'—Catholic
Unity," he wrote, "and have been in communication with
the Roman Bishop." [23] The way in which Dr. Sparrow described the incident shows that he was more amused than
worried by the students' conspiracy to turn the seminaries
(Virginia among the rest) into stations on a kind of underground railway to Rome. Like other seminary professors
before and since, he must have been familiar with the extravagances of which theological students are capable in
the stage of spiritual adolescence through which all seem
to pass in the course of training for the ministry. Faith and
doubt and self-righteousness combine to produce strangely
rank growths in the seminary atmosphere that veers so
rapidly from torrid to frigid and back again. But what the
professors rightly recognize as a phase of immaturity,
tedious enough to be sure, others—laymen and parish
parsons with short memories—may diagnose as disease
which, if it cannot be eradicated, must at least be isolated.
So it was with General. In a pattern that was to recur repeatedly in the seminary's history, the antic churchmanship of a few students thus succeeded in fastening upon
General a reputation for ultra-ism which the trustees
and the professors both were powerless to counteract.[24]
The Evangelicals began to send their men and their
money elsewhere.

[22] *Ibid.*, p. 202.
[23] Walker, *Sparrow*, p. 159.
[24] *Proceedings*, IV, pp. 77, 435, 447. For similar difficulties in 1867 and
1871, see also references in Turner, *Autobiography*, p. 211.

How serious this was for General in the long run is revealed by Heman Dyer in his *Records of an Active Life*. For when the outbreak of the Civil War closed Virginia to the theological students from the North who had, in the years between 1845 and 1860, found their way to Alexandria in increasing numbers, the distrust of General still ran so deep that the Evangelicals were unwilling to go to New York instead. In their opinion,

. . . though that institution was, in name and by profession, a General Seminary, established by the General Convention and under the supervision of a board of trustees appointed by all the different dioceses, yet it has been so managed as to become the tool and agent of a narrow-minded partisanship, and had alienated and disgusted a large portion of our Church. Under these circumstances it was necessary to make provision for such students as would not go to New York, and could not go to Alexandria.[25]

The result was the opening of the Philadelphia Divinity School under the auspices of Bishop Alonzo Potter—who years before had opposed the foundation of diocesan seminaries precisely because they might weaken the New York seminary.[26] It is a significant revelation of how people felt at the time that at the very moment when the trustees of General were meeting with disappointment in their appeals for funds, Heman Dyer found no difficulty in raising $40,000 with which to endow a professorship and a lectureship for Philadelphia.[27] The pleasures of paranoid ecclesiastical partisanship for both sides in the nineteenth century came at a high price.

Except in the forties, and again in the sixties, however, the quarrels between Tractarians and Evangelicals caused

[25] Dyer, *Records*, p. 268.

[26] J. H. Hopkins, Jr., *The Life of the Late Right Reverend John Henry Hopkins, First Bishop of Vermont*, p. 137. (Hereafter cited as *Hopkins*.)

[27] Dyer, *Records*, p. 269. $250,000 was raised for the Divinity School before 1865.

no prolonged disturbance within the confines of General itself. The professors answered the bishops' questions in 1844 with what tart patience they could muster, and in 1845 expelled the most contentious students from the seminary, with Professor Ogilby, the faculty member whom the Evangelicals most distrusted (next to the unfortunate Onderdonk), taking the lead in the proceedings. Thereafter they settled quietly down once more to their teaching.

Although the Evangelicals did not think so, the professors were an unusually heterogeneous group—more so than the faculties at the other seminaries of the time. While the weight was certainly on the Hobartian end of the scale, they nonetheless represented several types of churchmanship from the semi-Evangelical position of Professor Turner through the eighteenth-century-style conservatism of Professor Wilson to the unabashed Tractarianism of Professor Ogilby and his successor, Professor Mahan. Shortly after the death of Professor Turner in 1861 narrowed the spectrum at one end, it was broadened at the other by the appointment of an exuberant Ritualist, George Seymour. The variety of teaching offered was enriched still further in the seventies by the appointment of lecturers whose point of view did not happen to be represented among the permanent professors.[28] The professors, furthermore, permitted the free expression of diverse opinions within their ranks with an equanimity that Gambier would have done well to emulate.[29]

Similar self-restraint governed the relationship between faculty and trustees. Although there were occasional manifestations of crochetiness from each side, there appears to have been none of the open wrangling that jarred so many of the other seminaries—Nashotah, Bexley, Seabury, and Western. The most active trustees, whether

[28] *Proceedings*, V, pp. 98, 100.
[29] Turner, *Autobiography*, p. 237.

New Yorkers or not, generally shared the Hobartian point of view, so that they had less in common with Professors Turner and Wilson, perhaps, than with other members of the faculty; but even at their most interfering, they did no more than make Turner a little peevish (as he confessed in his *Autobiography*)[30] by urging him indirectly, through the medium of the examining committee, to put more stress on the "authority" of the Church in his classes.

Room at the Top

As early as 1832 it was recognized that the seminary would be better off with a permanent, resident head who could preside at faculty meetings, take responsibility for discipline in the seminary, and serve as a communicating link between faculty, trustees, and the Church.[31] But it was easier to acknowledge the desirability of instituting such an office than actually to find a place for it in the existing administrative structure, much less find a suitable candidate for it once it was established. As a result, the proposal was not finally acted on for nearly forty years. The principal reason for the long delay is probably that in the minds of the trustees it was taken for granted, at least until the Civil War, that only a bishop would be imposing enough to fill such a post.[32] A bishop would have a seat in the House of Bishops, where the basic theological curriculum was determined, as well as commanding respect from clerical and lay trustees alike. But although such a solution was easy to achieve in diocesan seminaries by simply

---

[30] *Ibid.*, pp. 186-189.

[31] *Proceedings*, I, pp. 365-366.

[32] For a different explanation, see W. W. Manross, "The General Theological Seminary: Growth and Progress since 1860," *Historical Magazine of the Protestant Episcopal Church*, Sept., 1936, p. 267. Dr. Manross suggests that the trustees deliberately delayed appointing a permanent dean until after the death of Professor Turner because they liked him too much to pass him over, and disliked his Evangelical opinions too much to appoint him. The references to the subject in Brand, *Whittingham*, II, pp. 49-58, point to the less personal reason elaborated here.

making the diocesan bishop "president" or "dean," it proved impossible to procure at General. The difficult position of the episcopate in New York after 1845, with Bishop Onderdonk's reproachful figure hovering for so many years in the shadows behind the Provisional Bishop, Horatio Potter, added another complication. In 1856 and 1864, however, attempts were made to induce William Whittingham, Bishop of Maryland, to return to General as "President" and professor. He had been a very popular professor from 1836 to 1840, the year of his election to the episcopate. But Whittingham would not come unless he could be sure of retaining his seat and vote in the House of Bishops after resigning his diocese, a condition which it proved impossible to meet.[33] It was doubtless the failure of the second attempt, in the course of which opposition was expressed to the very idea of electing a diocesan bishop to a professorship in the seminary, that finally convinced the trustees that they should stop looking for a Right Reverend President, and hunt for a Very Reverend Dean instead. They found him four years later. Nonetheless, in settling for a dean, the trustees did not entirely give up the more grandiose conception of the office which they had had earlier. The dean of General Theological Seminary has remained a monarch among deans to this day, bearing a detectable—if muted—resemblance to the mitred figure of the trustees' dreams.

From 1832 until the advent of the "real" dean in 1869, the seminary made do with a less impressive official, the dean of the faculty, whose responsibilities were limited to keeping an eye on the fabric, ordering the janitor about, and adding a report of his own to the sheaf presented annually to the trustees by the professors. The office rotated among all the professors in order of seniority, each holder serving for a year. In an effort to provide something more

---

[33] Brand, *Whittingham*, II, pp. 49-58.

than strictly academic supervision of the students, somewhat ambiguous "pastoral" responsibilities were appended
to the office in 1837;[34] and in an effort to improve com-
munications between faculty and trustees, the dean-for-a-
year was authorized in 1860 to attend all trustees' meetings, although without a vote.[35]

The "Rotatory Headship," as the trustees termed it,
was too amorphous an office to satisfy anybody. An office
that passed so rapidly from hand to hand could not provide the stability and direction desired. Most of the professors held their posts for such long periods, however,
that they came in time to constitute such a stabilizing
and directive force in themselves. Once they joined the
faculty, they tended to stay until they either retired or
died, as did the professors at Alexandria. For the first
thirty years after the seminary returned from its short
sojourn in New Haven the faculty's real core—Turner,
Wilson, and Moore—did not change at all. The element of
continuity which these men provided must have been a
factor of some importance in minimizing the ill effects of
the ecclesiastical tempests of controversy to which, because
of its "general" character, the seminary was peculiarly
vulnerable.

Studies

During this period of General's history the curriculum
was derived from the course of study prescribed by the
House of Bishops in 1804, depending heavily on seven-
teenth-and-eighteenth-century Anglican theology. Except
in the case of Professor Turner, there is little evidence of
the interest in German biblical and theological works that
was shown at Andover and, to a lesser extent, Virginia.
Knapp's *Theology*—a staple of theological study at Virginia from the days of Dr. Keith until Dr. Walker's retire-

---

[34] *Proceedings*, I, pp. 612, 617.
[35] *Proceedings*, III, p. 347.

ment in 1895—was dismissed by one of the professors at
General as "a poor substitute for Pearson on the Creed." [36]
A few, more recent treatises by American or English
authors were introduced: the *Exposition of the Thirty-
Nine Articles* by E. Harold Browne (pub. 1850-53),
Richard Trench's *Notes on the Miracles of Our Lord*
(pub. 1846), and germane selections from the writings of
Bishop Hobart and Henry Ustick Onderdonk, sometime Bishop of Pennsylvania. But the tone of the annual
reports presented to the trustees by the professors, as well
as the tone of the reports of the trustees' own committee
which sat in on the oral examinations that brought each
academic year to an end, suggests that the trustees kept a
watchful eye on the teaching materials used by the professors, and gave them no encouragement to experiment
with many deviations from the traditional course.

What this actually meant for a student who was preparing for ordination by a three-year course of study at General may be gathered from a typical report drawn up by
the trustees' committee on the examination of the students in 1855.[37]

The junior class was given instruction in the "Evidences
of Christianity," homiletics, the Gospels in Greek, Hebrew
(with particular attention to the portions of Genesis that
were included in the Lectionary for Sundays and Holy
Days), and the first three centuries of the history of the
Early Church. The evidences course was based on a reading of Leslie, Paley, Trench, Hurd (on Prophecy), with
extra material drawn from contemporary periodicals by
the professor himself to armor the students against the
"various assaults of modern Infidelity." Gresley's *Treatise
on Preaching* was the textbook for homiletics—a book
as dull as most treatises on the subject; and, in addition,
the students analyzed one sermon a week by a famous

---

[36] *Ibid.,* p. 174.
[37] *Ibid.,* pp. 23-28.

preacher of the past and practiced preparing sermon outlines on their own on texts assigned by the professor,
handing in four complete sermons before the end of the
year. The texts used in the study of the Bible were not
cited in the report; but in ecclesiastical history the basic
books were Mosheim and Gieseler, as they had been for
over fifty years.

The middle class was given instruction in the Epistles
in Greek, more Hebrew (with particular attention to the
portions of Isaiah prescribed in the Calendar for Sundays
and Holy Days), church history from Constantine to
Charlemagne, theology (an examination of the articles of
the Apostles' Creed), and a course that combined liturgics,
homiletics, and lectures on the "awful responsibilities, and
sacred obligations of the Ministry." The basic theology
textbook was Pearson, with "enlargements from Scott on
the Mediatorial offices of Christ, West on the Resurrection, Hobart on the State of the Departed, and H. U. Onderdonk on Eternal Punishment." In liturgics, as no single
textbook covered the subject adequately, lectures were
supplemented by reading assignments in Wheatly, Hooker,
H. U. Onderdonk on *Episcopacy*, and Percival on the
Apostolic Succession. Once a week, in the evening, for
much of the year the students met for practice in composing and delivering sermons and in reading aloud from
the Bible.

The seniors concentrated on church history from the
Second Council of Nicaea through the Council of Trent,
on theology, and on the Prayer Book. The texts used in
the theology class were Magee on *Atonement* and *Sacrifice;* Hardwick, Burnet, and Browne on the Thirty-nine
Articles; the *Homilies*; Hooker on the *Sacraments*; Water-
land on *Justification* and *Regeneration*; Horsley's *Visitation Charges*; and Jerram on *Infant Baptism*. Burnet and
White provided material for studies on the nature of "the
pastoral Office." As in the junior and middle years, prac-

tice in writing and delivering sermons continued, along with the reading of lessons and services from the Prayer Book.

In addition to their academic studies, almost all the students had jobs analogous to what would now be called "Field Work." They taught Sunday School or superintended a Sunday School in one or another of the city parishes in New York, Brooklyn, or across the river on the Jersey shore. And some sang in church choirs or functioned as organists. This was not a matter of policy or evangelistic zeal (although the students were not at all deficient in that quality), but of simple necessity. Money earned in this way kept the students at school.

A Perennial Dilemma

So comprehensive a course of study, when coupled with the opportunities for applying its lessons in the field, is a recognizable ancestor of the modern curriculum; and the modern seminary professors and students who complain that the comprehensiveness has been secured at the cost of study in depth in our own day might be startled to discover their objections being voiced by their predecessors a century ago. Professor Turner was dean in 1855, and his comment on the seminary's curriculum made this very point:

It is the prevalent error of most of our Seminaries of education, from those of the lowest to those of the highest grade, that efforts are made to teach too much within a limited period of time; and I cannot but fear that the remark applies to the General Seminary. The Course is usually regarded as one of three years; but, if the Christmas and Easter recesses are added to the summer vacation of three months, the actual time of study becomes contracted into two years; and so many subjects are crowded within this short period, that, even without taking into consideration the inadequate preparation of some members, it is impossible to do justice to all. Sufficient time for examining important Theological points on critical and exegetical difficulties cannot be spared; and the consequence is, that the knowledge required is often meagre, while the intellectual powers have but little time to act upon the topic under examination. Vague and indistinct views must necessarily be the result of such a system of daily propulsion. I am satisfied that, to make full preparation for the two daily lectures, and to attend the daily services, appropriating also sufficient time for the required compositions, is such a demand on the sedentary application of the Student, as in many cases would be likely to impair his physical health, and that without rightly strengthening his mental and religious constitution.[38]

If Professor Turner's criticism of the curriculum was to be repeated many times in the future, so was the trustees' failure to reply to it. Instead of simplifying the curriculum, they drew up plans to expand it. When the train's freight cars are full, it is always easier to couple on a few new ones than to unload and repack the old ones.

The first actual addition was instruction in vocal sacred music one evening a week, which began in November, 1855.[39] It proved short-lived, but that was due to the personality of the instructor, not to a change of heart on the part of the trustees. The Rev. John Henry Hopkins, Jr., was the teacher, the eldest son of the Bishop of Vermont; and he took on the task for love, not money, as he not only received no remuneration, but also had to buy a large portion of the books used in his class out of his own pocket. A sparkling companion, he was very much what the English call an "original," walking about the New York streets dressed more like Audubon or Walt Whitman than like a clergyman, hair and beard long and curling, and the wide, flowing shirt collar open at the throat. Like his father he had in abounding measure a

[38] *Ibid.*, pp. 16-17.
[39] *Ibid.*, p. 73.

musician's talents, a musician's taste—and, unfortunately,
a musician's obstinacy. Hopkins had a passion for plainsong; and as organist at the services held daily in the room
that served for a chapel at General, he would play nothing
else. When the professor whose turn it was to take the
service happened to be Dr. Turner, who insisted that the
more conventional Anglican chants be sung when he
was in charge, Hopkins refused to play at all.[40] Most of
the students agreed with Turner. They loathed plainsong; and as Hopkins was less adept at persuasion than
attack, they attended his classes only when made to. Even
the organ, offended perhaps by Hopkins's description of
it as an "inferior instrument," [41] remained glumly un-
responsive to his touch. After two years Hopkins wisely
resigned.

The other embellishments of the curriculum produced
less dissension, but only, perhaps, because it was years
before they were actually put into effect. In 1855 a committee of trustees was appointed to go over the course of
study, obtain suggestions from the professors as to ways
in which it could be improved, and make recommendations. It took two years to do so, issuing its report in
1857.[42] Three years later these were included in a report
from the standing committee,[43] providing the basis for a
reorganization of the seminary that was carried out piecemeal over the next twenty years as the straitened circumstances of the institution would permit.

The impetus for this movement for reform, which followed closely on the publication of the Muhlenberg Memorial in 1853, and coincided with the Memorial's after-
math of comment and discussion in the General Convention of 1856, appears to have been provided by two devel-

---

[40] Turner, *Autobiography*, pp. 215-238.
[41] *Proceedings*, III, p. 74.
[42] *Ibid.*, pp. 143-149.
[43] *Ibid.*, pp. 363-382.

opments which had begun to affect the Church so strongly that they could no longer be ignored.

The first was the development of new ways of thought in philosophy and science that appeared to bring traditional Christian beliefs into serious question. By the late 1850's it was becoming obvious that Christian thinkers would have to reexamine some of their hitherto accepted assumptions, and rephrase some of the old arguments of Christian apologetic, if they wished to continue to win the assent of educated men.

The second was the accelerating pace at which areas of the country were being opened for settlement. Coupled with a keener appreciation of the Church's responsibility to reach into other areas, long since settled, where its ministry had been either ineffective or nonexistent, this called for an expanding supply of clergymen. A generation before, the rector of Trinity Church in the city of Boston had refused to contribute anything to help build a country church in a village outside Boston, explaining in his kindly way that "the Episcopal Church is for ladies and gentlemen, and ladies and gentlemen do not live in the country." [44] But at mid-century Episcopalians took a less restricted view of the sphere in which they were called to minister. They were beginning to see that they needed not only more clergymen, but also clergymen of different kinds; and consequently some were beginning to wonder whether the old-fashioned pattern of uniform training was appropriate any longer.

Within the seminary itself the prospect of increasing numbers was an additional factor in inducing the trustees and the professors to appraise critically the old methods, as well as the subjects, of instruction. A heavy reliance on individual recitations and classroom drill was characteristic of almost all institutions of learning, whether

---

[44] Clark, *Reminiscences,* p. 34.

school or college or seminary, until after the Civil War; but this was only efficient where classes were relatively small. The same was true of the system of oral examinations then prevalent; for as it was customary for the examiner to allot twenty minutes of questioning time to each student in the class, a marked increase in numbers would either make the system impossibly unwieldy or reduce the examination rapidly to a piece of *pro forma* nonsense. At General in the late 1850's signs of precisely such an expansion began to appear. In 1857 nine men were enrolled in the junior class; in 1858 eighteen; in 1859 sixteen; and in 1860 twenty. There were thirty-eight students in all enrolled at General in 1858; six years later their numbers had doubled. The effect of this was magnified by the failure of the trustees to fill vacant teaching posts, which had forced the three remaining professors to divide up the duties of instruction in "Pastoral Theology and Pulpit Eloquence" and "the Evidences of Christianity," adding these to the responsibilities which they had undertaken already in their own departments.

Almost exactly one hundred years later the same forces —a radically changing climate of thought, an expanding field for missionary enterprise, demonstrably inadequate resources, and rapidly increasing numbers of students— have precipitated a critical appraisal of modern theological education in much the same way.

ж 5

General's High-thinking Professors
and Plain-living Students

THE PROFESSORS at General submitted their suggestions
for improving the curriculum separately in writing to the
Committee on the Course of Study in 1856. They make
depressing reading for anyone who has sanguine hopes of
finding permanently effective solutions for any educational problems; for the professors' letters amply demonstrate that many of the conditions that trouble modern
seminary faculties were already frustrating their predecessors a century ago. The criticisms of theological education
which had bubbled to the surface in the wake of the
Muhlenberg Memorial had centered on the failure of
the seminaries to train the students to read the service
properly, to preach interesting sermons with warmth and
conviction, or to tackle the practical tasks of the ministry
with either methodical responsibility or common sense.[1]
The seminaries had also been criticized for failing to encourage the students to develop a more mature personal
religion.[2] There was nothing novel about any of these
criticisms even in 1856; for the bishops, at a meeting of

---

[1] Alonzo Potter, *Memorial Papers, passim.*
[2] *Ibid.*

the General trustees in 1830, had emphasized the necessity of preparing men for *"practical* parochial tasks," and suggested that the study of Hebrew should be reduced to one year (instead of three), to give more time for learning the intricacies of sermon preparation and preaching techniques.[3] The professors were entirely aware of the criticisms (two of the three professors—Dr. Turner and Dr. Johnson—had been among the signers of the original Memorial), and they dealt with them inferentially if not directly in their suggestions; but their principal anxieties lay elsewhere.

The Professors Suggest Improvements

The three professors all agreed with the trustees that conditions beyond the seminary's control dictated an unavoidable expansion of the curriculum. Among themselves they were agreed as well, however, that the course of study was already so full that unless the time allotted to the traditional disciplines was somehow reduced, expansion of the curriculum would be impossible. The advances of philosophy and science presented problems to faith which obviously must be dealt with in the seminary. On the other hand, the fact that the students were entering the seminary increasingly ill-prepared in Greek, Latin, Hebrew, ancient history, and—to the horrified surprise of the professors—increasingly ignorant of the contents of the English Bible, meant that the seminary must begin instruction in languages, history, and the Bible at a more elementary level than it had ever done before. It was the familiar problem of how to stuff still more into an already overfilled trunk.

The professors' solution was not of a kind that would have reassured the bishops in 1830 (or in 1856). In effect, it was to reduce to a minimum the classroom time de-

---

[3] *Proceedings,* I, p. 332.

voted to the "practical" subjects—homiletics, liturgics, pastoral care; and instead to invite lecturers from outside the seminary to speak on these subjects, as well as on the new developments of philosophy and science. Professor Turner, agreeing that the manner in which most parsons read the service was abominable, was in favor of retaining the old system of requiring practice in reading of all the students during the entire three-year course; but he thought that homiletics could more wisely be confined to the senior year, when the students would have learned enough to have something to say that was worth hearing. He thought that liturgics should be squeezed back into church history where it belonged.[4] Professor Mahan was equally blunt about pastoral care:

The Duties and Relations of the Pastoral Office are an excellent theme for reading, observation, and quiet reflection; but, like most subjects of an immediately practical character, not exactly fitted for the Class-Room. I have little faith in any effort to *teach* ministerial or spiritual *tact*. Such things are learned not taught. At the same time, a few carefully prepared lectures, not by a Professor, but by some able and experienced Pastor, or Bishop, who should come before the students with the odor of the hay-fields, as it were, breathing fresh and sweet around him, would have the effect—which is all that is needed prior to actual experience—of awakening the minds of young men to the importance and sacredness of the subject.[5]

Mahan had an unusually incisive mind, and he had apparently given much thought to the philosophy underlying the seminary's pattern of instruction. He was therefore more prepared than were his two colleagues to prescribe in detail the proper scope and spirit of the lectures with which it was proposed to supplement the traditional

⁴ *Proceedings*, III, p. 161.
⁵ *Ibid.*, pp. 181-182.

course of study; and what he wrote is an interesting revelation of the educational theory of the period—made all the more vivid by reason of Mahan's refreshingly clear and robust style. Pointing out that among the subsidiary subjects of study "more or less necessary to the outfit of an accomplished ministry," [6] must be included, not only pastoral theology, but also *"The Evidences of Christianity, Theologia Moralis,* embracing *Casuistry* (a study too much neglected), *Canon Law, Rhetoric, Logic, Music,* and the like," [7] he stated:

To any one conversant with studies of this kind, and with the average abilities of the young men who enter the Seminary, it is manifest that the whole, or even the greater part of them, cannot be properly attended to in the routine of Seminary instruction. The attempt to take them all in overcrowds our limited time, and confuses and perplexes the minds of the Students. No School can possibly furnish all that a clergyman ought to know. Something must be left for after study.

A line must be drawn, in fact, between things *necessary to be taught,* and things *necessary to be learned.* The former, as a general rule, are dry, elemental, and skeleton-like—too abstract, too theoretic, too intricate, to be acquired by ordinary, unaided diligence in reading. They belong, therefore, to the Class-Room. They must be *taught*—line upon line, and precept upon precept. They are matters of routine and drill. The latter are more juicy, more attractive, more immediately and obviously useful, more easily picked up in the ordinary course of reading, experience, or conversation; and for that reason may be safely left to the enlightened industry and ambition of after-life. To introduce such studies into the Class-Room savors more of quackery than of solid education. . . .[8]

. . . I believe, however, that the system now generally pursued at the Seminary, viz., that of regular and constant class-room drill, might be judiciously *enlivened,* and so far im-

[6] *Ibid.*, p. 178.
[7] *Ibid.*
[8] *Ibid.*

proved by courses of *Lectures* on subjects of more practical and popular interest.

For example: the subject of *Apologetics,* or, to narrow the field, of *Evidences,* in reference to the semi-infidel, materialistic, or pantheistic drift of modern positive philosophy, is undoubtedly a matter of great and growing interest. The same may be said of certain questions of *infallibility, inspiration, authority,* and the like, which are already assuming formidable proportions in the mother country, and which the clergy now growing up, ought to be prepared for. But such things are not good subjects of class-room instruction. The able controversialist, whether against the absolutism of unreasoning faith on the one side, or against that of reckless negation on the other, is formed more by sound, general culture, than by any specific cramming with objections and answers. In modern warfare, muscle is of more avail than armor. The best defender of Christianity is the man who knows best what Christianity is. A particular study of multifarious issues and evasions is, with half-formed minds, more apt to shake the faith, to blunt the edge of the theological instinct, and to foster, in fact, a captious, undevout, and pragmatical turn of mind, than to raise up really able and well-grounded apologists.[9]

To lectures on these subjects (which he thought might be grouped under the headings of Infidelity, Romanism, and Sectarianism), Mahan suggested that others should be added in liturgics and Christian ethics. He concluded:

I can conceive, in short, of a *Course of Lectures,* extending over three years, embracing three or four or more subjects, numbering from six to twelve or twenty Lectures each Seminary year, attended by the Students, and open to the public, which should contribute largely to spiritual and intellectual culture, without being a tax upon the time that has to be given to drier and more elementary studies; for such a course the best talents in the Church, in this country, and perhaps in England, might be enlisted. Men of high standing should be

---

[9] *Ibid.,* pp. 180-181.

sought, men of eloquence as well as learning. The course should be entertaining as well as instructive. For that, to my mind, is a matter of no little importance. Of regular routine work the Students have enough. Hebrew, History, Hermeneutics, Systematic Divinity, and the like, are dry and hard studies; and a conscientious teacher, who understands the importance of system, can not well make them otherwise. Without Class-Room drill, which is not only hard work, but often somewhat of a bore, no solid foundation can be laid. Still, "all work and no play" is as bad for Students of Divinity, as it is for others. And it seems to me, that so far as the intellectual work of the Seminary is concerned, a little more "play," a little more diversion of a healthy kind, is precisely the thing most needed.

And the Lecture or strictly Professorial system—generally adopted on the continent of Europe—has undoubtedly one advantage over the Tutorial—which is preferred in the English Universities—that it gives larger scope to the *genius* of the Lecturer, or Professor; and is therefore more enlivening, more enkindling, more apt to communicate to the minds of Students a real enthusiasm for the subject-matter of instruction. But, why not unite the two methods? Having made a sufficient provision for routine work, why not concede something to that kind of influence, powerful, but not strictly definable, which is exerted upon young men by mere force of contact with superior and well-trained minds? an influence, I may observe, however, which depends somewhat on its *rarity*, and which the patient drudgery of the Class-room seriously impairs.[10]

The professors were all agreed that the study of Hebrew should be reduced from three years to two. Professor Turner felt that this would be feasible if the oral examination at the end of the year was stiffened so that the students were induced to take the language more seriously and study harder. (He pointed out that while the examining committee of trustees was not slow to blame the teacher if the class made a poor showing, it had yet

[10] *Ibid.*, pp. 182-183.

to fail anyone—a weakness which the students had not been slow to perceive.) Mahan, in view of the rudimentary command of the classical languages displayed by the students when they entered the seminary, was not so much in favor of prefacing the regular seminary course with a preliminary, preparatory class (an expedient suggested by Professor Turner) as of spending most of the junior year itself in grammatical study of Greek, Latin, and Hebrew, using the Septuagint, the New Testament, and some of the Greek and Latin Fathers as texts to be "read, parsed, and construed, as Xenophon or Caesar are read at school," [11] setting up a special Linguistic Department for the purpose. Admission to the middle year would depend on a demonstration of proficiency in the three tongues in the examination. To make this possible, Mahan was willing to postpone to the middle year the subjects usually studied in the junior year. As he considered the evidences material more suitable for lectures in any event, this really meant that only the study of the history of the Early Church would have to be sandwiched into the routine of recitation and drill planned for the middle year. And this, Mahan felt, might be still further trimmed by giving the juniors one lecture a week on the Church of the period of the New Testament and the Apostolic Fathers. In addition, he estimated that after so concentrated a study of Greek, Latin and Hebrew, the students would be able to cover the material assigned in the later biblical, theological, and historical work so much faster, that the time gained for the traditional subjects in the last two years would more than make up for the time relinquished in the first.

Professor Turner was the only member of the faculty to question the advisability of continuing to require that all the students pursue the same course of study. Recognizing by implication the need for practical men in the

---

[11] *Ibid.*, p. 179.

ministry emphasized in the Memorial, he suggested that it might be wise for the seminary to consider establishing two courses of instruction, the first being more strictly academic than the second:

The former might correspond, in a good degree, with the present; the latter might be limited to the English Bible, with such introductory accompaniments and illustrations as may be necessary and proper, and to the plainer English works on Theology and Ecclesiastical History. Thus some general and accurate knowledge might be secured of the English Scriptures, and of English Divinity; and practical and sensible men of religion and piety might be trained as effective laborers in the Lord's vineyard.[12]

It was Turner, also, who alone raised the question of a program of graduate study:

I will venture also to express my hope, that the time will come when the General Theological Seminary will be able to afford facilities for carrying on a Divinity Course to some high degree of excellence. Its best educated members, the most studious and careful examiners, who have assiduously employed their time and devoted their attention to the prescribed course, from its commencement to its close, know and feel, that they have done little more than lay a foundation on which to erect a superstructure hereafter if circumstances and opportunity allow. Would it not be a blessing to the Church if some arrangement could be made, whereby graduates might be enabled to pursue an extended course? To illustrate solely from my own Department: Is it not desirable that opportunity and facilities should be afforded to studious young men to go profoundly into the study of the Scriptures, so as to keep pace with the advanced literature of the age in that Department of Divine knowledge?—to be competent to meet the Jew, by an acquaintance with his own Rabbinical expositors?—the philosophic infidel, by an extensive acquaintance with geology, astronomy, ethnology, science, and phi-

---

[12] *Ibid.*, pp. 166-167.

losophy in general?—to become so familiar with the Bible, in its original tongues, and the prominent historical interpretations of successive ages, as to be able to settle every religious principle on the ground of Scriptural authority, the Protestant rule of faith?—and to maintain against errorists of all sorts, the Church's true and revealed doctrine, by a fundamental application of such learning as is demanded by the sound principles of exegesis? In this way a class of Divines might be raised, competent to fill, with honor to themselves, and unbounded service to the Church, any position which may require more than ordinary talent and learning.[13]

Besides submitting suggestions for improving the course of study, the committee had also asked the professors to comment on the question of appointing a "Pastoral Head" for the seminary. This obviously involved that responsibility for the spiritual health of the students as well as for their academic work and physical well-being which the seminaries had been accused of neglecting. As early as 1837 concern had been expressed by the trustees because the students, although a Christian family, were without a recognizable "father" in the seminary, and therefore uncomfortably close to being "sheep without a shepherd." [14] It was for that reason that the paternal figure of the dean of the faculty was reinforced with slightly enlarged powers, and the suggestion made that he or a substitute should pay a visit to every student's room at least once every two weeks during term time.[15]

The professors were unanimous in thinking this a ticklish subject; and they handled it gingerly. Professor Turner pointed out that the students were already subject to the pastoral authority of their bishop, their rector, and generally connected as well (supposing that they came from a parish outside New York itself) with a parish in the city where they worked on Sundays to earn their

[13] *Ibid.*, p. 167.
[14] *Proceedings*, I, p. 617.
[15] *Ibid.*, p. 612.

board and keep. "Pastoral" meant to him and his colleagues (and presumably the trustees, too) not just a
friendly response to human need; it carried with it the
obligation to judge on spiritual grounds the student's
fitness as a candidate for the ministry. This was obviously
the parish rector's responsibility; but the professors were
not at all sure that the seminary could or should be
asked to share it. Turner doubted that it was wise to
mix judgment of the student's academic and spiritual
fitness in this way, and was afraid that conscientious exercise of such a responsibility would bring the seminary
into collision with the student's bishop and home parish.
Mahan did not see how the seminary head could act like
a parish rector without turning the seminary into a
parish:

A Pastor implies a flock. A flock must be duly folded in a
regular congregation. A regular congregation, in a city like
this, especially if it is designed for the benefit of young men
mainly, must have all the usual facilities of worship, "in the
beauty of holiness"—good preaching, good music, a goodly
array of worshippers and hearers, a certain genial warmth, a
kindly intermixture of "old men and children, young men
and maidens," and many like things needless to mention.
The absence of these advantages makes it disagreeable to the
Students to attend Sunday worship in the Seminary, and more
disagreeable to the Faculty to require their attendance. A
Seminary Chapel *might* be made a model of devout, sober,
and yet beautiful Christian worship. It might be made a living
centre of Mission work in the City, of the very best kind.
As it is, however, there are no proper facilities for any
thing of the sort: and the appointment of a Pastoral Head
would have no other effect in this respect, than that, what
the Professors now feel as a divided, and therefore tolerable
burthen, he would have to bear in all its concentrated force.
The office would be a weariness and a disappointment to
him.[16]

---

[16] *Proceedings,* III, p. 183.

Professor Johnson made the same points, but added one of his own: that there were too few students to require the fulltime ministrations of one man; and that any clergyman willing to assume such a responsibility, therefore, would very likely be just the wrong man to do so:

If he were very zealous in his spiritual care, having so few to deal with, his intensity of feeling might make him overdo the matter, and so deal unwisely with the young men; dissecting their private, sacred feelings, and peering into their thoughts, and into the common faults of the spiritual man in conflict with the natural, tormenting the shrinking and delicate mind, and hardening the bolder and the coarser one —sacred feelings and common infirmities, which had far better be left to the ordinary influences of affectionate care, of Christian intercourse, and the general instructions of God's Word and Sanctuary, and to God's grace, than thus particularly dealt with. I should deplore it, if some such men as I have read of, and known, admirable men too, should be shut up to such a charge.[17]

The Trustees Concur

The trustees' committee was so impressed with the professors' suggestions that it adopted the principal ones in its own report, and they were repeated in 1860. A preparatory course was recommended for students who made a bad showing in the entrance examination, and an examination on the contents of the English Bible was to be added to the admission requirements. The committee recommended the introduction of the system of special lectures. It urged the building of a proper chapel, and the appointment of a chaplain whose duties, besides the pastoral care of the students, should also include the supervision of a chapel Sunday school and the visiting of the sick (in company with students). The establishment of fellowships for graduate study was advised. It was sug-

---

[17] *Ibid.*, p. 176.

gested that written, as well as oral, examinations should be given. And a revised curriculum was drawn up which, it was stated, was beyond the capability of the minute faculty of 1860 to put into effect, but which was intended to be a guide to faculty expansion in the future. The curriculum was a significant foreshadowing of the change from the text-centered curriculum of the past to the subject-centered curriculum of today:

CURRICULUM [18]

1. *Hebrew and Greek Languages.*
   (a) Exercises in translating and parsing Hebrew.
   (b) Critical explanation of certain passages in the Hebrew Scriptures.
   (c) Readings in the Septuagint and Patristic Greek.
       One Professor, and a Tutor if necessary.

2. *Philosophy of Christianity.*
   (a) Philosophical Introduction to the Christian Religion. By Lectures.
   (b) General principles and necessary basis of a Catholic Religion. By Lectures.
   (c) Morals, as deducible from a revealed Religion. By Lectures.
       One Professor.

3. *Dogmatic Theology.*
   (a) The Doctrines of the Church Catholic—The Creeds.
   (b) The True Doctrine of the Sacraments, in their aspects religious and moral.—What their efficacy, and what the cause and conditions thereof.
   (c) Special Dogmas—Rome—Calvin—Luther, &c., &c.— These considered historically and scripturally.
       One Professor—Text Books and Lectures.

4. *Pastoral Office and Duties.*
   (a) Homiletics—Sermons, Composition and Delivery.
   (b) Liturgics—value, use and history of Liturgies—Ameri-

---

[18] *Ibid.*, pp. 371-372.

can Prayer Book—its particular history and proper
use.
(c) Catechetics—Pastoral Instruction, public and private.
(d) Duties of Pastor to the souls of his flock.
(e) Duties to the bodies of his hearers.
One Professor for first 2—Chaplain, for last 3.

5. *Ecclesiastical Law.*
(a) History of Canon Law.
(b) The General Canon Law of the Church.
(c) Canon and Rubrical Law, and Constitution of the
Protestant Episcopal Church in the United States—
historical and explanatory.
One Professor—Lectures.

6. *Ecclesiastical History.*
(a) History of the Church General, with particular reference to the introduction of Dogmas.
(b) History of the Church of England; particularly of the
independent origin of the British Church.—The English Reformation.
(c) History of the Protestant Episcopal Church in the
United States.
One Professor—Text Books and Lectures.

7. *Evidences of Christianity.*
(a) Nature and need of Revelation, and herein of Inspiration.
(b) Objections considered and answered.
(c) Harmony of Science and Revelation.
(d) Internal Evidence derived from adaptation of Christianity to man's moral nature and necessities.
One Professor—Lectures and Tutor.

8. *Biblical Exegesis and Literature.*
(a) Critical examination and Exegetical study of the Old
and New Testaments in the original texts.
(b) Doctrines—history and harmony, or consistency of the
whole.
One Professor, and an adjunct, or Tutor.

But Nothing Is Done

Despite the approval with which most of these proposals were greeted, however, not one of the three professors lived to see them put into effect. Turner died in 1861. Mahan resigned in 1864 to take a parish in Baltimore, dying in 1870. Johnson retired in 1869, and died in 1873. These were the years of the seminary's desperate financial crisis. It could not manage to pay the professors it already had, much less engage new ones. Nor could it offer any fee to a visiting lecturer. The trustees were naturally preoccupied with the institution's plight, which in itself reflected a little embarrassingly on their administration in the past. The professors, on the other hand, had no power to adopt the reforms on their own, even if they wished to do so. All initiative remained with the trustees. Not until 1865 was permission given to the dean and faculty to invite lecturers to the seminary, and even then the approval of the standing committee was stated to be required before each invitation was extended.[19] So, despite grumbles that General was falling steadily farther behind the times,[20] things continued much as they always had. The professors included more lectures in their classes as a variation from the old recitation system; that was all. And despite the three professors' unanimous testimony to the futility of such a step, the dean of the faculty was given a second title: chaplain.

Along with the outbreak of the Civil War, the financial *débâcle,* and the sclerotic administrative structure at General, another factor in dissipating the momentum for reform generated in the 1850's was the almost complete turnover of the faculty in the course of the 1860's; for the new faculty lacked the experience, the authority, and—to some extent—the ability of the old.

---

[19] *Ibid.,* p. 714.
[20] *Ibid.,* p. 683.

Turner's successor was Dr. Samuel Seabury, grandson of the bishop, and for many years editor of *The Churchman* and rector of a city parish. Every bit as pugnacious as his grandfather, he had a cross-grained prejudice in favor of unpopular causes, in whose service he indulged a rather undiscriminating taste for the offensive. Infuriating opponents, not winning converts, was his forte. By 1861, however, he was old, set in his ways, and failing in health. Retaining his parish, he did not concentrate his ebbing energies exclusively on the seminary.

Mahan's successor was the Rev. George F. Seymour, the future Bishop of Springfield. Seymour was young, alert, intelligent, well-read, and an able teacher. But unlike Mahan, he was not so much forceful as effervescent. There was about him, small and quick as he was, a good deal of the fox terrier: the same bright-eyed, personal charm; the same spunk; and the same darting aberrations in judgment. As a strategist in the field of education or in church affairs, he was generally shrewd; but as a tactician, he was deplorable. This—quite apart from his controversial ritualistic idiosyncrasies—weakened his influence.

The professor of pastoral theology from 1862 to 1889 was the Rev. William E. Eigenbrodt, whose long career, despite his generous and kindly disposition and impeccable manners, demonstrated convincingly that in teaching simple industry is no substitute for ability. The man who defined genius as "the infinite capacity for taking pains" had not known Professor Eigenbrodt. Curriculum reforms of the kind suggested by Turner, Johnson, and Mahan would probably never have occurred to him.

The other addition to the faculty was temperamentally fully as committed to the *status quo* as either Seabury or Eigenbrodt. This was the Rev. John Murray Forbes, who became the seminary's first permanent head in 1869. In the sensitive area of churchmanship Forbes was unusually well-travelled; for he had not only gone to Rome, like Newman and Manning, but come back again. During his Roman period, furthermore, he had had an opportunity to acquire some expertise in the intricacies of seminary administration while organizing for Pius IX the American College for Priests in the Holy City. But although his contemporaries thought highly of him, his conduct of affairs at General suggests that he was as it were still suffering too much from travel-sickness after his ecclesiastical Grand Tour to be able to do either himself or the seminary justice during his deanship. Bereft, at least for a time, of any sense of humor, his manner varied between the solemn and the fretful. Overexposure to Rome had left him too tense to treat calmly the students' theological and devotional vagaries; and his administration bore the telltale signs of weakness: long periods of dismayed mumbling punctuated by sharp bursts of violent and arbitrary action. Consequently it was not until after he resigned in 1872, to be succeeded by Seymour, that the atmosphere relaxed sufficiently to make possible renewed attention to the curriculum.

Hardships of Student Life

The glacial rate of change in the course of study, in spite of so much talk about it, was duplicated when it came to improving living conditions for the students. Here too there was a good deal of discussion, but little action. The strong sense of corporateness embracing both students and faculty, which was made so much of at Virginia, was never much in evidence at General; and although it was asserted that the student body was "a christian family," [21] the familial regime appears to have remained for many years as permissive as the most emancipated modern could wish. After 1837, when an attempt was made to tighten discipline, chapel attendance was made compulsory, as

---

[21] *Proceedings,* I, p. 617.

was attendance at classes; but otherwise the students were still left very much to themselves—partly, perhaps, because most of the professors were so much older. They were given rooms in the seminary buildings; but aside from causing a fire hazard (no stoves could be installed without the dean's permission),[22] how they lived and what they ate was up to them.[23] Some, like their modern counterparts, took considerable interest in their surroundings, papering or painting their rooms themselves, and, as the trustees' Committee on the General State of the Seminary once reported, showing "much good taste . . . in the arrangement of their furniture and books, and the adornment of them with simple and uncostly, but beautiful engravings of some of the noblest works of Christian art." [24] Some, on the other hand, as the committee also felt compelled to report, showed a "marked neglect of cleanliness and good order . . . much carelessness . . . much want of the commonest neatness." [25] Apparently they shared the popular contemporary taste for chewing tobacco, a practice of which the committee, looking at the stained floors, could not speak "in terms of too decided reprehension." [26] Dirt and disorder could reach dismaying proportions as arrangements for washing and cleaning the rooms were always sketchy. Even the ideal standard set by the trustees only prescribed that "the floor of every inhabited room should be thoroughly scrubbed at least once a month, and the windows, woodwork generally, halls, and stairs once every three months." [27] The cost of living at the seminary—including only food, washing, fuel, and light (there was no room rent or tuition charge)—

[22] *Ibid.*, p. 612.
[23] For a time efforts were made to manage a seminary vegetable garden worked by the students. *Proceedings* I, p. 411. A similar expedient was tried at Kenyon.
[24] *Proceedings*, III, p. 94.
[25] *Ibid.*
[26] *Proceedings*, I, p. 660.
[27] *Ibid.*, p. 430.

was $70.95 in 1831 for each student (with two students to a room).[28] This was only 95 cents more than the rate "of unexampled cheapness" boasted of by Bishop Chase at Kenyon. But in six years it was half again as much;[29] and by the beginning of the Civil War it was over three times what it had been forty years before.[30] Although some scholarships were given to help to meet these expenses, there were never enough to release the students from the financial anxieties so frequently reflected in the records of the period.

Indeed, sickness and poverty appear to have been the two constant companions of the men at General during the first sixty or seventy years of its history. Poetic references to the beauty and "salubrity" of the seminary's site notwithstanding, the hollow by the river was an unhealthy spot. Whereas Virginia did not have a student die in course until 1890, hardly a year passed in New York without the withdrawal of students because of bad health; and often the dean's annual report would have one or two deaths to mourn. Some of these were due to the rapid spread of disease in a city which constantly outgrew its sanitary facilities, such as they were. One student died of "gaol fever" contracted while ministering to city prisoners, for example; and Professor Turner's death of what was diagnosed as typhoid might also be ascribed to urban dirt. But constant references to colds and the incidence of tuberculosis were evidences of the fatal effect of the dampness sucked into the low-lying buildings, whose heating was never adequate from year to year.

What no doubt contributed fully as much as the unhealthy location to spreading sickness among the students, however, was poverty—with its attendant evils: overwork and an inadequate diet. Even with the opportunities for

---

[28] *Ibid.*, p. 356.
[29] *Ibid.*, p. 615.
[30] *Proceedings*, III, p. 352.

part-time work available in the city, some men ran so short of money that they had to withdraw from the seminary for a time until they could put by a little in savings again; and the extremities to which students could be reduced are vividly demonstrated in Heman Dyer's memoirs:

. . . One day, a hot summer day, a student from the General Theological Seminary called on me and said that two or three students were staying at the seminary during the summer vacation. They had remained to pursue their studies, that they might make up some deficiencies, and at the same time be in the way of earning a little money in mission work in the city, and that one of them was very ill in his room and wished to see me.

As soon as possible I went, and found the young man very ill. He was alone, and almost an entire stranger to the few other students remaining. I spent an hour and more with him, and by dint of persevering inquiries I satisfied myself his sickness was more of the mind and heart than of the body.

I learned that in order to save expenses he had nearly starved himself in college; he had boarded himself in his own room until he became ill, and then a poor widow woman who had done some work for him, insisted that he should take his meals with her. This he did, but he could not pay; and when he left college he was in debt.

On entering the seminary he undertook to do some teaching, that he might pay his debt as well as meet his current expenses. This he had been doing the preceding year. The strain was too great, and he broke down under it; being of a nervous, sensitive nature he had kept his troubles to himself. None of the professors or students knew of his circumstances or what was needed. On leaving, I said, "You must now have some nourishing food, and when I call to-morrow, you must let me know how much you owe. Put down everything, add it up, and let me know the amount; that is all I care to have." I then made the necessary arrangements about food, and such care as he needed, and left.

The same afternoon I saw Mrs. Banyer and Miss Jay, and

briefly stated the case. They at once authorized me to act for them, and furnish all that was necessary.

The next day I called at the seminary, and found the young man in much better spirits; and instead of giving the amount of his indebtedness, he had written out a detailed statement of his affairs, showing what his debts were, and for what they had been contracted. It was a clear case of a high-spirited, high-toned, conscientious young man, trying to pay his own way through a long course of study, without any means except such as he could earn as he went along. The result was, he greatly overtaxed a delicate and nervous frame, broke down his health, and became unable to earn any money, or even to pursue his studies. We can admire the heroism of the man, but doubt the wisdom of his course.

I returned to Mrs. Banyer and Miss Jay, and reported the state of affairs financially. Several hundred dollars were necessary to pay his debts and meet his immediate necessities in the way of clothing, etc. This sum they gave me, and added a handsome amount to enable the young man to go into the country and spend a month or two in regaining his health. This was a noble and generous act; but it was like them to do it, and I may add, that they looked after his wants afterwards, until his ordination.[31]

That was in the early 1850's. It shows how rudimentary the seminary's organization was nearly forty years after its beginning that the students went to Dyer for help (no seminary professor or trustee, presumably, being accessible), and that the debt (which was not insubstantial in a day when "several hundred dollars" would have comprehended the entire salary of the janitor at General— and, no doubt, of more than a few parish clergy) was met through the generosity of John Jay's daughters, who were both staunch Evangelicals, rather than through the agency —if not the funds—of the seminary directly.

The establishment of a refectory under a matron and four assistants in 1867 may have helped to improve the

---

[31] Dyer, *Records,* pp. 239-240.

students' diet;[32] but the strain imposed by the necessity
of part-time work was still an important factor in im-
peding the development of anything more than a minimal
routine of corporate worship and study in the 1870's. Dean
Forbes complained to the trustees in 1871

. . . that, during the two years he has now held his present
office, he is satisfied that the whole body of Students have
never once all met together in the Chapel at the same time,
whether for prayers, or on an occasion of the administration
of the Holy Communion, or for any special instruction provided for them. During the last Advent season the Dean
prepared with care, and delivered a course of lectures to the
Students on a subject of great practical importance, intending
to follow it with a similar course during the season of Lent;
but not more than about one-half the Students were present
at any one time. The Right Rev. the Bishop of Western
New York kindly offered to deliver a short course of lectures
to them on the subject of Prophecy. The attendance was
about the same, and the reason is that, apart from the hours
of daily service and of recitation, there is no hour, morning,
or afternoon, or evening, in which some of the Students are
not engaged in the necessary work of helping to support
themselves by some work outside the walls of the Seminary.[33]

The Brighter Side

Yet for all the hardships and frustrations of their seminary
life, the students were not subdued. When funds could
not be procured with which to redecorate the dingy chapel
and purchase a new organ to replace the one which had
so tried the musical genius of John Henry Hopkins, Jr.,
the students raised the money themselves by holding a
concert.[34] And the record of faculty head-shakings in the
troubled 1840's and 1870's reveals that the seminarians
were quite as argumentative and quick to debate con-

[32] *Proceedings*, IV, p. 58.
[33] *Ibid.*, pp. 441-442.
[34] *Proceedings*, III, pp. 562, 597.

troversial ecclesiastical issues then as are their better-fed and better-off counterparts in the present day. On one occasion the juniors offended the trustees' examining committee with their "incessant talking and indecorous levity." [35]

The professors, however, except in rare instances deliberately refrained from subjecting the students to a tight rein. In resisting pressures to be strict disciplinarians, and require complete theological and behavioral conformity from the students, Turner the Evangelical, Mahan the Tractarian, and Seymour the Ritualist were at one. It was in part disagreement with this policy that impelled Forbes to resign. The unruly conduct of the juniors in 1860, for example, was defended on the ground that "the Examination of the Junior Class, occurring in a room exposed to all the noises of the streets, and on Wednesday (the day complained of), being disturbed by the talking and frequent going in and out of numerous visitors, the attention of the examining Professor, as well as that of the Class, is much distracted." [36] Instead of the repressive measures which the trustees hoped for, it was suggested that a better way to encourage sobriety and industry among the students would be to single out the best among them for special honor. "The prospect of reward," the trustees were reminded, "is as legitimate an aid to the sense of duty, and at least as powerful, as the fear of censure." [37] Such studied moderation was the product of compassion as well as of a sense of proportion refined by experience. Mahan, who had taught boys in the Episcopal High School at Virginia before coming to New York to teach men at General, declared in the course of a detailed consideration of the disciplinary problems of the seminary that "every educational institution is necessarily somewhat

---

[35] Ibid., p. 319.
[36] Ibid., p. 397.
[37] Ibid., p. 423.

of a *hospital* in its character: it deals with the sick rather than with the whole; it has among its inmates some who are growing better, and some (perchance) who in spite of every effect grow worse." [38] In that statement the "(perchance)" is significant. It reflects the basic optimism tempered with caution, the ingrained reluctance ever to give up hope, that is characteristic of both the real teacher and the true parish priest. The professors at General were no less unwilling than their colleagues at Virginia and Gambier to submerge the teacher in the censor, or the censor in the judge. Within the seminary in the formative years of its history, as in their ministry outside it, they tried to keep faith with the vision of the character of the Christian Church that Dr. Turner eloquently described in a matriculation address to the juniors in Advent, 1849: the Church that "kindles, on the shore of the ever-troubled sea of mistiness and doubt, that lofty beacon-light, which, supplied with the holy oil of the sanctuary, shall never go out, but burn and flame and blaze in a celestial splendor, until its divine warmth and illumination shall have dissipated error, and shall have animated and attracted to itself all the tempest-tossed and perishing." [39]

---

[38] *Ibid.*
[39] Turner, *Autobiography,* p. 229.

ж 6

In Another Part of the Forest

WHILE Bishop Meade, Bishop Hobart, and Bishop Chase were acquiring experience of the mingled satisfactions and frustrations of running a theological seminary, Bishop Griswold of the Eastern Diocese (which included all the New England states except Connecticut) was growing increasingly eager to try the experiment himself. General had been in its East Building but a year, Virginia had just moved to its hill outside Alexandria, and the students at Gambier were only beginning to prepare their raw log cabins for the first winter above the Kokosing, when Griswold broached the subject publicly in an address to the annual convention of the diocese that met in September, 1828, in Bellows Falls, Vermont:

The General Theological Seminary is an institution wise and useful. I was among the first to bring forward the motion for its establishment; and hope, while I live, to be among its supporters. But, as must have been expected, it diminishes the number of our candidates, and causes a loss to this Diocese of some of its most promising young men. The advantages of such a Seminary must, of course, be far greatest to the Diocese, in which it is located. But we ought to banish from our minds all local prejudices, and party feelings, to view the Church as one, and to rejoice that it prospers in any place. Yet, we are allowed to love ourselves as well as we love our neighbors, and we must not neglect those, who come under our most immediate care. Whether a Seminary for instructing our candidates in this Diocese be practicable, or, all things considered, expedient, I shall not venture even to give an opinion; but it is our duty, so far as it may be in our power, in some way to induce more of the young men, whom we bring forward to the ministry, to labor in this Diocese.[1]

Nine months later, on June 17, 1829, the Massachusetts diocesan convention (each of the components of the Eastern Diocese also held an annual convention of its own) appointed a committee "to inquire into the expediency and practicality of adopting some plan for Theological Education in the Eastern Diocese, and to present a memorial on the subject to the next Diocesan Convention." [2] The composition of the committee afforded proof of the seriousness with which the convention regarded the matter. It included two prominent laymen, Edward A. Newton of Pittsfield and Henry Codman of Boston, and two of the leading clergymen of the diocese, George Washington Doane and Alonzo Potter.[3] Newton and Codman were active, interested, and rich; both were to be connected with diocesan efforts to improve theological education for many years. Doane had many things to recommend him: he was a protégé of Bishop Hobart's; he had gained some experience in the field of education at Washington College in Hartford before coming to Boston; and by his position as assistant on the Greene Foundation at Trinity Church in the city of Boston, as well as through marriage to a niece of Gardiner Greene, he had a strong

[1] John S. Stone, *Memoir of the Life of the Rt. Rev. Alexander Viets Griswold*, p. 341. Hereafter cited as Stone, *Griswold*.
[2] *Journal of the Convention of the Protestant Episcopal Church in the Diocese of Massachusetts*, 1829, p. 9. Hereafter cited as *J. M.*
[3] *Ibid.*

base of support within the diocese. Full of energy and
ideas, witty, charming, he concealed an exceptionally
strong-willed personality behind a smooth and graceful
manner. It had not yet become apparent that his vivid
imagination was prone to overheat in a crisis—a serious
flaw in one whose appetite for power was only equalled
by his delight in exercising it. Potter was even more experienced in educational affairs, having held the professorship of mathematics and natural philosophy at Union College in Schenectady before coming to the rectorship of
St. Paul's, Boston. Less ebullient than Doane (whom he
had known when they were undergraduates together at
Union years before), his sensitive appreciation of varied
points of view, and his extraordinary gift for anticipating
—and forestalling—dissension had already gained his parishioners' affection and respect. In characteristic fashion,
his major contribution to the committee was to urge that
Bishop Hobart should be won over before any definite
plans were made,[4] and—presumably with Griswold's approval—eventually to write a tactful letter on the subject
himself to Bishop Hobart.[5] This was a wise precaution, as
Hobart's determined opposition to the planting of a
seminary in Ohio had immeasurably multiplied Bishop
Chase's difficulties five years before.

Neither Hobart's reply to Potter nor the committee's
final report have been preserved; but it is probable that
both were discouraging. Addressing the convention of the
Eastern Diocese in September, 1830, Bishop Griswold was
sufficiently disheartened to state that there appeared "little
probability of our having a theological school in this
diocese." [6] As an admittedly rather watery substitute, he
suggested that a qualified clergyman might take a few

[4] Stone, *Griswold*, pp. 341-342.
[5] *Hopkins*, p. 133.
[6] The entire address was printed in *The Banner of the Cross*, Nov. 26,
1831, p. 51.

students into his house to study—an establishment on the lines of the old-fashioned "School of the Prophets." The tone of his address indicated that he was not confident of managing even that. Little did he foresee that within a year just such a modest establishment would indeed be in operation, and that the theological school of which he had begun to despair would be formally organized, at least on paper.

The "Massachusetts Episcopal Theological School" of 1831

The worker of this miracle was Potter's colleague on the 1829 committee, George W. Doane. In December, 1830, Doane's rector, the aged and ailing John Sylvester John Gardiner, died at Harrogate in England while "taking the waters" in an effort to regain his health, and Doane was elected to succeed him. To take his place as assistant, Doane approached John Henry Hopkins of Pittsburgh. Hopkins, a former lawyer, was thirty-nine (some nine years older than Doane), a man whose High Church leanings were congenial, whose energy was as indefatigable as that of Doane himself, and whose protean gifts as a preacher, teacher, composer, musician, artist, architect, and educational theorist had already won him a considerable reputation. Doane's first invitation was declined; but when, in the course of a visit to Boston, Hopkins divulged that the principal reason for his wish to remain in Pittsburgh was his hope of establishing a diocesan seminary there, Doane resourcefully set to work to magnify the attractiveness of the post he had to offer by coupling with it the possibility of starting the long-hoped-for seminary in Massachusetts. Using Hopkins's reputation as bait, he procured letters from Bishop Griswold and others warmly endorsing the proposal to organize a seminary. Using the letters as bait,

he then urged Hopkins to withdraw his earlier refusal in
view of the enticing opportunities now beckoning. The
Pennsylvania diocese meanwhile played into his hands by
tacitly rejecting the plan for a seminary in the West.[7]
That decided Hopkins; and with the reluctant approval
of his vestry, he accepted the call to Boston.

At the diocesan convention which met in June, 1831,
steps were accordingly taken to establish "The Massachusetts Episcopal Theological School." [8] The name, the location, the organization, and the choice of trustees, visitors, and faculty had all been carefully decided on in advance by Doane himself,[9] and were adopted by decisive
majorities (as the rector of Trinity had planned) despite
a last-minute attempt by Alonzo Potter to defeat the proposals on the ground that the seminary would offer un-
welcome competition to General, was being put in the
wrong place, and was too big a job for one man—even if
the man was Hopkins. Once the resolutions were adopted,
however, Potter wrote to Hopkins assuring him of his
hearty support.

The seminary was to be located in Cambridge, where
it would be close to the Harvard Library, and yet near
enough to Boston "to enjoy its benefits and escape its
disadvantages." [10] Its organization was conventional. The
Board of Trustees was to consist of six clerical and six
lay members, all appointed by the convention. The Board
of Visitors was to consist of all the bishops having jurisdiction in the New England states together with the
secretaries of the conventions of those states. The visitors
had authority to visit the seminary whenever they chose,
and were "to report to this Convention deficiencies, or

[7] The dominant influence in the diocese was that of Philadelphia, where
interest was divided between General and Alexandria, with no disposition to encourage possible competition anywhere else.

[8] *J. M.,* 1831, p. 14.

[9] *Hopkins,* pp. 138-139.

[10] *J. M.,* 1831, p. 14.

to propose amendments in its course of theological instruction and discipline." [11] The bishop having jurisdiction in Massachusetts was to be chairman of the Board of
Trustees and president of the Board of Visitors *ex officio*.

The clerical trustees appointed by the 1831 convention
were the Rev. Messrs. Asa Eaton of the City Mission,
James Morss of St. Paul's, Newburyport, G. W. Doane of
Trinity, Alonzo Potter of St. Paul's, Theodore Edson of
St. Anne's, Lowell, and Thomas W. Coit of Christ Church,
Cambridge. Of these, all except Potter and Edson were
cronies of Doane. The lay trustees were mainly from
either Trinity or St. Paul's: Gardiner Greene (Doane's
uncle-by-marriage), George Brinley, Dr. J. C. Warren, and
Edward Tuckerman. The remaining two were from outside Boston: Joseph Foster from Cambridge, and Edward
A. Newton, Doane's friend from Pittsfield. In the fashion
of Gambier (but not Virginia), two of the trustees, besides the bishop himself, served also on the faculty. Asa
Eaton was made professor of ecclesiastical history and the
nature, ministry, and polity of the Church; Thomas W.
Coit was professor of Biblical learning and the interpretation of Scripture; and Bishop Griswold was to be professor of sacred rhetoric and pastoral care. The remaining
member of the faculty, and the only one to be a resident
and full-time, was the professor of systematic theology,
who was John Henry Hopkins himself. The official opening of the seminary was arranged for Easter Monday,
1832.

Hopkins arrived in Boston in July, purchased a house
in Cambridge a few weeks later "about a quarter of a
mile from Harvard College on the high road to Boston," [12]
and towards the end of September took in four students
and began instruction forthwith. To make it easier for
him to devote the major portion of his time to the infant

[11] *Ibid.*, p. 16.
[12] *Hopkins*, p. 138.

seminary, he was given no pastoral duties at Trinity, being required only for the services.

Yet, ironically enough, the seminary which had been
so rapidly brought into being was, within a few months,
to be hurried equally rapidly out of existence. And the
man primarily responsible was, as before, George Washington Doane.

Doane's interest in theological education was genuine
enough; but in 1831 and 1832 it was by no means his
principal one. Nor was his parish. He was working to put
the diocese in his pocket. Very much the Hobartian young-
man-in-a-hurry, he had grown impatient with Griswold's
studiedly unobtrusive administration, and longed to get
things moving up-Church. Griswold had chosen a com-
plimentary text for his sermon at Doane's institution as
rector of Trinity: *He must increase, while I must diminish* (John 3:30); but Doane's activities in the next few
months must have made even the gentle Griswold feel
that the text was almost uncomfortably apt. With the
help of an intimate friend, William Croswell, rector of
Christ Church, Boston, who had followed him from
Connecticut at his suggestion, Doane started a church
newspaper, *The Banner of the Cross,* to publicize his
opinions. His next step was to strengthen the High Church
forces by importing Hopkins. And at the 1831 convention
he consolidated the power he had sought, arranging the
election of his supporters to fill almost every place on
every committee of importance, including the standing
committee. The new seminary was only part of this Grand
Design.

Griswold understood what was behind all this, and be-
haved with his usual discretion, confident that time would
show the wisdom of his policy. He wrote to a friend:

I am well aware that I am generally thought to be deficient
in energy and decision, perhaps justly. But very few, if any,
of those who so judge know the difficulties of the situation

in which I have been placed. To unite in one body, and keep at peace and in harmony, our churches and clergy, thinly scattered over five States, has been a work which required more prudence, study and care than is generally supposed. There is always some danger of doing too much, unless a man were perfectly wise and good. It is perhaps better to neglect doing ten good things, than to do one which is injurious and wrong. Had Bishop Hobart pursued in this Diocese the same course as in New York, the result, in my belief, would have been very different; and they who attempt to introduce his policy here, may at length be convinced of it.[13]

He did not have long to wait. For Doane was too young, too inexperienced, too much of a partisan not to over-play his hand. His adroit manipulation of the 1831 convention, so successful at the time, in retrospect disturbed the conservatives and aroused the spirit of contrariness that never more than half slumbers in the Yankee. Next time they would not be so manageable. As president of the standing committee in the months that followed, he was so high-handed, and ignored Alonzo Potter (the one clerical member not in complete sympathy with his views) so completely that Potter resigned, and—unwilling to lead a factional dispute that deeply offended his instinctive craving for harmony—gave up his parish and left the diocese. Potter was replaced by yet another former Union college mate of Doane's, John Seely Stone, who was as sincere a partisan on his side as Doane was on the other; and the old alliance between Trinity and St. Paul's, hitherto considered essential for the conduct of diocesan business, dissolved in recrimination and bad feeling. Finally, in April, 1832, Doane arrayed himself openly against the bishop himself. Strongly in favor of requiring the full three-year term prescribed in the canon of all candidates for the ministry (a policy he had commended in *The Banner of the Cross* three months before),[14] he

---

[13] *Ibid.*, p. 133.
[14] *The Banner of the Cross*, Sat., Jan. 21, 1832, p. 84.

got the standing committee to refuse its consent to Griswold's proposal to dispense from the last few months of
their three-year candidacy two Harvard graduates who had
been studying all year under Hopkins and satisfactorily
passed their pre-ordination examinations. All Griswold's
friends were scandalized. Under Doane's leadership the
Bishop's "Board of Advice" was plainly functioning instead as a "Board of Control."

Among those horrified was Hopkins.[15] He disliked party
politics and distrusted party managers. He respected bishops in practice as well as in theory. And he venerated
Griswold. In November he had been approached about
accepting election as Bishop of Vermont (a jurisdiction
Griswold had just resigned) and at first declined to consider it; but by late spring of 1832 his position at Trinity,
in view of his disapproval of Doane's course of action,
was becoming embarrassing. By the end of April all that
kept him in Massachusetts was the theological seminary.
The seminary, however, was no stronger than it had been
when he came. Its only building was the house he had
bought himself. Its operating expenses were paid entirely
out of his own pocket. There was no endowment; and
the only pieces of equipment so far acquired were a
minute book for trustees' meetings and a few printed
copies of the seminary's constitution and bylaws (which
had not yet been paid for). Accordingly, Hopkins consulted the vestry of Trinity to see if $10,000 could be
raised for the seminary endowment as a sign that the
institution's continuance was seriously intended. He discovered that his friends were very willing to establish a
trust fund which would pay the professor of systematic
theology's salary so long as Hopkins was the professor (at

---

[15] His position is detailed in his *Defence of the Convention of the
Protestant Episcopal Church in the State of Massachusetts against certain Editorial Statements of the Paper called "The Banner of the Cross."*
The conduct of the Standing Committee is discussed on p. 11. (Hereafter
cited as Hopkins, *Defence.*)

that point Hopkins's only remuneration came from his assistantship at Trinity); but they would give nothing to the seminary. Such caution was by no means unique. Jay Cooke endowed a professorship at Gambier in just this way for his personal friend, the Rev. Sherlock Bronson. But it did not reassure Hopkins that support for the seminary would outlast his own popularity, which, in view of the dissension troubling the diocese, was likely to prove an undependable commodity. On May 31, 1832, he was elected Bishop of Vermont, and accepted. His departure deprived the seminary of its only building and its only resident professor.

A few months later the seminary's most influential trustee departed as well. At the diocesan convention in June, 1832, Doane retained his seat on the standing committee, but otherwise suffered a total defeat in his attempt to return himself and his friends to office. Having lost the election, he lost his head and his temper too. Late in the afternoon, after over half the lay delegates had gone home, he and his friends tried to maneuver the convention back into their control by questioning the legality of the vote on a legal quibble. They managed to prolong the convention, but not to alter its result. A few days later Doane published in *The Banner of the Cross* an editorial "Manifesto" in which, "speaking the truth, and endeavoring to speak it in love" [16] (the clergyman's time-honored way of warning his audience that he is about to be deliberately offensive), he accused his opponents of a number of picturesque misdemeanors—not omitting "treason." Hopkins was not unfair when he called the "Manifesto" an "eloquent Philippic, displaying abundant talent and ingenuity, but sadly deficient in sobriety and justice, to say nothing of christian charity and discretion." [17] Meanwhile a friend of Doane's, Edward A. Newton, began

---

[16] *The Banner of the Cross*, Vol. I, No. XLIV, Saturday, June 30, 1832.
[17] Hopkins, *Defence*, p. 25.

circulating a petition calling on the recently-elected Massa-chusetts delegates to the General Convention to resign in favor of the unsuccessful Doane slate, which "ought to have been elected." He threatened to make trouble in future diocesan conventions if they refused. At Griswold's request, Hopkins published a *Defence of the Convention* in answer to the Doane forces which was in the best tra-dition of Elizabethan controversy. It included a reprint of the "Manifesto," letters from Griswold and other dele-gates to the diocesan convention, and a critique of Doane's editorial and policies by Hopkins himself that was kindly, dignified, and devastating. Some Massachusetts men were still so angry in October, when Doane was elected Bishop of his native New Jersey, that they tried to prevent his consecration. In the uproar surrounding Doane's leave-taking, the seminary disappeared utterly. Not until 1834 was it even mentioned again. At the convention in that year, William Croswell, Doane's old crony, who had been appointed "Secretary to the Trustees" in 1831, plaintively mentioned that the bill of $27.00 for the minute book and printing was still outstanding.[18] The convention paid it.

The first attempt to launch a seminary in Massachu-setts, therefore, did not so much fail as evaporate. The seminary had, as it were, slid down the ways smoothly enough; but as the builders' attention had been diverted at a crucial moment, it had sunk like a stone almost as soon as it hit the water. As a result the diocesan leaders went back to their drawing boards with a renewed respect for the importance of sound principles of hull construc-tion. Years were to pass before they dared do much more than cautiously revise the old blueprints. One mistake was not repeated. Never again did they commit the folly of opening a seminary that had not a penny behind it. But one opportunity was not repeated either. Doane and

---

[18] *J. M.*, 1834, p. 31.

Hopkins took with them any hope of drawing together
High and Low Churchmen in support of a common seminary. The friends of General in the diocese who had cooperated in the 1831 undertaking did not do so another
time.

The Massachusetts "Protestant Episcopal Theological Seminary" of 1836

Four years later, however, a second try at founding a
seminary looked very much as if it might succeed. The
year before, the convention had set up a committee to
"consider the expediency of establishing a Protestant
Episcopal Seminary in the Diocese of Massachusetts." [19] It
consisted of Bishop Griswold, two of the 1831 trustees—
Edson and Tuckerman, Doane's successor at Trinity—
Jonathan Wainwright, and Professor Simon Greenleaf of
the Harvard Law School, a parishioner at Christ Church,
Cambridge. The first thing it did was to authorize the
Rev. John A. Vaughan, Griswold's successor as rector of
St. Peter's, Salem, to go out and raise money. He spent
three months at it, with the result that the committee
reported to the 1836 convention that Rhode Island had
agreed to raise $25,000 in ten years with which to endow a
professorship, that St. Paul's in Boston had pledged
$12,000 (Trinity and Christ Church—significantly—had
pledged nothing), and that sites worth $10,000 had been
offered for the seminary in Lowell, Worcester, Newburyport, Taunton, Northampton, and Pittsfield. The convention agreed that a $200,000 endowment was needed, but
gave permission for the seminary to open when $100,000
was in hand. In the course of the session a number of
parishes pledged themselves to raise $28,000 in five years;
the convention itself assumed responsibility for another

---

[19] J. M., 1835, p. 34.

$25,000; and the total amount promised from all sources was calculated to have reached $104,000.[20]

Emboldened by Vaughan's reports of success, the committee had drawn up a plan of organization for the seminary, and even gone so far as to get a bill through the General Court incorporating the institution. The bill as passed was unsatisfactory, and was consequently returned to the legislature; but the plan of organization was approved. It was similar to the one adopted in 1831. The only change was in the composition of the Board of Visitors. That body was now to have five members appointed annually: two from Massachusetts, and one each from Maine, New Hampshire, and Rhode Island. It was to report to the Massachusetts convention. The appointments to the Board of Trustees reflected both a desire to recognize the interest shown by the other New England dioceses (with the exception of Connecticut and Vermont), and also to retain the services of men who had already acquired experience of the difficulties involved in setting up a theological seminary. The clerical members were James Morss of St. Paul's, Newburyport; Theodore Edson of St. Anne's, Lowell; John A. Vaughan of St. Peter's, Salem; Jonathan Wainwright of Trinity, Boston; and Nathan B. Crocker of Rhode Island. Morss and Edson had been trustees in 1831. The lay members were the Hon. Jeremiah Mason of New Hampshire; Henry Codman and William D. Sohier of Trinity, Boston; Edward Tuckerman of St. Paul's, Boston; Edward A. Newton of Pittsfield; and Simon Greenleaf of Cambridge. Codman had been a member of the 1829 committee. Tuckerman had been a trustee in 1831, and a member of the committee in 1835. Newton had been a member of the 1829 committee and a trustee in 1831. Greenleaf had been a member of the 1835 committee. No professors were appointed; but it was

[20] *J. M.*, 1836, pp. 46-48, 49-53.

hoped that Alonzo Potter, who had taken up the professorship of moral philosophy and political economy at Union
College after leaving St. Paul's, would head the seminary.

A year later these bright prospects had vanished. Potter
declined all offers to come back to Boston. Differences of
opinion developed over the proper "character" of the seminary (in which churchmanship played a part).[21] Most
serious of all, to men who remembered 1831-32, no money
came in. 1835 and 1836 had been good years for making
pledges. William Appleton, a prominent member of St.
Paul's, Boston, noted in his diary that the year 1835 had
been "one of unparalleled prosperity";[22] and in 1836, he
remarked that "Labour is far beyond the price of any
former period: Journeymen Mechanics get from two to
three dollars a day and the girls in the Factories at Lowell
get two and a half dollars a week besides their board." [23]
1837, however, proved to be an abysmal year for paying
pledges. Appleton had thought that "a reckoning day
must come, and as I think, before the ensuing year
closes";[24] and he was right. Panic swirled through the
financial world in New York at the end of March, and
spread rapidly throughout the country.[25] When the diocesan convention met in June, it could not discover that
the trustees of the seminary had taken any action; and in
view of "the great commercial and mercantile embarrassment now pervading the community" [26] it decided that
for the moment nothing more should be done. In this it
was undoubtedly wise. Bishop Hopkins, between 1832 and
1837, had put into effect an ambitious plan for a school
for children and a seminary for theological students in

---

[21] Stone, *Griswold*, p. 400.
[22] Susan M. Loring, ed., *Selections from the Diaries of William Appleton 1786-1862*, p. 45. (Hereafter cited as *Appleton Diaries*.)
[23] *Appleton Diaries*, p. 50.
[24] *Ibid.*
[25] *Ibid.*, p. 52, *et seq.*
[26] *J. M.*, 1837, pp. 38-41.

Vermont, into which he threw his whole fortune. By 1841 it was all gone, with debts outstanding which burdened Hopkins for years.[27] As late as 1854 a Boston creditor had him arrested when he came to give a Price Lecture at Trinity; and he would have gone to jail if the Dexter brothers had not paid the debt for him.[28] (The law permitting the imprisonment of debtors was not repealed until 1855.)

Yet, although the plans laid down in 1836 had been ephemeral, they had not been entirely without result. On January 28, 1836, Miss Betsy Varney, a forty-seven-year-old parishioner of John Vaughan's at St. Peter's, Salem, died of cancer. She left an estate of $12,406.55; and on the day before she died, she had her doctor, George Osborne, the son of her old employer (there was no social stigma to working in a household in that period), draw up a will in which she left $500 "to the new Episcopal Seminary in Massachusetts." [29] She would not place any time limit on the bequest, saying to Dr. Osborne, "Well, you can pay them the $500 whenever they get a Charter." [30] Thirty-one years later, Dr. Osborne did as she had directed, making her the Episcopal Theological School's earliest benefactress.

The trustees, however, apparently heard nothing of Miss Varney's bequest at the time. John Seely Stone obviously thought he was pronouncing the epitaph on a closed chapter of diocesan history when, in 1844, he wrote in his biography of Bishop Griswold (who had died the year before):

The whole work was thus brought to a silent but immovable stand, and what may be termed the favorite object of the

[27] *Hopkins,* pp. 202-205.
[28] *Ibid.,* p. 295.
[29] G. Osborne to E. S. Rand, Jr., Dec. 2, 1867 (ETS Archives: "Before 1866" folder).
[30] *Ibid.*

Bishop left to slumber for the remainder of his life. I say to slumber; for it is believed that, so far as endowed, schools for theological learning shall be approved by the cool, second thought of the present and the coming age, the demand for such a school in the Eastern States still exists, and must ultimately enforce effectually its claims, and wake up effectually the plans and measures, which have fallen asleep. Whether such endowed schools *will* be approved by that second thought, is a different question,—and one, which need not here be agitated. It will be enough to say, that the best theological Seminary, which the Eastern Diocese ever had,—perhaps the best, that any Diocese will ever have,—was found by his students in Bishop Griswold's own house and parish at Bristol. There are many reasons why such *practical* theology, as was taught there, will ever, in the main, be found better than that, which is, to so great an extent, taught amidst the dreamy speculations and the scholastic subtleties of most, if not all, of the endowed institutions of Theological learning, whether in our own, or in other lands.[31]

The future dean of the Episcopal Theological School sometimes had a gift for prophecy.

The Greenleaf "Feeler"

The "slumber" to which Stone referred, nonetheless, was neither deep nor dreamless. On February 15, 1839, Professor Greenleaf wrote a letter to Alonzo Potter, at Union College:

Rev. & Dear Sir
    A few friends of the plan of an Episcopal Theological Seminary in this State, are still directing some attention to that subject, & it is not improbable that it may soon be distinctly moved again. I have been requested to act with them; but before I decide, I wish, if it be not improper, to know whether you could be induced to take charge of the Institution. I am clearly of opinion that to defer the opera-

---

[31] Stone, *Griswold,* p. 401.

tion till an adequate sum is raised to erect large buildings, & support several professors, is virtually to postpone it indefinitely. The project, which appears to me most feasible, is, to locate the Seminary in this place, say, on the Mount Auburn road, & select a suitable professor, who will at the same time take the Rectorship of the Church here, which consists of only about thirty families, but can pay six to eight hundred dollars salary. In that case we can commence operations with a capital of fifteen thousand dollars, & this can without doubt be obtained. Instead of the erection of expensive buildings, I should advise the purchase of one of the ample mansions on the road I have mentioned, which would cost very far less, & might be enlarged, or others built, as the Seminary might prosper. I suppose the emoluments of the principal, at the *beginning,* to be not less than twelve hundred dollars, besides the house; & probably fifteen; to be augmented as above. I see no hope of success in any other plan; & I cannot bring myself to more than this, without first knowing whether the principal would be acceptable & useful as my parish minister; & this is the reason, & I hope will be received as an apology for the liberty taken in thus addressing you.

Requesting the favor of as early a reply as may consist with your convenience, I remain,

> Dear Sir, with great respect,
> Your very Obt. servt.
> Simon Greenleaf [32]

Whether due to haste or to a sudden access of self-consciousness on the part of the writer, Greenleaf's letter rather came apart at the seams towards the end; but its point was clear. Potter wrote a quick reply on the letter's unused back page, and sent it back. As he was considering whether or not to accept his recent election to the post of Assistant Bishop of Massachusetts, and had promised to say nothing of his intentions until the opening of the diocesan convention (which was still four

---

[32] ETS Archives: "Before 1866" folder.

months away), he could not give Greenleaf a definite answer. But he was as discouraging as he could discreetly be.
While confessing that if he became assistant bishop, some
such arrangement as Greenleaf proposed would be "perfectly agreeable . . . if it was so to others," he warned
that he saw "very little prospect of such a termination to
this matter."

William Appleton's Proposal

In 1842 the project stirred again. This time the prime
movers were William Appleton of St. Paul's, Boston, and
his rector, Alexander Hamilton Vinton (Stone had resigned in 1841 to become rector of Christ Church, Brooklyn, New York). On April 30 Appleton recorded in his
Diary: "Went to Cambridge with Mr. Vinton; called on
Mr. Greenleaf, much talk as to Theological Seminary:
I said, 'Now is the time to begin; if you Gentl. will put
things as they should be, I will purchase the House opposite the Craigie [Longfellow] place, if it is to be had for
ten thousand dollars.' " [33] The next day he noted: "Communion Sunday. I have never before felt so much interest
in Missions; I feel much inclined to give the balance of
my income to religious objects, not confined to Missionaries, but to education of ministers & workers for Christ. I
feel that it is a true test of a man's religion, his desire to
impart it to others." [34] On Monday morning he added:
"My mind dwelt most of the night on the subject of which
I was contemplating last evening. I think my true course
is to spend my income as above stated. Amory [his son and
business associate] fully agrees with me in the course I
propose." [35]

The excitement which these ideas had generated indicates that the whole subject was something of a novelty to

[33] *Appleton Diaries*, p. 93.
[34] *Ibid.*
[35] *Ibid.*

Appleton, as, indeed, was the intensity of religious feeling which lay behind it. Until 1842, certainly, Appleton himself would have said that he was not a religious man —in the way, for example, that his daughter Sarah's father-in-law, Amos Lawrence, had been for years, with his fervent piety and innumerable charitable interests. How and when he changed (insofar as so personal a development can be traced) is of importance. It helps in part to explain why the plan for establishing a seminary in Massachusetts was to develop in the way it did.

William Appleton was the son of a Congregationalist minister who died in a typhus epidemic when the boy was nine, leaving a widow with five children to bring up on an estate no bigger than that left by Miss Betsy Varney. When he was about twenty, Appleton took what patrimony was his—less than a thousand dollars, came to Boston, and in a little over twenty years made himself one of the richest men in the city. He was a small man, pale and emaciated from the nervous dyspepsia that plagued him, quick and sometimes abrupt in manner, but thoughtful, observant, an unerring judge of men, and with a sixth sense about making money. Although a generous supporter of St. Paul's from Jarvis's time on, and an appreciative friend of both Alonzo Potter and John Seely Stone, his practice of religion was dutiful rather than devout, characterized by a keenly discriminating moral sense unwarmed by any very lively faith, and remarkable only for its honesty and absence of cant. At fifty he wrote: "I feel the value of religion and desire my children should be religious more than everything else";[36] at fifty-one he took Communion for the first time;[37] at fifty-two he was confirmed.[38] Yet even then, the entry in his *Diary* revealed little change in his feelings:

---

[36] *Ibid.*, p. 51.
[37] *Ibid.*, p. 52.
[38] *Ibid.*, p. 63.

Sunday. It is about a year since I first went to the Communion; I feel satisfied that I did right in so doing; I have through life thus far always had a great respect for religion & for many years felt the sinfulness of my nature. I went this day with my dear Amory & was confirmed by Bishop Griswold; this I did in part as an example to my children, at the same time feeling the additional pledge was my duty.

Not for the last time, however, a father whose connection with the Church had been maintained principally out of concern for the well-being of his children found himself led farther than he had anticipated. The *Diary* entries for March, 1842, tell in a touchingly homely way of Appleton's crisis of faith:

March 2nd. Harriet [a daughter] had a party of Ladies and Lads the last night, of about sixty. I do not like them.
25th, Good Friday. Attended prayers at the Chapel in the morning, sermon by Dr. Vinton in the Church; attended Price lecture at Trinity and at our Chapel in the evening; very full.
27th, Easter Sunday. Our dear Mary Ann went for the first time to the Communion: I felt it much. Of the many, very many blessings that I have, that of our children appearing to have religious feelings, I feel most. I have felt more as I think a Christian should feel this day, than for many; I will most earnestly pray that I may give myself up to my Maker. I believe, Help, Lord, my unbelief. *28th*. Had a long conversation with Mr. Vinton, quite unsettled in my mind. I then went to Mr. N. Appleton's Store and met Mr. J. K. Mills who said to Mr. Appleton, "I went to hear Dr. Vinton and saw Wm there, was told he went three times each day to Church." I said it was the season of our Church for many services, rather apologizing, &c. Awoke in the night with a feeling as if I had discovered in a dream my difficulty; it was that I was not willing to give myself up to my Maker, that I was disposed to give the World more than the half of my heart, that I was not willing that a portion of my friends should know that I went to meet religious men, that I made excuses for going to a place of worship other than on Sunday,

that, in fact, I was ashamed to acknowledge myself the follower of Him who died for my sins; such were my sensations,
I could not again get to sleep. I awoke my wife, told her of
some of my feelings; when I left my room I felt as if I wished
an opportunity of showing myself to the whole World and
to declare that henceforth I would make religion my first
and great object of life. *29th*. Went at 8 o'clock to Prayers
where I had a conversation with Mr. Vinton, told him my
feelings; he encouraged me by saying it was the work of God.
30th. I find myself quite happy and satisfied with the resolutions to be a whole Christian. At lecture in the evening, much
pleased and enjoyed the service much.[39]

One month later, Appleton and Vinton stood on Professor Greenleaf's doorstep in Cambridge.

In the years that followed, Appleton was to have his
spiritual ups and downs. Sometimes he was chagrined to
detect in his friends "something like doubting in their
minds as to the reality of the change." [40] But the change
was real and enduring, nonetheless. It inspired in him a
determination to further the spread of the gospel and
relieve human suffering by gifts and work for churches,
hospitals, charitable societies and individuals, that only
ended with his death in 1862.

Vinton's part in the transformation of his conscientious
but circumspect parishioner should not be underestimated. Every parish parson learns by experience that Holy
Week and Easter often fan into flame the feeling of guilt
that smolders in the half-hearted and semi-committed;
but not every parson can handle the crisis with the solid
wisdom and decision of Vinton, who, as a physician, had
been cool and circumspect himself until his vigils at the
bedsides of the dying sent him first into the Christian
Church and then into the ministry. Like his predecessors,
he brought special gifts to St. Paul's and Boston just when

[39] *Ibid.*, pp. 90-91.
[40] *Ibid.*, p. 116.

they were needed. A big man, with a leonine head and resonant diapason of a voice, there was about him a quiet massiveness, a sense of power in reserve, that was irresistibly impressive. Potter and Stone had brought into the Boston chill something of the gentle warmth of Gluck's *Orfeo*: they touched and charmed. But if they were like Gluck, Vinton was like Brahms: he compelled. Phillips Brooks, who was still a boy when Vinton first came to St. Paul's, said that "the movement of his words was like the heaving of the tide and not the sparkling of the spray";[41] and Bishop Clark, a colleague, said of his sermons that they were "not merely painted on the memory, but *burned in,* so that they became indelible." [42] He was especially effective with men of business like Appleton, touching the vital core where faith determines action. Episcopal merchants in Boston during much of the nineteenth century were not generous men as a rule. Hopkins found that out in 1832. Appleton, in the same year, had been fairly typical when he took stock of himself at forty-five, and noted with detectable satisfaction that at least he was not a miser: "I do not feel anxious to make money for the sake of having it, and should as soon spend my whole income as not if I could do it with a belief that it would do more good than harm" [43] (the obvious conclusion being that it most certainly would not). Nor had this changed (though Appleton had) more than ten years later. In 1844, Appleton's dour comment on the meeting to organize the City Mission was: "I find such sensitiveness among those who take part in this charity, that I almost doubt if it will be useful";[44] and after the diocesan convention three months later, he noted with equal lack of enthusiasm: "They got through, but a poor display of

[41] Packard, *Recollections,* p. 298.
[42] Clark, *Reminiscences,* p. 95.
[43] *Appleton Diaries,* p. 39.
[44] *Ibid.,* p. 110.

Christian practice." [45] Yet there appeared exceptions to this as the century wore on; and it is significant that most of the exceptions were men who regularly attended St. Paul's Church. Among the parishioners in Vinton's time were most of the original benefactors and trustees of the Episcopal Theological School: Amos Adams Lawrence, Edward Sprague Rand, Robert Means Mason, Richard Henry Dana, Jr., John Phelps Putnam, John Appleton Burnham, and its founder, Benjamin Tyler Reed. They were to be no less zealous in well-doing than William Appleton. The inescapable conclusion is that in the list of those who exerted a profound influence on the development of theological education in Massachusetts, the name of Alexander Hamilton Vinton should stand among the first.

The call on Professor Greenleaf did not come to anything. Griswold was failing. He died in 1843, and for a year or so, his successor, Manton Eastburn, encouraged Massachusetts men to go to his own old seminary, General, in New York. Eastburn's enthusiasm cooled sharply, however, after the uproar over the inroads of Tractarianism in 1844; and in 1845 Appleton tried again. On February 10 he noted: "Meeting at the Bishop's in relation to a Theological Seminary; I had a long talk with Mr. Mason about it." [46] At the diocesan convention in June a committee was appointed to take up the cause of "Theological Education in the Diocese" [47] once more under the chairmanship of Bishop Eastburn. Other members were the Rev. Charles Mason of St. Peter's, Salem, the Rev. Edward Ballard of St. Stephen's, Pittsfield, William Appleton, William F. Otis, and Edward S. Rand, Jr., of St. Paul's, secretary of the standing committee. Appleton, however, was

---

[45] *Ibid.*
[46] *Ibid.,* p. 118.
[47] *J. M.*, 1845, p. 41.

the dominant force. The committee was directed to report to the convention in 1846.

In June, 1846, Appleton made three significant entries in his *Diary*: "*June 3rd*. Went to Cambridge to see Mr. Greenleaf in relation to Seminary. *9th*. All dined at Brookline; rather in confusion, but all will come right. *12th*. The Convention closed its session with my proposition for a Divinity School; it was well received; but whether it will be carried into effect is doubtful in my mind. I think much good would be derived by the Institution, but God will devise all for good." [48]

The Appleton Indenture

The proposition which was "well received" was a radical departure from previous plans. Its core was an Indenture[49] made on May 9, 1846, between William Appleton and four members of his family: two sons, Francis and J. William Appleton, and two sons-in-law, Amos Adams Lawrence and John Singleton Copley Greene. The part of the Indenture which most delighted the convention was Appleton's consignment of bank stock worth $25,000 to this group, with the proviso that if it was matched within two years by gifts of an equal amount from other sources a seminary was to be opened. This was the first time that anyone had not only pledged, but paid. But unlike Miss Varney, Appleton set a time limit on his gift. After two years, if the matching funds had not been raised, the bank stock was to be returned to him at his request; and even if the $50,000 was in hand, so that the seminary was actually incorporated and functioning, no more than $25,000 was to go to it from him. Any over-plus from a sale of the stock was to come back to Appleton and in the meantime he was to receive all dividends. Nothing could have re-

[48] *Appleton Diaries,* p. 120.
[49] The Indenture is printed in full in *J. M.,* 1846, pp. 48-53.

flected more clearly Appleton's low opinion of the zeal and generosity to be expected of the convention.

From the point of view of the future, however, the novel fashion in which the seminary was to be organized was more important than the way in which it was to be endowed. The convention was to have no part in it. The Bishop of Massachusetts was to be a member of both the Board of Trustees and the Board of Visitors *ex officio,* and was to preside at all trustees' meetings when present. The remainder of the Board of Trustees (six clergymen and six laymen as in the past) was to be elected at a meeting of the contributors to the endowment which was to be called as soon as $50,000 was in hand. In a fashion reminiscent of the somewhat complicated method by which some of the trustees of General had been provided, the number of votes accorded to the contributors was to depend on the size of the contribution—one vote for every thousand dollars contributed (up to ten), with two or more contributors being permitted to join together to constitute a vote where their individual contributions were smaller than a thousand dollars. Once the Board of Trustees had been elected in this fashion, the association of contributors was to be dissolved, and henceforth the board was to be self-perpetuating, all vacancies being filled by vote of the remaining trustees. To this board, once constituted, all the funds held by Messrs. Appleton, Lawrence, and Greene were to be consigned. The only provision limiting the trustees' administration of the funds was an order that no more than one quarter of the funds and property of the institution should ever be vested "in real estate for the accommodation of the School and its officers." But that, like other directions in these "Fundamental Articles," could be overridden or changed if three fourths of the trustees and visitors concurred.

The professors were to be appointed by the trustees; but it was suggested that the appointment of tutors or subordinate instructors should be delegated to the professors, subject to whatever limitations the trustees cared to impose. As for the duration of professorial appointments, the Indenture ordered that "to secure a reasonable degree of independence, the Professors shall hold their offices during good behavior, subject to removal by the Trustees on trial for neglect of duty, incapacity satisfactorily to perform their duties, immorality, holding and avowing doctrines, or adopting practices inconsistent and irreconcilable with the doctrines and order of the Protestant Episcopal Church of the United States." The trustees were authorized to "appoint one of the Professors President of the School, with such powers as they deem proper and expedient." [50] They were to regulate the admission of the students, the term, and the course of study. As at General and Gambier, anyone who wished to endow a professorship or scholarship was to be permitted to nominate the holder subject to the approval of the trustees.

In addition to the Bishop of Massachusetts, the Bishops of Connecticut, Rhode Island, Vermont, New Hampshire, and Maine were to constitute a perpetual Board of Visitors if they chose to accept the appointment (if one refused, his successors were not to be offered a second chance), and they were to appoint their own presiding officer. They were to "have and enjoy all the powers by law incident to the office of visitors of eleemosynary institutions." These, as stated in the Sixth Article of the Indenture, were considerable:

It shall be the duty of the said visitors to inquire into, and examine the state and condition of, the said institution, and all matters and things relating thereto. They shall take care that the statutes, by-laws, rules and regulations of the institution be, at all times, faithfully observed and obeyed, and that wholesome and proper discipline be enforced in said

---

[50] *Ibid.*, pp. 51-52.

school. They shall correct and reform all abuses from whatever cause arising. They may sustain appeals from any order,
decree, act, or doing of the Board of Trustees, relating to any
Professor or other officer of said institution, and, on hearing
thereof, confirm or vacate the same; provided that such order,
decree, act, or doing of the Trustees, shall remain in full
force until vacated by the visitors, on such appeal. No re-
versal of any act, or doing, of the Trustees, shall be effectual
to vacate the same, unless agreed to, and concurred in, by three
fourths of the whole number of visitors.[51]

The self-perpetuating Board of Trustees, the provision
that the professors hold office during good behavior subject
to removal only after an official trial where charges had
been presented and answered, and the constitution of
the visitors as a board of appeal with power to reverse as
well as to criticize the actions of the trustees were all new.
Nor were they duplicated in any other Episcopal seminary
of the period. Their derivation is impossible to trace beyond dispute; but it seems very probable that the framer
of the Indenture had carefully studied the fundamental
articles and supplemental statutes of Andover Theological Seminary. They were available in print; and in them
every one of the Indenture's novel provisions was duplicated. Andover's donors had themselves personally appointed the original members of the seminary's self-perpetuating Board of Trustees.[52] After careful deliberation,
they had also magnified the powers of the visitors, raising
them above the modest eminence occupied by such bodies
as Harvard's Board of Overseers to the clouded heights
where sat in judgment those mysterious and awesome figures, the visitors of the colleges of Cambridge or Oxford.[53]
And early in Andover's history an appeal to the Supreme

---

[51] *Ibid.,* pp. 52-53.
[52] Woods, *Andover Theological Seminary,* pp. 222, 233-234. The trustees
of Phillips Academy were nominated by the donors, and were, in turn,
constituted trustees of the seminary by its donors.
[53] *Ibid.,* pp. 121, 262-268.

Court of the Commonwealth had established that no professor could be removed except after a trial at which, if he wished, he could be represented by counsel.[54] The head of the faculty at Andover, furthermore, was a president appointed by the trustees.[55] There was in the Andover statutes, however, no such explicit statement as appeared in the Indenture stressing that the provision for tenure was "to secure a reasonable degree of independence" for the professors. In that, Appleton's plan was unique.

To the disappointment of the historian, there is nothing to indicate who was responsible for importing these novelties into the old design for a diocesan school. Appleton's son-in-law, Amos Adams Lawrence, had gone to school at Franklin Academy in Andover;[56] and while spending a term at Andover when he had been rusticated from Harvard, had had a good deal to do with the seminary.[57] Appleton himself, however, as his *Diary* indicates, always thought out the details of his benefactions very carefully; and the fact that Rand's report to the convention stated that the committee had matured no plan of its own before Appleton's was submitted to it,[58] suggests that the credit rightly belongs to him.

Appleton soon discovered that Massachusetts was no more ready to support a seminary in 1846 than it had been ten years before. The skepticism recorded in his *Diary* at the close of the convention was amply justified. Declaring that it had a "profound sense of the liberality manifested by Mr. Appleton . . . and of the importance of the object, which he has in mind," the convention appointed a large committee of laymen from parishes all over the diocese to raise the money needed in order to match Apple-

---

[54] *Ibid.,* pp. 172-173.
[55] *Ibid.,* p. 182.
[56] W. Lawrence, *The Life of Amos A. Lawrence,* p. 6.
[57] *Ibid.,* pp. 13, 16.
[58] *J. M.,* 1846, p. 48.

ton's offer.[59] Nothing could have been more ominous. Effective diocesan committees in that day rarely numbered more than five at most. The appointment of a committee as big as this one hinted at a fear that a great many bushes would have to be beaten if the $25,000 was to be found. Even the wording of the resolution—"profound sense of . . . liberality . . . importance of the object . . . in mind"—was a bad sign. Corporate bodies seldom content themselves with admitting to a sense of someone else's liberality and nothing more if they have the slightest intention of emulating it. The committee never made a report; and the 1847 convention never asked for one. Appleton did not try again.

Yet although Appleton's attempt to provide the diocese with a seminary had been as abortive as the rest, it was to have an enduring influence. Benjamin Tyler Reed had been present at the conventions of 1845 and 1846. Twenty-one years later he had an Indenture drawn up creating the Episcopal Theological School. In general form, and frequently in the very wording, it was a copy of William Appleton's. The involved financial provisions did not need to be repeated, for the conditions of Reed's gift were different. But the other special features—the freedom from control by the convention, the self-perpetuating Board of Trustees nominated by the donor, the provision for professorial tenure, the Board of Visitors with the powers "incident to . . . visitors of eleemosynary institutions"—all were there. One regrets that Appleton had not lived to see it. He had built better than he knew.

---

[59] *Ibid.*, p. 69.

Part II

A NEW SCHOOL

✖ 7

Mr. Reed Creates a School

BENJAMIN TYLER REED was a Boston businessman who, like William Appleton, took a keen interest in shipping, railroads, and banks. He was actually a connection of Appleton's through the Ipswich branch of the family, but fifteen years younger (he was born in 1801) and not a bit like Appleton in appearance or manner. His people had been Marbleheaders for generations, merchants and seafarers trading with the West Indies. His maternal grandfather was one of the hard-bitten band of Marblehead men who fought with such determination at Trenton and Saratoga, and the story in the family was that he had piloted the boat which rowed Washington across the icy Delaware. Reed took after them. He was a big, ruddy, vigorous man with the fringe of wiry whisker, the weather-beaten face, and the quarterdeck manner of a sea captain. He had helped to put himself through Harvard (he was in Ralph Waldo Emerson's class) by teaching school in the vacations —keeping one lesson ahead of his pupils, and thinking nothing of staying up all night at a country ball and driving to school the next morning still wearing his dancing pumps. Nor was he less energetic at seventy. Bishop William Lawrence used to recall how he had watched Reed racing his sleigh down the Brighton Road on wintry afternoons behind horses that no one else dared to drive. All his life he had an appreciative eye for a spirited horse and a pretty woman.[1]

In the business world Reed was indomitable. At fifty he was heard to say that he had already made and lost two fortunes. With each reverse he turned to something else with an unperturbed resourcefulness that amazed his rector, Dr. Vinton. By the 1850's he had made enough money to "retire" and devote his full energies to managing his financial interests.

Most of Reed's family correspondence was destroyed after he died, but a few fragments were preserved which reflect characteristic qualities of his personality. In 1840, for example, he wrote to a sister who was touring in Germany:

I hope this week or next to accomplish the object of a hard summer's work by opening the Eastern Railroad for travel to Portsmouth, as I have all the season made two visits to Newburyport & one to Portsmouth weekly. E. [his wife, Elizabeth Hooper] is afraid I shall be too much at leisure after the Road is done. If I find time hangs heavy on my hands I may take it into my head to cross the Atlantic in one of Mr. Cunard's steamers. . . .[2]

Thirty years later his letters revealed not the slightest diminution of activity. Sitting down to his desk at 5:15 on

---

[1] Except where otherwise stated in the text, the biographical material on Benjamin Tyler Reed is drawn from a letter written to Prof. A. V. G. Allen by Reed's nephew, the Rev. W. R. Woodbridge, July 14, 1904 (ETS Archives: "B. T. Reed" folder).

[2] This excerpt from a letter dated Oct. 16, 1840, was sent to Dr. Allen in 1904 by Reed's niece, Lucy Woodbridge, along with excerpts from a few other Reed letters for possible inclusion in the history of the School on which Dr. Allen was working at the time (ETS Archives: "B. T. Reed" folder).

a June morning in 1871, with the rest of the household still asleep, he wrote:

I expect to go to Portsmouth on Wednesday and shall probably extend my journey to Union, Ossipee, and possibly to Conway. . . . We don't have our railroad in operation as fast as we expected, and I must go there and drive them up. I had hoped when I became so near seventy that my days of driving younger men would stop: but in many respects I find myself as young as my juniors.[3]

Reed was an enthusiastic traveler. He spent several months in Europe in 1832 and 1850, went twice to Cuba, and in 1859 rode the western railroad to the end of the line at St. Joseph, Missouri. In 1870 he went clear to San Francisco with Vinton and other friends to attend a missionary conference as a delegate of Emmanuel Church, stopping on the way back to visit Yosemite, which had only been opened to the public the year before. The only family letter of his to be preserved in full dates from that trip:

Salt Lake City   April 24/70
Sunday eve'g

Dear L.

As you will probably never have another letter from me in this far off place, 2715 miles from Boston, I will write you a short letter for all the family in N. York.

The weather the first two days was damp & cold, then two quite warm, & two pleasant but cool coming over the mountains, which at first I thought for hundreds of miles—as we rode the tops of them apparently on a great level plain—were tame compared with the White and Green Mountains; but the last hundred miles before we entered this basin were magnificent.

I was surprised when I arrived here last evening to find myself so little fatigued by a whole week's constant travel day and night, without so long an interval as I had in New

---

[3] Letter dated June 10, 1871 (ETS Archives: "B. T. Reed" folder).

York—when I should certainly have visited Lamartine Place [his sister's house] if I could. As it was I made my fellow travellers anxious about my arrival. I was the last to join them all in the cars at Jersey City. We started with 17, & the party was made up to 25 before we arrived here.

Mrs. Howe [wife of the Bishop of Pennsylvania] was the only lady till we took a school-mistress going to Sacramento into our car.

We had morning & evening prayers daily. The sound of many gentlemen's voices as they sang the hymns while the car was rattling over the road was magnificent. Dr. Paddock [the future Bishop of Massachusetts] acted as chaplain, having a clear voice, and as my prayer book was better print than the others, he used it constantly. It has been all about this country and to Cuba with me often these last twelve years, and I shall appreciate it more than ever.

This morning Dr. Vinton preached in the Bishop's Church, and as it has on it a large sign "Independence Hall," I presume it is used for dancing and all other purposes. The clergy and all our laity were much pleased with Dr. Vinton's sermon —the three men in the fiery furnace.—From that service I went at 1 P.M. to hear Brigham Young & his Councillor preach poor trash and find fault with Dr. Todd. It is said there were 6500 people in the audience—4000 women & a more stupid, ordinary set I never saw in my life. Either of our four servants were more intelligent looking & handsome than any woman in the audience.

We shall leave here tomorrow evening & expect to arrive at San Francisco Wednesday evening—& hope to get letters there from you.[4]

Reed's letters reveal a temperament more expansive and uncomplicated than Appleton's: a charcoal drawing, so to speak, as opposed to an etching. Yet in important respects the two men had much in common. Both were intellectually honest. Both were acutely aware of how difficult it was to be at the same time a successful businessman and a

---

[4] ETS Archives: "B. T. Reed" folder.

good Christian. Both knew they failed. And both minded. Both men, furthermore, hit upon the same way of atoning for what each interpreted as a serious personal failure: the establishment of a theological seminary. Appleton's efforts have already been described. Reed must have first entertained the idea even earlier, for he confided his intention to his rector, John Seely Stone, in the 1830's, not long after moving to Boston and becoming an Episcopalian.

As Stone's son-in-law, Professor A. V. G. Allen, recalled years later:

He [Reed] had been a successful man of business but he had worked hard for his money; it had not come to him in easy ways. In order to succeed he had been forced to identify himself with business, to give it time and energy and thought, and therefor to sacrifice the cultivation of those inward spiritual graces for which he hungered, whose pursuit he felt to be the highest aim of man.

Later he had made successful ventures, by one stroke almost doubling his fortune. This increased his sense of gratitude. Early in his life the idea came to him of aiding those whose business it would be, unlike his own, to devote themselves to exclusively spiritual ends. Under the preaching of Dr. Stone, rector of St. Paul's, Boston, in the thirties, he had gained and deepened his religious experience. At this time, and partly in consequence of a serious illness, he lamented to his pastor the consciousness of contradiction under which he lived, devoting himself to the world in order to succeed, while yet desiring to devote himself to God. During many years, the plan was maturing of making the great, what seemed to him the only, reparation.[5]

Dr. Huntington Suggests a Plan

Although the ups and downs of his fortune prevented Reed from doing more than harbor the idea at the back

[5] A. V. G. Allen, "The Early Days of the Cambridge School," in *Church Militant*, Apr., 1904, p. 6.

of his mind for most of his life, by 1866 he felt secure
enough to begin to make definite plans. Like Appleton
twenty years before, he went first to his rector. Frederic
Dan Huntington of Emmanuel Church, Boston, the young
parish of which Reed had recently become junior warden,
was as interested as Reed in fostering theological education within the diocese. President of the standing committee, chairman of the committee on new parishes, and
chairman of the executive committee of the Board of Missions, he was keenly alive to the opportunities for what
would now be called "church extension" which could only
be grasped if the diocese could attract increasing numbers
of men into the ministry. Familiar with the Cambridge
scene as former Plummer professor at Harvard (he had
been an Unitarian minister before entering the Episcopal
Church in 1860 at forty-one), he was aware of all the advantages which had drawn Hopkins, Greenleaf, and Appleton to choose the town as the site for the abortive seminaries planned in the past. He had himself cherished the
hope that some day a seminary would be located there
once more, close to Harvard.[6] Reed's confidential admission that he was considering founding just such an institution, therefore, received his instant encouragement.
Indeed, to strengthen Reed's resolve, Huntington went to
the trouble of drawing up a plan of his own for the seminary and had it copied out (his own handwriting was ex-
ecrable) for Reed's benefit:

I. *The Need*

One of the foremost wants of the Protestant Episcopal Church
in this Diocese is a Divinity School. Among the advantages
that might be expected from such an institution are the following, viz. 1. That it would train candidates for the Sacred
ministry who would be the more efficient and useful *here* for
being educated in a knowledge of our people, our literary

[6] A. S. Huntington, *Memoir and Letters of Frederic Dan Huntington*,
p. 246.

habits and our peculiar religious wants, culture, and modes of thought. 2. That it would provide the Church in Massachusetts with young men in the lower order of the Ministry or yet engaged in the preparation for it, who would be able, on Sundays, to render services much needed, as assistants in the Parishes or in the Missionary-Stations. 3. That it would tend to awaken interest in the Sacred office, to predispose earnest young men to seek admission to it, to supply the urgent demand everywhere existing for the increase of a living ministry, and to bring honor and power to the Church as the Kingdom of our Lord Jesus Christ.

II. *The Place*

Such a School should be situated in Cambridge, because 1. The Professors and Students would have access, at small expense, to the Libraries, Lectures and general literary benefits of Harvard University; 2. They would be near enough to Boston for practical purposes; and 3. They would be, there, in an atmosphere more favorable to Study than would be found in Boston itself.

III. *Instruction*

The curriculum of Study should be substantially such as is generally pursued in Theological Seminaries, being embraced in a course of three years in extent, and including departments of exegesis, the Hebrew and Greek languages, Biblical antiquities, Systematic Divinity, Ecclesiastical History and Rituals, Homiletics, Church Government and Discipline, Pulpit Eloquence and the Pastoral Care. For this instruction there should be two resident Professors; with lecturers visiting the School at certain Seasons of the year.

IV. *Apparatus*

Apart from the University Library, there should be a Library of Text and Reference Books especially adapted to the uses of the School, and belonging to it. This might be small at first; but it would probably be steadily increased by donations.

Two Rooms of proper form and size would be sufficient to

accommodate this Library together with the classes in all the offices of instruction.

V. *An Accessory Church*

While the above outline exhibits what is absolutely essential to an institution for the intellectual part of an education in Theology, there remain spiritual and practical parts of such an education, which are commonly too much neglected. It is for want of these that young men often enter the Ministry and take charge of Parishes, who are well furnished as Scholars, but are not properly qualified to deal with men, with children, and with families, as Pastors, Rectors, or Missionaries. Every Divinity School ought to be immediately associated with a local Church and Parish, which should be in itself a constant School for this practical and religious training.

A Church of this kind is particularly wanted in Cambridge, not only for this special purpose, but to attract to our Household of Faith and Worship many young men in the various departments of the University, besides young people and families residing in the place, who would be soon interested in a *thoroughly vital and working Parish, with an earnest ministry.* The entire religious condition of the Community in Cambridge renders this a favorable time for the introduction of such a movement.

There should therefore be erected, in connection with the proposed Divinity School, and not very far from the Colleges (probably on the open lands toward North Cambridge) a Church building, including, with other arrangements, the apartments necessary for the exercises of instruction. The moral power of the institution would be much increased by the impressions of dignity and permanency which gather about a visible structure.

This Church should be kept open for the worship of God, and the Seats should be free to all people. Any lectures before the School, that should be adapted to interest and benefit the public, might be held here. There should especially be a Service, with preaching, on Sunday evenings.

Both Rectorship and Pastoral Charge of this Parish should be vested in the two Resident Professors until such time as, in the judgment of the Board of Trustees, the attendance and income of the Congregation should authorize the employment of another minister as a Rector, when such Rector should become one of the yearly lecturers in the School. The incidental expenses of the Church edifice should be defrayed from the weekly offertory; the remainder of the offerings to be applied in Charity at the discretion of the Rector.

VI. *Government*

1. The Bishop of the Diocese, the Resident Professors, and the Rector of the Church, should constitute the Theological Faculty for the management of the internal discipline and the educational and spiritual concerns of the School. 2. The financial and general business-regulation of the institution should be committed to a Board of Trustees, consisting of the Bishop and the Clerical and lay members of the Standing Committee of the Diocese, who should also have the appointment of the Professors and other instructors. In case, however, that a Rector of the Church should be appointed, as provided in Section V.—and that the Parish should be canonically joined to the Convention of the Diocese, the Wardens and Vestry should be chosen by a majority of the adult males who should have been, according to the Records, regular worshippers at the Church for one year; and the Rector should be chosen by such Wardens and Vestry acting together with the Board of Trustees. The duties of the Rector as an instructor in the School should be assigned by the Trustees, and agreed upon between them and him.

VII.

The purchase of the land, the erection of the Building, and the entire preparation of the form of the institution, previous to the acceptance of the trust by the Trustees, should be committed to three responsible gentlemen, communicants in the Protestant Episcopal Church, one from each of the Parishes of Emmanuel, Trinity, and St. Paul's Churches in Boston, appointed by the donor of the fund, and acting according to his designs.

VIII. *Estimates*

2 Professorships—($35,000 each)	$70,000
Lectureships Foundations—	$ 5,000
Library—	$ 5,000
Land and Building—	$30,000

Total $110,000[7]

Huntington had not been nicknamed "the Major General" in his college days for nothing. This clear and carefully-thought-out plan was a prophetic foreshadowing of the Episcopal Theological School. Two features of it were especially interesting. Section VII. suggested a small executive committee to get the project underway which was reminiscent of the group of four to whom William Appleton had entrusted his $25,000 in the Indenture of 1846. It also reaffirmed the traditional necessity of appointing representatives of the three biggest parishes in Boston to any diocesan committee which had serious business before it. Reed did not forget this. Section V. introduced for the first time the notion of making the seminary a preaching station as it were from which to evangelize Harvard College in order to win adherents to the Episcopal Church. At the very least such a seminary, with a flourishing church associated with it, would be a rallying-point for young Episcopalians who were studying in Unitarianism's most famous stronghold. The prospect was bound to appeal to a man like Reed, who was a devoted friend of his old college, and who could not but know that fellow-alumni, like his friend Rand, Emmanuel's senior warden, had preferred to send their own sons to Gambier rather than risk having their faith shaken in Cambridge. Simon Greenleaf, in his letter to Alonzo Potter in 1839, had suggested that theological education and parochial tasks could be profitably combined; so there was nothing novel about

---

[7] ETS Archives: "F. D. Huntington" folder.

that. But it was significant that Huntington's proposal never mentioned Greenleaf's parish, Christ Church, so strategically located just across the Common from the Yard. Huntington knew the parish too; for he had been befriended by the rector, Nicholas Hoppin, in the days when he was thinking of leaving both Unitarianism and the Plummer professorship for the Episcopal Church, and he had worshipped at Christ Church for some months. Hoppin's ministry, however, appears to have been oriented toward the town, not toward the college—an emphasis of which his supporters in the parish strongly approved; and Huntington must have decided that no help in devising a more vigorous ministry to Harvard was to be expected from that quarter. Certainly his emphatic reference to the need of *"a thoroughly vital and working Parish, with an earnest ministry"* seems an oblique way of saying that in his opinion Christ Church at that time showed none of these characteristics. Much more was to be heard of this in months to come.

The Attitude of Harvard

What Reed and Huntington probably did not know, at the time of their first discussion of the project, was that the Harvard Corporation was as anxious to see an Episcopal seminary placed in Cambridge as they were, and for much the same reason. The members of the corporation were most of them much too confident of the superior virtues of Unitarianism to be afraid that enlightened young men might easily be enticed into so atavistic a relic of antiquity as the Episcopal Church; but they were uncomfortably aware that Unitarianism had given Harvard such a bad name in other parts of the country that the enrollment—compared to that of other colleges of a more orthodox background—was slipping. And in 1866 it occurred to some of them (notably the Rev. Edward Everett Hale, Huntington's successor as minister of the South Con-

gregational Church, a man of the broadest sympathies and
most genial nature) that an effective way of assuring prospective parents that their sons would be safe in Harvard
hands would be to facilitate the establishment of some
orthodox seminaries close by in Cambridge to whom the
Harvard library and free lecture facilities would offer
tempting advantages. In December, accordingly, formal
overtures were made to the Methodists by a committee of
the corporation to see if the contemplated Methodist "Institute of Theology" could not be placed in Cambridge,
and as much publicity as possible was given to their proposal by having it promptly printed in full in the newspapers. The corporation offered the Methodists free use of
the Harvard College Library, the Harvard Museum and
its lectures, admission to all university and undergraduate
lectures, and—for a small fee—admission to lectures at
the Law School and Scientific School as well. It also offered
to help the Methodists to find a proper site for the seminary. The letter concluded:

It only remains, sir, for us to speak with great frankness of
the advantages which we suppose the College will receive
from the neighborhood of such an Institution as that which
you propose.

We know that a board constituted like yours will be disposed to consider such advantages accruing to the oldest
university of New England and so to that of the whole community. You yourself heard the suggestion made by Hon.
Mr. Dana to the overseers. We believe that those suggestions
as to the great value to the University of an enlargement in
the means of the study of theology and a consequent enlargement in the religious influences of Cambridge upon a thousand young men assembled there, approve themselves to the
whole community. We have been told that one of the newspapers suggested that scientific indifference to religious truth
imagined to exist in any institutions for secular education,
might lower the devout tone of an institution for the training
of Christian ministers. We certainly do not believe that any

such indifference exists at Cambridge, but if there did, we feel sure that the officers of any school of Christian instruction would be only glad to meet it and to conquer it. Certainly we would not urge the proposals which we have the honor to submit to the government of the Institute of Theology, if we did not believe that the presence of the Institute in Cambridge would be as great a benefit to the College as we hope the vicinity of the College will be to the Institute.[8]

The committee's letter was signed by the secretary, Edward Everett Hale. Had Huntington or Reed talked with friends in Cambridge about Reed's plan? It seems likely. One of Huntington's acquaintances from Harvard days was Richard Henry Dana, Jr.—the "Hon. Mr. Dana" who, as reported in Hale's letter, had been the man to urge on the Harvard overseers the advantages of having other theological seminaries in Cambridge. Dana was an enthusiastic Episcopalian. He had been a parishioner of St. Paul's, Boston, and then become one of the organizers of the Church of the Advent. A great devotee of Gregorian chant, he had been accustomed to singing merrily with his children at the breakfast table—in plainsong. High Anglicanism could hardly have been carried further. He must have had a great deal more to do with initiating the approaches to the Methodists than meets the eye, for within ten days of sending off the letter to the Methodists, Hale wrote to Dana:

In the matter of the Methodist Theological School, I have drawn, under the instruction of the Committee, as earnest a letter and as good a statement as I could.

The advantages to the Methodists are very great. The two libraries, the Museum,—and twenty-five free courses of lectures annually—make in themselves a preparatory school for their pupils.

---

[8] The letter was printed in local newspapers. An undated clipping of it is in the ETS Archives: "1866-67" folder.

I cannot but think that the measure would be advanced,—
and the Cause of Religious Learning as well—if *at this time,*
gentlemen in the Episcopal Church were willing to move for
a foundation at Cambridge for a theological School. That
would shew the Methodists that they need fear no trap on
our Unitarian side—and it would stimulate the Corporation
also.

Will you think of this? I suggested it to Mr. Samuel Eliot
and Mr. Ben Rotch, who are on the Library Committee, where
I met them,—and I think they thought there would be an
advantage in a Consentaneous [*sic*] movement of the sort.

Some of the Methodist gentlemen are a good deal interested
in the plan.[9]

On December 28, before even replying to Hale, Dana
sent the letter straight to Benjamin Tyler Reed. He told
him that, in answering Hale, "I shall not name your plan
to him, as I consider it a secret. I send the note to you,
that you may act your pleasure." [10]

No Sooner Said than Done

Dana's letter, which probably included not only Hale's
note but also a copy of the letter to the Methodists as well,
appears to have been the decisive factor in stirring Reed to
act. At no time in the past had so many things combined
to favor the enterprise. The necessary money was available,
for Reed's fortune now exceeded one million dollars. Not
only did friends high in the councils of the diocese warmly
support his plan, but also friends at Harvard as well. In
the Appleton Indenture of 1846 and in Huntington's
scheme were two concrete proposals for the organization
of a seminary which Reed could adapt as he chose. It was
not a bolt from the blue, therefore, that struck him on a

---

[9] E. E. Hale to R. H. Dana, Jr., Dec. 25, 1866 (ETS Archives: "1866-67"
folder).

[10] R. H. Dana, Jr., to B. T. Reed, Dec. 28, 1866 (ETS Archives: "1866-67"
folder).

Saturday morning early in January, 1867, when the realization came to him with inescapable force that his cherished scheme was really in his grasp at last, but that, as the project had not been mentioned in his will, it could still come to nothing if he should die suddenly during the weekend through an illness or an accident. Once that idea had occurred to him, it was not in Reed's character to delay one moment longer. He bundled up some negotiable securities worth just under one hundred thousand dollars, added to the package Huntington's plan for the school, and hurried out to look up a friend and associate, the lawyer Edward Sprague Rand. Rand, as his colleagues in various activities used to complain, was always difficult to find. By the time Reed finally met him on State Street, the banks had shut. But Reed was not to be put off. He thrust his bundle into Rand's hand and told him what he had in mind, thus making Rand on the spot the first trustee of the Episcopal Theological School. Rand, with the Yankee conscientiousness that was typical of him, "took the School home with him in his pocket, and sat up with it all day Sunday, never leaving the house" until the banks opened on Monday morning and he could safely deposit with them his valuable charge. Emmanuel Church did without the services of Senior Warden Rand that Sunday, and had to depend instead on the offices of Junior Warden Reed. That, at any rate, was the tale Rand used to tell to his friends in after years.[11]

Reed's intimations of mortality were, happily for him and happily for the School, a shade premature. He was not to die until 1874, by which time he had had the pleasure not only of seeing the School successfully established on its permanent site and the major portion of the build-

---

[11] Letters from Irving Winslow to Bishop William Lawrence, and Irving Winslow to J. W. Suter, undated (ETS Archives: "B. T. Reed" folder). Probably written when researches were being made in the School's history in preparation for the celebration of the Fiftieth Anniversary in 1917.

ings originally contemplated completed, but of sitting in the place of honor at the School's second Commencement in 1872 with "a look on his face of profound satisfaction, of deep inward serenity and happiness." [12] But the gratifying stage of development which the School had attained before his death was due in large part to the speed and decision with which he and his colleagues acted to bring the School into being, once he had made up his mind to do so. Not only Reed, but Rand and all the rest, worked on the plan during the remainder of 1867 as if none of them expected to live to see New Year's Day, 1868. The legal document setting up the School's basic structure was drawn up and signed on January 22. Most of the faculty appointments were complete by the end of April. The Act officially incorporating the School was passed by the General Court in May, and signed on the first of June. The School's first permanent dean was in residence in the School's temporary quarters by October, and was joined by the School's second resident professor in December. The School's first service of worship was held on the third Sunday in Advent; and on January 1, 1868, the first student appeared in the late afternoon—to begin his studies almost the moment he had been relieved of his coat and thrust into a chair beside the study fire.[13] It had taken just short of a year to translate intention into actuality.

While the credit for this achievement belongs rightly to a large number of men from as far away as Philadelphia and Alexandria who cooperated to help put the School on its feet, the chief share belongs to Reed. For his part in the enterprise was not simply that of providing the money. He knew what kind of theological school he wanted. From the correspondence that passed between members of the group that aided him, it is clear that he sketched the broad out-

---

[12] Allen, "The Early Days of the Cambridge School," *Church Militant*, Apr., 1904, p. 6.

[13] A. V. G. Allen, Speech at Alumni Banquet, June 4, 1907, p. 36 (ETS Archives).

lines of the School himself, and with rare perspicacity chose men well fitted to fill in the details of his proposal and then put it into effect. The members of the first Board of Trustees were remarkable for the way in which they complemented one another in their several talents. That was Reed's doing, who knew each man well and personally nominated him for membership on the board. In the same fashion Reed personally chose the members of the first Board of Visitors. But nowhere did he show better judgment than in his selection of the man to whom he committed the task of drawing up the School's constitution, making out its first curriculum, and choosing the first faculty. This was not Huntington, who was too occupied with his parochial and diocesan duties even to accept the post of lecturer in the new School,[14] but Francis Wharton, rector of St. Paul's Church in Brookline. Wharton did all that Reed asked of him, and more. He was the School's first dean of the faculty, although he served for only three months; and through his friends in Philadelphia, New York, and Providence, he raised the money (to which some of his own was added) that purchased the parcel of land which was the nucleus of the School's permanent site—the small piece on which the Chapel now stands. As Professor Allen wrote long ago, Wharton is to be ranked with Reed himself as a founder of the School.[15]

Francis Wharton

In January, 1867, when he probably first became associated with Reed's scheme, Francis Wharton was not quite forty-seven years old. He had been ordained only five years before, and St. Paul's had been his first parish. Any-

[14] F. D. Huntington to an unnamed person—probably J. P. Putnam, secretary of the Board of Trustees, Apr. 23, 1867 (ETS Archives: "1866-67" folder).

[15] Helen A. Wharton, *Francis Wharton, A Memoir*, p. 176. Correspondence between Wharton and Reed and the trustees in the ETS Archives ("1866-67" and "1868-71" folders) amply substantiates Allen's assertion.

one who did not know him, and met him walking along the Brookline roads, might well have wondered how he had ever been called to such an exclusive and fashionable little parish—with its modish Gothick church designed by Upjohn and its wealthy parishioners—for Wharton was anything but impressive to look at. Short and plump, he rolled from side to side when he walked, like a sailor on the stage. He was half-bald, with a little, fair fringe of beard that ran down one cheek, under his chin, and up the other cheek. His eyes were a sparrow's eyes—sharp, bright, quick; and his voice (due to an affliction of the throat which was ultimately to cost him his life) was as high and shrill as a cricket's. Helplessly impractical about common household tasks, he was as careless of his clothes as the most absentminded of professors, and ingenuously grateful to those who tidied him up or helped him "tidy away": his wife; his German manservant, Franz (whose moustachios *à la Victor Emmanuel* were the talk of the neighborhood); or capable boys in the parish like young William, the son of Amos A. Lawrence. Fond of animals in a somewhat inexpert way, he was habitually accompanied around Brookline by an enormous Saint Bernard, which often followed him into church and lay amiably panting beneath the pulpit during the service. People in trouble always found Wharton kind and warmly sympathetic, but solemn and humorless people were disconcerted by him. His conversation bubbled airily along, glinting with a sometimes mischievous wit, savoring the absurdities and incongruities of life in a way that reminded his friends of what they had heard or read of Sidney Smith,[16] abounding in original turns of phrase that were vivid, spontaneous, and unexpected. Bostonians, inclined—except in the case of Dr. Holmes—to talk that was almost angularly functional, could be put off by such grace, unless it was sanctified by Bostonian origins. And

---

[16] Wharton, *Francis Wharton*, p. 172.

Wharton was no Bostonian. Like Lucretia Hale's suavely omnicompetent Lady, he came from Philadelphia. Some, therefore, were inclined to dismiss him as superficial (Rand, for one, does not appear to have been entirely comfortable with him),[17] until, in an unwary moment, they found themselves transfixed by an observation so exceedingly acute that it was rendered painless only by the patent friendliness of the speaker. For the roly-poly exterior was deceiving. Those who listened to Wharton's sermons (he composed them with such facility that at one time he had a backlog of fifty in a drawer waiting to be used)[18] soon realized that behind the chubby face and chirpy voice was an intellect of uncommon breadth and depth. Versatile without being diffuse, blessed with an uncommonly retentive memory as well as a ready tongue, he had read every book he could get his hands on in law and philosophy and science, history and theology and literature, and could in a moment draw apt illustrations from these sources to give weight to any point he wished to make. Nor did he depend on books alone. Before at length entering the ministry, he had been a successful lawyer as well as a prolific writer on legal subjects, the editor of two church periodicals, an itinerant lay preacher, a professor, and an accomplished tactician in church conventions, both diocesan and general. Practical experience in such an unusual range of fields had taught its lessons too.

Although Wharton's personal appearance was unimpressive, his parishioners knew that his background was as distinguished as theirs. He had been born in 1820 into a family that had been prominent in Philadelphia since the time of William Penn. A great-grandfather, Joseph

---

[17] Rand did not know Wharton at the time when Reed first threw them together in the organization of the School. Correspondence between them from 1867 to 1882 in the ETS Archives begins in a friendly vein on Wharton's part, but grows progressively chillier in tone as the years advance.

[18] Wharton, *Francis Wharton*, p. 178.

Wharton, Quaker though he was, had been such a grandee that everyone called him "The Duke"; and his country estate had been so handsome that two years after the old man's death the ill-fated André had chosen it as the site of the "Meschianza." [19] Francis Wharton's father, Thomas Isaac, had been a well-known lawyer and something of a writer himself. He had taken a turn at editing a periodical, and had been the author of *Wharton's Digest* and *Wharton's Reports*. It was he who had urged his son to take to the law, notwithstanding an inclination to the ministry, immediately after Wharton graduated from Yale in 1839. The father had not misgauged his son's abilities; for after being admitted to the bar in 1843, Wharton had conducted an increasingly lucrative practice for twelve years while doing considerable writing on the side. He had produced treatises on criminal law, pleas, state trials, the law of homicide, and (in conjunction with Stillé) on medical jurisprudence. These were of such excellence that they went through a succession of revised and expanded editions throughout his lifetime and beyond. A re-edited version of the twelfth edition of his treatise on *Criminal Evidence* was issued as recently as 1955; and the tenth edition of a treatise based on his work on *Criminal Law and Procedure* was issued in 1957.

The death of Wharton's first wife, however, only two years after their marriage, brought this period of his life to an end. In his grief his mind turned to thoughts of the Christian ministry which his father had persuaded him to renounce years before because of his weak voice. He took up lay preaching in mission stations about Philadelphia for a time, combining the work with his law practice; then in 1856 gave up his law work altogether, bought a wagon, loaded it with Bibles and religious tracts, and set out to make a circuit of the upper Missouri Valley with a friend, distributing the reading material to farms by the

---

[19] *Ibid.*, p. 1.

roadside as they went. In the course of their journey they passed through Gambier, where Wharton was so taken with the beauty of the place and the interest of the work being undertaken at Kenyon under the enterprising Lorin Andrews that he agreed to return. After the tour was completed, accordingly, he came back to assume the offices of professor of English history and literature, logic and rhetoric, and lecturer in constitutional law to boot.

Wharton's stay at Gambier lasted six years, and during that time he contrived to continue to carry on a variety of activities which would have killed a lesser man. In addition to his regular lectures and class sessions, he entertained constantly, and often brought sick or unhappy students back to his house to stay for weeks or months until they had been nursed back to health or better spirits. The array of mission stations on the outskirts of Gambier still existed as it had in Chase's time, and he frequently rode out to one of these as lay preacher to conduct a service or Bible class on a Sunday, as well as conducting an exceedingly popular Bible class for the Kenyon students in the basement of Rosse Chapel. With the aid of men like Dr. May of the Virginia Seminary and Dr. Heman Dyer, he edited *The Episcopal Recorder* and *The Protestant Episcopal Quarterly Review,* a responsibility he had assumed before leaving Philadelphia. In 1857 he carried on most of the work of the committee on hymnody set up by the General Convention in that year, work from which came the progenitor of our present Hymnal.[20] In the same year he delivered a second course of lectures at Virginia, the first course (on *Religious Elements connected with the Colonization of the United States*)[21] having been given in 1856. Each year he traveled back and forth between Philadelphia and Gambier, charming so many young Philadelphians into following him back to Ohio to study at Ken-

[20] *Ibid.,* pp. 50-62.
[21] Walker, *Sparrow,* p. 230.

yon that he acquired among his friends something of the reputation of the Pied Piper.

It is hardly surprising, therefore, that in 1859 nervous exhaustion and a return of his chronic throat trouble forced him to take a year off. He did no teaching; but, as was typical of him, spent six months in Europe—most of it in Germany to perfect his command of the language. All the time he was there, a stream of articles and editorials retailing his observations of European scenes and customs came from his pen. This régime restored him to health. He returned to Philadelphia, was married for the second time, and by September, 1860, was back in Gambier writing in his accustomed high-spirited way to urge his new bride to follow him as soon as she was able, reporting that the news of his marriage had so over-stimulated the cook during the preserving season that all the closets in the house were "like little organ lofts, fluted with bottles of brown tomatoes, green peas, and yellow peaches ranged in rows for the sake of symmetry" [22]—an analogy worthy of Dickens.

The outbreak of the Civil War the following spring, however, ended this lighthearted idyll. Lorin Andrews marched off to military service, and returned shortly after, only to die from the effects of exposure. The number of students dropped away. Wharton's interest turned more and more to preaching—but to preaching in a part of the country where the atmosphere was less charged with the tensions generated by a nervous, suspicious, and intolerant Evangelicalism. Bishop McIlvaine ordained him after a few months of private study in 1862, and shortly afterwards he was called to Brookline.

It would have been unlike Wharton to have allowed himself to be swallowed up by local, parochial affairs once he became rector of St. Paul's, any more than he had confined himself exclusively to professorial tasks

---

[22] Wharton, *Francis Wharton*, p. 152.

while at Gambier. No quietist, his interest had been deeply engaged in the war, and in his sermons he did not shrink from attempting to interpret its significance to his people. His father had been an old-line Whig, a friend of Henry Clay's; his sister had married a rich plantation owner in the South; and Wharton himself was a staunch Democrat who had shown as little liking for abolitionism and the Republicans as his friends, Dr. Packard of the Virginia Seminary, or Bishop Meade. But he was no Copperhead. He put the Confederacy and its aims in a geographical and historical perspective that Lincoln would not have disavowed; and almost from the beginning of his time in the parish he took an active interest in what he considered much the most important issue raised by the war: the rehabilitation of the Negro. This meant (as he reminded his congregation on Thanksgiving Day, 1863, in a sermon so impressive that the vestry had it printed) not only temporary relief, but "the determination to remove that prejudice which in the North, and particularly at the North-West, refuses to receive the negro as part of the industrial energies of the land." [23] He continued, in words which have lost neither their timeliness nor their solemnity in one hundred years:

If, in the present state of the country,—if, in view of the liberty we are giving to so large a part of the negro race, and the military debt we are accumulating to them, we do not remove this prejudice; if we do not receive the Africans to a free home, and to the full rights of labor in this our land, or, if that be impracticable, to give them adequate homesteads elsewhere,—we shall, I think, be eternally branded as a nation dead to generous impulses, and faithless to the most sacred trusts. The question is not the political one of emancipating these particular slaves, for that is already done; but of saving those whom, for our own purposes, we have already emancipated from moral and physical ruin. To this work the

[23] Francis Wharton, *A Willing Reunion Not Impossible*, p. 22.

intelligence and humanity of this country are most solemnly pledged.[24]

When the Protestant Episcopal Freedman's Commission was established by the Board of Missions in October, 1865, Wharton was one of its leading spirits. He traveled about among the churches to urge support of the Commission's work in providing education, practical and secular as well as religious, for the freedmen, warning his hearers that "we cannot exclude the negro from the range of promises which these represent, without excluding ourselves." [25]

It was this man who now, at Reed's invitation, turned his attention to organizing the Episcopal Theological School. No one was better qualified. The task was one which he had wanted to undertake for years. He knew Virginia and Gambier and the Philadelphia Divinity School, and had analyzed their virtues and shortcomings.[26] He was a friend of Bishop Meade, Bishop McIlvaine, and Bishop Potter (in earlier days his influence in the Diocese of Pennsylvania had been so great that he had been nicknamed the "lay Bishop"). He had been associated with Sparrow, Packard, May, Dyer, and Milo Mahan in other enterprises in the past. His acquaintance with theological professors, furthermore, went beyond the Episcopal Church to include men like Dr. Park of Andover. He had specifically discussed the problems of theological education with many, if not all, of these men. The fruits of this experience were to be clearly embodied in the constitution of the new school.

---

[24] *Ibid.*

[25] Protestant Episcopal Freedman's Commission, *Occasional Papers, January 1866*, p. 9. The Appendix contains an "open letter" to the freedmen from the ministers of all the Christian denominations in Selma, Alabama, which, in the light of recent history, is not without a certain morbid interest.

[26] A. V. G. Allen, MS. notes for a history of ETS (ETS Archives: "A. V. G. Allen" folder).

¤ 8

Dr. Wharton Creates a Constitution

THE CONSTITUTION of the Episcopal Theological School is to be found principally in two documents: the Indenture of January 22 and the Act of Incorporation of June 1, 1867; for the later bylaws were based upon these, being in the beginning simply a repetition of the Fundamental Articles laid down in the Indenture itself. The Act of Incorporation was entirely Wharton's work. The Indenture, however, was a much more complex document in which the traces of many other hands are to be seen as well: Reed, Rand, Huntington, and even Bishop Eastburn. In general outline as well as in the actual wording of most of its provisions, it is an updated revision of William Appleton's Indenture of 1846—as if the author had taken the text of Appleton's document (which was printed in the *Journal* of the diocesan convention of 1846), substituted different names, crossed out a phrase here and added a phrase or entire article there in order to adapt it to Reed's purpose. Reed himself had been a delegate to the 1846 convention, and Rand had actually been secretary of the committee which had included Appleton's Indenture in the report which it had presented to the convention; so either man could have suggested such a procedure. As the provisions of Appleton's Indenture harked back to the founding of Andover in 1808, and as they were carried over into the basic articles which have prescribed the School's organization and even its operation right up to the present day, the School's constitution may be said to have exhibited from the very beginning that "continuity of Christian thought" which has been the dominant theme of the School's most brilliant teachers throughout its history. No composer, intending to establish the essential character of a symphony or tone poem by the statement of the central musical motif in the very first bars of the composition, could thus have done so more aptly than Wharton.

Cambridge

The Indenture naturally specified that the new School was to be situated in Cambridge.[1] This was in accordance with Reed's intention of establishing what amounted to two institutions in one: a theological school and, at the same time, a missionary outpost for Episcopalians at Harvard. But the founders thought it wise to provide as well for moving the School elsewhere should the need arise. Article Eight read: "In case the Trustees shall hereafter consider that the welfare of the Institution demands, or that its interests and those of the Protestant Episcopal Church will be promoted by, the removal of the said School from Cambridge to some other place in Massachusetts, they shall have the right, with the consent during his life of the founder, and with the approval of the Board of Visitors, to make such removal."[2]

---

[1] Some of the trustees had second thoughts about the desirability of a location in Cambridge, but not until a few months after the Indenture had been drawn up. Allen, MS. Notes (ETS Archives: "A. V. G. Allen" folder).

[2] Indenture—Protestant Episcopal Theological School of Massachusetts, p. 8.

Mention of the "interests" of the Protestant Episcopal Church suggests that this was intended in large part to reassure the friends of Reed's general plan who were deeply apprehensive about locating a theological school in any university town, and particularly in Cambridge. Many years before, Bishop Kemp had strenuously objected to attempts to found a seminary at William and Mary because of what he called the "infidelity" of the college,[3] and this had helped to determine the Education Society to shift Virginia from Williamsburg to Alexandria. The "infidelity" of Harvard was obvious to all. Reed and his associates did not confide their secondary purpose in placing the school in Cambridge to their friends outside Boston, but it is doubtful if it would have made much difference had they done so. Dr. Packard of Virginia wanted the School to be located well away from the contagion of heresy which would, he thought, be virtually irresistible in Cambridge.[4] John Seely Stone, now at the Philadelphia Divinity School as holder of the Griswold lectureship (for which his old friend, Heman Dyer, had raised the endowment), agreed with Packard.[5] So, probably, did Dyer.[6] And so did Professor L. W. Bancroft, a young but highly-thought-of graduate of Virginia who was teaching at Gambier.[7]

The Article was also intended to reassure in the same way those who objected to Cambridge not only because it was too close to Harvard but because it was too close to

---

[3] *Virginia Seminary*, I, p. 135.

[4] Allen's note: "Dr. Packard's fear was Unitarianism. He thought it dangerous to be placed in its headquarters & feared the stigma might be placed upon the School. People in the church would be afraid of it— etc. etc. A great mistake" (ETS Archives: "Allen's Notes" folder).

[5] Stone to Dyer, Nov. 1, 1873: ". . . the mere fact of our School's having been, by what I pronounced, from the start, a mistaken policy, located by its founders in *Cambridge* . . ." (ETS Archives: "J. S. Stone" folder).

[6] *Ibid.*

[7] Bancroft to E. S. Rand, Feb. 15, 1867 (ETS Archives: "1866-67" folder).

Boston. In 1831 Hopkins had picked on Cambridge as the place for his seminary because it was safely removed from the distractions and temptations of city life. In 1867 Huntington thought that it still was. He had said so in his plan for the School. But others were more skeptical. Boston was within half an hour's journey of Harvard Square by horsecar. Perhaps the seminary would be better off a bit farther out of town in Waltham.[8] Dr. Park on his Andover hill-top was an articulate proponent of the wisdom of keeping theological students well out in the country "unspotted from the world";[9] and he was by no means alone in his opinion. The trustees of General had talked seriously of moving the seminary out of New York City altogether in 1860. Since then the seminary's exhausted financial condition had diverted their attention; but Dean Forbes in 1870—only three years after the Episcopal Theological School had been settled at Cambridge—would open the question once more for General, proposing that it forsake Chelsea for the innocent joys of rural Mamaroneck.[10]

---

[8] This was the opinion of a minority among the first trustees (ETS Archives: "Allen's Notes" folder).

[9] Allen's recollection: "Prof. Park of Andover admired isolation—To have the School in Cambridge would seem like theology competing with the university—suggest comparisons, etc." (ETS Archives: "Allen's Notes" folder).

[10] Article Eight, needless to say, has never been invoked. There is no evidence that Reed or Wharton really expected that it would be. But the doubts about Cambridge which prompted the inclusion of the Article in the Indenture proved very long-lived. One hears echoes of them to this day.

Within the School there appears to have been talk of moving only once. In 1955 some members of the Board of Trustees and the faculty became concerned at the way in which the School's vastly increased size had virtually dispelled the old, intimate, familial atmosphere in which both faculty and students had been knit together in an affectionate, if (as in any family) occasionally peevish group—an atmosphere which had ever since 1867 been considered one of the School's most highly valued features. It was suggested that one way of partially recapturing it would be to move the junior and middle classes away from Cambridge

A Lay Board of Trustees

The entire responsibility for Reed's "Cambridge School" (as it soon came to be called) was vested in a self-perpetuating Board of Trustees. The members of this body had to be residents of the diocese in which the School was situated, and forfeited their membership if they moved away; but otherwise the Articles placed no restriction on the choice of men for the position. The Articles did not say that they had to be clergymen or that they had to be laymen. But Reed's choice of the first board left no doubt of his personal wishes in the matter. At the beginning there were only three members: Edward S. Rand of Emmanuel, Boston, the friend to whom Reed had entrusted the bundle of securities a few days before the Indenture was drawn up; Judge John Phelps Putnam of St. Paul's, Boston, Reed's own lawyer and the future executor of his estate; and the Hon. Robert Charles Winthrop of Trinity, Boston, a former United States senator, sometimes mentioned as likely to be the next president of Harvard.[11] All three were lawyers; all three were laymen. Also, it will be noted, they represented (as Huntington had advised in his plan for the School) the three Boston parishes of Emmanuel, St. Paul's, and Trinity. At the three men's request, Reed almost at once consented to add two more members to the board, nominating Amos Adams Lawrence and James Sullivan Amory to the vacancies thus

---

to an estate on the North Shore similar to the one recently occupied by Gordon Theological College. There the first two years could be spent in a less harried and scattered way in a community similar in scale to the old School of former years. The seniors would spend their final year on the Brattle Street site, free to make the most of the opportunities offered by Harvard and by the city itself, in an atmosphere of considerable independence. The proposal promised so revolutionary a change in the School's organization, and presented at the outset so many obvious difficulties that it was quickly discarded.

[11] Henry James, *Charles W. Eliot*, I, p. 187.

created.[12] They, too, were laymen. Lawrence was the son-in-law of William Appleton, and had been one of the parties to the Indenture of 1846. Amory was Appleton's nephew. Both men had prospered in business, and were vestrymen of St. Paul's, Brookline—Wharton's parish. They were not strangers to Reed (Lawrence's brother, Dr. William R. Lawrence, had been one of the prime movers in the establishment of Emmanuel Church in Boston in 1860); but it was Wharton who suggested their names to him. Their election filled the board's roster. It was to remain unchanged until 1882, bringing the School safely through the first, crucial fifteen years of its history.

By appointing only laymen to the Board of Trustees, Reed did not intend to compel the trustees to follow his example willy-nilly. Throughout the Indenture he and Wharton were careful not to tie the trustees' hands. But he did intend to set a strong precedent. The trustees, although strongly criticized at various times for doing so, have chosen to follow it ever since, thereby perpetuating a feature of the School's organization which was unique then, and is unique still. No other theological school, so far as is known, has a Board of Trustees from which all clergymen—including the bishop of the diocese—are by common consent traditionally excluded. The phenomenon, as Dean Hodges said with characteristically deft understatement at the School's Fortieth Anniversary, "perplexes the uninitiated." [13] Bishop William Lawrence at the Fiftieth Anniversary called it a "great experiment." [14] Yet in instituting the practice, neither Reed nor Wharton set out to be revolutionary or to perplex anyone.

---

[12] The number of trustees has been increased since: to seven in 1889, nine in 1913, eleven in 1922. There are now fifteen trustees, and the number can be increased to thirty if the board desires. The requirement that all trustees be residents of the Diocese of Massachusetts was lifted in 1911.

[13] "Fortieth Anniversary Alumni Banquet," p. 7 (ETS Archives).

[14] *ETS Bulletin*, June, 1917, p. 89.

There was no radical doctrine or theory behind their action. It had, indeed, some obvious roots in the immediate past. Both Appleton and Huntington had envisaged committing the task of establishing the theological school initially to a small group of three or four trustees, all of whom were laymen. But they had gone on to suggest that once the school was organized, these trustees should resign their power into the hands of a new board which would be composed of both clergymen and laymen in the conventional way. Huntington, in an effort to wedge the school firmly into the framework of the diocesan structure, had even suggested that this new board should consist of the bishop and standing committee. It was this step which Reed and Wharton did not take. Their reasons were pragmatic. Based upon what they knew had happened elsewhere in the not-too-distant past, they simply thought that a lay Board of Trustees would work better.

One of Wharton's last services to the School was to make all this unmistakably clear in 1885, when the trustees were under strong pressure from Bishop Paddock and others to bring the School into line with other seminaries by appointing the bishop and other clergymen to the board. By that time Reed, Rand, Putnam, Lawrence, and Amory were dead. Wharton had left Cambridge three years before. Only Winthrop remained, and he wrote to ask Wharton's opinion of the proposal. Wharton obliged with a statement so succinct that a copy was placed in the School archives where it could be consulted should the matter ever be raised again; for corporate bodies have short memories. He wrote:

I should regard it a great perversion of the purpose of the Seminary to make the Bishop a Trustee. I drew the Charter, & I not only knew Mr. Reed's intentions in this matter, but I fully concurred in his reasons. In England's great Universities the Bishops do not form part of the bodies by whom even the professors of Divinity are nominated. In this country, the presence of a diocesan Bishop in a diocesan School has been always held mischievous. Bishop McIlvaine always said this imperilled Gambier; Bishop Meade at the end of his life declined to interfere in Alexandria Trustee meetings; Bishop A[lonzo] Potter in the framing [of] the Constitution of the Philadelphia Seminary, put in two or three other Bishops, on the ground that a single diocesan Bishop would by his presence greatly embarrass the Board: the N.Y. Seminary is preserved from this difficulty by having *all* the Bishops members, who neutralize each other by uniform disagreements.

To have even a *good* Bishop a member as diocesan would cripple your independence. You can consult him far more efficiently if he were simply, as in England, a mere overseer or visitor. And a *bad* Bishop,—or an able, despotic ecclesiastic, such as De Koven or Whittingham!—you would either have to spend your time in fierce antagonisms, or make the School his puppet. Your only course is to keep the Bishop where he is.[15]

It is interesting to hear in this way, via Wharton, that Bishop Meade may have had second thoughts about the impetuosity with which he had once practiced amateur carpentry in the Virginia chapel, and that Bishop McIlvaine had repented of his tugs-of-war with the trustees and faculty at Gambier. But it was not Evangelicals alone who concurred in Wharton's diagnosis. A report from General in 1872, expatiating suavely on the advantages which it enjoyed compared with mere diocesan schools, made precisely the same point:

5. The [General] Seminary being in the government of the whole Church, and every Bishop having a visitorial power, is protected against extreme views. The *via media* is secured by the structure of the Institution. A Diocesan School will naturally take its cue from its Bishop, or other local circumstances of influence. And if a young man wishes to be edu-

---

[15] ETS Archives: "1884-86 (Feb.)" folder.

cated for a particular Diocese, and be patterned after a particular Bishop, he may properly prefer the local school. . . .[16]

Reed and Wharton in 1867, furthermore, had had no need to look farther afield than their own diocese to discover the embarrassments that can arise under a strong-minded and opinionated bishop. Manton Eastburn had by then been Bishop of Massachusetts for over twenty years. In that period his people had learned that he had many fine qualities. He was, in the words of Henry Codman Potter (who was Eastburn's assistant at Trinity when Reed was organizing the School), "absolutely constant, and absolutely fearless; and this last made him a champion whose instinct of loyalty to a friend was at once chivalric and imperious." [17] Any clergyman or layman who came to Eastburn's house with a complaint that had in it the least hint of slander always left much more rapidly than he had entered, his ears red from the wigging he had received.[18] He was equally forthright in his conservatism.

---

[16] *Proceedings,* IV, p. 542.

[17] H. C. Potter, *Reminiscences of Bishops and Archbishops,* p. 66.

[18] *Ibid.* Potter was present when a committee from a suburban parish called on the bishop to complain (falsely) that their rector was addicted to opium. The actual grievance behind the complaint was that the rector, who had been taking his meals in the house of a vestryman, had stopped doing so because he thought the food poor. The offended wife had prodded her husband into trying to stir up trouble for the rector in this fashion.

Eastburn at once expressed his grief at the serious charge, and said, "I suppose, gentlemen, you wish me to take canonical action in this painful business, and I shall proceed to do so. But, to that end, it is necessary that the charge should be presented to me in writing, and that you should subscribe your names to it." This understandably threw the committee into confusion. "We couldn't sign any paper," they said to Eastburn, "We merely wished to come and tell you what you have heard, and leave the matter in your hands."

Eastburn's reply, as he forthwith showed them the door, is classic: "Though you know that a clergyman's reputation is well-nigh as sensitive as a woman's, you will do all you can to destroy it; and when you are asked to subscribe to your own accusation you will refuse. Do you know, gentlemen, what your rector would do if he were a layman? *He would horsewhip you*—and so would I! Good morning, gentlemen."

Born in England, from which he had come to the United
States in 1813 at the age of twelve, he solemnly drank the
Queen's health every year on her birthday. He went out
riding accoutred in the Regency-period jockey cap, short
jacket, and yellow leggings popular in his boyhood instead
of the topper, frock coat, and long trousers more conventional in post-Civil-War Boston. His hair was always
brushed forward to an up-curled point on either side of
his head in the mode that had gone out of fashion with
Washington Irving. And his notions of the world were
equally static. He was once heard to say that he had never
changed his religious views since he was seven, and his
congregation, listening to his sermons, saw no reason to
doubt him. Bishop Clark, another of Eastburn's onetime
assistants, said of him that "for all modern phases of
thought he had an unmitigated contempt." [19] As "modern"
meant anything which had come up since 1808, it included the Tractarian Movement and all that had sprung
from it; and it was from this that trouble arose. For Eastburn was as much of a stickler in requiring conformity
with what he considered proper church practice as in
everything else. When, in Bishop Hopkins's expressive
phrase, "novelties disturbed his peace," he had no com-
punction about disturbing everyone else's peace until the
novelties were discarded. If there were flowers in the
chancel, he refused to enter it. If a clergyman turned east-
ward to say the Creed in a service at which the bishop
was present, Eastburn would admonish him in a per-
emptory whisper to "turn 'round"—repeating the command with increasing vehemence until the cowed ecclesiastic did as he was bid. Although on the most cordial terms
with the Roman Catholic Bishop of Boston, the courtly
Fitzpatrick, he would have no truck with the "Romish"
innovations of the Church of the Advent, refusing to visit
it for confirmation for thirteen years. Amos A. Lawrence,

---

[19] Clark, *Reminiscences*, p. 104.

a close friend, had remonstrated with him in vain over this partisan rigidity. All this Reed and Wharton knew. They were in complete sympathy with Eastburn's Evangelical views (and he with theirs); but they did not wish the School's admissions policy or its course of study restricted to conform with his prejudices. They had no desire, therefore, to associate so granitic a figure with the government of the School. He was not even told what was afoot until the organization was virtually completed.

Difficult though it may be today to conceive of establishing a theological school—or any other major ecclesiastical project—in so quiet, simple, and independent a fashion, with no official reference to the diocesan convention or even the standing committee, there seemed nothing odd about it at the time. Massachusetts laymen had been accustomed to taking the lead in diocesan affairs in this way for years. Unlike the laymen in many other dioceses, they did not leave the initiative to the clergy or the bishop. While the Church in Boston had shown signs in the 1820's of the same inertia that hampered Chase and McIlvaine in Ohio and distressed Meade in Virginia, the ministries of Potter, Stone, Vinton, and Huntington had gone far to dissipate it—and particularly in the congregations from which came the founders of the Episcopal Theological School. In the formation of new parishes, furthermore, laymen had been bold from the first: in St. Paul's in Boston, Grace Church, Emmanuel, the Church of the Advent, and St. Paul's in Brookline. In the very months when Wharton and Reed were organizing the School, one of the trustees, Amos A. Lawrence, was engaged in planning a new church for the Longwood section of Brookline, where he and his brother lived. So little did this depend on official approval or encouragement, that the Lawrences were prepared to present the edifice to "some other Evangelical denomination" if protests from the two richest members of St. Paul's scared the standing committee into refusing to authorize the establishment of a second Episcopal parish in the town.

The founders of the School, furthermore, were quick to assume and exercise responsibility partly because they had been so long accustomed to occupying positions of power in the official administrative structure of the diocese itself. Reed, Rand, Winthrop, and Lawrence served as Trustees of Donations; Reed, Rand, Winthrop, Lawrence, and Amory were on the committee on the increase of the Episcopal Fund. In 1864 Winthrop and Amory had been on the standing committee; and Reed had been on it in 1865. In 1866 the Massachusetts lay delegation to the General Convention consisted of Rand, Winthrop, Lawrence, and Amory. In themselves, therefore, these men were a link with the official "establishment" of the diocese that was much closer and stronger than would appear at first glance.

Preserving the Endowment

In their preference for a board composed entirely of laymen—and such distinguished laymen at that—it must not be supposed, however, that Reed and Wharton were blind to the mistakes which lay trustees, too, can make. They were not uncritically partial. The citizens who had served on the boards of General, Gambier, and Virginia had been no less solid and respectable men of affairs who had acquired a reputation for skillful management of money and property. But they had shown little evidence of this as trustees. While they could seldom be accused of overpaying the professors, when it came to buildings they had uniformly been overcome by a *folie de grandeur* reminiscent of Louis XIV. Blithely committing tomorrow's money to pay today's construction bills, they had almost bankrupted the institutions of which they had been appointed guardians. In addition, the trustees of General had doled out the endowment spoonful by spoonful to ease the pangs of a yawning operating deficit until the seminary had almost died of financial malnutrition in the 1860's. A man like Reed, who had made three fortunes by lucky investment and lost two, was far too conscious of the unaccountable vagaries of business cycles even to attempt to dictate investment policy to future trustees; but he could at least prevent the endowment from being squandered as it had been elsewhere. The final Article of the Indenture read:

No part of the fund of one hundred thousand dollars hereby given shall be expended in the purchase of land, or the erection of buildings for the use of the said School; but the same shall be kept constantly invested, and the income thereof shall be applied to the payment of the salaries of the Professors and Lecturers and the necessary expenses of the School; provided however, that nothing herein contained shall be held to forbid or prevent the investment of any portion of the said fund in real estate for the purposes of income.[20]

This went further than Appleton's Indenture, which had permitted "one fourth part of the funds and property of the institution . . . [to] be vested in real estate for the accommodation of the School and its officers." The restriction was a wise one without which it is highly likely that the School would not have survived its early years of financial hardship. For at least two of the trustees, like their forerunners elsewhere, were of the opinion that an ample site and impressive buildings were so vital to the School's prestige in the eyes of the world that the School should not even open before these had been obtained.[21] There seems little doubt that they would have used the endowment for this purpose if they could; and as the

---

[20] *Indenture*, p. 9.

[21] One of these was James Sullivan Amory, although he later completely reversed his position. See J. S. Stone to J. S. C. Greene, June 20, 1867; J. S. C. Greene to E. S. Rand, July 10, 1867; and J. S. Amory to E. S. Rand, Aug. 28, 1867 (ETS Archives: "1866-67" folder).

School's independence of diocesan control deprived it of
the sympathy which might be expected to attract financial
support from the local parishes or from the bishop (a
backlog on which both Virginia and Gambier could depend), once the endowment was gone, there would have
been nothing to take its place. Reed's restriction, however, prevented this from happening. He, Wharton, Stone,
Huntington, and Rand were agreed that the effectiveness
of a school is derived from its professors, not from its
buildings. As the endowment income was expected to
amount to a little over $6,000 a year, Reed was ensuring,
in this final Article, that there would always be money
available with which to pay the salaries of two resident
professors and four nonresident part-time lecturers (calculated at the generally accepted level of $2,000 a year
for a professor and between $500 and $1,000 a year for a
lecturer).[22] The knowledge that these salaries could always be paid regularly and on time would free the School
from an anxiety which had hitherto burdened, and sometimes embittered, the atmosphere in every other seminary
of the Church. With such a faculty, furthermore, the
School could function adequately, if not very comfortably,
even with no property of its own at all. As Wharton
pointed out, the professors could hold classes in their
houses (as Hopkins had done in 1831), and the students
could be boarded in the town in the fashion of theological
students at the German universities.[23] The problem of
ministering to the students at Harvard would have been
more difficult to solve under such Spartan conditions; but
Lawrence saw a way out even there. He suggested that if
the School could find or afford nothing else, it should
ask Harvard College for permission to use Holden Chapel
for lectures and worship for a year or two in return for

[22] "Schedule of expenses of Seminary for one year," in Wharton's hand,
undated, probably drawn up in May, 1867 (ETS Archives: "1866-67"
folder).

[23] Wharton to Rand, Mar. 22, 1867 (ETS Archives: "1866-67" folder).

payment of a modest rent.[24] Lawrence presumably knew that the Harvard Corporation would look with favor on such a proposal: he had, after all, been treasurer of Harvard College for many years.

The Board of Visitors

While the Bishop of Massachusetts and the clergy were deliberately excluded from the Board of Trustees, however, they were not shut away from all connection with the School. On the Board of Visitors they were carefully given the dominant position. There was nothing novel about such a board in those days; the Harvard Divinity School had one, and so did Andover. The Article prescribing their duties, furthermore, was copied almost word for word from Appleton's Indenture. The visitors were to enjoy "all the rights and powers by law incident to the office of visitors of eleemosynary institutions" [25]—a phrase which was a good deal less ambiguous in 1867 than the trustees and faculty of the Episcopal Theological School liked to pretend in a later day when the visitors had become a nuisance to them. According to the Article the board was to "inquire into and examine the state and condition of the School, and all matters and things relating thereto." It was to "take care that the Statutes, Articles, Regulations, By-laws, and rules be at all times faithfully observed and obeyed, and that wholesome and proper discipline be enforced in the said School, and . . . correct and reform all abuses from whatever cause arising." [26] Unless Huntington completely misunderstood Reed when the two men had their second talk about the organization of the School, it was originally intended that the visitors should have as influential a voice in the School as the Harvard overseers of the period did in the affairs of

---

[24] Wharton to Rand, Apr. 23, 1867 (ETS Archives: "1866-67" folder).
[25] *Indenture*, p. 7.
[26] *Ibid.*, p. 8.

the college, even to approving formally faculty appointments.[27] This would have been natural; for Huntington,
Reed, Rand, Winthrop, and Lawrence were all Harvard
men, and constantly active in the business of the college.
But second thoughts led to a change in this plan—second
thoughts which almost certainly came from Wharton.
Wharton was not a Harvard man, and it is plain from
his letter to Winthrop in 1885 that he was influenced by
English, rather than local American, precedents. In his
view, the Board of Visitors was to be both a watchdog to
see that the School continued to carry out the intentions
of the founder, and a referee to be called in whenever the
School's governing body had become hopelessly divided
against itself. Otherwise, the visitors were not to interfere with the administration, and they were to have
nothing to do with faculty appointments. In keeping with
this view, the only part of the Article in the Appleton
Indenture which Wharton deleted was the phrase specifically affirming the right of the professors to appeal to
the visitors against the trustees—a right which had been
used at Andover exclusively to stave off dismissal. And
when the trustees could not agree among themselves on
where to establish temporary quarters for the School in
the late spring and early summer of 1867, Wharton suggested to Rand that the disagreement should be referred
to two of the visitors for settlement.[28]

The bishop was to be a member of the Board of Visitors
and president *ex officio*. The other members were to be
"three ministers of the Protestant-Episcopal Church, canonically and actually resident within the Diocese in which
the said school shall be situated, and three laymen of the
said Church residing within such Diocese." [29] The first

---

[27] F. D. Huntington to B. T. Reed, Feb. 14, 1867 (ETS Archives: "1866-
67" folder).

[28] Wharton to Rand, May 9, 1867 (ETS Archives: "1866-67" folder).
Rand's answer, if any, is not extant.

[29] *Indenture*, p. 7.

members were to be appointed directly by the trustees. Future vacancies were to be filled by the board itself— but only by compliantly electing whomever the trustees thought fit to nominate, a Yankee *congé d'élire* which was no more popular with the visitors than its more ancient English counterpart was with cathedral chapters. The first Board of Visitors, although technically elected by the trustees, was in fact chosen by Reed, and reflected the same concern with parochial and family relationships that had earlier governed his choice of the trustees themselves. The president, Bishop Eastburn, was, of course, also rector of Trinity. The three other clerical members were Frederic Dan Huntington, rector of Emmanuel, William R. Nicholson, rector of St. Paul's, Boston, and John Singleton Copley Greene. Greene was one of the sons-in-law of William Appleton whose names had been on the Indenture of 1846. Entering the ministry, like Wharton, late in life, he had been rector of Grace Church, Newton, for a time until ill health compelled him to resign, whereupon he had been succeeded by the Rev. Peter Henry Steenstra. He was a grandson of Copley, a nephew of Lord Lyndhurst, and a lifelong friend of Winthrop, Lawrence, Amory, and Stone. The three lay members were Judge Joseph Story Fay, a prominent Cambridge citizen and a conservative churchman; Robert Means Mason, Lawrence's cousin and senior business partner, the son of Jeremiah Mason (who had been a trustee of the seminary provisionally planned in 1836); and Dr. George Cheyne Shattuck, dean of the Harvard Medical School, a pillar of the Church of the Advent, and (like Winthrop) a trustee of General.

Despite Wharton's careful drafting, however, the Board of Visitors never worked well. In the composition of the board and in the role envisioned for it, there was an inherent contradiction which proved irreconcilable, resulting in frustration for everyone concerned. Wharton's

conception of the visitors as composing principally a court
of last resort, with considerable power to intervene in
School affairs where necessary in order to resolve difficulties that might arise within it, had sound traditional
warrant; but except at Andover it had no roots in local
practice. It is true that it had been Appleton's conception,
too; but Appleton's board had been sufficiently awe-
inspiring—and sufficiently far removed from the immediate locality of the School—to make such a role seem
natural. It was to have consisted of the Bishops of Connecticut, Rhode Island, Vermont, New Hampshire, and
Maine acting in concert, a group which in 1867 would
have included, besides Manton Eastburn, John Henry
Hopkins, John Williams, and Thomas March Clark.
Wharton's board was neither so august nor so scattered. Its members, furthermore, were familiar with only
one kind of visitor, the Harvard overseer, who was not so
much an impartial referee as a keenly interested partisan
bent on influencing educational and administrative policy.
President Eliot in his Inaugural Address in 1869 said:

The real function of the Board of Overseers is to stimulate
and watch the President and Fellows. Without the Overseers,
the President and Fellows would be a board of private trustees,
self-perpetuated and self-controlled. Provided as it is with
two governing boards, the University enjoys that principal
safeguard of all American governments—the natural antago-
nism between two bodies of different constitution, powers, and
privileges. While having with the Corporation a common
interest of the deepest kind in the welfare of the University
and the advancement of learning, the Overseers should always
hold toward the Corporation an attitude of suspicious vigi-
lance. They ought always to be pushing and prying. . . .[30]

For "Overseer" read "Visitor"; for "President and Fellows" read "Trustees"; and the passage becomes a precise

---

[30] James, *Charles W. Eliot*, I, p. 232.

description of the way in which the Board of Visitors of the Episcopal Theological School did its best to behave during almost its entire existence. It became, in other words, what Professors Washburn and Nash years later aptly called a "Smelling Committee." [31] This was, of course, the very role which Reed had first envisaged for it, and then deliberately discarded on Wharton's advice. And because he had discarded it, the visitors scanned the Indenture in vain looking for a grant of powers which would enable them to exercise such a role effectively. In the course of their visitations they made not the slightest attempt to ascertain whether or not the trustees and faculty were carrying out the intentions of the founder. Instead they criticized the attendance at chapel services,[32] and tried to tell the professors how they should conduct the services,[33] and how they should teach.[34] The trustees, most of whom—being loyal Harvard men—were fully as bemused by the overseer model as were the visitors themselves, accepted these attentions blandly, employing them when they chose as a weapon with which to prod the professors into making changes which the trustees wanted.[35] On the other hand, the professors (including Wharton himself for a time) were surprised, not to say dumbfounded, by what seemed to them perverse interfer-

[31] Faculty Meeting Records, Vol. II, March 12, 1910, "Report of the Committee on the Board of Visitors," p. 3. Nash and Washburn (the committee) were in favor of continuing the board in this capacity, stripping it of all power, and making it entirely advisory. "Thus constituted," they wrote, "a Board of Visitors might prove a real help. Every academic body is in danger of becoming academic to excess, unconsciously removing itself from vital contact with practical life. Friendly critics might give material aid and stimulus to the Faculty." This, too, shows no comprehension of the board's function as planned by Reed and Wharton.

[32] "Memorial to the Trustees from the Board of Visitors," June 14, 1881 (ETS Archives: "1880-81" folder).

[33] Ibid.

[34] The Board of Visitors to the Trustees, Jan. 29, 1883 (ETS Archives: "1883" folder).

[35] The Trustees to Dean Gray, June, 1881 (ETS Archives: "1880-81" folder). This letter was written by Rand.

ence in matters which were none of the visitors' business.[36] The visitors were surprised that the professors were surprised, replying rather snappishly that if it wasn't their business, it certainly ought to be, and that either the composition of the Board of Trustees or the Article prescribing the powers of the visitors should be changed forthwith to make it their business.[37] It was just such a proposal which prompted Winthrop to elicit from Wharton a statement of Reed's intentions with regard to the School's government in 1885. Nor was this case of mistaken identity ever cleared up. An apparently invincible ignorance permanently obscured the outlines of Reed and Wharton's plan. Basing their position firmly on a fundamental misconception, the visitors remained an anomaly to everyone, including themselves. They did not demur when the faculty suggested to the trustees that the Board of Visitors be stripped of its power to "correct and reform all abuses" in 1910, and obligingly went out of existence altogether in 1944 when the faculty decided that they should.

Freedom for the Professors

In view of the prickly forbearance with which professors and visitors had treated one another over the years, the attitude of mournful benevolence assumed by the faculty in reports written when it was finally getting rid of the board is more than a little diverting; but that the faculty should have taken the initiative in a matter of this kind, instead of leaving it to the trustees or to the visitors themselves, was completely in keeping with the spirit of the original Indenture. The peculiar composition of the Board of Trustees and the duties assigned to Wharton's stillborn

---

[36] Wharton to A. V. G. Allen, Aug. 26, 1881; P. H. Steenstra to Allen, Sept. 12, 1881 (ETS Archives: "1880-81" folder).

[37] The Board of Visitors to the Trustees, Oct. 30, 1885 (ETS Archives: "1884-85 [Feb]" folder).

Board of Visitors, as well as the sections dealing specifically
with the faculty as such, had been alike framed with one
object in mind: that of giving the professors an independent, even a dominating, voice in the affairs of the School.
In other seminaries of the period, the professors, no matter
how deeply they might be respected as individuals, were
little more than monitors under the trustees—teaching
what the trustees told them to teach in the way the trustees
told them to teach it. This was as true at Virginia as it
was at Gambier or General. In times when heated ecclesiastical controversy had made people nervous, a man who
revealed signs of independent thought could be abruptly
dismissed from his post. Even as the Episcopal Theological
School was coming into being, just such a wave of accusa-
tions, investigations, resignations and dismissals was about
to break over luckless Bexley. Shrewdly aware of these
dangers, Reed and Wharton were determined to insu-
late the professors against any threats of interference from
the outside so that they would be free to do the best work
of which they were capable. Professor A. V. G. Allen, in
composing notes for the history of the School which he
did not live long enough to write, recalled:

Dr. Wharton's idea was "freedom"—such an adjustment as
should secure for the teachers "freedom." He saw how institutions had been hurt or wrecked. This he believed to be
the ideal of the Anglican Church in the great age of the
Reformation. It was the meaning of the Gospel—its freedom
of the Children of God.

All the standards of the Anglican Church pointed in this
direction. The object in breaking from the Roman Church
had been to secure it. When the Reformation formularies
were studied by themselves apart from this ideal they became
dull dogmas, hard and narrow and small—when seen as
agencies of freedom they meant life.[38]

---

[38] Allen, MS. notes (ETS Archives: "Allen's Notes" folder).

Freedom from financial worry, freedom from episcopal domineering, freedom from the "pushing and prying" of anxiously orthodox committees or of a passion-swept diocesan convention, freedom from fear of dismissal: Reed and Wharton intended to secure them all. The Fifth Article of the Indenture, in words taken in large part verbatim from Appleton's document of twenty years before, read:

The said Trustees shall appoint such Professors, Lecturers, and Officers for the instruction and government of the School, as they may deem proper; prescribe their duties, fix their salaries, and define their powers. They may remove such Lecturers and Officers at their pleasure. To secure a reasonable degree of independence, the Professors shall hold their offices during good behavior, subject to removal by the Trustees on trial, for neglect of duty, incapacity satisfactorily to perform their duties, immorality, holding and avowing doctrines, or adopting rites, ceremonies, or practices inconsistent and irreconcilable with the doctrines, ritual and order, discipline and worship, of the Protestant-Episcopal Church in the United States of America, as set forth in the Book of Common Prayer and the Canons of the said Church, or for violation of the provisions of the Second Fundamental Article hereof. . . .[39]

"Lecturers and Officers," according to the custom of the day, were not generally considered permanent posts. Offices often rotated from one member of a faculty to another. Lecturers were usually nonresident and part-time, like the local rectors and bishops who delivered lectures at Virginia or General. Technically, they were not members of the faculty. The intent of the Article, therefore, was that the basic, stable faculty of the School—the resi-

---

[39] *Indenture*, pp. 6-7. In tune with the practice at Virginia, no professor was to be either a trustee or a visitor. Reed and Wharton, however, were even more strict: they excluded lecturers from these offices.

dent, full-time teachers—should have tenure.[40] On this provision Professor Allen commented:

One of the features of the School which it owes to Francis Wharton is the sense of perpetuity in office which is secured by a provision that they have the right of trial, etc. in case of alleged failure, etc. To this point Dr. Wharton attached the highest significance. The incapacity must be proved and demonstrated. Of course it hurts an institution to accumulate dead weights, incompetent men in its teaching staff—or men obnoxious for other reasons. But it hurts it more when they are dismissed in any arbitrary fashion. The passion for justice is very deep in the life of students. A wound incurable has been inflicted when injustice has been done.

The old rule which prevailed quite generally in theological schools in the last century, down to a late date in the century, was to appoint to positions elderly men who had broken down in the pastoral work—or to assume that men who had won distinction in the pulpit were for that reason best fitted to guide the training of the theological student. That usage has now gone by. It is better as a rule to take young men and train them for the position, or men still young who have served in parishes (but not too long) whose aptitudes are suited for the work of teaching and who have been watched and found competent.

But the main point is that the life of a school centers in its teachers. They must be efficient, they must be scholars, thoroughly up in their respective departments, full of devotion

---

[40] This has been whittled down to conform with the practice common among academic institutions of the present day. By 1943, tenure was conferred only on full professors, and then only after a preliminary term of three years. Although mitigated by the modern custom of appointing members to the faculty, including instructors, for three-year terms instead of from one year to the next, the retreat from the system instituted by the founders has perforce made a considerable portion of the faculty in certain periods more vulnerable than Reed and Wharton wished. This becomes apparent when it is realized that throughout the nineteenth century and part of the twentieth, members of the faculty were made professors as soon as the trustees and faculty had decided that they ought to be permanent additions to the staff. These appointments were usually made when the men were still in their late twenties.

and interest in their work, and not only so but successful as
teachers in inspiring others by interesting them in their work.
They can not interest others unless they are profoundly interested themselves. But for their best success, they need the
assurance of certain tenure of position. The rivalry and
competition which may be allowed in the university, tho'
even there it does injury, the fear that at any moment they
are liable to removal, for incompetency as compared with
others, or for teaching what is regarded as "false doctrine" by
irresponsible factions, weakens them till they do not do their
best work. The competition among rival colleges, the tests of
success applied, the immediate effects of popularity—all these
are singularly out of place in the theological school. The
simple words that if they are to be removed it shall be "upon
trial" gives them a fair chance. That is all which is asked.

Of course there is here a practical difficulty—but it is best
solved by practice than by theory.

The great thing is to be slow in making appointments—
and apply the tests most thoroughly at that stage.

The great reason for the success of the School is that the
Trustees in making appointments have conferred with the
Professors until unanimity has been reached. Harmony and
freedom have thus been secured. Those who know theological
seminaries are aware of the evil that reigns when this harmony
is lacking. For religion is a most sensitive sphere, etc. and
religious and ecclesiastical quarrels are the most unpleasant
of all quarrels.[41]

"The Great Doctrine of Justification by Faith"

In their anxiety to guarantee the greatest possible degree
of freedom to the professors—and to the trustees in their
choice of professors—Reed and Wharton, in fact, made
only one limitation, which was set forth in the "Second
Fundamental Article" referred to in the Article establishing tenure for the professors. But they considered the
limitation so vital as a protection of the School's basic
character that the "Second Fundamental Article" was the

[41] Allen, MS. Notes (ETS Archives: "Allen's Notes" folder).

only one which, by the terms of the Indenture, they directed could never be changed or amended in the future.[42] It read:

The instructions and teachings of the said School, and of its Professors and Lecturers, shall always be in conformity with the doctrine, ritual and order, discipline and worship of the Protestant-Episcopal Church in the United States of America, as set forth in the Book of Common Prayer and the Canons of the said Church; and shall at all times embody and distinctly set forth the great doctrine of Justification by Faith alone in the Atonement and Righteousness of Christ, as taught in the "Articles of Religion" commonly called the Thirty-Nine Articles, according to the natural construction of the said articles (Scripture alone being the standard) as adopted at the Reformation, and not according to any tradition, doctrine, or usage prior to the said Reformation, not contained in Scripture.

Each and every Professor and Lecturer appointed in the said School, shall, before entering upon the duties of his office, subscribe to a solemn declaration that his teachings and practice shall in all respects conform to this Fundamental Article.[43]

---

[42] *Indenture*, p. 6.

[43] *Ibid.*, p. 4. The "solemn declaration" was drawn up by John Seely Stone to replace a draft submitted by the trustees which Stone considered too restrictive in its phrasing. He achieved a form that satisfied him in 1868, and all members of the faculty have been required to subscribe to it on first taking up their appointment at the School. The declaration reads: "We, whose names are hereto subscribed, having been respectively elected, or appointed Professors, Lecturers, or Teachers in The Episcopal Theological School of Massachusetts, & having accepted such office, DO HEREBY, in the presence of Almighty God, solemnly promise & declare, each for himself, that the Instruction & Teaching, given by us in the said School, shall always be in conformity with the Doctrine, Discipline & Worship of the Protestant Episcopal Church of the United States of America, as set forth in the Book of Common Prayer & Offices, & recognized & enforced in the Constitution & Canons, of the said Church; &, in particular, that such Instruction & teaching shall always be consistent with, &, at all proper times, shall embody & distinctly set forth the great Doctrine of 'Justification by Faith only' in the Atonement & Righteousness of Christ, as taught in 'The Articles of Religion,' commonly called 'The Thirty-Nine Articles,' as finally adopted

In adopting this method of preserving the character of
the School unchanged over the years, Reed and Wharton
were taking a leaf out of the book of the founders of
Andover, who had attempted in precisely such a fashion
to prevent their seminary from ever being infected by the
heretical Rationalism which had driven Orthodoxy from
their beloved Harvard. But the simplicity and brevity of
Reed's Article, compared with the pages taken up by the
Andover counterpart, testifies to the essential simplicity
and sobriety of Reed's intention. "Justification by Faith
alone" was a watchword of the Evangelicals. Bishop Mc-
Ilvaine had written a book about it. Professor Bancroft
of Gambier, commending Reed's Article, wrote, "When
the doctrine of the free justification of the Sinner through
faith in a Saviour crucified and risen is surrendered, then
everything is surrendered." [44] Bishop Eastburn rarely
preached on any other theme; and in later years the
trustees were to say that the Second Article so exactly
reflected his own beliefs that "it might be said to have
come from his pen." Nothing had more disturbed and
aroused the Evangelicals than the way in which Newman
had transformed this doctrine into something unrecog-
nizable to them in *Tracts for the Times* (a disturbance
reflected in the wording of Reed's Article). The inclusion
of the Second Fundamental Article in the Indenture
simply meant, therefore, that the Episcopal Theological

& settled under Queen Elizabeth, in the years 1562 & 1571: according to
the natural construction of the said Articles, & not according to any Tradition, Custom or Usage prior to the Reformation not contained in Scripture: it being understood that, in our Interpretation of the said Prayer
Book, Offices & Articles, nothing shall be taught, as a matter of Faith
necessary to Salvation, which 'is not read in Holy Scripture, or which
may not be proved thereby.'

"And we do further severally promise that our public Preaching &
practice shall, in all respects, be conformable to the declarations now
made" (from the copy in Stone's handwriting deposited in the ETS
Archives: "1866-67" folder).

[44] L. W. Bancroft to E. S. Rand, Feb. 4, 1867 (ETS Archives: "1866-67"
folder).

School was to be staunchly (although not necessarily narrowly) Evangelical. Rand made this clear in an official letter to Wharton which he intended to show to wealthy Evangelicals in order to interest them in the School: "It is . . . the desire, and, so far as is in their power, the fixed determination of the Trustees that the School should be *decidedly Evangelical* in its character, influence and teachings—that it shd be for New England what the Phil School is for the Middle States and Gambier for Ohio & the West. . . ." [45]

Reed himself, furthermore, laid down a policy for faculty appointments in accordance with this intention by sending the following letter to the trustees on January 26, 1867, only four days after the Indenture had been drawn up and signed:

Gent: It is my anxious desire that in appointing Professors or any officers for the Episcopal Theological School at Cambridge, that they and their successors should be selected from the Evangelical class, who believe in the doctrines of the church as declared at the Reformation, & free from any of the isms of the day.

I would by all means avoid the appointment of men, who would magnify the forms of the church above its teachings, or who would institute any of the ceremonies of the Papal Church. [46]

That, too, was "for the record."

---

[45] Rand to Wharton, Apr. 6, 1867 (ETS Archives: "1866-67" folder, appended to Wharton's brief "on the organization of the School").

[46] Reed to the Trustees, Jan. 26, 1867 (ETS Archives: "1866-67" folder).

꙰ 9

The Body Stirs to Life

THE SELECTION OF MEN to fill the posts of professor or lecturer was committed by the trustees to Wharton and John Seely Stone,[1] but they were not left without guidance. Huntington, who knew Harvard and Cambridge better than most Episcopalians, submitted a long memorandum to Reed on the choice of professors which was considered so valuable that it was handed on to Rand, who carefully kept it. Three principal considerations, in Huntington's opinion, made the finding of the right men especially important—more important, perhaps, than it might have been in an earlier day or in another place.

Dr. Huntington's Job Description

1. It will be essential to the prosperity of the undertaking itself. No endowment however ample, no patronage however munificent, no local advantages or academic *prestige*, can avail to make a theological Institution flourish, if it is compromised or prejudiced from the outset with ill-qualified Teachers. It will be only a fine establishment without pupils. In this case, the Institution has its whole character to create.

---

[1] E. S. Rand to F. Wharton, Apr. 6, 1867 (ETS Archives).

Its only claims on confidence or attendance will be in the known moral and intellectual power of those Teachers. Obscure men will not do. Small men will not do. Onesided men will not do. There must be a most exemplary piety, unquestioned ability, unimpeachable learning, and a large style of manhood. It deserves to be remembered that the existence of so many Divinity Schools, already established, puts additional emphasis on this requirement. If students are not strongly attracted to a particular school by superior officers, they can easily turn to some other. We cannot even depend on our own diocese. The facilities of travel and rapid intercommunication make it quite easy for young men to go from Mass$^{ts.}$ to Ohio and Penn$^{a.}$, much more to New York and Connecticut. Except when the Bishop has great personal popularity or uncommon strength, there is,—as is constantly seen,—not force enough in the mere diocesan sentiment to prevent the passing from one diocese to another. Probably still other competing Seminaries will arise in other Dioceses, as they grow; at least this will be prevented only by the eminent excellence of those that come first in time.

2. The importance of the Choice is seen again in reference to the Church at large. Every seat of learning, and especially one that trains men for the sacred ministry of Christ, is accountable for an influence beyond itself. It affects the public welfare. It sets in motion trains of causes that reach on, multiply themselves, and are felt without limit. It educates educators. It moulds men that mould Parishes, and thus the lives of countless people. It stamps them with truth or error, charity or bigotry, the spirit of concord and brotherly love or the spirit of division and suspicion. And it is no abstraction in the Institution that does this. The living men that teach the lessons do it.

3. At Cambridge the reasons for placing in the chairs men of the kind referred to are peculiarly urgent. No intellectual atmosphere, no literary tone, no standard of criticism, is like that. I am constantly struck with the difficulty that even able and accomplished men, reared in other parts of the country, find in seizing and apprehending what we may call the philosophy or spirit of the place; and yet a good degree of such

apprehension there must be, in those that enter into the scene as instructors or preachers, or else they miss the mark. It is safe to say, I suppose, that there is no literary society in this country where the genuineness, the thoroughness, or comprehensiveness of a Teacher's mind would be likely to be subjected to more trying tests than there.

Of course the question comes up, therefore, what the qualifications would be. Without adventuring so far as to undertake a complete catalogue of them, I only ask leave to allude to a few to which my mind has particularly turned, and which impress me as worthy of deliberate regard at this stage of your great enterprise.

First, the qualities to be desired in a Theological Professor are not the same as those that are desirable in a Rector or Preacher,—even in the best of Rectors or the most persuasive and successful of Preachers. It may even be said, I suppose, that so distinct and *un*like are these callings, the one from the other two, and so dependent is success in them on *separate* elements in the constitution of the mind and different mental habitudes, processes, kinds of discipline, modes of thinking and expression, and acquirements, that it is even improbable that a man who succeeds best in the pulpit will be a ready, competent guide to students in theological science. No doubt, one of the former class may do some good in a Divinity-School by a kind of sympathetic action; but unless he has a scientific mind and culture he is not the man for the place. Impressing religiously mixed congregations, made up of men, women, and children, is one thing,—a high and holy vocation. Conducting a class of scholars through the discriminations and subtleties of theological systems, so as to build them up into wide and strong thinkers, is another.

Secondly, a Theological Professor, especially in this age and in this region, ought to be perfectly free from those religious *onesidednesses,* whims, or sentimentalities,—sometimes called *isms* and sometimes *hobbies,*—which are not of the substance of the Common Faith, which limit a teacher's command over the respect and confidence of the clearest-sighted pupils he attempts to teach, and which almost insensibly, in a critical community, expose him sooner or later to ridicule. For instance, take three of these forms of sentiment (they are very apt to be erected into dogmas and to characterize the whole man before he is aware) which are found in individual cases in our own Church: viz. Calvinism, Ritualism, & Millenarianism. No one of them is any part of the recognized, standard theology of the Church. A man may personally hold either of them, and be a Churchman notwithstanding. A minister may, if he pleases, teach either of them to his own flock, and take the necessary risks and responsibilities. I say nothing of their truth or falsehood. But no one of them has any business in a Theological School. No one of them is a component part of Evangelical and Catholic Divinity. Either of them would restrict a Professor's influence and power in the School you are to have the honor of establishing, would array opposition against it, injure its name, and prejudice its success.

Thirdly, it appears to be eminently desirable that a Professor at Cambridge should have a generous intellectual appreciation, some acquaintance with the later results of scholarly research in other departments than his own, acute knowledge of the relations of modern Science to Revealed Truth, and a considerable tact and judgment in dealing with that class of topics. He must mix much with other men, who are Masters in the several Departments and picked from the world of students, be compared with them, have his measure taken by them. If he blunders or trips, he loses his hold. We need to have our Church represented at Harvard University by men quite up with the times, going to the bottom of questions, careful what they say, looking all round the subjects they handle, large enough as well as good-tempered enough to meet their equals on handsome terms, knowing what has been thought and said by the best heads. There are doubtless spots where another class of teachers would get on and accomplish something; but, even for the man himself, I could hardly conceive a more mortifying or more painful position than, without a good degree of this sort of furnishing, to undertake what would be required just there.

Fourthly, I ought not to pass entirely by a topic which, without your excellent moderation and good-sense would perhaps be the most perplexing and dangerous of all. You know very

nearly, I have no question, what I would say of Church-parties
and of tendencies to Ecclesiastical extremes; because, being
my parishioner, you have observed my course as a Rector and
may be supposed to understand my principles. I have certainly
nothing in them to conceal from anybody,—tho', so deep and
settled is my aversion to the whole spirit, chicanery and
phraseology of party-politics in the Church, that I can rarely
indeed bring myself to refer to them in any way. Our Blessed
Lord has given us other, better, purer, nobler, happier work.
The one supreme and indispensable requisite in the matter of
doctrine in this School should be that the pure Gospel of our
Lord and of his Evangelists and Apostles should be taught
in it, just as it lies on the face of the Gospel:—repentance and
newness of life; justification and sanctification; the cross and
the righteousness of the Redeemer; and the Holy Trinity. This
system of doctrines should stand out clearly, beyond mistake,
as it has been held by the great body of English Divines since
the Reformers, as it was held in the Primitive Church before
the Romish usurpation. The whole theory of sacramentalism
—ritualistic, semi-Romish theology and practice—we put aside
at once and forever from the start. This being determined,
this Evangelical theology should be so taught, in my judgment, as to come in its due and just proportions, as our
Church in all its system of Doctrine, Discipline and Worship,
has held and administered it. The Church itself should be
presented always as the Divine means of drawing souls to the
Saviour and edifying them in Him. It should be honored,
reverenced, loved, obeyed, in all its laws, ordinances, rubrics,
canons, as the best Gift of God—after Christ whose Body it is
and the Inspired Word of his Salvation—to this world, and
most especially to such a nation as ours. But it is very clear
that there are at least two ways of holding and teaching this
Evangelic Truth. One is the polemical, partisan way. The
other is the positive, gracious way. You know the difference as
well as I, and the different results:—the Saviour's own kingdom growing blessedly on the one side,—mischief, poison,
pride, wrath, strife on the other. It would be easy to point out
examples in Bishops and Presbyters. The great host of the
devout and earnest Churchmen occupy, and always will, the

middle ground. This Divinity-School ought, by all means, to occupy it. It is wide enough for such Bishops as Burgess and Williams at the East, Lee and Whipple at the West, and Coxe and Bedell at the Centre. The first and the last mentioned are admirable representatives of it. I thank God for your disposition to abide by this true—only true, Scriptural basis. It is solid and will remain. Let the School stand firmly there, biding its time, and it will be secure. As long as parties continue to exist, let it treat them with impartial respect, fairness, and kindness, but know as little of them as it can. Let it shift to either extreme, and it might as well never have been planted.

Unquestionably other wishes will be made known to you or to your representatives, directly or indirectly, and not without plausibility. I shall not argue against them, for I hate such work. We have got a solemn duty before us in repressing and destroying if we can this rising ceremonialism; but bitter, angry, disorderly demonstrations to the opposite excess will not help us. It is true, there are some inconveniences always in a moderate and independent course. But there are glorious satisfactions in it. . . .[2]

Huntington's long, careful diagnosis was so judicious and so accurate that, as with his plan for organizing the seminary, it contained a strong element of the prophetic. It prescribed qualifications which have governed the selection of men to fill positions on the faculty of the Episcopal Theological School throughout almost its entire history, and which are no less apt today. The Harvard of President Hill's closing years has been denigrated as a bit of a backwater by men who lived through Charles W. Eliot's turbulent reforming régime; yet even in that long-vanished, semi-pastoral Cambridge, Huntington already discerned the familiar characteristics of intellectualism which the future was to magnify so greatly.

[2] Huntington to Reed, Feb. 14, 1867 (ETS Archives: "F. D. Huntington" folder).

Gathering a Faculty

Wharton and Stone, in their efforts to find professors who would fill such exacting requirements, cast their net wide. Old friends and associates like Heman Dyer, Henry Codman Potter, John Singleton Copley Greene, Edwards A. Park of Andover, and Samuel Batchelder of Cambridge suggested candidates. So did complete strangers who had heard what was afoot.

The first man to be approached was Professor Bancroft of Gambier. Wharton knew something about him from his friends in Ohio. Rand knew something about him because Bancroft had been teaching his son. The trustees wanted a young bachelor who could take students to live with him in one of the School's houses until money could be raised with which to build a proper dormitory, and Bancroft fitted that need.[3] But Bancroft refused repeated invitations to come to Cambridge. Harvard's reputation for insidious heterodoxy frightened him off,[4] and he went to the Philadelphia Divinity School instead. (This may have been as well, for Stone's daughter-in-law, Mrs. Kent Stone, wrote from Gambier that Bancroft's brand of Evangelicalism was so heady a mixture that one of his most eager pupils had recently "left his church altogether, joined the Plymouth Brethren openly, and been immersed.")[5]

Bancroft himself suggested that the trustees call Dr. John Cotton Smith of New York, the son of Gambier's president, saying that he would very probably accept as he "must leave parish work";[6] but at this ominous revelation

[3] Rand to L. W. Bancroft, Feb. 28, 1867 (ETS Archives: "1866-67" folder).
[4] Bancroft to Rand, Feb. 15 and March 9, 1867 (ETS Archives: "1866-67" folder).
[5] W. G. Smith and H. G. Smith, *Fidelis of the Cross: James Kent Stone*, p. 107.
[6] Bancroft to Rand, Feb. 14, 1867 (ETS Archives: "1866-67" folder).

the trustees shied off.[7] A third candidate sent in his own name. This was Dr. Joseph Muenscher, who had left Massachusetts some twenty-five years before to become professor of biblical literature at Gambier. After he had been eight years at Gambier, the subsidy from New York which supported the chair had ceased; and when an offer of a professorship at Jubilee College had had to be withdrawn because no money turned up with which to pay him, Muenscher had returned to parish work for fourteen years, retiring just before 1867 to devote himself entirely to biblical scholarship.[8] Muenscher had supporters in Boston, but the trustees decided that he was too old. They did not think Dr. Alexander H. Vinton too old, but Dr. Vinton did [9] (which was no doubt a relief to Amos A. Lawrence, who had heard from friends in Philadelphia that Vinton had grown "somewhat dry with smoke").[10]

The greatest disappointment in the hunt for a faculty came when Vinton's neighbor in Philadelphia, Phillips Brooks, refused to accept appointment. Brooks, in everyone's opinion, was uniquely fitted to perform the double function, so essential to the School as Reed planned it, of preparing men for the ministry and simultaneously spearheading an evangelistic mission to Harvard. Two years after the great Commemoration Service for the Harvard war dead, Cambridge was still talking about the prayer which Brooks had delivered on that occasion. As Stone wrote to Rand:

His [Brooks's] mind was trained there. It is a powerful mind; &, while he is decidedly Trinitarian and Evangelical, he has not about him those repellent points & forces, which would shock & drive off the Unitarian elements, by which he would

[7] Rand to Bancroft, Feb. 28, 1867 (ETS Archives: "1866-67" folder).

[8] Muenscher to S. Batchelder, Jr., Mar. 27, 1867 (ETS Archives: "1866-67" folder).

[9] Vinton to Rand, Apr. 5, 1867 (ETS Archives: "1866-67" folder).

[10] Lawrence to Rand, Mar. 23, 1867 (ETS Archives: "1866-67" folder).

be surrounded. He understands the New England mind & training; & he would meet that mind, in its present state of training, with an influence, which would draw it in the right direction, instead of driving it away still further from the truth. . . .[11]

The possibility of combining parish work with a professorship was so attractive that Brooks hesitated for several weeks before giving his answer. But the parish was too amorphous, existing at that moment more in fancy than in fact, and he finally decided to stay where he was in Philadelphia.[12] His caution was vindicated when Bishop Eastburn and the standing committee, in giving permission for the establishment of a new church in connection with the School, noticeably did not give permission formally to divide Christ Church parish.[13] Nicholas Hoppin firmly opposed even that.[14] Reed, Wharton, Amory, and Winthrop—who were Brooks's keenest admirers—had to wait for another year before the call from Trinity, Boston, gave them a second chance to emphasize (this time successfully) the opportunities that awaited Brooks at Cambridge.[15]

In the end, therefore, as often happens in the Church, Wharton and Stone—having looked in vain for men to occupy the principal professorships—agreed to assume the responsibilities themselves. To assist them, they obtained the services of Henry Codman Potter, Eastburn's assistant at Trinity; Peter Henry Steenstra, who had succeeded J. S. C. Greene as Rector of Grace Church, Newton; and Alexander Viets Griswold Allen, who was combining a ministry at St. John's, Lawrence, with graduate study at

---

[11] Stone to Rand, Mar. 19, 1867 (ETS Archives: "1866-67" folder).

[12] Brooks to Rand, Mar. 29, 1867 (ETS Archives: "1866-67" folder).

[13] Bishop Eastburn to the trustees, May 11, 1867 (ETS Archives: "1866-67" folder).

[14] Hoppin to Rand, May 14, 1867 (ETS Archives: "1866-67" folder).

[15] R. W. Albright, *Focus on Infinity: A Life of Phillips Brooks*, p. 129, *et seq.*

Andover. As Potter (whose assignment was to deliver some twenty lectures each in "Polity" and "Homiletics") resigned in 1868 to accept the rectorship of Grace Church, New York, the faculty was reduced almost at once to four, with Wharton taking on Potter's subjects. This was to be the entire faculty of the School until the coming of George Zabriskie Gray in 1876. Allen was only twenty-seven and a bachelor, so it was intended from the beginning that he should fill the place of resident professor earlier contemplated for Bancroft. Stone, too, was to live at the School and devote his full time to it. Steenstra and Wharton continued to live in their parishes for a short time, adding the teaching responsibilities to their ordinary pastoral duties, but both found the double task too taxing. Steenstra became a resident professor in 1869; Wharton, in 1871.

Reed would have been happy to have Wharton made permanent dean,[16] and for a time Wharton was willing to fall in with his wishes. But he was selfless enough to recognize, after some thought, that the School would be better served if Stone became its head instead. At seventy-two Stone was still vigorous, and a lifetime in the ministry in Maryland, Connecticut, Pennsylvania, New York, and Massachusetts had given him an opportunity to contract friendships in every part of the Church. As an acknowledged leader among the Evangelicals, he would lend the School prestige in a way that Wharton himself could not hope to do. Furthermore, as the former rector of every one of the men concerned in the establishment of the School, he could command their affection and respect to an unique degree. Wharton therefore accepted appointment as dean of the faculty for only three months, during which time Stone was occupied in delivering the last of his lectures at the Philadelphia Divinity School, selling

---

[16] Allen, MS. Notes (ETS Archives: "Allen's Notes" folder).

his house at Croton Falls, and making arrangements to
move to Cambridge. As soon as these tasks were completed, Wharton resigned in Stone's favor. He also yielded
him the chair of systematic divinity, which Stone wished
to occupy, although it was the chair above all others which
Wharton would have very much liked to keep for himself.[17] In October the faculty met formally for the first
time in Rand's law office, appointed Allen secretary,
stated officially that "in the opinion of this faculty, it is
expedient that the Dean should be presiding officer of the
faculty, and its executive representative, to act for it in all
matters during its recess," [18] appointed Stone, Wharton,
and Steenstra to confer with the trustees in drawing up a
course of study for the School, and committed to Stone
the task of drawing up bylaws for the School. With that,
the formal establishment of the Episcopal Theological
School was complete.

The First Course of Study

The curriculum, as shaped in the ensuing months, was
strongly traditional. It was principally the work of Stone,[19]
to whom Wharton had deliberately ceded the dominating
role once he became dean, himself studiedly retiring to
the background.[20] The foundation of the curriculum was
the course of study prescribed by the bishops in 1804;[21]
and in the early years the textbooks employed, where they
did not come directly from the 1804 list, were almost

---

[17] *Ibid.*

[18] ETS Faculty Record Book, Vol. I, first entry.

[19] Allen, MS. Notes (ETS Archives: "Allen's Notes" folder).

[20] This is clearly reflected in the correspondence. After July, when
Stone became dean, Wharton letters no longer appear in the file, although
they are numerous before that date. Wharton made it clear that this
action was deliberate on his part when, some years later, the appointment of Dean Gray precipitated a discussion between Stone and Wharton
as to the appropriate responsibilities of dean and professors respectively.
See Stone to Rand, Mar. 27, 1876 (ETS Archives: "1875-76" folder).

[21] *A Statement of the Trustees of the Episcopal Theological School,
1873*, p. 19.

always ones which were being used as supplements to it in that period at Virginia and Gambier, if not at General. Among the books cited in the School's first catalogue in 1869, for example, were Pearson on the Creed, Burnet and Browne on the Thirty-nine Articles, Paley's *Evidences*, Leslie's *Short Method*, Butler's *Analogy*, Burnet's *Pastoral Care*, Hooker's *Ecclesiastical Polity*, Bishop White's *Memoirs*, and the *Constitution and Canons*, Wheatly on the Book of Common Prayer, Knapp's *Theology* (standby of Drs. Keith, Sparrow, and Walker), Gesenius's Hebrew Grammar, Tischendorf's New Testament, Robinson's *Harmony*, and Bingham's *Origines Ecclesiasticae*. The chief signs of modernity were the substitution of Guericke, Kurtz, and Neander for Mosheim in church history, and the introduction of works by Ellicott and Westcott in New Testament.

The principal emphasis of the course of study, in keeping with Stone's own predilection, was very strongly biblical rather than historical or theological:

FIRST YEAR.—The studies of this year are mainly Elementary, introducing the class to a knowledge of the Hebrew language; of the Origin, Contents, Antiquities, and Canonicity of the books of the Old and New Testaments; of the principles of Sacred Hermeneutics, and of the Evidences of Christianity.

SECOND YEAR.—The studies of this year are chiefly Exegetical, Doctrinal, and Historical; applying the principles of Hermeneutics to a fuller interpretation of the sense of Scripture, both in the Old Testament and in the New; developing their Doctrinal System; and tracing the History, sacred and secular, of the Divine Dispensations.

THIRD YEAR.—The studies of this year are mostly Constructive, exhibiting the Scriptures—as the Record of Revealed Theology, the "Lively Oracles" of God—in their relation to the *building up* of the live Church of God in its Inner Life and its

Outward Polity, its Ministry and Worship, its Canon Law and Practical Working.[22]

What this meant for a student in terms of actual courses during the three years of his stay may be gathered from the detailed synopsis published for 1873, when the School had achieved an enrollment of eleven students and, after five years of experience, had worked out in stable fashion the details of its plan of instruction:

THE JUNIOR CLASS ATTENDS:

I. THE PROFESSOR OF HEBREW. [Steenstra]—Study of Hebrew language begun, and continued through the three sessions of the term. (Text-books: Van der Hooght's Biblia Hebraica, Conant's Gesenius' Grammar, Robinson's Gesenius' Lexicon.) Introduction to Old Testament begun. Principles of Hermeneutics.

II. THE PROFESSOR OF BIBLICAL INTERPRETATION. [Steenstra]— Critical Readings in the Greek of the New Testament,—the Gospels and the Acts of the Apostles. Lectures on the Peculiarities of the New Testament Greek.

III. THE PROFESSOR OF ECCLESIASTICAL HISTORY. [Allen]—*First Session.*—History of Jewish Church begun. *Second Session.*— History of Jewish Church completed; History of Apostolic Church begun. *Third Session.*—History of Apostolic Church completed. (Text-books and books of reference: Kurtz's Sacred History, Milman's History of Jews, Schaff's History of the Apostolic Church, Neander's Planting and Training of the Christian Church.)

IV. THE PROFESSOR OF HOMILETICS AND PASTORAL CARE. [Wharton]—Evidences of Christianity begun, and continued through the whole term. (Text-books and books of reference: Paley, Butler, McIlvaine, &c.)

---
[22] *Ibid.*

THE MIDDLE CLASS ATTENDS:

I. THE PROFESSOR OF BIBLICAL INTERPRETATION.—Hebrew Studies continued. Introduction to Old Testament continued, giving account of origin of the several books, their collection into the Sacred Canon, and History of the Text. Lectures on the Characteristics of Hebrew Poetry. Exegesis of select portions of Psalms and Prophets, with particular reference to Messianic Prophecy. (Text-books and books of reference as usual.) Through the whole term, Greek of New Testament continued, with Lectures. Introduction to New Testament on same plan with that to the Old Testament. Exegesis of Epistle to Romans, and of some minor Epistles. Lectures on Principles of Textual Criticism, and Sacred Hermeneutics. (Text-books: Tischendorf's Greek New Testament, Robinson's Harmony of New Testament, Winer's New Testament Grammar, Robinson's New Testament Lexicon, Westcott's Introduction to the Gospels, Ellicott's Life of Christ.) Through the whole term.

II. THE PROFESSOR OF SYSTEMATIC DIVINITY. [Stone]—The Exposition of the Creed begun, and continued through the term.

III. THE PROFESSOR OF ECCLESIASTICAL HISTORY.—*First Session.* —History to year 323. Recitations, Lectures, and Essays. History of Doctrine commenced. *Second Session.*—History continued to the great Schism between Eastern and Western Churches. Recitations, Lectures, and History of Doctrine continued. *Third Session.*—Lectures on History of the Middle Ages, with reference to authors, and Essays by students.

IV. THE PROFESSOR OF HOMILETICS AND PASTORAL CARE.—*First Session.*—Liturgics. (Text-books: Wheatly, Blunt, Mant, Blakeney.) *Second Session.*—Apologetics, with reference to Modern Skepticism. Lectures. *Third Session.*—Apologetics continued. (Text-books: Aid to Faith, Birk's Bible and Modern Thought, Barnes's Apologetics.)

THE SENIOR CLASS ATTENDS:

I. THE PROFESSOR OF BIBLICAL INTERPRETATION.—On the Old Testament: the general course of second year continued and completed. On the New Testament: the general course of second year continued and completed.

II. THE PROFESSOR OF SYSTEMATIC DIVINITY.—Exposition of Creed continued and completed. Exposition of Thirty-Nine Articles begun.

III. THE PROFESSOR OF ECCLESIASTICAL HISTORY.—*First Session.* —History of Reformation Period, XIV. and XV. Centuries. Lectures by Professor and Essays by students. History of English Church begun. History of Doctrine continued. *Second Session.*—History of English Church completed. History of Doctrine completed. *Third Session.*—Lectures by Professor and Essays by students. History of American Episcopal Church. Lectures on Course of Modern Thought.

IV. THE PROFESSOR OF HOMILETICS AND PASTORAL CARE.—*First Session.*—Church Polity. (Text-books: Hooker, Litton on the Church, and Episcopacy tested by Scripture.) *Second Session.* —Church Polity and Homiletics. (Text-books: Bridges on Christian Ministry, Burgon on Pastoral Office, Shedd's Homiletics.) *Third Session.*—Pastoral Care. (Same text-books, with Baxter's Reformed Pastor.) [23]

This formal plan of study was, of course, no more exhaustive then than its counterpart would be today; the students had other opportunities for instruction. Those who were both inquisitive and energetic could attend lectures at Harvard (the Free Lectures which Edward Everett Hale had cited in his effort to tempt the Methodists into Cambridge). Those who were badly prepared for the regular work had no choice but to attend preparatory classes under the guidance of a special tutor,[24] just as

---

[23] *Ibid.*
[24] ETS Trustees Minutes, Dec. 14, 1868.

their fellows had had to do at Gambier and Virginia. All, if they wished, could belong to the Reed Brotherhood, a student society whose members sought to improve one another's skill in composition and elocution by weekly exercises and occasional public recitations;[25] and all were expected to attend the weekly "Faculty Meetings"—adapted from those at Andover and Virginia—where senior sermons were preached (and criticized) one week, and where professors and students joined in "prayer and simple religious conversation" the next.[26]

The Body and the Spirit

Thus by 1873 the Episcopal Theological School—with its Board of Trustees, its Board of Visitors, its faculty, its students, and its course of study—had achieved a recognizable and enduring form. Despite the changes wrought in the course of a century, a theological student of today looking back would identify it at once. The curriculum may seem a trifle bare and austere, and decked out with utterly unfamiliar textbooks; but its skeleton is obviously the same as that of its bigger, fatter, more elaborately garbed modern descendant. Like the Trustees Minutes, the Faculty Minutes of the late 1860's and early 1870's already reveal a business agenda differing only in its comparative brevity from the agenda of a century later: approving class schedules, revising the catalogue, tinkering with examination and admission requirements, making exceptions for special students, recommending men for the degree, arranging for special preachers or speakers and making plans for Commencement, or—extremely rarely—giving the dean authority to take disciplinary action in the case of an unusually refractory student.

Even the School's physical setting acquired enduring form with singular rapidity. In 1867-68, when Dean Stone

[25] *ETS Catalogue,* 1870-71.
[26] *Ibid.*

and Professor Allen were holding Sunday services for Harvard students and busily preparing one man for the ministry on weekdays in rented quarters on Coolidge Hill, the site on Brattle Street which was to become the School's permanent home was a rough field stretching from the Hastings house (now "Hodges House") to the Matthews house (2 Phillips Place, now fled down Brattle Street to make room for "Sherrill Hall"). But within just over ten years the School's central quadrangle had come to look much as it does today, and much as it did in the prophetic master plan drawn up by the architects, Ware and Van Brunt, before building started. First came St. John's Memorial Chapel, built by one of the visitors, Lawrence's partner, Robert Means Mason, in 1869. Alumni, aware of their professors' generally *degagé* attitude to religion's cultic aspects after three years of taking part in the School's traditionally "Low and Dry" pattern of daily worship, have sometimes expressed surprise that the Episcopal Theological School, alone among seminaries of the period, should have been given a very large and handsome house of worship before it was given anything else; but the explanation is simple. The trustees had Harvard students and faculty in mind primarily, not theological students. (Nor were their expectations disappointed; for although the School's small group of students and professors rattled about at daily services for years—both looking and feeling a little ridiculous, according to Professor Steenstra[27]—on Sundays the chapel was well filled, much to Nicholas Hoppin's annoyance and somewhat at his expense.)[28] Amos A. Lawrence himself built the dormitory, Lawrence Hall, in 1872. The "Recitation Halls & Library" —Reed Hall—followed in 1874-75; and the Refectory

---

[27] Steenstra to Allen, Sept. 12, 1881 (ETS Archives: "1880-81" folder).

[28] Gardiner M. Day, *The Biography of a Church*, pp. 51-52. Over one fourth of the communicants of Christ Church parish deserted it for St. John's Memorial Chapel, as did "many of the more prosperous parishioners."

and kitchens were added in 1879 by John Appleton Burnham, Mrs. Amos A. Lawrence's cousin (and a Brookline parishioner under both Stone and Wharton). That completed the architects' plan. The next addition to the quadrangle, the John Gordon Wright Library, was not to appear until 1912.

Yet though the Body of the School was thus in a sense recognizably complete early in its history, it was an inert Body still. It had yet to feel the power of the animating Spirit that ultimately springs up within every institution, knitting its loose-strung frame together, giving it life and energy, inspiring it to revealing and effective action, and impressing upon it over the years a peculiar and distinctive character. Such a Spirit does not spring up overnight. Nor can it be forced into the Body by the craft or determination of its fabricators. In a school it wells up gradually, almost imperceptibly, as a result of term after term of faithful corporate performance of a common task: teaching and study.

What the Spirit of the Episcopal Theological School would be, neither the founders, nor the professors, could have foretold with accuracy at the outset. Its basic structure and its course of study seemed to them (and was) conventional. When they spoke of its function, they tended to describe it analogically—as intended to be for New England what Gambier was for the West or Philadelphia for the Central Atlantic area. It was for the moment no more than the impersonal institutional embodiment of a generalization. What it was to be in itself would depend on what the professors became together.

Anglican Features

Even in infancy, however, a body will reveal signs of the nature of the spirit to whose promptings it will give natural and efficient expression in maturity, and it does not seem fanciful to detect in the constitution of the School in its earliest days similar signs that point to the individual character which it would later come to possess. These indicated that it would be profoundly Anglican, giving indigenous expression within an American environment to the spirit and philosophy which had belonged especially to the English Reformers of the sixteenth century. The observation, in the light of the specific references to the Reformation in the School's founding documents, may seem so obvious as to be simpleminded, but it is more complex than appears on the surface.

One distinctively Anglican feature of the School's organization was its conscious debt to the past. Its debt to the living was great; for professors in the other seminaries and laymen throughout the Church—both High Churchmen and Evangelicals—cooperated with signal kindness and goodwill to speed Reed's venture. But as the first part of this history should have demonstrated, the School's debt to the past was very great indeed. Reed and his associates did not have to start from scratch. When they came to draw up a plan of organization and a plan of studies, they were able to draw upon nearly sixty years of experience in the opportunities and pitfalls of theological education obtained at Gambier, Virginia, General, Philadelphia, and —parent of them all—Andover. For that reason they were able to act with a confidence, speed, and decision which would otherwise have been impossible. But the manner in which they contracted that debt was equally significant. They were misled neither by a lust for novelty nor by a fear of it. They treated the time-honored and traditional with respect, but they did not appropriate it uncritically or thoughtlessly. They were haunted by no passion for a premature and superficial consistency. They compromised. They were amiably practical. And they knew there were limits to their wisdom and their power: they knew when to stop, and wait. In just such a fashion had their spiritual ancestors gone about reforming the Church of England three centuries before, pragmatically employing treasures old and treasures new in a way that was learned without being pedantic, and spontaneous without being ignorant. Seen in this light, the institution of a lay Board of Trustees was a typically Anglican paradox. On the surface, what could appear more illogical than to frame the governing body of a theological school in such a way that none of the school's graduates would ever be able to serve on it? This was, however, a *modus vivendi* arrived at after ascertaining what certainly appeared to be the lessons of recent history and then applying them to present circumstances. Behind this expedient, as has been said, was no intricate system of doctrine, no conscious theory. Other boards, differently composed, had worked rather badly; this one might work better. That was its sole purpose. No other conclusion was meant to be drawn from it. Reed and his associates had neither a doctrinaire distrust of ecclesiastics nor a doctrinaire confidence in laymen, as other aspects of their plan for the School demonstrated. If their action appears today to have a deeper import than it did to them, it is precisely because it is so vivid an example of an attitude which has been characteristic of that part of the Christian Church which has looked to Canterbury for guidance—whether in the days of Cranmer and Parker or in the days of Tait, Davidson, and Temple: an attitude of refusal to acknowledge anything overridingly decisive about the claims of an immediate, obvious, rational consistency, either of theory or policy. It is a refusal which both Rome and Geneva found incomprehensible, perverse, and intolerably vexing in the sixteenth century; and those who have been temperamentally sympathetic with their point of view (both without and within the Anglican fold) have been alternately bewildered and exasperated by it ever since. Behind it are presuppositions basic to Anglican theology which Hooker expounded meticulously in his *Laws of Ec-clesiastical Polity,* and which the professors of the Episcopal Theological School, if they remained true to their institutional heritage, would be called upon to work out for their own day.

In addition to a disposition to take history seriously and a shrewd sense of *choses possibles,* the School at its outset also showed a respect for the world of secular learning (and a lack of fear of it) which was equally profoundly Anglican in nature. This was not true of Stone and his Evangelical colleagues, but it was certainly true of Reed, Wharton, and their Boston friends. The decision to place the School in Cambridge close to Harvard was in the very spirit of the Anglican Reformers, for whom—in a far older Cambridge—learning and faith had fused to give life new direction and purpose. In their time the Reformers, too, had encountered the skepticism, the chill rationalism devoid of faith, that always hangs like ground mist in academic halls, and they had been disquieted by it; but they had not run away. And because the world of learning and the world of faith had not been permitted to drift apart, the two great English Universities, Oxford and Cambridge, had continued from the days of Wycliffe to be seed-beds from which had sprung virtually every movement that had periodically revitalized the English Church. In the nineteenth century still, within college parlors and combination rooms, skeptic and believer, historian, scientist, mathematician, philosopher, and theologian argued and reasoned together over the port, as their predecessors had done: propounding theories or jettisoning them, refining doctrines, each bringing the resources of his own special field of learning to bear on the discussion with a deceptive ease of manner, and discovering in the course of it—perhaps for the first time—the nature of the unexamined presuppositions which underlie all conscious thought and serve as lenses through which the eye of the mind looks out upon the world. In the 1860's and seventies something of the same atmosphere existed in the American Cambridge, and Reed carefully put his School right in the middle of it. He felt sure that it would do both Cambridge and the School good. Thereby he decisively rejected the doctrine of separatism, the disposition to subdivide the world of experience into isolated and mutually hostile enclaves, which in one form or another had bedeviled Rome since the Council of Trent, conquered much of non-Anglican Protestantism, and dominated American Christianity throughout the first half of the nineteenth century.

Equally significant as an indication of its future character was the dominant part which laymen had played in the establishment of the School, and the cooperation which they had received from the clergymen whom they had asked to assist them in the task. At the School's Fiftieth Anniversary, Bishop Lawrence was to point out that a precedent for the work of Reed and his associates could be found in the Constitution and House of Deputies of the Protestant Episcopal Church, in which the laity had deliberately been given an equal voice with the presbyters and the bishops. As he said, "No single change can be made in Prayer Book or Creed, even though the bishops and clergy are unanimous upon it, without an affirmative vote of the laymen of the Church." [29] But the precedent could, with equal force, be carried back still further. Such a pattern of collaboration recalls the alliance of ecclesiastical administrators, university dons, civil servants, and thoughtful merchants which brought about the English Reformation—the basic purpose of which had been to liberate the layman (sometimes much against his will) to assume once again the responsibilities of an active, informed, mature Christian. Indeed, in the founding of the

---

[29] *ETS Bulletin,* June, 1917, p. 89.

School there is a curious parallel between the links of friendship, business, and family relationship that drew Appletons, Lawrences, Masons, Winthrops, Amorys, and Reeds together and the ties that three centuries earlier had linked Cecils, Bacons, Walsinghams, Mildmays, Knollyses, Dudleys, and Tudors. Nor is it fanciful to see, in the lifelong association that bound Stone to his Boston friends, a reflection of the bond forged between the Princess Elizabeth, Cecil, and the two court chaplains, Mathew Parker and Richard Cox, in the days of Henry VIII and Edward VI—a bond which subsequently neither years of court intrigue nor the crochets of old age ever quite severed. Allowing for the inevitable differences between Tudor England and Yankee Boston, there is even a startling similarity of tone in the letters written by Stone to his onetime parishioner, Edward S. Rand, president of the Board of Trustees, and those written by the ageing Bishop Cox of Ely to his somewhat temperamental and unpredictable sovereign: the same evidence of real personal affection, the same note of confident judgment stemming from long experience in spiritual matters, and the same slight quaver of temporal insecurity. It is a similarity not without pathos. *Indignatio principis mors est*, wrote Cox at a particularly tense moment in the 1570's; "another Rand [on the board] would be *death!*" [30] echoed Stone's colleague, Professor Steenstra, in not dissimilar circumstances almost precisely three centuries later.

Another echo of the Reformation was, of course, the deliberate selection of "Justification by Faith only" as the one doctrinal foundation stone which future builders of the School would not be at liberty to reject. What this meant had been expounded in the Thirty-nine Articles: "We are accounted righteous before God, only for the merit of our Lord and Saviour Jesus Christ by Faith, and not for our own works or deservings. Wherefore, that we

---

[30] Steenstra to Allen, Jan. 6, 1882 (ETS Archives: "1882" folder).

are justified by Faith only, is a most wholesome Doctrine, and very full of comfort. . . ." Reed and Wharton had made no attempt to identify the doctrine with any particular dogmatic theory. They had explicitly directed that "Scripture alone" was the standard by which it was to be interpreted, and they had not tied the Bible to any mechanical doctrine of inspiration. They were concerned with a principle, not a formula. The principle of Justification by Faith in Christ, as Professor Drown was later to point out, "emphasized the Person of Jesus as the heart and centre of Christian faith and of Christian life." [31] The principle of the supremacy of Scripture, in Drown's words, "emphasized the fact that the Bible is the supreme source for our knowledge and understanding of Christ, and that it therefore demands thorough and critical study, unhampered by theories put upon it from outside." [32] Although the reformers of the sixteenth century were by no means agreed on the meaning or appropriateness of the words *sola fide,* they were at one in their devotion to Christ and in their keen interest in the Bible as the source of their knowledge of him: Colet, Erasmus, Luther, Ximenes, Loyola, Pole, Calvin, Zwingli, d'Étaples, and the men and women of Reformation England. A similar devotion was, as Professor Allen testified, at the heart of Reed's religion;[33] and the letters of his associates show that this was true of them as well. As with the Anglican Reformers, this broadened rather than narrowed their sympathies. "Though a pretty rigid Episcopalian, I have no prejudice against any body of men who love the Lord Jesus Christ . . . . The older we grow, the more we value simple piety, wherever we find it, and the less importance we attach to sects," wrote Amos A. Lawrence in 1856.[34] This sympathy extended beyond the borders of Protestantism,

---

[31] J. A. Muller, *The Episcopal Theological School 1867-1943,* p. 25.
[32] *Ibid.*
[33] Allen, MS. Notes (ETS Archives: "Allen's Notes" folder).
[34] Lawrence, *Life of Amos A. Lawrence,* pp. 120-121.

and—often a still more acid test—did not exclude Episcopalians whose point of view was not at all like that of
Lawrence himself. In the 1840's a note in his diary relative to the conduct of the affairs of the Cocheco Company,
which he and Mason owned, recorded: "Went to see the
Bishop this week about sending a Roman Catholic clergyman down to Salmon Falls to look after the spiritual interests of the girls [in the mill], of whom one third are
Irish." [35] Three years after the establishment of the School,
Lawrence wrote to an Evangelical organization asking to
have his name removed from its membership list because
of its extreme manifestation of partisanship:

The Church consists of all those who love the Lord Jesus
Christ and obey his precepts. And of all the denominations
into which, through human weakness and ignorance, it has
become divided, I believe the Protestant Episcopal Church is
the best. On that account I joined it nearly forty years ago,
and my love for it has increased since. But this does not prevent my loving Christians of other denominations and acting
with them; and especially it does not prevent my living and
acting with those of my own denomination who entertain
opinions in which there are "shades of difference." No doubt
this movement to make all men of one mind will gain ad-
herents, and churchmen may become so hostile to each other
as to divide the Church many times; but all this will not make
men agree, nor will it advance the cause of truth nor the
cause of religion.[36]

There was in this the same irenic note struck by Huntington in his analysis of the qualities that ought to be required in men chosen for professorships in the School, but
there was also a hint of a more positive attitude towards
the differences that divide Episcopalians than had been
implied in Huntington's uniform disapproval of all
Church parties. That Lawrence was not unique in this

[35] *Ibid.*, p. 53.
[36] *Ibid.*, pp. 236-237.

attitude is shown by the list of donors to the School's sub-scription fund, which included, besides the expected names, those of Martin Brimmer, Nathan Matthews, George C. Shattuck, Richard H. Dana, and "the Church of the Advent."

American Dress

Yet notwithstanding its Anglican, and even English, char-acteristics, the School was not to be an exotic. The found-ers of the School did not suffer from the chauvinism that had occasionally afflicted their fathers' generation, and was to become an increasingly serious weakness in the gen-erations that were to follow. They felt "at home" in Eng-land, and moved with unselfconscious ease, like visiting cousins, in English society. But they had no thought of setting up in Cambridge a school modeled on an English pattern, even though the architects were popularly sup-posed to have carefully designed an "English" setting for it. There was no desire to copy the atmosphere of Cuddes-don—half college, half monastery—or to create a minia-ture reproduction of the pattern of life which obtained in Oxford or Cambridge colleges. From the start, the cor-porate life of the School was distinctively American—at first by accident, but then by design. By force of circum-stances it began in a house, where Professor Allen and the students lived and ate and studied together—with visita-tions periodically from Stone, Wharton, and Steenstra. This was a duplication of the "School of the Prophets" which had been the staple of theological education in America since the eighteenth century, and its atmosphere was strong enough to survive the move to Brattle Street and then into Lawrence Hall. As Edward L. Stoddard of the Class of 1871 recalled:

The Episcopal School was housed in a large square wooden building on Brattle Street a few hundred feet north of the beautiful memorial chapel, which was then standing. There were not more than ten or twelve students and I think that all were accommodated in that building and that each had a room to himself. We took our meals in the same house, sat around the same table, and formed a genial and affectionate fraternity. Not being satisfied with the food, we organized during part of the year a society to run the kitchen & dining room. Two students took charge for one month and then passed on the gracious task to another couple. Each pair endeavored to surprise the others by improving the quality & cheapening the cost of the food; and I remember distinctly that during some months this was effected: the cost per student falling from the original price of $4 to $3.75 & even $3.50 a week. . . . With the exception of Prof. Allen, none of our instructors ever came to our student dormitory or mingled with us outside the class rooms. We had no forum exercises, no debates, no general discussion churchly or secular, nothing but the routine of daily recitations varied by lectures in the case of Prof. Allen. . . .[37]

Professor Allen himself, speaking to the alumni in 1907, said of those days, "We were a small family. The school existed in poverty and obscurity and amid much opposition, but no family was ever happier than we were in those earlier years, the first five years when the School dwelt in tabernacles—or, to change the phrase, in its own hired house. We had family prayers according to the prayer book. The order for family prayers was said instead of the regular morning and evening prayer. It helped to cultivate the family feeling in the school. . . ." [38] It was reluctance to hazard losing this old-fashioned informality and simplicity that kept the School from moving its daily service out of Professor Allen's boarding establishment to the Chapel until 1872, three years after the Chapel had been

[37] E. L. Stoddard, "Memoir," written at the request of Bishop William Lawrence in 1927 (ETS Archives: "Notes by W. Lawrence, E. L. Stoddard, C. J. Palmer" folder).
[38] "Fortieth Anniversary Alumni Banquet, June 4, 1907," pp. 36-37.

consecrated. The full service of morning and evening
prayer did not entirely replace an elaborated form of
family prayer until 1894, after Dean Hodges had come to
the School. The same familial pattern of life and worship
had obtained at Gambier, Virginia, and General (although
it began to change after the death of Professor Turner);
but at the Episcopal Theological School the atmosphere
of the "School of the Prophets" demonstrated unusual
staying power. Despite the concentration on academic excellence in classroom (and faculty meeting), the School
was for many years more like a domestic household than
anything else. From this stemmed the informality, the
sense of intimacy between dean, professors, and students
reflected so vividly in the recollections of alumni, and also
what was perhaps the inevitable corollary of such qualities,
a deeply ingrained distrust of "ceremony." Airs and
graces seem more often pretentious than appropriate in a
household where means are modest, quarters close, and
everyone has a chore to perform. From the first, the
Deanery and the faculty homes were almost as freely open
to the students as Lawrence Hall itself, with the professors and the students dropping in on one another frequently. In Dean Gray's time the Deanery, with its wealth
of nooks and crannies, was the favored setting for vigorous
games of hide-and-seek, with the dean himself—tall,
heavy, red-faced—playing along with the rest, and thun-
dering down the stairs at the game's climax to get "home"
safe before he was caught. Fifty years later there was a different dean, Dean Washburn, but the atmosphere was
just as informal, and just as uproarious. One of the famous
sights was Dean Washburn, "by an astonishing combination of suppleness of limb and ramrod erectness of body,
giving an imitation, behind the sofa, of a man going down
the cellar stairs and coming up again with a jug of cider." [39]
Professor Steenstra, throughout his forty years of teaching,

---

[39] Muller, *Episcopal Theological School,* p. 168.

never failed to express disapproval of every attempt to introduce the slightest morsel of academic or ecclesiastical pomp. At a Matriculation Service in 1895 or 1896 Dean Hodges wore an academic hood for the first time, and when asked why, replied, "Because it was given to me." In a lecture the following day, Steenstra, without the slightest variation in tone or emphasis, dictated the following: "The combination of the late priestly history with the earlier composite prehistoric histories resulted in the first six books of the Old Testament. The next thing we'll see will be the Dean wearing cap and bells if someone gives them to him." [40] Grudgingly donning a surplice at Commencement, Steenstra would then comfortably crown this ceremonial attire with a straw hat to keep off the sun, just as every winter he would firmly wear galoshes at all chapel services to keep out the damp. These idiosyncracies were entirely harmonious with the fundamental character of the School. If there was about them something of the same quality of "plain living and high thinking" that also characterized Virginia in the days before Angus Crawford introduced more stylish ways, there was also something unique: an angularity, a certain snap and bounce as peculiarly indigenous as New England granite.

Such, then, were the identifying characteristics of the Episcopal Theological School. It was a body with English traits, Anglican in its nature, its lineaments revealing many traces of Reformation influence—but a body clothed unmistakably in genuine American homespun. Homespun suits of that day were usually plain, serviceable, a trifle old-fashioned in cut, and a bit scratchy where they touched the skin. But they wore like iron. Within a Body so clad, the Spirit would grow.

---

[40] *Ibid.*, p. 126.

THE INDWELLING SPIRIT

✠ 10

"Where the Spirit of the Lord Is"

The Symbolism of Reed Hall

The architectural integument of an educational institution is not always a helpful guide to the nature of that institution's essential spirit. As the years pass and buildings multiply, a Babel of different styles eventually results —all shouting at once—in which what was once a clear individual voice may at length be lost. At the Episcopal Theological School, however, it appears that the architectural setting was an enigmatic guide even from the first. The Chapel, it is true, was a thoroughly straightforward piece of work, and dominated the entire site. But after the Chapel, the most conspicuous building was Reed Hall; and that pile, although connected by a "cloister" to Lawrence Hall on one side and to Burnham Hall on the other, has never seemed to have any clear relation architecturally to the other buildings. Within a year of its completion it was described in the *Catalogue* of 1876-77, in a phrase delightfully redolent of Yankee caution, as "somewhat unique," a dry confession of mystification which has stuck to it ever since. Professors and students in more recent years have been less restrained: one calling the building "a paralyzed centipede," another saying that it looked like "a friendly pterodactyl." And uniformly deprecated in this manner, Reed Hall has for almost a century crouched resignedly on spindly arches at the other end of the School from Brattle Street in the mood of gentle depression so often inspired by helplessly awkward bulk.

Yet despite its ungainly shape, there have been occasions—particularly in springtime—when Reed Hall, in a departure from its everyday mood, has imparted to the School backwater behind it an air of subtly foreign grace. Perhaps this is less detectable now that automobiles, intruding into every vestige of open space, have given so much of Cambridge the appearance of an elderly lady whose dress sense has been lamentably disoriented by an uncontrollable passion for the most raucous pieces of costume jewelry; but in the 1940's, when the last of the Gray or Washburn poplars had not yet had to be replaced by Taylor gingkoes, the grace was still evident. Sitting on the steps of Winthrop Hall on a clear afternoon in the May Reading Period, and surveying the scene before him, a student would find that with the sunlight shimmering in the poplar tops and outlining the steeply-pitched roof and stepped gables of Reed Hall against a pale sky, it took no effort of the mind to imagine St. John's Road a slow-flowing canal, and himself transported to some small, quiet town in the Low Countries which might have served as the background for a painting by Brueghel or Teniers. The scenic effect was as quaintly charming as it was unexpected.

Few of those who remarked upon this transformation gave it more than a passing thought. At most, they explained it as a chance effect created by an architectural caprice typical of mid-Victorian eclecticism. But they were mistaken. There was nothing capricious about the choice of stepped gables or other "Dutch" ornamental details for

Reed Hall. On the contrary, a scrutiny of the architects' drawing of the quadrangle originally projected for the School suggests that these details are, rightly interpreted, the vestigial syllables of what was intended to be an explicit architectural expression, along with the Chapel, of the School's guiding spirit as the architects understood it. They were meant to "say something." Only, as with other ancient inscriptions, rather unsatisfactory execution in the first place, combined with years of exposure to the weather, have made the "lettering" too faint to be readily deciphered.

Henry Van Brunt and William R. Ware were the School's first architects. They designed and built the Chapel, Lawrence Hall, Reed Hall, Burnham Hall, and the Old Deanery. Their ingenuity and engineering skill were considerable. In designing a wing for the Harvard Library (Gore Hall) in 1877, for example, they are credited with having originated, in association with Justin Winsor, the stack principle of library construction which has since been copied by all libraries of large size the world over.[1] So far as the School is concerned, however, what is especially interesting about Ware and Van Brunt is that they seem to have been exuberantly inventive symbolists in their approach to architecture, employing symbolism not only in their choice of surface ornament, but in the ground plan and general external appearance of their buildings as well. There was in this much more than simply the deliberate resort to an antique style—such as Gothick—in the manner of Holland or Nash, Scott or Upjohn. Ware and Van Brunt apparently liked to hint at a deeper meaning underlying whatever obvious function the building which they were designing was intended to perform. They did this by making the building —at least on the outside—look as if its function was quite

---

[1] Samuel Eliot Morison, ed., *The Development of Harvard University . . . 1869-1929*, p. 610.

different. The "machine-for-living" concept of design, it is safe to assume, would have struck them as tediously dull and spiritless; and they would probably have dismissed the skyscraping products of our modern, almost self-righteously graceless functionalism as not only unimaginative, but superficial. Their buildings were never bald "statements." They were "interpretations": *metaphors* in stone.

The two architects won their reputation (and probably the commission to design the Episcopal Theological School as well)[2] by designing the Memorial Hall at Harvard; and this familiar Cambridge landmark vividly illustrates their approach. In its final form, the Memorial Hall was to contain a large "commons" where the undergraduates could eat, and an amphitheater suitable for large lectures or concerts or academic ceremonies. At the same time, it was to enshrine the memory of the College's Civil War dead in an atmosphere suitably dolorous and majestic. Most architects might have considered a collegiate or classical style suitable for such a building, whose function was clearly secular; but not Ware and Van Brunt. They saw in these functions deeper implications. In the Yard the College Library was at that time housed in a building modeled on the chapel of King's College, Cambridge, England, the stalls of the worshippers being replaced in the Harvard adaptation by alcoves for readers. Perhaps this provided the two architects with their initial inspiration. For when Memorial Hall finally stood complete in 1878, after having been eight years a-building, what Cambridge residents saw was not primarily an auditorium or a hall at all, but instead a vast, cruciform structure surmounted by an enormous clock tower. It was unmistakably a cathedral: a cathedral consecrated to learning. And

---

[2] Amos A. Lawrence was as actively involved in the building of the Memorial Hall as he was in the formation of the Episcopal Theological School. Lawrence, *Amos A. Lawrence,* pp. 230-233.

to make clear precisely how communion with the Eternal Verity was to be achieved in the Newest Dispensation, the lecturer's platform was placed just where the high altar would have stood in the parent edifices of the past.

Sometime between 1869 and 1873—the same years in which they were carrying forward the construction of Memorial Hall—Ware and Van Brunt were asked to draw up plans for the Episcopal Theological School; and in complying, they once again indulged their taste for architectural metaphor. The School was to be a theological establishment devoted to corporate study and worship. Its function was obviously religious. Other architects, taking this into account, would have designed (and elsewhere usually did design) something in the collegiate or monastic style. Ware and Van Brunt, however, did nothing so obvious. The School was intended, in addition to its other function, to be the parish for Harvard Episcopalians. Its constitution, furthermore, had been drawn up by men who believed deeply in the value of freedom (for professors and students as well as for everyone else), and who believed as well in the basically religious character of the secular world. Reed, Wharton, Lawrence, and their associates spoke of this in their letters to one another, and must have said much more in the course of conversation. By 1869, furthermore, something of this character had already begun to appear in the development of the course of study and in the teaching of the professors themselves. It was these features which Ware and Van Brunt seized upon to symbolize in the architectural setting which they designed for the School. For a chapel they created what was clearly a parish church, with seats arranged in rows facing the chancel rather than ranging longitudinally along the sides of the building in collegiate fashion. The style was generally identified as English Gothick; but it could equally well have been Flemish or German in inspiration, for a church exterior very like that of the Chapel appears in the background of Brueghel's famous painting of "The Blind Beggars." The rest of the School the two architects laid out as a miniature mediaeval town. It had one street of houses (Lawrence Hall), a guild hall (Burnham), and—in a position of appropriate prominence—what in the original sketch is indisputably an *hôtel de ville*. Like its mediaeval models in Flanders or northern France, this *hôtel de ville* had an open arcade on one side of the ground floor (an eminently suitable marketplace for St. John's Society auctions of the future!), meeting-rooms for the citizens on the floor above, and was surmounted by a tall, thin pinnacle of a belfry. The belfry was a telltale device the meaning of which any nineteenth-century architect knew how to construe. It stood for freedom. It was the symbol of municipal liberties: personal liberty for the serf who found refuge within the town's bracing wall, and liberty for the community, which could manage its own affairs secure against interference or control by neighboring feudal princes outside—be they dukes or barons or prince-bishops. Did Ware and Van Brunt intend by their appropriation of this symbol to stress the fact that the Episcopal Theological School was an imperial "free city" in the feudal heartland of Unitarianism or a commune free of all save token allegiance to the prince-Bishop of Massachusetts and the lords spiritual and temporal of the diocesan convention? Or did they mean simply to emphasize the reality of a freedom at once more general and more profound? The records do not tell. But the *hôtel de ville* motive, significantly, was never discarded. It was realized in Reed Hall. The difficulty, unfortunately, was that in the process of realization, the original conception was so changed that its meaning was almost obliterated. The reason, as usual with theological schools, was lack of money. In an effort to trim costs, the ambitious scale of the building was reduced. The roof was lowered and its lines simplified. The window openings were made smaller. In place of the gradual ascent of a series of peaked cubes culminating in the belfry, the central core of the building was changed so that it rose sharply in a triangular sweep to stepped gables on four sides. The all-important belfry itself—the key to the design—shrank and dwindled to a spindly cupola that looked disconcertingly like an overgrown narwhal's tusk. What had begun as a symbol ended as mere architectural conceit. In 1938 the hurricane knocked the cupola askew; and Dean Washburn (who had always thought it a slightly ridiculous oddity) was delighted to hear that the contractor would charge more for straightening it up again than for taking it down altogether.[3] It was removed. After that Reed Hall seemed squatter than ever; and all that was left to hint at the meaning of Ware and Van Brunt's essay in architectural metaphor were the stepped gables and the arcade (now impenetrably disguised as "The Cloister"). It was not enough.

Nonetheless, despite the mute unintelligibility to which storm and poverty have reduced a major portion of their design, the two architects deserve credit for keen perception in their choice of symbols at the School's beginning. The high steeple crowned with the Cross of Christ—in its shadow the belfry symbolizing Freedom—and beneath them a group of buildings which were styled to evoke, not the world of cloistered peace or aristocratic privilege, but the world of trade, craftsmen, crowded streets, the world of ordinary men: what could have been more apt? The spirit which Ware and Van Brunt sought to capture in stone, Professor Allen expressed in words not long before his death, when he attempted to assess the significance of the School's development over the years:

. . . And as to the work that has been done—the School has remained true to the principles of the founder which inspired

---

[3] *ETS Bulletin*, Dec., 1938, pp. 1-2.

him to his generous deed. In so doing and while it has been waiting, the world of religious thought and inquiry, after many vicissitudes appears to be returning once more to the evangelical principle that the personal Christ is Christianity. The relationship of the individual soul to the personal Christ in faith and love and obedience is the ground of salvation and of hope for mankind. This is the inspiration alike for the study of the Bible, or history, or of theology.

In this conviction the School has found the largest scope for freedom of inquiry in every department related to theological study. Very early in its history was it seen and acknowledged that any attempt to restrict freedom would be futile. The effort would have been vain, even had it been contemplated, to mould its students after any one ecclesiastical pattern. The School was to be as comprehensive as the Church itself. All that has been asked for on the one hand has been freedom of research and freedom of utterance, conceding on the other freedom to criticize, to accept or reject. To educate the student for this large freedom has been the predominant aim. For the rest, *Tros, Tyriusque mihi nullo discrimine agetur.*[4]

Freedom to Change

The freedom which Professor Allen and his colleagues prized so highly was manifested from the first in one significant and sensitive area: the curriculum. Alumni who have returned at various times to the School over the years, and been startled to discover that the texts which served them in their student days have disappeared entirely from the reading lists—Oesterley and Robinson or Driver nudged into obscurity by Pfeiffer, for example, and Pfeiffer in turn consigned to oblivion by Noth or Bright—would discover as well, if they consulted the old catalogues, that such changes have been characteristic of the School from the very beginning. In 1895 the faculty stated in its annual report: "Every endeavor of the schol-

---

[4] ETS Archives: "Allen's Notes" folder.

ars, every labor of the critics, every utterance of the men by whom the Holy Spirit speaks today, every new book, every most recent question, we must bring into the class-rooms of the School." [5]

This was not a new idea. The professors had been doing just that since 1868.

In its ability, if not in its desire, constantly to revise the courses and the assigned reading, the School was for some time unique among the seminaries of the Episcopal Church. Men like Turner, Wilson, Mahan, Sparrow or Grammer were not less up-to-date in their reading than Steenstra, Allen, and Wharton; but the bylaws governing their seminaries made it almost impossible for them to express changing contemporary interests or points of view by introducing new material in the classroom. Dr. Sparrow actually *reduced* the references to modern, secular litera-ture in his questions on apologetics when he went from Gambier to Alexandria.[6] At General and Virginia the rules explicitly directed the professors to use in their in-struction "such works only as are included in the course of study which has been, or may be recommended by the House of Bishops" [7] unless they had gained prior approval from their colleagues and also (although this was not al-ways categorically stated) from the trustees. The profes-sors at General dared to bring in Browne to supplement Burnet on the Thirty-nine Articles only in the most gin-gerly fashion;[8] and it will be remembered that Professor Walker of Virginia was sharply reproved in the late 1870's for introducing books "not in the syllabus" without ob-taining permission from the trustees.[9] From the first, how-ever, the constitution of the Episcopal Theological School imposed no such restriction. The trustees were charged

[5] *ETS Catalogue*, 1895-96.
[6] Walker, *Sparrow*, p. 392.
[7] *Virginia Seminary*, II, p. 598.
[8] *Proceedings*, III, pp. 21, 78, 174.
[9] *Virginia Seminary*, I, p. 252.

with general responsibility for the instruction (as they were, indeed, for everything else); but from the beginning they delegated all decisions in this department to the faculty. This gave the professors a freedom which they used generously.[10]

As a result, the School *Catalogues* from 1869 to 1900 (when the editors ceased to include book lists in the Course Calendar) are illuminating guides to the reading which the professors found to be so valuable that they commended it in turn to their classes. It was by no means one-sided reading; for although some of the books amplified the professors' opinions, others were authoritative statements of very different points of view. Most of the new books were of English or German origin, with a sprinkling of French, Danish, Dutch, and American. The Continental influence was so marked, indeed, that in another echo of the English Reformation, the School might legitimately be said to have performed in these years something of the function of the White Horse tavern in the English Cambridge of three centuries before, serving as a

---

[10] An unsuccessful attempt to curtail this freedom by introducing what might be called the "general consensus" principle was made in 1873, when Nathan Matthews tried—in Dr. Allen's words—to "buy up the School."

Matthews was an active and generous Boston Churchman, a worshipper at the Church of the Advent, who had grown rich by adroit speculation in real estate. He had built a new dormitory for Harvard, established scholarships, and had been among the first contributors to the School's building fund at its beginning. It was natural, therefore, that when the trustees were anxious to purchase land adjacent to the Brattle Street site in 1872-73, they should write to Matthews, among others, asking for money. Matthews, in reply to their appeal, offered to give the School $100,000 if steps were taken to assure that the School's "Trustees and Faculty . . . fully represent the great body of Churchmen." This would have doubled the School's endowment.

The trustees were at first disposed to accept Matthews' offer. Amos A. Lawrence offered to resign in favour of some trustee of more conservative hue whom Matthews presumably would nominate. Further communication revealed, however, that Matthews had in mind even more extensive changes. He wished a Board consisting of "two Low Churchmen and three High Churchmen, two of whom should be conservative." This convinced the trustees that Matthews wished to change the School's basic character, and they consequently declined to accept his gift.

little "Germany" from which the teaching of Continental theologians and biblical scholars radiated out to the Church at large. Andover had performed a similar function under Leonard Woods and Moses Stuart fifty years before.

The first names to disappear from the School reading lists were those of the seventeenth- and eighteenth-century English divines, with the exception of Hooker, Butler, Pearson, and (in pastoralia) Baxter and Burnet. Knapp's *Theology* (which was to continue to be a basic text at Virginia for another twenty years) was discarded after the first year. In their places appeared more recent authors: Van Oosterzee, Stuerm, Baumstark, Christlieb, Neander, Ullmann, Hagenbach, Kurtz, Tulloch, McIlvaine, Onderdonk, Litton, McIlhenny, and Milman. In 1878-79 Dorner's *Person of Christ* was listed for the first time, along with Maurice's *Religions of the World,* Bryce's *Holy Roman Empire,* Ranke's *German Reformation,* Greenwood's *Cathedra Petri,* Hampden on *Scholasticism,* and other works by Delitzsch, Martensen, Nitzsch, Reichel, Guizot, and J. B. Mozley. In 1884-85 Matheson's *Introduction to German Theology* was assigned, as well as Julius Müller's magisterial two volumes on *Sin,* Perowne's treatise on *Immortality,* and Hoefling on *Baptism.* The *Catalogue* for 1889-90 listed for the first time Dean Stanley's *History of the Jewish Church,* Rothe's *Theologische Ethik,* Harnack's *Dogmengeschichte,* Baur's *Versoehnungslehre,* Seebohm's *Oxford Reformers,* the Renaissance histories of Burckhardt and Symonds, lives of Luther from the differing points of view of Koestlin, Kuhn, and Michelet, Ranke's *History of the Popes,* Creighton's work on the popes of the Renaissance, Hodgkin's *Invaders of Italy* and Lea's *Studies in Church History.*[11] In 1890-91 the New

---

[11] In the supplementary list of books appended by the bishops in 1889 to the Course of Study of 1804, the names of Christlieb, Ullmann, Hagenbach, McIlvaine, Milman, Dorner, Bryce, Delitzch, Martensen, Mozley, and Ranke appear.

Testament department directed the juniors to use Professor Thayer's *Dictionary,* the New Testament introductions by Salmon and by Bernhard Weiss, Weiss's *Biblical Theology of the New Testament,* lives of Christ from the different points of view of Edersheim and Keim, resorting where necessary to Meyer's or Godet's commentaries, and to Alford's commentary on Romans. At the same time, in systematic divinity the juniors were to become acquainted with Caird's *Philosophy of Religion,* Harris's *Philosophical Basis of Theism,* Martineau's *Study of Religion,* Browne's *Metaphysics and Psychology,* Pfleiderer's *Philosophy of Religion,* Lotze's *Microcosmus* and *Philosophy of Religion,* Butler's *Analogy* (the one holdover from the texts of the past), and Green's *Prolegomena to Ethics.* The middlers that same year were reading Dorner, Martensen, Matheson, Mulford, Wilberforce, Pearson on the *Creed* (once again a faint echo of the past), and Browne on the Thirty-nine Articles (another echo). The seniors, in addition to continuing with Dorner and Martensen, were reading Maurice on *Sacrifice* and *The Kingdom of Christ,* Ritschl, Baur, Hooker, and Charles Gore's *Christian Ministry* (which had been first published in England two years before). Only a few months after its publication, Illingworth's *Personality, Human and Divine* appeared in the *Catalogue* for 1894-95; and Herrmann's *Communion of the Christian with God* was introduced into the curriculum in 1897-98. Over the years in this fashion the students' reading was guided by a list which was both authoritative and up-to-date. There was nothing faddish about it, however; some of the history books and theological treatises were still on reading lists for courses at the School in the 1940's.

Improving the Curriculum

At the same time that the professors were revising their reading lists, they were seeking ways of improving the

instructional framework itself. From the School's very beginning they appear to have tinkered almost constantly
with the machinery of examination schedules, degree requirements, and the organization of the various courses.
Not that they had illusions about what they could accomplish. They were as conscious as their colleagues at General and Virginia of the fact that with only three years
available for study, a seminary course could be neither exhaustive nor comprehensive. Echoing the words of Samuel Turner years before (and anticipating the words of
their successors in 1963), the professors reported in 1886:

The period which the Church allows for preparation for
Orders may be all that can be required as a rule, yet it is a
very brief period for what the clergy need, and for what many
students desire. All that can be done in any preparation is to
teach men how to study, to start them on their way. In three
years they evidently cannot cover much ground. Another year
immediately following would be worth much, far more than
several after an interval.[12]

George Seymour had said much the same at General in
1874.[13]

In what time was available, however, the faculty did
what it could to tailor the curriculum both to the interests and talents of each generation of students and to
what the professors interpreted as the special needs of the
time. One way in which they did this was by expanding
the curriculum—offering additional elective courses (usually, in the early years, on some aspect of religion and
"modern thought"), inviting to the School a specially
qualified lecturer from outside (like John McCrady, Professor of Zoology at Harvard, who lectured on the relations of science and religion in 1876), or (after 1890) by
encouraging properly qualified students to undertake in-

---

[12] *ETS Catalogue*, 1886-87.
[13] *Proceedings*, IV, p. 737.

dependent study under the guidance of one of the professors. Another way was by varying the methods of teaching, replacing the old-fashioned classroom recitation which had dominated colleges as well as schools in the 1860's with a more elastic system of lectures, examinations, papers, and seminars as time went on. By 1889 they had evolved a pattern of instruction recognizably similar in spirit and general outline to the one familiar to students today, as is revealed in the Faculty Report of that year:

In our methods of study we do not yield but rather insist upon large liberty of thought, wide as well as thorough reading, and the frank expression of opinion. Text-books are used as far as their use seems wise. But the instructor's work is not the hearing of lessons so much as the inspiring and guiding the students to thought and research. The men are thus led to realize that the real work of the School must be their own work, and not the instructor's work for them. The lecture of the instructor leads naturally to the essay or thesis of the students; and these both lead to the "seminar" where the instructor and his class discuss as fellow-students the subject of the evening.

In these and other ways, the instructors and students are brought naturally into close and intimate relations. While each recognizes the position of the other, a spirit of comradeship exists between them; professors and students meet upon the play-ground as well as in the class-room; the professors are as much at home in the students' rooms as are the students in the professors' houses. Thus lifelong friendships are formed and spiritual bonds created which strengthen as years go by.[14]

---

[14] *ETS Catalogue,* 1889-90. Since 1890, the only major change in the system has been the addition of the senior tutorial, which was instituted in 1928. It is debatable whether that addition—along with more recent ones such as junior preceptorials and junior orientation—can be fairly considered to constitute an improvement in the quality of the teaching when contrasted with the teaching carried on in the years before World War I. In Professor Muller's opinion, the significance of devices like the tutorial was that they enabled a much larger School to regain the educational advantages which it had possessed earlier, when it was small.

A third way was by radically revising the entire course of study. And a study of Faculty Reports reveals that in the course of just under a century, the School has unveiled a "New Curriculum" roughly once every twenty years. Typical in its revelation of the mixture of motives and the correlation of experience winnowed from other seminaries and graduate schools that have figured in every revision was a paragraph in the Faculty Report for 1890 announcing the advent of what might be called "New Curriculum I":

We propose to make a change next year in the order and arrangement of the studies. Hitherto we, with other schools of our Church, have distributed the several studies quite evenly over the three years. The chief advantage of this method has been that it has enabled the student to keep in touch with all the studies from the beginning to the end of his course. But on the other hand, the overwhelming disadvantage has been that he has not been able at any one time to throw his interest decidedly into any one, two or three lines of work; his time, interest and thoughts were liable to be scattered, and to cause his work to lack distinctness and effectiveness. To do thorough work in six or seven studies at the same time is beyond the ability of most men. Following to some degree the line adopted in many divinity schools, we shall so arrange the work that while three or four studies may be engaging the student's attention at one time, the emphasis will be laid on only one or two lines. Speaking roughly, the main stress will be laid on the Scriptures, Greek and Hebrew, in the Junior year, on History in the Middle year, and Systematic Theology and Practical Theology in the Senior year; though it will be understood that these studies over-lap and touch each other.[15]

Although time may have blurred the memory of it, the bishops' Course of Study of 1804 had recommended such

---

[15] *ETS Catalogue*, 1890-91

a progression from Bible to history to theology; and it will be remembered that some of the professors at General had suggested revising their curriculum in somewhat the same direction in 1856-57. The tendency to reintroduce curriculum devices which had been used, discarded, and forgotten in an earlier day was, indeed, characteristic of the periodic reforms of the curriculum. The reformers rarely delved into the past to discover what their predecessors had done. As a result, they often repeated history without realizing that they were doing so. Discovering this, in doing research for his history of the School in 1942-43, Professor Muller (who had himself been a keen reformer of the curriculum in the 1920's and 1930's) observed with wry amusement, "Verily, there is nothing new under the academic sun." [16]

One need not even go outside the School itself for vivid examples of the ups and downs of fortune suffered by instructional devices. In 1879 Dean Gray and his colleagues voted to stiffen the School's requirements by henceforth awarding a certificate of proficiency to men who had successfully passed all their course examinations, reserving the degree for men who had taken, in addition, a general examination covering the entire three-year course and submitted two senior theses. Some years later the certificate and the general examination both dropped out of sight. But not forever. The certificate was resurrected in 1931, lapsed into comparative desuetude again in the 1940's, and was brought out and dusted off afresh in the 1950's. The general examination (its roots in the School's own past apparently forgotten) returned by way of Harvard in 1928 in four-fold form (with an oral): church history, Bible, theology, and practical theology. But its practical theology component withered away (or was swallowed up by the other three) almost at once, only to be restored

---

[16] Muller, *Episcopal Theological School,* p. 184.

(as usual, as an "innovation") in 1963. The senior thesis requirement was simplified in 1884, only one thesis being required after that year; that practice, in turn, was abolished in 1924, when the thesis was discarded for all save honors candidates; and in 1941 the thesis was made optional even for them. For twenty years after 1941 the thesis faded gradually into virtual extinction. Then in 1963 it was made mandatory for degree candidates all over again.

These changes were not wrought out in a vacuum to conform to an *a priori* assumption. If there was an *a priori*, it was the student body; and nowhere was the professors' constant preoccupation with the students and their idiosyncracies more clearly reflected than in the fluctuations of electives. The search for a mean whereby the students would be free to study what they wanted while learning what they must had few intermissions. In Dean Gray's and Dean Hodges' time men could petition to be released from required courses in order to take special courses at Harvard; and to encourage them it was customary for many years for the faculty to place a list of recommended Harvard courses on the School bulletin board at the beginning of each term. Of the courses at the School, before 1920 less than one third were elective. After 1920, however, the proportion oscillated markedly. Between 1920 and 1924 about two thirds of the total course of study was made up of electives. The proportion declined to one third once more between 1924 and 1947, rose sharply to three fourths in 1948, dropped back to one third again in the 1950's, and flooded in once more in 1963 to cover virtually the entire curriculum. In similar fashion, after the custom of scheduling a reading period in January and May was established in 1929 (modeled on that of Harvard), the size of the reading period assignments approved for each course by the faculty in different years rose and fell like the tide. In 1929, 400 pages of reading per course could be assigned, 600 in 1930, 400 in

1931, 300 in 1931-32, 400 in 1933, 500 in 1934, 300 again in 1935. Harvard and the students seem to have jointly played the part of the moon in determining these tidal fluctuations; for the size of the Harvard reading assignments (always lower) was promptly reported to the faculty by the students, and accepted as a decisive guide. But why the Harvard assignments varied so from year to year does not appear.

Committees charged with reforming the course of study, whether in a school or college, naturally tend to attribute to the product of their deliberations an intrinsic value which a broader historical perspective reveals it does not possess. In the light of one hundred and fifty years of formal theological education even the most highly touted articles of academic machinery in any period are seen to have an extrinsic and contingent merit only, great though that merit may be. In an allied field, an illustration of this is the recent sharp decline in the popularity of the "great issues" courses which were introduced into colleges amid such acclamation twenty years ago. What is significant, therefore, about the changes in the School's curriculum is not so much what particular devices commended themselves to the faculty at various times, as that the changes were frequent, and that they were initiated by the professors themselves. This meant that at no period in the School's history were the professors forced to use tools in their teaching which had been selected or passed down to them by someone else. The impact of their teaching was the greater because the basic framework of instruction was their own creation.

A Cooperative Enterprise

It is equally significant that while the professors were the master-builders in this enterprise, they did not labor alone. Almost from the beginning the students took an active and articulate part in working out what seemed best for the

School, whether in worship or in instruction or in some other phase of the common life. Their opinion was seldom the determining factor in decisions; but the minutes of faculty meetings show that it was given considerable weight nonetheless. Very early in the School's history, in fact, the professors appear to have voluntarily assigned to the students rights rather similar to the familiar ones which Bagehot in his political essay reserved to the Crown in Britain: "the right to be consulted, the right to encourage, and the right to warn." In 1893, William Lawrence consulted the students about the chapel services, the conduct of which was theoretically his responsibility alone as dean.[17] (This was an area in which, like seminarians everywhere, the students showed themselves especially opinionated.)[18] In 1902, Dean Hodges took student advice into account when he had to decide whether to retain John W. Suter or Henry B. Washburn as instructor in church history for a second year.[19] The students were also formally included in the discussions held when plans for retooling the curriculum were being laid in 1939, 1947, and 1962. At other times they could always express their opinions in private conversation or, in moments of particular tension, by petition. The first such petition was submitted in March, 1874, a request for weekly communion services during Lent; and the faculty replied in a communication for which Dean Stone (after consulting Bishop Paddock) supplied the matter, and Professor Allen the tactful manner, agreeing to meet the students precisely halfway by holding fortnightly communion services instead.[20] The same judicious combination of sympathy and restraint characterized the faculty nearly seventy years later, as is revealed in the following laconic minute from the faculty

---

[17] H. C. Robbins, *Charles Lewis Slattery*, p. 68.
[18] Dean Hodges' Journal, 1894 (ETS Archives).
[19] *Ibid.*, 1901-02.
[20] ETS Faculty Record Book, I.

meeting of May 2, 1940: "A petition of twenty-three Juniors [most of the class] to be excused from a final examination in Pastoral Care was discussed without action. Professor Taylor was requested to persuade the Juniors to take
the examination."

In these and other less formal ways an atmosphere of
mutual confidence and respect was created, to which innumerable reminiscences attest. It made the School not
just a corporate, but a cooperative enterprise. In such an
atmosphere the influence of individual teachers could be
exerted with unusual ease and power. This was a vital
element in the School's development; for as Bishop William Lawrence used to remark[21]—and as every alumnus
learns as death and retirement take their toll of the masters under whom he once studied—it is the teachers who
make every school.

---

[21] William Lawrence, *Beginnings of the Episcopal Theological School,*
p. 27.

ⅹ 11

Dean Stone and Dean Gray

THE FIRST of the teachers in order of rank was John Seely Stone, who had been associated with Wharton in gathering a faculty, and personally had drawn up the first course of study. He was seventy-two when he became professor of systematic divinity and dean in 1867, eighty-one when he retired in 1876, and eighty-six when he died in the study of 2 Phillips Place, the house which a group of his former parishioners at St. Paul's, Brookline, had purchased for his use when the School moved to Brattle Street from Coolidge Hill in 1869. He was physically and mentally agile until the very onset of the stroke that killed him. As a teacher, however, his influence was in the realm of character rather than of ideas. In the classroom he was not effective. For all his extraordinary vitality, at seventy-two his mind was attuned to currents to which younger minds were no longer sensitive or sympathetic. His theological opinions were neither rigid nor harsh. Like his friend, Dr. Sparrow of Virginia, he was more Arminian than Calvinistic in his thinking.[1] But he was old-fashioned. In class he was much more interested in display-

---
[1] ETS Archives: "Allen's Notes" folder.

ing with appreciation the ingeniously articulated apparatus of theological argument which had been admired in
his youth than in stimulating the students to think for
themselves. The arguments had on them both the patina
and dust of years. Dr. Stone lovingly drew attention to
the patina; but his students were conscious only of the
dust. E. L. Stoddard, who had become an Episcopalian
while at the Harvard Divinity School and left in mid-
course to join the ETS class of 1871, remembered that
"Dr. Stone did not profess to teach, but rather to hear
recitations" [2] and that the Doctor accepted "that anti-
quated fossil *Paley's Theology* . . . as a modern funda-
mentalist the first chapter of Genesis." [3] Dr. Allen recorded in his notes that Stone "taught Pearson and Burnet
—and when the boys were not ready, was only too ready
to recite for them, more intent on seeing the nice argument of Pearson and Burnet receive justice than to secure
knowledge on the part of the student." [4]

Dean Stone's Legacy

Dean Stone's real gift to the School was a spiritual one.
Many of the things that demanded his attention were
mundane enough—notably the everpresent task of finding
money with which to pay the stream of niggling household bills incurred in running the School, a task which he
performed conscientiously, although with none of the
brisk firmness that characterized his successors, Gray and
Lawrence, both of whom were administrators *con amore*.
What was far more important, however, was the gentle,
restrained, quiet way in which he slowly drew professors
and students together, gradually instilling habits of co-
operation and attitudes of mutual confidence which would
bear fruit in years to come. By his very presence, he

[2] ETS Archives: "E. L. Stoddard" folder.
[3] *Ibid.*
[4] ETS Archives: "Allen's Notes" folder.

helped to reassure those outside who were warily doubtful of the orthodoxy of a School established so near Harvard; and within the School itself he fostered a spacious
atmosphere of faith and trust which was spontaneously
congenial to his own nature. It was he, furthermore, who
evolved the administrative pattern traditionally followed
in the School since his time, whereby the power of the
executive is vested in the faculty rather than in the dean
alone. "We have never supposed that it was the intention
of your Board to make the other members of the Faculty
mere personal assistants of the Dean," the professors wrote
to the trustees in March, 1876, in a communication of
which Stone himself was the author, "but rather to make
him what he, as presiding officer, naturally is,—primus
inter pares." [5] The professors, however, were only able to
assume "that the Faculty, as a whole, is charged with the
instruction, discipline and religious culture of the
School" [6] because Stone intended that they should. He did
not wish to see virtually all executive power delegated to
the dean, as was the case at General under Forbes and
Seymour and those who came after them (although he
told Rand that had he wanted to assume such power,
Wharton would have agreed).[7] His relationship with the
trustees was so close, moreover, that he could have over-
ridden faculty opposition any time he wished by manipulating affairs behind the scenes just as McIlvaine had done
with dramatic success at Gambier in 1840; but he scrupulously refrained from doing so. Instead, he used his friendship with the trustees to build up the faculty's position
more strongly.[8] Like Dr. Sparrow at Virginia, Stone

[5] ETS Archives: "1875-76" folder, in an envelope marked "Letters respecting powers etc. of the Dean, March, 1876."

[6] Ibid.

[7] Ibid.

[8] Fairness begets fairness. Wharton differed with Stone in a discussion
of the dean's powers in 1876, and Stone informed Rand of this. When
Rand got in touch with Wharton to suggest a quiet discussion of these

wished to exert within the School only so much influence as his colleagues would willingly accord him out of affection and respect for his experience and sound judgment. In view of his own position of seniority among the leaders of the Church, to say nothing of the youth of Steenstra and Allen, this was a remarkable gesture which only a man of great strength of character and little or no personal vanity would have made; and his successors faithfully followed the example which he had so deliberately set.

Stone was not stodgy in his interpretation of what is, and what is not, a proper way of carrying on the work of the Church. When a friend who was thinking of becoming a lay street-preacher wrote to ask his opinion, Stone replied:

I have not enough acquaintance with the mode & the results of street-preaching to enable me to gauge the matter. I am decidedly in favor of Lay-effort in the service of Christ: &, in theory, street-preaching is as good as pulpit preaching; but I suppose the former requires a peculiarity of talent. Street-preaching ought, I should think, to be somewhat like Colporteur's talk: i.e. full of Christ, in simple, strong language, & guided by good common sense & much practical experience. And I think no one can tell whether he is called of God to this kind of labor but the individual himself, moved by what he feels within, & guided by what he knows of his own abilities & experience in things without. . . . Never run the risk of fighting against God, in thought, word or deed by opposing those who are striving to work for Him, though not

---

differences, however, Wharton declined, preferring—as he said—to put his own opinion in writing so that Stone and the other professors could "have an opportunity of knowing & replying to, if they desire, whatever I may say." Wharton concluded, "I have a great unwillingness to express any opinion which is not open to this correction." Wharton to Rand, April 1, 1876, (ETS Archives: "1876" folder). The stormy disputes which unsettled General under Forbes, and Gambier under McIlvaine, Short, and others amply illustrate what happened when openness of this kind was lacking.

in your own way:—and the advice may be carried to another case: never fight against God by opposing what He is manifestly striving to work in & by yourself. In this case, however, we need to be well assured that He *is* striving to do a particular work by us, before we undertake it.[9]

Such moderation and charity, however, were not maintained without effort. Stone had strong opinions of his own, and had been an active member of the Evangelical party too long to be able to resist adopting a partisan tone on occasion. Party strife invaded the seminaries in the 1870's just as it had done in the 1840's, and its echoes ring in a letter which Stone wrote to his old friend, Heman Dyer, on June 13, 1870:

What a grand thing is that gift of Mr. Some-One to the Fairfax Seminary! I suppose good Dr. Sparrow begins to think there is a slight possibility that he may not have lived wholly in vain. Dear old fellow! I wish he might become just a *leetle* saucy by way of self-assertion. If he could only get the notion —even for a little while—that he is something, it would do him a deal of good. From my heart I rejoice with him in view of the bettered prospects of the old School of our prophets. . . . I hope that, in future, the proportion of real, God-called, Christ-commissioned & Spirit-sanctified graduates from the old Halls may be greater than ever, & that of graduates who are otherwise may be less than ever. I express this hope, because I have seen enough of Theological Schools in the course of my life to know that the most Evangelical faculty cannot insure an unmixed succession of Evangelical graduates: nor can the most rigid High Ch. Ritualistic Faculty insure an unmixed Succession of highflying Church Dolls. Even our Genl. Theol. Sem. can't make *all* its Students what it would. . . . I have had letters of inquiry from the Genl. Semy. New York—& from St. Stephens, Annandale,—seeming to indicate that all are not satisfied with the training which they there get. Dear

[9] Stone to C. Wyntrop, May 19, 1869 (ETS Archives: "J. S. Stone" folder).

brother, what a state of things in our Church does your letter disclose! Oh ho! bitter as is my grief over the trial that has befallen me, I say unhesitatingly that I *can* respect the man who honestly follows his logic & his convictions straight into Ultramontanism;—but I *cannot* respect the—what shall I call them?—who, at Bridgport & elsewhere, play their dishonest pranks under the shade of our once really Protestant Episcopal Church. Oh! How I should rejoice to see a new Pentecost, letting loose ten thousand tongues of fire, to confound the folly, & consume the fraud, that have been brought in among us.—O Lord! How long?[10]

In this letter Stone did not speak lightly of respecting men who followed their logic clear to Ultramontanism, as his correspondent well knew. He was referring to the defection of one of his sons to Rome which had taken place only a few months before. In these years when he was burdened by anxiety over the future of the School, both because of its limited financial resources and because of the hostility to it of many men in high places in the Church, there was always lingering in the background the cloud of this personal tragedy as well. The extraordinary impress which Stone's kindliness and restraint left upon the School becomes easy to understand in the light of this episode, of which everyone in Cambridge (although they said nothing of it to Stone) was sympathetically aware. It reads like a Victorian melodrama.

James Kent Stone, the most brilliant of Stone's children, had been born in 1840, and from the first had shown signs of the vivacity, imagination, wit, and intellectual gifts that later distinguished him. He was an unusually articulate child with a very warm and affectionate nature, and he grew into a tall, handsome, athletic young man. Entering Harvard in 1856, he spent two of the next four years in Europe, studying throughout 1860 in Göttingen, and returned only after the Civil War broke out, graduating

---

[10] ETS Archives: "J. S. Stone" folder.

with the class of 1861. He enlisted in the army, was invalided out at the end of 1862, was ordained, became professor of Latin at Kenyon, and in 1863 married the daughter of Harrison Fay of Brookline, a former parishioner of his father's (the Fay and Stone children had made up the volunteer choir when Stone was rector of St. Paul's). In 1867 he became president of Kenyon. He was very popular with the students; but his point of view, which was becoming steadily more High Church, alarmed both McIlvaine and the professors at Bexley, and Kent Stone resigned after a row in 1868 to accept the presidency of the more sympathetic Hobart College. A year later even Hobart had come to seem too Low for him, and he resigned to enter the Roman Church. His wife's death after the birth of their third daughter in 1869 (like the death of Manning's wife in the case of a more famous convert) made Stone free to enter the priesthood. After removing the children from the care of their Grandmother Fay, placing them in a convent (where the second daughter soon died of pneumonia), and then arranging to have them formally adopted by a childless Roman Catholic couple in California, Kent Stone became a Paulist in 1870. A few years later he joined the more austere Passionist Order, to which he devoted the rest of a very long life (he died in 1921 in his eighty-second year). The suffering into which Kent Stone's conversion to Rome plunged his parents, himself, and his children was deep and prolonged. The memory of it still echoed in a letter which he wrote to his youngest daughter in 1920, when communication between them had been restored after almost a lifetime of silence. (He had seen the children once or twice in the interval, but had forbidden their adoptive parents to reveal to them that he was their father.)

You may have wondered why I did not send you some relic of the past. I had none, dear. When I gave my children away,

I destroyed everything. Household goods, furniture, etc. were stored at Geneva, N.Y., Hobart College; I wrote and gave orders to have everything sold by auction. The proceeds were given to the Sisters at Manchester. . . . Then I made a bonfire in the rear garden of the Paulist Fathers of everything combustible,—Mss., old letters, poems, etc. There were a few precious things left. (My books had been given to the College.) I kept them in a rosewood box,—some simple jewelry, memento of the past, that would never return,—pictures of "Mama and Nellie and Ethel" (there were none of you, O my little one), and (Dear Lord help me!) *her ring*. I weighted the box with pieces of iron, locked it and then when darkness fell, I took it down to the end of the old abandoned pier, which in those days, ran out from the foot of 59th Street and then with a prayer, an anguished prayer, I dropped it into the Hudson River, where the waters were deep, and there it must be today, covered over, sunken in the silt of that river bed. After that, for fifty years, nothing broke the long sad silence.[11]

The atmosphere of intense, overwrought emotion which is evoked in this letter also prevailed in Cambridge and Brookline at the time of Kent Stone's conversion. Most people thought that Kent Stone had gone mad. His former brother-in-law, James Fay, who had been his closest boyhood friend, tried to have him officially certified insane (in order, no doubt, to gain custody of the children). What Dean Stone felt, he confided only to Heman Dyer:

Ever since my great affliction, I shrink from publicity, & I long to walk the little remainder of my way behind a Screen. . . . I suppose you will say, that I ought not to shrink from effort; but—"Have pity on me, have pity on me, O ye my friends; for the hand of God hath touched me." I cannot enter into explanations. Let me carry my wound unseen, till we come, where alone it can be healed, into that Divine Light,

---

[11] Smith and Smith, *Fidelis of the Cross*, p. 422.

where, at last, the reasons of all God's dealings will be manifest.[12]

Yet mother and father respected their son's right to do what he felt he must, appalling as it seemed to them. They kept in touch with him as long as they lived; and long letters passed between them—his often combining fervent expression of the happiness which he had found in the Roman Church with questions about the School or messages of good will for Phillips Brooks, for whom he had always had much admiration.[13] Many years later Father Fidelis, as Kent Stone was called, returned to Cambridge, and stayed for a night or so with his sister and brother-in-law, the Allens, in the house in which his father had died. Dr. Allen offered to take him to prayers in the Chapel; but Father Fidelis declined: "he said he too would go to prayers—his own—so he went for his Breviary." [14]

Dean Stone's Last Lesson

John Seely Stone had no illusions about his ineffectiveness in the classroom. But when he told one of the students that he was "entirely too old to learn the trick of teaching," [15] he was modestly limiting the field to the one area in which his competence was not great. Everywhere else he taught unforgettable lessons. By his faith and dignity in sorrow, by his lack of bitterness, by his unaffected courtesy (which was never without a twinkle of humor), he gave the students of his day, in Bishop Lawrence's words, "a high conception of the calling of the ministry, and of their work as preachers and pastors." [16] Nor was his teaching

---

[12] Stone to Dyer, May 31, 1870 (ETS Archives: "J. S. Stone" folder).

[13] Smith and Smith, *Fidelis of the Cross,* pp. 147, 149, 167.

[14] From a letter written c. Sept., 1893, and quoted in C. L. Slattery, *A. V. G. Allen,* p. 137.

[15] Recollections of J. G. Bacchus, '73, *ETS Bulletin,* June, 1917, p. 72.

[16] William Lawrence, *Seventy-Three Years of the Episcopal Theological School, Cambridge,* p. 13.

confined to the students alone. One of the last of his
lessons, and by no means the least effective, was in the
form of a "correspondence course" whereby he sought to
prepare George Zabriskie Gray to succeed him with a
minimum of upset and misunderstanding in the late
spring of 1876. Gray was inclined to be brusque, and to
act the part of a "new broom" with an outspoken direct-
ness that ruffled feelings when not the least offense had
been intended. He knew nothing of New England or,
in particular, Cambridge; but from letters and personal
interviews Stone was aware that Gray was keenly interested in the Chapel ministry as a part of the responsibility
of the deanship, and was already making plans to assume
vigorous control of it as soon as he took office. Stone,
therefore, wrote to him on February 12, 1876—long
enough before the time of his coming for Gray to digest
what he had to say—to welcome, to inform—and to warn.
It was a superbly tactful and wise letter:

Dear brother,

I sent you, the other day, a brief acknowledgement of the
rect. of yr. letter of the 6th, promising to write again after
advising with the rest of the Faculty. They have been with
me this morning, & I hasten to fulfill my promise. It gives
me pleasure to say, that the Faculty will be glad to have you
undertake not only the *teaching* of "pastoral Care" to the
Students, but also the *discharge* of pastoral duties to the
congregation: including their organization for Christian work,
so far as circumstances will permit. You know that we are
not a *parish,* in the ordinary sense of the word; & that the
people have nothing to say, or to do, in choosing their Pastor.
The Instrument of Donation, which puts our Trustees in
possession of the Chapel, simply makes it the duty of the
Faculty to maintain public worship & preaching, without providing any additional compensation for such service. In this
state of the case, the Faculty, finding as much work as they
can well do in their labors as Professors, have been unable

to do any thing in the way of pastoral work, except so far
as merely *official* acts have required; and I have no doubt
that what you propose in the way of such work will be most
gladly recd. by the people, as well as seconded by the Faculty.
We shall let it be known as soon & as widely as we can in a
quiet way, that you will become the pastor of the Congregation, & be encouraged to train them in your own way, to all
kinds of Church Work.

As to Dr. L[angdon, the new Rector of Christ Church] we
are not particularly apprehensive of losing our Congregation
through his influence; though our new arrangement with you
will doubtless operate favorably in retaining what we have, &
possibly in gathering in others. In Cambridge, however, the
Episcopal Element is not super-abundant; & the New England
mind is not given to easy shifting of pastoral relations. We
need not expect, therefore, any great, or sudden rush of new
members into our congregation. Those, who already attend
the Chapel, have been drawn by the one, or the other of two
influences, that of a *free* Chapel, or that of our recognized
evangelical standing: these influences will, I think, retain
those who have come; & occasionally, perhaps, draw in some
new families; especially if Dr. L[angdon] should attempt any
marked following of Dr. H[oppin's] 's *ritualisms.*

But though N.E. people are not given to any easy shifting
of pastoral relations, yet they are much given to running
after extra services, especially if popular in character. This
is clearly seen here in Cambridge, when Mr. Brooks preaches
for us. It has become a settled understanding in the public
mind, that he is to preach in St. John's the 3rd Sunday evening of every month; & on those evegs. the Chapel is always
crowded, sometimes to overflowing, with University Students,
& people of all Denominations. These services are highly
prized by both Trustees & faculty; particularly as bringing
Mr. B. himself into growing sympathy with & interest in our
School.

In your contemplated work among our congregation, you
will have a free field before you; but in distributing among
our Faculty the labor of *preaching,* I fear the case will be
somewhat different. In my position as Dean, I have felt a

delicacy, which has led me to leave this matter to mutual agreement among ourselves. Our *morning* congregations are generally fair; but our afternoon congregations are always slim, generally *very* slim; & I fear our Professors would hardly be willing to be restricted to the latter. But—suppose you assume the *whole* duty of supplying the pulpit; & then, when you need help, call on one or other of us to assist you,— sometimes in the morning, & sometimes in the afternoon. In such an arrangement, I think the Faculty would cheerfully acquiesce. For myself, I can speak without hesitation; & I think I may safely say the same for the rest. Professors Steenstra & Allen would be glad of such a relief; & Dr. Wharton, I am quite sure, would be indifferent *when,* or how *often,* he should be called upon to preach. Please let me hear what you think of this proposal. Meanwhile let us be faithful in prayer that God will guide all our counsels, & bless all our labors to the promotion of His own glory, & the best good of our School, with brotherly love & sweet peace among us all.

In coming from N[ew] J[ersey] to Mass. you will, I doubt not, become conscious of a change, greater or less, in your circumstances & in the feelings, which they tend to inspire. I was born in Mass. & have spent many years of my life in Boston, & its immediate neighborhood; while at the same time, I have been made somewhat familiar with N[ew] Y[ork] & Philada. & the State between them. On this point, therefore, I feel qualified to speak. Let me say, then, in few words, that the people of Boston are slow in forming a judgment of a newcomer among them; but when they have had sufficient opportunity for judging, if they find him a true man, worthy & sound, they adopt him as one of themselves, & stand by him through *thick & thin.* For yourself, as an expected stranger, I have no fear. You will come among us quietly, as we await you; take up your work modestly as it meets you, & do it earnestly as God gives you strength; & gradually you will find hearts warming to you, & hands held out to help you, as well as minds ready to judge you fairly, if *slowly,* &, in due time, yourself "strong in the Lord" & in an assured position of credit & of usefulness, which I pray you

may long hold & fill, with abundant satisfaction to yourself,
& to those among whom you are to labor & to dwell.

Yr. affectionate friend & brother
John S. Stone[17]

George Zabriskie Gray

George Zabriskie Gray was professor of systematic divinity
and dean from 1876 until his death in 1889. In many ways
he was not at all like his predecessor. The difference was
one not only of age and personality, but of background.
Gray was only thirty-eight when he became dean of the
School; and his face proclaimed the man: ruddy cheeks,
bristling muttonchop whiskers, and sparkling eyes that
looked as if they might pop right out of his head whenever he was amused or interested or angry. Vigorous,
decisive, quick-tempered, and utterly without guile, his
bowwow abruptness of manner was the defensive weapon
of a fundamentally shy and sensitive man. He was a New
Yorker born and bred (except for an interlude of schooling in Geneva, Switzerland). He had grown up in the
Dutch Reformed Church, and had not decided to be confirmed in the Episcopal Church until he had reached his
junior year at New York University. His theological
training had been obtained at Virginia and (after the outbreak of the Civil War) at Philadelphia; and until his call
to Cambridge, his ministry had been spent entirely in
New York or New Jersey. In 1876 he was rounding out
eleven years as rector of Trinity Church, Bergen Point,
New Jersey. Before entering the ministry he had received
training also in business. His father was a rich man, and
Gray himself had independent means.

The effect on the School of the shift of responsibility
from the old dean to the new one was immediate and

---

[17] ETS Archives: "J. S. Stone" folder.

marked. In the files of School correspondence, the Stone letters with the slanting "s," abbreviated "ye" for "the," and long eddying sentences reminiscent of the eighteenth century disappeared abruptly, to be replaced by Gray letters in a clear, round, legible hand and a style equally clear, almost crisp. Discipline within the School was tightened. The administration became brisk. From the first, Gray managed the day to day financial affairs of the School with an aplomb which had always escaped Stone. He even reduced to surprisingly docile frugality the recalcitrant department to which, in a moment of half-irritated amusement, he once gave the appropriate nickname of "The Refractory." Partly because of his earlier business training perhaps, and certainly because his independent income made him immune to tensions from which Stone, for one, had never been entirely free, he maintained with the trustees an easy rapport subtly different in quality from the relationship which had prevailed between the trustees and his predecessor. The trustees had loved and admired Stone, just as later trustees were to love and admire Dean Hodges and Dean Washburn, but they felt at home with Gray. They thought of him, obviously, as one of themselves. And Gray felt at home with them—rather more at home than he felt with the faculty, much as he liked and respected his colleagues. Only his successor, Dean Lawrence, appears to have had the capacity of being equally at ease in both worlds. Like Stone, however, Gray scrupulously refrained from trading on his intimacy with the trustees in order to get his own way after he had failed to obtain it in faculty meeting. Trustees or visitors who criticized the rather thin and uninspiring weekday services in the Chapel, for example, might discover afterwards to their surprise that the dean had for some time felt just as they did, although in the face of the satisfaction with the *status quo* expressed by Steenstra, Allen, and Wharton he had done nothing; but Gray himself would not say anything until the trustees brought the matter up first.[18] When money ran really short, he told Amos A. Lawrence not to pay the dean's salary at all rather than pay the other professors piecemeal or late.[19]

As a pastor, Gray excelled. His interest in the Chapel congregation instilled renewed vigor; the number of Harvard students regularly attending the services increased; and the congregation itself became much more like a regular parish. He built the Deanery at his own expense, and made it not only a center for the School, but almost for the neighborhood. After Gray's death, William Lawrence said in a memorial sermon:

The college boy, coming from a happy home, found here his second home; and young Harvard graduates throughout the country look to that house with gratitude for their warm reception. The theological student seldom entered that he did not find another before him. The Deanery was the School's hospital, for there the sick student was carried. The western bishop, the missionary, the traveller, all found the same welcome. To neighbors, friends, and strangers as well, the door stood ever open. And even the study door was rarely, I may say never, shut.

It was a home where envy, sordid ambition and petty rivalries were unknown. His genial heart, his humor, his sense of honor, his sympathy with all that is pure, lovely and of good report were caught by all who entered.[20]

Like Stone, Gray was not as effective in the classroom as he was outside it. He was a conservative Evangelical when he came to the School, and in the early years he taught simply what he had learned at Virginia sixteen years before. The classes consisted principally of recita-

[18] *E.g.,* G. Z. Gray to W. R. Huntington, Nov. 29, 1883 (ETS Archives: "1883" folder).

[19] Gray to Lawrence, Jan. 22, 1881 (ETS Archives: "1880-81" folder).

[20] William Lawrence, *George Zabriskie Gray D.D.—A Memorial Sermon,* p. 33.

tions on Van Oosterzee, Pearson, and Browne. In 1876 the trustees at Virginia, it may be remembered, suggested to the professor of systematic divinity that it would be a salutary exercise for the students to commit the Thirty-nine Articles to memory. In 1882 Dean Gray directed his students at the Episcopal Theological School to learn the Thirty-nine Articles by heart—in Latin. When they protested, he relented only to the extent of permitting them to memorize them in English instead. But Gray grew. He was a talented linguist, and stimulated by the Cambridge atmosphere he began to read widely in contemporary German theology. The results of his reading he promptly brought into the classroom, although his method of presenting new material was slightly impetuous. Bishop Lawrence, in his memoir of the School's early years, said that Dean Gray "threw his somewhat undigested conclusions at the students, sometimes in such a way as to confuse or stun them, and when they asked Dr. Allen what the Dean meant he was unable to tell them." [21] Yet while the students were battered by chunks of ill-digested theology, they were not bludgeoned by a dogmatic authoritarian. When the Board of Visitors suggested a return to the textbook-and-recitation method of instruction in 1883, after the faculty had resolved to abandon it gradually in favor of the lecture and seminar, Gray in reply described his approach to teaching in a spirit that the modern ETS alumnus would instantly recognize as familiar:

In the Department of Homiletics and Pastoral Care, while assigning books for reading, I use none in the room, because none suit me nor the students. I lecture on the clergyman's personal life, preaching and pastoral work. I require frequent sermons and skeletons of sermons, wherein the men show their assimilation of what has been learned in these lectures,

---

[21] Lawrence, *Seventy-three Years of ETS,* p. 18.

and also in the other department under my care. These sermons are also criticized and discussed in class.

The other Department is Systematic Divinity, including
Evidences and Ethics. Here, I use text-books throughout, but,
instead of catechising the men on the portions they are pre-
sumed to have studied as directed, I spend most of the hour
in either delivering oral lectures, or in supplementing the
book on such points as the inquiries of the students suggest.
I also, in different books, require written abstracts of the
lessons.

The difficulty with all text-books in this Department, is
that they reflect the position and opinion of the authors, so
that, unless supplemented, they would render the students
disciples of the men in question, instead of independent and
intelligent theologians. This is true of all books beyond the
rudimentary grade, to a great degree.

Again, it seems to me that men should be encouraged to
ask questions, and have their inquiries met, instead of merely
having questions asked of them.

Each year makes me feel, therefore, that the strict textbook method must render students narrow in scholarship,
one-sided in churchmanship, indifferent to the love of truth,
and indisposed to independent thought.

Our men, furthermore, are unusually qualified for abstruse
study, and unusually aware of the questions now debated.
Therefore it would be to them intolerable, unsatisfactory,
and dangerous to confine study to learning lessons by rote.[22]

Gray's emphasis on wide freedom for the students
sprang from his understanding of the essential catholicity
of the Church, a quality that he emphasized in his preaching and teaching. He spoke of it with typical clarity in
the Baldwin Lectures which he wrote shortly before his
death:

If anything is evident, it is that the Church shows that it is
Apostolic and Catholic by endorsing no Theology and com-

<hr>

[22] ETS Archives: "1883" folder.

mitting itself to no scientific results. There are many systems or schools of Christian thought within the allowable limits of adherence to the Creed and Prayer Book. There are many theories of particular subjects, such as sacraments, ministry, atonement, eschatology, and others more or less important, many theories even of the very organization of the Church. But the Church identifies itself with none, regards all as only approximate at the best, and authorizes no man to speak for it as to the final definition of anything.[23]

In his last report, Gray stated that "the ministry which cannot deal with human needs intelligently or sympathetically, because ignorant thereof, nor speak in manly and brotherly language, may win respect for its piety and admiration for its erudition, but still only find its claim to lead men ignored. . . ." His contemporaries did not ignore George Zabriskie Gray.

---

[23] Lawrence, *G. Z. Gray—Memorial Sermon*, p. 25.

✹ 12

The Teaching of Francis Wharton

DEAN STONE taught in the School for nine years; Dean Gray, for thirteen. Francis Wharton taught for fourteen years—from 1867-68 to 1881-82. His subjects were liturgics, church polity, canon law, and (for a few years) homiletics, pastoral care, and apologetics. He was always ready to take on whatever no other member of the faculty wished (or felt competent) to tackle. At Gambier in the fifties and early sixties, Wharton had been a very popular teacher. Dr. Allen, who was one of his students there, later bore witness to his influence:

I gained from him a deep and lasting interest in literature. He was, by constitution, a Humanist of a higher order, with an instinctive perception of the quality and meaning of life, with a deep sympathy for all human manifestations. He was a very interesting man, making all that he touched interesting. From him I gained also my first conception of the picturesque aspects of history, and my first conviction of its value as a psychological revelation of the soul of humanity. The same fascination and sense of living reality of things he carried into his work as a lay-preacher. I recall the crowds that flocked to the basement hall of Rosse Chapel to listen to his lectures on the Acts of the Apostles. It was no ordinary man who could have drawn students from their rooms, or people from their homes, on those winter evenings, as he did for successive weeks, to such an uncouth, ill-ventilated, badly lighted room.[1]

The Disconcerting Dr. Wharton

At ETS, however, Wharton's influence appears to have been greater outside than inside the classroom, precisely as was the case with Stone and Gray. The difficulty lay not with anything old-fashioned about his methods; for he always lectured instead of relying on recitations, and there was nothing out-of-date about the reading which he recommended to his classes. He was as responsible as anyone for opening the School to the influence of contemporary Continental theology and history (he reviewed books in German for the learned Andover Seminary periodical, *Bibliotheca Sacra,* edited by Edwards Park). Indeed, the real trouble seems to have been that he was not old-fashioned enough. He expected the students to carry on independently their own basic study of the elementary material, and employed the lectures as a commentary, providing extra information or a larger perspective which supplemented and illuminated, but was no substitute for, the assigned reading. At a time when the men were being called on for nothing more than simple recitations in every other class, this was disconcertingly unconventional. It did not fit the students' somewhat narrow conception of what a class in a theological school ought to be like. As a result, while they found Wharton stimulating and amusing (another disconcerting feature—*ought* a theological professor be *amusing* in class?), they were confused and a little disapproving. This is clearly reflected in the recollections of E. L. Stoddard, '71:

Dr. Francis Wharton was born to be a delightful companion as host of a dinner party, but as a Prof. of Homiletics &

---

[1] Smythe, *Kenyon College,* p. 178.

Liturgics he was a scream. I speak as a fool when I say that had I not been a studious wretch, determined to learn all there was to know about the Church of my choice I should have been graduated as ignorant of homiletics or liturgics as if I had been one of the newly enfranchised slaves of the South. Dr. Wharton was witty, full of anecdotes and clever in argument, but the only thing I ever learned from him was how one could disobey rubrics and even canons and not get found out.[2]

Dr. Wharton might justly have replied to this that if Stoddard had not been "a studious wretch, determined to learn all there was to know . . ." he did not belong in the School in the first place.

Stoddard's reference to Wharton's teaching with regard to rubrics and canons recognizably embalms a reaction not uncommon among zealous, but not very knowledge-able, students when their teacher addresses himself to the tricky task of distinguishing between the spirit and the letter of a law. Professor Muller used sometimes to provoke a similar reaction fifty years later when he contrasted the literal and the genuine, historical meaning of the Confirmation Rubric. This was a distinction about which Wharton, as a trained lawyer, knew a great deal, and about which he felt strongly. Dr. Allen said that Wharton "was inclined to fall back upon the larger rubric of common sense in interpreting the Prayer Book, which would keep the Church true in the main to its standards, while preventing the scrupulosity which insisted on fulfilling obsolete or inconvenient injunctions, no longer necessary to the Church's welfare." [3] Students, anxious to find a secure base in some invulnerable formulary, whether rule or creed, naturally were made uneasy by this, particularly when it was expressed with pointed learning, as in the fol-

[2] ETS Archives: "E. L. Stoddard" folder.
[3] Wharton, *Francis Wharton*, p. 179.

lowing passage which is taken from one of Wharton's articles, but which, Allen says, originally figured in one of his lectures:

. . . from the attempt to establish as a perpetuity subtile and minute theological definitions . . . difficulty flows. No truth is more generally conceded, and yet more practically repudiated, than that which affirms the multiplication of differentia by the specification of definitions. We think that we will make a new definition which will be complete and minute and exhaustive enough to settle all controversy; but instead of this it only creates as many new controversies as it contains words. The statute of frauds, for instance, which was adopted in England for the purpose of preventing frauds and perjuries consequent upon purely oral proof of contracts and wills, provided that contracts and wills should, with certain exceptions, be in writing, and should be proved in a particular way; but there is no word in the statute of frauds which has not been the subject of innumerable suits, and of the most intricate distinctions and subdistinctions. The bull Unigenitus was to settle the Jansenist controversy, but it did not do so, for we had at once not only a multitude of new questions as to the meaning of each sentence in the bull Unigenitus, but up sprang the still more radical question whether, as to matters of fact, the Pope had the right to publish any bull at all. So far as concerns the Thirty-nine Articles, hardly had the church adapted herself to them, when new articles were called for, and the Lambeth formularies were constructed in order to settle questions as to the divine sovereignty left open by the Thirty-nine Articles, and the Westminster Confession followed, making still more minute and precise the Lambeth formularies. Had we not passed from the creed-making period, it is difficult to say to what extent we should have gone on defining the definitions of our definitions. We went, however, far enough to generate in every direction controversies almost implacable. It is remarkable that these contests were not as to the essence of the faith. As to the Thirty-nine Articles, there was a general feeling of submission; but when it came to the rubrics, then followed revolt, and one side provoked a schism, and the other accepted it, for the sake of a posture or a garb. Scarcely less worthy were the controversies by which, through excessive minuteness of definition, other communions were disturbed. . . . Words change; circumstances change; that which is rational enough at one time ceases to be rational at another, and becomes destructive instead of recuperative. Not that the cardinal facts of the universal creeds are not universally binding; not that our more intricate formularies may not be retained as articles of peace; but they should not be maintained as to matters in which they were based on theories merely local or temporary, simply to become articles of war. And if retained, they should not be sub-defined. . . . How can it be otherwise than that both the ethical and spiritual elements in Christianity should recede from the vision exclusively occupied with the imposition of new tests drawn by arbitrary *a priori* argumentation of old? Why should we be surprised if, in an era in which this with many is the dominant idea, those permeated with this idea should consider logical orthodoxy to be the ruling note of Christian life? . . . What could be more logically precise than the orthodoxy of the leading members of the court of Edward VI; yet, if we leave out that hapless boy, and his still more hapless cousin, whose coronation throne was her scaffold, where can we find a group of men more oblivious of moral duty than those who appear and disappear, murdering and murdered, plundering and disgorging, in that turbulent court? Or, if we proceed further, can we fail to be struck with Cromwell's dying cry, "If I had assurance, as I had, I was elected; if elected, elected forever; if elected forever, elected to holiness"; and as we hear this, omit to remember the strange dissimulations, the unscrupulous stratagems, the disloyalties to the cause of freedom which once he held so dear, by which that splendid and haughty career was marked? Can we forget the massacres and perfidies which went side by side with the Synod of Dort? Or can we forget that at a time when our New England divines were entering on a new era of creed-making, when some of the greatest of human intellects were absorbed in the application of a differential calculus to all mysteries, Whitefield arrived in New England, preaching a gospel that was to seize the heart, and moralize the life, and can we forget the uproar and contumely with which he was received, and how the finest of all distinctions were launched at him to shut him out, accompanied with the coarsest of anathemas to stun him? Or can we fail to be struck with the strange union, in the hymns of some of the noble French ladies who took up Calvinism as a party cry, of strict dialectic theology with amative sentiments far from strict? It is true that the minute formularization of metaphysical theology is by no means inconsistent with a holy life. It is true that many men engaged in this work have been eminently holy. But it is also true that when these formularies, thus elaborated, became party standards, when to the heated mind salvation depends on them, then the ethical element subsides.[4]

The combination of legal and historical learning, shrewd powers of observation, and an ear for the cadences of English rhetoric probably made Wharton too formidable a teacher for many of his students. They were bewildered by his propensity for mixing together superficially disparate subjects and disciplines. But to men like Allen these same qualities made him endlessly fascinating. Even in their nineteenth-century stylistic dress, his articles still have force and freshness. Speaking of prayer in a paper on "Certain Legal Analogies" which he once read before the Massachusetts Clericus, for example, he stated:

It would not be considered a petition cognizable by . . . a court for a petitioner to say, "I want an equal division of all the real estate in my neighborhood," or "I want to have another man's patent right transferred to me simply because he is rich and I am poor." A petition, to be received as such, must assume certain fundamental rules of justice, and must submit to these rules. So it is with prayer. Prayer, in the right sense of the term, is submission to certain general laws, and an entreaty that the petitioner may be brought within their operation. It is not prayer to ask that a risky investment may

---

[4] Francis Wharton, "Church Parties as Apologists," *Bibliotheca Sacra,* July, 1880, pp. 445-449.

be made good, or that a house which negligence or parsimony leaves uninsured should not be burned down, or that a constitution damaged by indulgence should be repaired. It is an insult, not a submission, to God to offer a prayer which assumes that his laws are absurd. . . . In other words, to seek to upset the general system of law governing the universe in order to procure exceptional benefits to ourselves is not prayer, but revolt. It is a petition without a judge, a litigation without a law, and a prayer without a God. Prayer, in its true sense, involves a submission of the heart to the divine law, and a supplication that of this law we may become ministers. This is not mystic quietism. So far from this, it involves far greater activity and practical effectiveness than does the idea of revolt from law and seeking special privileges above the law. . . . True prayer is, "not *my* will," but "*thy* will be done." [5]

In a paper on "Involuntary Confessions," he had this to say about the effects of guilt "lodged in the intent":

. . . every lunatic asylum bears witness to the . . . cases of imbecility in which the unexecuted purposes of sin—purposes which had only been thought over, but at the same time nursed—are babbled out, and with all their coarse consequences told by the tongue of age. The muscular hand of youth kept the curtain down—and the secret though nourished sin was thus concealed. But when the power of self-restraint weakened—when the cords and rings of the curtain decayed—then the secluded contents of the heart—these unexecuted sins, now exhaling phantoms by their very exposure —rise and spread themselves in their deformity before the public gaze. Sometimes overt acts follow, and we hear of sudden falls in old and heretofore correct men—falls, however, which were not sudden, for there were back-stairs in the heart down which the culprit had been for years descending. Sometimes the act is one of imagination only, but is talked of in the gross familiarity of senility. But however this phenom-

[5] Francis Wharton, "Certain Legal Analogies," *Bibliotheca Sacra*, April, 1883, pp. 221-222.

enon may exhibit itself, it is a part of that grand system of
Providence, by which guilt is lodged in the *intent,* and by
which, as a compensation for human law, which judges of
the overt act alone, the intent incloses in itself its own retri-
bution.[6]

The Anglicanism of Francis Wharton

Wharton's resort to law to illuminate theology, like his
employment of theology to explain psychological phenomena, was not just a quirk. Probing with absorbed
interest beneath the surface of things, he perceived relationships and unifying patterns underlying historical
events and personal experience of which many of his contemporaries were unaware. Central to his thought was the
conviction that infallible principles are revealed only in
and through fallible forms[7]—flexibility of form, indeed,
being the prerequisite for stability of life.[8] Hence his
emphasis on the necessity of changing the letter of rubric
or canon from age to age in order to preserve unchanged
the spirit behind it. Hence, also, his devotion to Anglicanism. For the comprehensiveness of Anglicanism at its best
—the broad, generous, profoundly law-abiding (but not
legalistic) outlook of Hooker—seemed to him not only
personally congenial, but basically true to the spirit of
life itself. As a result he was actually more comprehensive
in his point of view than most Episcopalians of his day,
and certainly broader in his sympathies than some of his
colleagues at the Episcopal Theological School. Rand, as
revealed in his hostility to Nicholas Hoppin and Hoppin's
mild ritualism at Christ Church, was a strong partisan
among the Evangelicals. Huntington, on the other hand,
was a moderate who, in the interests of a united Church,

---

[6] Francis Wharton, *Involuntary Confessions,* p. 20.
[7] Francis Wharton, "Romanticism in its Relations to Rome," *Bibliotheca Sacra,* July, 1871
[8] *Ibid.*

sought to obliterate or ignore all party distinctions. Wharton alone anticipated the modern point of view of men like William Temple, seeing in the various church parties a sign of the pluralism essential to the Church's vitality. For Wharton did not consider the parties as merely corporate expressions of the sentiments or prejudices which ebb and flow within a single denomination. Their counterparts, in his opinion, could be found in every Christian church—called into being in every instance to bear witness to a genuine aspect of the Christian truth which the spirit of the times in that particular period momentarily endangered. "I conceive," he wrote, "that the existence of a succession of parties, sweeping the surface without decomposing the substance of the Church, may be used apologetically, as showing its essential unity, ubiquity, and perpetuity."

Stimulated by the controversy as to church parties in England, to which Gladstone, Lecky, and Newman had contributed, Wharton expressed his views in an extended essay in 1880, two years before he resigned his position at the School. Using the history of the Church in Europe and America since the Reformation as a general background, he suggested that all the church parties in whatever denomination represented one of roughly seven points of view, each of which had become popular more or less in chronological sequence whenever the one-sidedness and weakness of the view which immediately preceded it in popularity had begun to be obvious. These seven he listed as the Dogmatic, the Ethical (the party of "religious moderatism"), the Evangelical, the Institutional, the Sacramentarian, the Ritualistic, and the Broad. In order to demonstrate that these distinctions were not coincident with denominational boundaries, he adroitly selected examples of each (not without a gleam of mischief) from the most unexpected sources—looking, for example, not chiefly to Anglicanism, but to the New

England of the Puritans for illustrations of institutionalism, sacramentarianism (the "leather mitten ordination of
Mr. Israel Chauncey"),[9] and ritualism ("when we walk
through that sumptuous room in Memorial Hall in which
banquet the students of the now largest college of Puritan
institution, have we the heart to criticize the costumes of
the eminent Puritan divines, whose portraits hang on
walls mounted by grotesque mediaeval gargoyles, relieved
by Chrysostom sculptured in his chasuble, and Bossuet in
his rochet?").[10]

The purpose of the article, however, was not simply one
of historical analysis. Wharton had another point to make.
He wished to demonstrate that the point of view which
was being expressed in the teaching of Steenstra and
Allen, and for which the School was widely criticized, was
not heretical or dangerous, but rather the most recent (and
therefore as yet unfamiliar) manifestation of the spirit
which had earlier found expression in the party forms
which the passage of time had now rendered acceptable.
Employing the term "Broad Church" to describe this
point of view (while at the same time indicating that as a
description of a party the term was unsatisfactory), Wharton wrote:

If . . . we are to particularly distinguish as broad churchism
the critical school, which is now, in all Protestant communions, engaged, it may be boldly, in inquiring into the
authenticity of the several particles of the canonical Scriptures;
in determining what is the sense of these Scriptures when
relating to facts established by physical science; in comparing
current theological dogmas with the conclusions of psychology and sociology; then we may recur to the position with
which we started, and inquire whether it is inconsistent with

---

[9] Wharton, "Church Parties as Apologists," *Bibliotheca Sacra*, July,
1880, p. 460.
[10] *Ibid.*, p. 464.

the nature and traditions of the church that we should regard investigators of this class as advance guards, who from the very order of things, start forth instinctively to struggle on frontiers on which the church may be assailed, and to entrench themselves on the assailants' own ground.

The struggle at present, let it be remembered, is for the possession of posts which, if manned by the church, would not only strengthen it, but add to its sway. What if by Christians it should be proved that in the patience of God's eternal purpose, the earth, filled as it now is by beings who may endure for countless ages, should have been for countless ages in evolution before it was fitted to become their habitation? Would it in any way lessen our conception of the divine power and wisdom should Christians unite in demonstrating that the dust, from which Scripture tells us the first man was framed, was in itself the pregnant germ of future ascending as well as multiplying life? Would the authority of the sacred text, would our sense of the dignity of man, be diminished, if Christian apologists should occupy the position that in the breast of the first man God implanted a germinal moral sense, to flow, swelling and refining from age to age, through the breasts of his descendants? Would the authenticity and authority of the canonical Scriptures be weakened, if Christian critics should show that passages heretofore suspected are spurious; and that these Scriptures, as well as all other authoritative records, when they unite substantial unity with circumstantial discrepancy, conform to what is an unvarying incident of complex documentary truth? . . . It may be that the party, if it be a party, which boldly, yet in Christian loyalty, enters into the field of textual criticism, destroying the untenable and fortifying the tenable, may make the field of textual criticism one of the chief outposts of the truth. And so it may be with those who seize on the theory of development, cosmical or individual, and on that field erect the banner of Christ, proclaiming that it is in accordance both with his word and mode of working that seed and germ are made pregnant with protoplastic power; and that in the beginning he framed them, thus wonderfully endowed; and that over their propagation and variation in development he

watches; and their multiform fruit he will at last gather into
his many-mansioned house.[11]

Wharton's summing up was majestic:

As we proceed from the centre to the outposts, the battalions into which the bearers of the faith are divided separate, as we have seen, more and more widely, and in the
outposts at which they are stationed acquire more or less of
the distinctive culture they go forth to possess. As these very
battalions, when their term of service is over, return home,
then does this distinctive culture, so far as it is alien, pass
away; and the nearer they approach the centre, the nearer
do they approach each other. The time will come when they
will mingle in a common host about the throne. But as this
time draws nigh, each will have something to impart, as well
as something to retain. Each has its conquest to divide, and
its primordial faith to retain. This faith is evangelical—belief
in Christ for us, and Christ in us, Christ the propitiation for
our sins, and Christ giving us new life. But around this central
faith are ranged subordinate banners, won in many hard fields
—that of institutionalism, vindicating the right of the church
to historic continuity; that of ethics, exhibiting the depend-
ence of morality on religion; that of sacramentarianism, maintaining the reality of things spiritual; that of free thought,
claiming all the domain of intellect as subservient to the truth.
As we ourselves approach the period when we will be dis-
banded from earthly service, we will not become less evangelical. But we may find ourselves more and more sacramentarians
in the true and pure sense; more and more impressed with an
appreciation both of the ethical and of the institutional sides
of the faith; more and more loyal to the catholic creeds; and
more and more fearless in appealing to reason as, co-ordinately
with revelation, the factor by which these creeds are established.[12]

---

[11] *Ibid.*, pp. 466-468.
[12] *Ibid.*, p. 470.

Resignation

Bishop Lawrence used to say that Wharton's real interest was in the law, and that this gradually weaned him away from the School. But the truth is a little more complicated than that. Wharton had gracefully yielded the deanship to Stone in 1867, and scrupulously refrained from what he thought might be interpreted as interference, even staying away from faculty meetings whenever he could. Stone, however, interpreted this restraint as a sign of indifference rather than of scrupulosity (he appears never to have realized just how much power Wharton had really exercised in the School's first six months of existence); and for this, as well as other reasons, Stone and the trustees looked elsewhere for a successor in the mid-1870's, when it came time for Stone to retire. Wharton was deeply hurt. He did not intend to accept the deanship; but in view of what he had done for the School, he did expect to be invited to consider such an appointment. Instead, Rand sent James Sullivan Amory (the trustee whose innate tact and sympathy made him throughout his period of service on the board the unofficial liaison with the faculty) to suggest that in order to save the board the embarrassment of having formally to reject Wharton's name if it was proposed, Wharton write a letter to Rand officially declining to consider accepting the deanship even should it be offered.[13] Wharton refused to do anything of the kind. The interview was a painful one for both men.[14]

---

[13] Although Wharton did not know it at the time Amory came to call, Stone and Rand had already been in touch with Gray for some months. Gray had come to Cambridge to see Stone once during the summer, had corresponded with Rand, and had already indicated his provisional willingness to accept the deanship whenever it was formally offered to him (ETS Archives: "1875-76" folder).

[14] The report of Amory's call is contained in a letter from Amory to Rand, Oct. 17, 1875 (ETS Archives: "1875-76" folder). The trustees were additionally embarrassed because they wished to offer Gray, together with the deanship, the chair of professor of homiletics which Wharton held.

But Wharton undoubtedly understood that the trustees wanted a dean who was a strong preacher, an energetic pastor, and a businessman as well as an administrator. The progressive weakening of his voice, if nothing else, would have been enough to disqualify him there; and while he was an adequate administrator—like Stone himself—he was certainly not an impassioned one. His theological position, furthermore, was now too advanced for his appointment to serve the purpose of reassuring the Evangelicals as would the appointment of a man like Gray. He therefore held no grudge. When the faculty—a little nervous over exchanging the gentle Stone for the ebullient Gray—asked the trustees before Gray's arrival for a clear ruling which in effect would restrict the dean's powers to conform to the pattern set by Stone, it was Wharton who alone stood out, quietly asserting that it would be wiser to discuss the matter openly and frankly with Gray himself.[15] But it was after this that he understandably turned with renewed interest to the law, teaching a course at Boston University, and, at the School, amazing the students by correcting proof for his legal texts "before, after, and even during class." [16] In 1881 he asked for sabbatical leave,[17] and resigned the following year without returning to Cambridge, pleading his wife's poor health.[18] There is an air of mystery about this final episode in the story of Wharton's close association with the School; for Wharton's wife, in her memoir written after her husband's death, said that it was Wharton's own poor

---

On Oct. 18, at a trustees' meeting, Wharton was accordingly formally relieved of the homiletics chair, and it was awarded to Gray. To sweeten an already sufficiently bitter dose, the treasurer, A. A. Lawrence, and Amory were made a committee "to consider whether any addition can be made to the salary of Dr. Wharton" (Trustees Minutes, Oct. 18, 1875).

[15] F. Wharton to J. S. Stone, March 27, 1876, 2 letters (ETS Archives: "1875-76" folder).

[16] Muller, *Episcopal Theological School*, p. 22.

[17] Trustees Minutes, Sept. 1, 1881.

[18] *Ibid.*, Sept. 26, 1882.

health which forced his resignation, and the letters written at that time from Europe (where the Whartons went to recuperate) bear her out. Dr. Allen came across a minute referring to this when he consulted the trustees' records twenty years later in the course of gathering material for his contemplated history of the School, and made a cryptically sympathetic comment: "1882. Dr. Wharton resigned in a pathetic letter, because it is brief and formal and so much behind it." [19]

In 1883 Wharton returned to Philadelphia, but the election of a fellow Democrat, Grover Cleveland, to the presidency in 1884 portended yet another shift. In 1885 he was appointed examiner of claims or solicitor for the Department of State in Washington. Out of this came the three volumes of the *International Law Digest*; and no sooner was that published than he undertook, on the side as it were, the editing of *The Diplomatic Correspondence of the American Revolution*. He died in 1889, only a few months before Dean Gray, proofreading indefatigably to the very last.

Throughout much of the School's history the deans and professors who taught for a longer term of years have overshadowed Wharton in the popular mind. The anecdotes lovingly retold at School dinners recaptured his quaint appearance and odd ways, but nothing more. There can be little doubt, however, that Reuben Kidner's tribute to him at the time of the Fiftieth Anniversary was just. Wharton was not only the author, with Reed, of the School's constitution and basic structure, he was also, beyond any question, its real spiritual and intellectual founder.

---

[19] ETS Archives: "Allen's Notes" folder.

⌘ 13

Peter Henry Steenstra: Valiant for Truth

THREE YOUNGER MEN were primarily responsible for elaborating the academic structure of which Wharton had laid the foundation. To it, they contributed valuable elements which were peculiarly their own. Of the three, two had been appointed at Wharton's own suggestion when the School began: Peter Henry Steenstra and Alexander Viets Griswold Allen. The third, Henry Sylvester Nash, attended the School when Wharton was still teaching, and joined the faculty the very year he resigned—partly in order to fill his place. Among them, the three men carried on most of the instruction in Old Testament, New Testament, ethics, and church history throughout most of the School's first fifty years. They also taught a great deal of theology as well—so much so that Dean Gray, with a touch of tartness in his tone, once permitted himself to wonder aloud if his own class was not perhaps an unnecessary repetition since its subject matter was already being dealt with so enthusiastically elsewhere. Because each of them spent his entire teaching career at the School (as did Kellner and Drown), it enjoyed from the outset the good fortune of having the pattern of instruc-

tion develop consistently under the same teachers year
after year—the same good fortune from which General
had profited under Samuel Turner and Bird Wilson,
Virginia under William Sparrow and Joseph Packard, and
even Gambier (in more meager fashion) under Marcus
Tullius Cicero Wing.

Steenstra the Straightforward

Of them all, Steenstra was the oldest. When the School was
founded, he was thirty-five. He served as professor of
biblical interpretation (more especially of the Old Testament) from 1867 until 1907, when he retired. He died in
1911. He was a Dutchman, born in Donjum near Franeker
in Friesland, where he lived until he was eleven; and he
never entirely lost his accent. In the year in which he
retired, one of the juniors writing home to tell his mother
about his first week at the School, described Steenstra as
"a man of ninety or a hundred years old, who says 'Godsch'
instead of God." [1] He was early exposed to hardship. One
year after his mother and father had brought Steenstra
and his two younger brothers to the United States and
settled in St. Louis, his father died; and his mother
died four years after that, leaving the three orphans to be
cared for by the strict Baptists who had taken the family
in during the father's illness. Poverty interrupted his
college career, but friendship completed it; for when his
pastor in St. Louis was made president of Shurtleff College in Illinois, he took Steenstra with him, and his young
protégé duly graduated (at twenty-five) in 1858. For a year
thereafter Steenstra did missionary work around St. Louis.
Then he met and married a young schoolteacher who had
come west from Massachusetts. Within a year they were
both on their way back to her home state, where Steenstra
had received a call to the pastorate of the Stoughton Street

[1] ETS Archives.

Baptist Church in Dorchester. In 1864 Steenstra was confirmed in the Episcopal Church, ordained, and made
rector of Grace Church, Newton. Three years later he
came to the School.

Steenstra's salient characteristic was his uncompromising honesty. It showed in his face. He had a firm mouth,
slightly drawn down at the corners, and eyes that looked
gravely out on the world from beneath straight brows that
were always faintly knit together as if Steenstra were
either concentrating on some difficult thought or else
feeling a little cross. He had his wiry hair cut close to his
head in a "no-nonsense" style; and his only concession to
the contemporary mode was a long, rather thin and
straggly chin beard. This ornament turned white long
before there was a fleck of gray anywhere else on his head,
giving him for some years the oddly youthful look of a
fledgling actor badly made up to play the part of a grandfather. In the very bad portrait of Steenstra which hung
in a dark corner of Paine Hall in the 1940's, the beard
looked as if it would come off altogether if one gave it a
stout tug.

People who met Steenstra, however, did not need to
deduce the straightforwardness of his nature simply from
his looks. He revealed it unmistakably the moment he
opened his mouth. Even in his letters he was almost
frighteningly frank. Reading those that have remained,
one is reminded of the delightful phrase which Maynard
Smith once so aptly applied to Erasmus: that no one could
look a gift horse in the mouth with a more penetrating or
more unblinking scrutiny.

The incident which best illustrates Steenstra's mono-
lithic honesty of mind was told by Bishop Lawrence. On
his way to a Matriculation Dinner one year, he discovered
that Steenstra was about to skip the dinner in order to
go home and prepare a lecture for the following morning.
When Lawrence asked him why he didn't give "last year's

lecture instead," Steenstra laconically replied, "Because I don't believe it." [2]

Professor Joseph Cullen Ayer of the class of '87, however, could testify that Steenstra's able use of the blunt reply dated even further back. At his ordination, so Steenstra once told Ayer, Bishop Eastburn, just before the service began, turned to him and said, "I must ask you a question or two, Mr. Steenstra,—purely formal, you know, purely formal—Who wrote the Pentateuch?" Steenstra, who had already begun the probing of biblical sources which was to occupy him the rest of his life, unhesitatingly replied, "I don't know." In 1864 this was tantamount to professing ignorance when asked "Who wrote Gray's *Elegy*?" Eastburn promptly drew himself up to his full height, and demanded that Steenstra explain what he meant. "That," said Steenstra, "would take more time than I have or than you would care to give!" The Bishop, for once met by an honesty as ruthless as his own, limply subsided, and the ordination proceeded without another word being said.[3]

Teaching Methods

Although Steenstra's scholarly opinions changed throughout his life, and his lectures with them, he worked out a satisfactory method of teaching early in his career and stuck to it. In 1907 he was still conducting his classes in much the same fashion which he described in a report to the Board of Visitors (who, it will be remembered, wished classes limited to recitation) in 1883:

Exegesis

The methods made use of in the Department of Exegesis may be grouped under three heads: 1. Lectures, generally delivered

---

[2] The classic locus for this oft-told tale is Lawrence, *Seventy-three Years of ETS*, p. 15.

[3] *ETS Bulletin*, July, 1931, p. 7.

slowly, so as to become dictations; 2. Recitations; 3. Essays and Disputations. The methods vary from year to year and even from day to day. The adoption of one or the other is usually determined by the nature of the subject to be studied, or by the availability or the contrary of suitable text-books. The method of essays and class-room disputations is of less frequent use than I could wish, because of the demands it makes on the students' time.

The best way to give an idea of my method, will be to describe the course of the current year.

N.T. Course

1. Lectures on the origin and genuineness of the gospels, and on the principles of textual criticism. On these subjects I lecture, not only from preference of that method, but also because of the want of available text-books that present them in the shape in which I think it best to bring them before the student.

2. Exegesis of the Gospel of St. Mark with the Junior Class, and that of St. John with the Middle and Senior Classes. Here I vary. On difficult passages, as for example, the prologue to St. John's Gospel, the conversation of the Saviour with Nicodemus, the sixth chapter of St. John, I dictate my exegesis. Elsewhere I question the student, or explain in freer conversational manner.

O.T. Course

Here I pursue essentially the same plan. This year, however, I have introduced a new feature. Instead of requiring two hours a week of O.T. study from the Senior and Middle Classes, I require only one, and give the second hour to such as choose the study voluntarily. My reason is this: experience has convinced me that Hebrew and O.T. studies, by reason of their difficultness, are for most students a mere waste of time. Few pass beyond the low mark required to pass canonical examinations. They either have not the perseverance, or they lack the ability to pursue them profitably. I felt that I could do more for the few volunteers, if the others dropped out. Thus far I am satisfied that the experiment is a good one. I am now studying select psalms with the Middle and Senior Classes as a required study, now translating and explaining myself, now calling on the class to do so; and I translate and explain the Book of Job to my volunteers. The advantage of this latter exercise is twofold: first, it imparts to the apt student one hour more insight into the character and genius of the Hebrew language and of Hebrew thought than he could get in six hours of ordinary grammar and dictionary work in his own room, however little that can be dispensed with; and secondly, it gives him some knowledge of a biblical book which it would be impossible to read at all in the ordinary recitation method, with even the highest class of students. For, after all, a course of three years, divided among the various branches of theological study, leaves but a small number of hours for each.

In conclusion, let me call attention to a prevalent and practically very influential diversity of opinion as to the work of the exegetical teacher, to which I am persuaded such criticisms of my own efforts as have from time to time reached me may be traced back. The first question which every incumbent of a chair of exegesis must ask himself is this: am I placed here to give my students a generally and necessarily superficial knowledge of the Old or New Testament (as the case may be), together with that interpretation of sundry pivotal passages or classes of passages which the doctrinal school to which I belong accepts? or, should my endeavor be to train the student to study the Bible intelligently for himself, to make him aware of principles and methods, and embue him with the spirit of patient and truth-loving research? In a word, shall I give results, or show by precept and example how to reach them? Now I am far from denying the legitimacy and expediency of the first of these methods in many cases. It is as impossible and as unnecessary that the great majority of the parish clergy of any communion should be able, scientific exegetes, as that they should be thorough and logically-thinking systematic theologians. I admit too that I have never yet had a class without one or more members for whom I felt that my method was not the best—did not render as much assistance as another might have done. Nevertheless, from the very first I have held that in my case the second answer to the above question was the right one, and have endeavored to act accordingly. I held that although this School was specially pledged to the maintenance of certain fundamental dogmatic conceptions, it was not designed to be a mere traditionary propaganda, but that its very location in this university town, where everything so powerfully tends to awaken the spirit of scientific inquiry, indicated the end to be aimed at by its instructors. I concluded that the special work of this School was not simply to prepare men for canonical examinations, but rather to cultivate the spirit and capacity of independent thought and investigation —to furnish impulses to ever-fresh inquiry, rather than convey the results of the labors of any past generation. How far I have fallen below the realization of my own ideal, no one knows half as well as myself. But it would grieve me exceedingly should I find that I have seriously misconceived the thoughts and designs of the founders, and benefactors of the School.

Respectfully submitted,

Feb. 22, 1883   P. H. Steenstra[4]

The visitors, and the juniors who found themselves exposed to the fierce winds of the higher criticism the moment they entered his class, may have thought that Steenstra was a radical; but they were mistaken. He disliked change. Looking back over their forty years of friendship, Dr. Allen said of him at the time of his retirement:

I [first] met him in 1867, calling upon him at Newton in his study. He was one of the most conservative men that I ever knew. It was like pulling teeth every step that he took. You have hardly any conception of what the steps were we were taking. In those early days we were discussing very painfully the question whether the date of the received chronology was true; whether or not the world was actually made in the year four thousand and in the spring of the year,—to

---

[4] "Reply to the Board of Visitors" (ETS Archives: "1883" folder).

be exact on March 25th, and that the evening and the morning of March 25th were the first day. It took us some time to make up our minds that the days were periods, and we were very much exercised over the question as to whether the deluge was partial or complete. Those were the questions that Dr. Steenstra also was very conservative on; and we groped painfully along through the difficulties.[5]

The Cost of Truth

Steenstra himself once observed that "people often suppose that only labor of the hands makes men sweat. But whoever would buy Truth will have to pay for it in drops of sweat. There are books—and the Bible, on hundreds of its pages, is one of them—whose contents are not to be got at without exhausting, I might truthfully say, agonizing labor." [6] One of his daughters said to him one day, "It seems so much more easy and natural to look upon the Bible as the higher critics do." She was taken quite aback when he blazed out in reply, "Easy! Do you find it easy?" [7] It was the tone as much as the words which revealed to her the depth of the struggle Steenstra had been through.

The emotional cost, indeed, of the continual battle within himself whereby intellectual honesty had to win daily victories over his natural repugnance to change and his attachment to the precepts of his Calvinistic, Baptist background was very severe, so severe that in 1884 Steenstra had a nervous breakdown. For four years he suffered from fainting fits which would come on him without warning; and the feebleness of health which afflicted him is clearly evident in his handwriting. All the attacks but one fortunately occurred in his home; but in November, 1888, he became unconscious while returning to Cambridge

---

[5] "Fortieth Anniversary Alumni Banquet, June 4, 1907," p. 34 (ETS Archives).

[6] C. M. Addison, "P. H. Steenstra—Memorial Sermon," *ETS Bulletin*, Nov., 1911, p. 9.

[7] *Ibid.*, p. 10.

from Boston on the horsecar, was arrested on a charge of drunkenness, spent the night in a Boston police cell, and was arraigned before the Municipal Court the following morning. The misery which this caused him may be imagined; but it is typical of him that in the midst of his intense humiliation his first thought was of the School, and of the way in which its reputation might suffer if the case received publicity in the newspapers. The newspapers, however, remained sympathetically silent; and Harcourt Amory, the secretary of the Board of Trustees, who had his Uncle James's tact and sensitivity, wrote to him at once to assure him of the trustees' sympathy and understanding.[8]

Bearing deep emotional scars, therefore, and yet indomitable, Steenstra was one whose pupils of later years would notice, in the words of Charles Addison, that "his eye would flash and his voice tremble as he told us the truths that had cost him so much, even as we listen to the old soldier tell the fortunes of the war he was a part of, and learn more from the voice and the eye than the accurate books of the closet historian."[9]

Professor Steenstra's Apologia

Steenstra did not publish much. He translated the Books of Judges and Ruth for Lange's *Commentary*, produced chapters on Hebrew history and literature in Wright's *History of All Nations*, and a series of lectures on *The Being of God as Trinity and Unity* which well exemplify his clear, careful, restrained style in which the banked fires only occasionally burst forth in a withering aside or passionate statement of conviction. Biblical learning, however, was developing so rapidly that by the time Steenstra

---

[8] This incident is recorded in a number of letters from Steenstra, Dean Gray, Harcourt Amory, and Steenstra's doctor written in November, 1888 (ETS Archives: "1888" folder).

[9] Addison, "Memorial Sermon," *ETS Bulletin,* Nov., 1911, p. 10.

had anything ready to be published, he usually found
that it was so out-of-date that he himself put it to one side.
And as he left so little behind him, it is appropriate that
he should be permitted to make once again—this time
in print—the *apologia pro vita sua* which he made *viva
voce* at the dinner marking his retirement in 1907. As
befitted the occasion, he was the last speaker, having been
preceded by Bishop Lawrence, Dean Hodges, Washburn,
Allen, Nash, and Mr. Kellen, one of the trustees. His
speech is printed just as it was taken down by the stenog-
rapher hired especially for the evening:

Our President has followed the old advice, "Set your best
wine before your guests first, and after they have well drunk,
bring on that which is worse." The worst is now coming.

The fact is, I have been thinking for some days as to what
to talk about on this occasion, and I have not been able to
find anything.

Soon after I was appointed to a teachership in this School,
I met with two Baptist ministers. One of them said to me, "I
am glad that you have that appointment, for now you will
get your D. D." Not that I had ever expressed a wish for the
title; but the desire for it had taken possession of his own
mind, so that the best wish he could have for me as a friend
was that I should get the natural result of my appointment to
a professorship in a Theological School. Well, the D. D. came
in time; but I knew no more after it than before.

The other was a scholar, a professor in the Newton Theological School, Dr. Hackett, a name that ought to be better
known than it is in this country; for he was one of the most
earnest, most thorough, most efficient and successful biblical
scholars that this country has ever produced. He came from
the Andover Seminary, and long before I became acquainted
with him had attained to an eminence in biblical scholarship
that entitled him to rank with the greatest professors of the
great old Andover School. I went to see him for the special
object of gaining some light on points that I was troubled on.
What those points were I will not enlarge on now. I went

with him to the School and heard him give a lecture. I went for several weeks to his lecture room, not so much because I was interested in what he was delivering, as to get a general insight into the way in which he imparted instruction.

After coming out of the lecture room, we walked about Newton Centre, and he said to me, "Now, I suppose you feel very much gratified by your appointment and anticipate a great deal of happiness." I said "Yes." "Well," said he, "You will find that it has its dark side as well as its bright." Just what he meant I did not know, and I will not guess at it to-night. It did have its dark side in my own experience, but the dark side was all outside. I do not think any really dark days ever came inside of my relations to the School. (Applause) My relations with the Faculty—always excepting our present Dean (Laughter), who is one who is fond of calling me a chronic kicker—my relations with the Faculty have been pleasant from beginning to end. My sense of obligation to the Trustees, to the early friends of the School, all of whom, or nearly all, have gone to the better land, demands gratitude for their service and reverence for their characters. I do not think it would be possible to find a set of men more worthy to be directors of a Theological School than those who were charged with that work at the beginning of this Institution. I do not think that there were ever any men who were so ready to bear burdens, to endure trouble and pain; no treasurer so ready to advance money and advance it endlessly, as was the Treasurer of this School at the outset. So that my relations with the School inside, with all its authorities, including bishops and Board of Visitors—although of the Board of Visitors we seldom see much, and I cannot say honestly that I have ever greatly missed their visits (Laughter)—all of these were pleasant. My retrospect over forty years in that respect may be compared to the memory of a calm voyage. I do not say that we have not had momentary disturbances or darkening of feelings now and then, but these things soon passed over. There was no man that ever left this School with whom at parting I did not shake hands, and who did not shake my hands with honestly friendly Christian feeling. (Applause)

My colleague of forty years standing [Dr. Allen] recently

wrote a letter, a copy of which was sent to me,—a letter for which I thank him because of the generous spirit it manifested, and its kindly tribute to my work. In that letter he said that my forty years of work here had been forty years of "singular uneventfulness." That is true. But isn't it also true that if you look for uneventfulness or eventfulness to the outside life, the same may be said of every scholar, no matter in what line of scholarship he may be engaged? The theologian who pursues a particular line of investigation, or the geologist or zoologist, all the scholars whose work does not directly address the people—all that class of men lead uneventful lives.

And yet my forty years here, looked at from the inside, have been eventful in one respect at least. During that forty years there has been a great transition in theological thought—in theological thought with respect to that which forms the basis, has furnished and still must furnish the basis of theological thinking, the Bible. This was indeed a great transition— a transition the greatness of which I believe few of us yet understand—the bearing of which upon the practical life and teaching of the Church, I believe, few of us yet comprehend. And the mediation of that transition within the limits of this School it was both my task and my privilege to conduct. It was *an event* of which I think few theological teachers have experience: an event to me, an event to my students, an event which in the very nature of the case can hardly be repeated once in a century.

When I came here I was under the still strong influence of the old theory about the Bible. What was that theory? To put it in one word, it was the idea of a book revelation. God had revealed himself to us, and that revelation was in the book, that revelation was the book, and that book had been written by infallibly inspired men.

I had difficulties with these two conceptions from the time I was twenty years old, and I had them when I came here. For thirty years I was turning over all that I could lay hands on of what had been written—in Germany, of course—on the origin of the Pentateuch. For there the battle began. Its results of course took in the whole Old Testament. Fought out there, it was fought out for the Bible as a whole.

For long years I felt that to talk of infallible inspiration was to talk of what, psychologically speaking, was an impossibility. Even almighty power cannot inspire a man infallibly unless he converts the man into a mere typewriting machine. Given a prophet, given a man, a thinking man, a feeling man, a man who looks back, a man who looks forward, a man who looks sideways—*that* man, inspired as he may be, can never be inspired infallibly.

These questions were discussed, and the analysis of the Pentateuch was carried on year after year, and resulted in book after book, and theory after theory. One thing about it: all the theories agreed that Moses did not write the Pentateuch, that the Psalms were not written by David (at least, most of them were not), and that in the historical part of the Old Testament—even in the oldest portions of it, there were a great many inaccuracies, inaccuracies not merely of science, but in history. And it was not until Wellhausen published his epoch-making book that we really got light on the subject.

You see, all this work had been something like the making of a card picture by a child, or a map cut up into forty pieces —which pieces the child tries to arrange in such a way as to give the complete, true and accurate form of the map.

It was, however, several decades before Wellhausen wrote, that the solution was suggested in the University of Strassburg by Reuss. The suggestion heard there by one of his pupils, Graf, was by him worked out afterwards, presented in various forms by several other men, and finally demonstrated to be true by its results by Wellhausen, who undertook to compare the results of the literary analysis with the historical notices both in the historical and the prophetical books of the Old Testament. That threw light over the whole. That was really the liberating book, even though Wellhausen did not originate the theory. Reuss had seen the whole thing —had in fact instigated the successful process. But no one had worked it out with such convincing power and force as Wellhausen. The moment I read his book, I had the answer and the solution of all my doubts and difficulties; and for the last twenty years I have been trying to impart what I had learned to the successive classes of this School.

And now, I want to say one more word in closing, and that is this: Do not imagine for a moment that this transition from one view of the Bible to another view necessitates a doubt or uncertainty as to Christianity. A good many people, of course, are afraid it does; but it isn't so. The more I study the history of the way in and through which God revealed himself to the Hebrew people, and through them to the world; the more I study the history which began in Ur of the Chaldees (a city, not of Babylonia, but—as I am persuaded— of North Mesopotamia), and led up and up and up until it culminated in the Christ; the more I feel that that history is its own self-sufficient guarantee. The more I study it, the more I feel that if this is not the truth, then the truth is unattainable for man. The more I study it, the more I feel that from the very beginning the inevitable outcome was in the mind of God, and (although in shadowy form) in the minds of his best representatives on earth—his prophets—the men who entered into his purposes and into his thoughts, and whom he guided by the insensible influences of his spirit. To us, at all events, the thought readily suggests itself, almost at the opening of this history, that it must end in *God becoming man*.

How is it then, you may ask, that there seems to be such diversity of opinion nowadays? Here is Dr. Crapsey, tried for denying one creed statement, and, moreover, denying another which, though it did not enter the trial, is of infinitely more importance than the Virgin Birth: to wit, the Resurrection of Christ. Here is a young man in Ohio, following in Dr. Crapsey's footsteps. Here are other doctrinally eccentric people all around. Here is a man comes to preach in the Chapel of Harvard College two or three years ago, and says to the students, "My young friends, you may be shocked at what I am going to say, but I have ceased to believe in a personal God. God is force."

How is it that men talk in that way? It is not because they know so much about the Bible, and it is not because they have made this same transition of which I have been speaking. Not at all! It is because somehow or other the materialistic spirit has diffused itself over the world in consequence of the extension of physical science and its misinterpretation by a great many retailers of science to the people. For to most of us science is represented by its onhangers rather than by its original cultivators. No doubt the physical nature of that with which science deals contributes its influence. It has become almost impossible for men to regard anything as existing except matter. It is that that has got into people. They are not under the leadership of the biblical critics; they are under the dominion of pseudo-scientists who undertake to interpret that of which they either have no real knowledge, or, if they have, interpret it as if there were nothing to be considered but matter. You and I are nothing but atoms of matter in the view of such scientists. Reduce everything to terms of matter, and your Christianity, your whole religion, in fact your very personality, falls to pieces. Your future is gone. Your God is gone. You have nothing left but force. And that is something you cannot understand, and cannot explain.

Now, I am not an enemy of science. Far from it. But just as I would oppose a theologian entering on expositions of the ethics involved in scientific facts, so I certainly feel strongly the impropriety of men whose whole lives are spent in material investigations, whose minds are attuned to such investigations and consequently dulled to metaphysical and spiritual thoughts and feelings, undertaking to instruct men in theology, or rather against theology.

What we have to do, brethren, is to *stand up for Jesus!* That hymn we sang tonight went to my soul: *"Stand up, stand up for Jesus!"* What is it that draws converts to this Christian Science, as it is called, of "Mother Eddy," who has lately stirred up a great mess here in Boston? It is not that, certainly. Nor is it the fact that somebody thinks he has had a headache relieved by this doctrine. It isn't anything of the kind. Men want to commune with God; and as Jesus said, "No man can come to the Father except through me," so man feels that in order to come to the Father he must have a mediator. In other words, he needs an Incarnate God. And it is because these Christian Scientists preach—notwithstanding their many absurdities—the Jesus of the Gospels, and bring that Jesus in direct contact with the weary and heavy-laden soul, that multitudes of simple people flock to them. Bring that Jesus with his love and his mercy to the sinful, to the downtrodden. Bring that Jesus and his words to bear on all the ills of life and on all the joys of life and on all the hopes of life, and you will get people to come back to the Church. They leave our churches because they have heard so little of that old Jesus without whom Christianity is simply not Christianity.

Do not think that I, in saying this, am throwing a side glance at Unitarianism. It is not that. I was reading the other day a sermon by Dr. Channing, on finishing which I said to myself, "Well, if I could preach like that I should like to preach for twenty years!" It was full of the Gospel of Jesus Christ. And that was the way with most of the old Unitarians. I have heard Unitarian preachers whose sermons today would be looked upon in many of our pulpits as very old-fashioned —as in fact "Evangelical," as people used to say.

We must come back to Christ—to the Gospel of Christ. Not to the Christ of metaphysics; not to the Christ of theological reasonings; but to the Man Jesus, the God-Man, who gave himself for man, and who said, "In my Father's house are many mansions. I go to prepare a place for you. I am the Way, the Truth and the Life. I go to prepare a place for you. If it were not so, I would have told you."

I hope to come back and be present at some future reunions. (Applause) But if I knew that this would be my last word, I would say, my dear brethren—my dear friends—my dear, old pupils: "Stand up for Jesus." Do not let science, do not let errant notions of the day lead you astray. You have already seen what evils result when Christ is neglected. Take his words. Make them your daily study. And bring them home to the hearts of your hearers, to the hearts of your individual parishioners, and you shall have *fruit unto life everlasting*. (Tremendous applause)[10]

Nearly thirty years before, preaching to a country congregation, Steenstra had said, "When I go forward to join

---

[10] "Fortieth Anniversay Alumni Banquet, June 4, 1907," pp. 45-53 (ETS Archives).

the glorious succession of teachers who in all ages have
instructed the Church of God, I wish to feel that I, the
lowliest of them all, who could but lisp and stammer
where the least of them spoke eloquently, had this in
common with the best and greatest, that Truth was my
theme and Truth my aim." [11] Surely he had his wish.

Steenstra's Successors

The spirit of uncompromising honesty and scrupulous
scholarship, however, did not depart with Steenstra. He
had been assisted between 1886 and 1907 by Maximilian
Kellner, first as instructor, then as assistant professor; and
Kellner served as professor of the language and literature
of the Old Testament from 1907 until his retirement (due
to a weak heart) in 1922. Kellner's chief contribution to
the School lay outside the classroom; for although he had
within him the makings of an Orientalist of ability, he
submerged the retiring scholar in the ministering friend,
leaving learned treatises unwritten in order to play an
emollient role in the daily life of the School for nearly
fifty years. (After his retirement he continued to be very
much a member of the School community until his death
in 1935.) His combination of diffident courtesy, efficiency,
and a warm interest in everything—buildings and
grounds, the Refectory, the expediting of faculty business,
or the recurring anniversaries, both happy and sad, which
punctuated individual lives—made him as valuable as
he was (or tried to make himself) unobtrusive. But in his
chosen field he was also an excellent teacher. He had not
much interest (or ability, Steenstra said) [12] for interpretation; but language and source-tracing were delights to
him, and his delight was contagious. In Hebrew he was a
superb drillmaster; and his interest in Near Eastern
archaeology enabled him to establish vividly the connec-

[11] *ETS Bulletin,* November 1911, p. 14.
[12] ETS Archives: "1894" folder.

tions between the history and religion of the Hebrew people and the ancient civilizations of Egypt, Assyria, and Babylon. Kellner was never more interesting, Dean Washburn remembered, "than when his lecture-room walls were covered with photographs of Oriental bas-reliefs, when he made it clear that Israel was one of the nations and that its history and religion were at least in large measure a product of international association. He made us see that the Hebrews were a central and not an isolated people." [13]

For eight years after Steenstra retired, the interpretation of the Old Testament was principally in the hands of Hughell E. W. Fosbroke, who was brought from Nashotah to be a lecturer in 1908, became professor of the history and religion of Israel in 1909, and remained at the School until 1916, when he resigned to become dean of the General Theological Seminary. Fosbroke, like Steenstra, had had to fight his own way through to the conclusions of the higher criticism. When Henry Sylvester Nash, in one of his prayers, spoke of "the prophet's passion for righteousness and truth," he might have been describing Fosbroke, whose lectures on the Books of the Prophets were instinct with a burning earnestness not soon forgotten.[14] His departure left a vacant place that was not filled for nearly ten years.

In 1925, Charles Lincoln Taylor, Jr., who had graduated from the School in the class of 1924, joined the faculty as a teaching fellow, became an instructor in 1930, assistant professor in 1932, professor in 1937, and dean in 1944. Until his resignation to become the first executive secretary of the American Association of Theological Schools in 1956, he *was* the Old Testament department, much as Steenstra had been between 1867 and 1886. Tay-

[13] H. B. Washburn, "Maximilian Kellner: A Memorial Sermon," *ETS Bulletin,* Apr., 1936, p. 12.
[14] H. K. Sherrill, *Among Friends,* p. 33.

lor had Kellner's contagious enthusiasm for the Hebrew
tongue, Steenstra's unbendingly forthright approach to
biblical criticism (as well as Steenstra's distrust of "ceremony"—amounting almost to physical discomfort), and
Fosbroke's deeply serious moral emphasis. In addition,
he had a gift peculiarly his own—a sensitivity to the use
of words which made him an unusually felicitous trans-
lator. The two evenings when the juniors went to the
Deanery to hear him read aloud his reconstruction of the
"Memoirs of the Court of David" (I and II Samuel) and
the Book of Jeremiah were to students in the 1940's always
among the highspots of the year. In his elective courses in
the Psalms or (in alternate years) Jeremiah, the way in
which the text sprang to life as he sensitively pared away
glosses and accretions—replacing archaisms or erroneous
translations with words of his own choosing that were
never bald or artificially contorted, but always simple,
fresh, and natural—was both illuminating and moving.
In the same way, his reading of the lessons or the prayers
in the Chapel, because of its deliberate, quiet concentration on meaning, and its disciplined economy of voice,
had unusual evocative power. His students were sometimes taken aback at what he obviously expected them
to accomplish with easy grace, such as preparing a three-
column version of Amos in which the book was pruned
to its pristine shape (with an explanatory commentary
attached) or memorizing generous portions of the Psalms
or sections of the Prayer Book. In 1948, a senior reeled
out of his oral general examination gasping, after the dean
had benevolently asked him to "give your five favorite
Collects for the Day, and recite them from memory." But
the students, even when awestruck by what he demanded
of them, always knew that he demanded more of himself.
Like his predecessors, Dean Taylor, by the unassuming
loftiness of his conception of the ministry, gave to the
men of his day a renewed sense of the sacredness of a

calling which can ennoble men who in themselves are giants neither in stature nor in spirit. By the force of his own example he demonstrated the power of a conviction expressed by Steenstra many years before:

That age and that church uniformly produce the highest results in Christian character in which faith and thought go hand in hand. The mind desires and seeks to grasp in the contents of its Christian faith, hope and experience; not primarily to convert its faith-assurance into intellectual certitude, but much rather to become more and more fully conscious of the wealth that is its own and to add to its love and gratitude the noble tribute of intelligent adoration.[15]

---

[15] P. H. Steenstra, *The Being of God as Unity and Trinity*, pp. 4, 5. The present professor of Old Testament is the Rev. Harvey H. Guthrie, Jr., who first came to the School in 1958.

✖ 14

Dr. Allen and Continuity

WHAT STEENSTRA was to the Bible, Allen was to church history.

Alexander Viets Griswold Allen, as his name suggests, was a New Englander and an Episcopalian born and bred: one of the few among the early leaders of the School of whom this could be said. His father had been a parson before him. In personality he appeared very different from Steenstra, for he was small, inclined to plumpness, quiet in manner, with a beautifully musical and soft voice, and with eyes that twinkled amiably behind rather large pince-nez; seated in a classroom he looked very much like a downy little saw-whet owl. But, like Steenstra, he had gone through deep and painful searchings of the heart in the years before he came to the School. Discovering the writings of John Stuart Mill, George Eliot, Strauss, Feuerbach, and Baur in his college days at Kenyon (where he had gone from his father's Vermont rectory just as Heman Dyer had thirty years before, because of the low tuition), he had had the Evangelical creed of his childhood shattered, and only reconstructed another, more spacious and vital one after a careful reading of Coleridge, F. W. Robertson, and J. F. D. Maurice (whose enthusiastic disciple he had become). Despite the completion of his preparation for the ministry under the impeccably orthodox guidance of Edwards Park at Andover, his Broad Church leanings were sufficiently well-known in Massachusetts to make Wharton tread warily when arranging to have him appointed to the School. ("I am going to try to get you in," he told Allen, "but I shall have to be very cautious.")

Allen the Teacher

Allen's methods of teaching were conventional. He was for some years the youngest member of the faculty (in 1867 he was only twenty-six); but he had no craving for novelty. He taught much as his elders did, and throughout his career was seldom in the forefront when revisions of the curriculum were proposed. His reading lists were constantly revised; and in the seventies and eighties it was principally through him that many of the contemporary German and English books made their first appearance in the School. But, like Steenstra, once he had arrived at a way of teaching which seemed supple enough for his purposes, he tended to stick to it regardless of the altering fashions in pedagogy. In the last years of his life a "New Curriculum" far more radical than the one brought out in 1890 was postponed almost indefinitely because Dr. Allen—like Professor Packard at Virginia—thought the old ways "good enough." Except for the use of one, principal textbook in class as a basis for discussion, a device he discarded in the late 1880's, his classes in 1907 (the year before his death) were conducted in much the manner described by him twenty-five years before:

In teaching Church History, I use a text-book which contains a condensed summary of the principal events and movements in the history of the Church. The students are assigned a portion of this hand-book, and are expected to make themselves familiar with the facts it contains, preparatory to meeting in the class-room. In the class-room it is my custom to examine the students on the portion of the text-book assigned, in order to ascertain their familiarity with its contents, and in order to impress events upon the memory by recitation. I then lecture or comment upon the events whose history we are studying in order to bring out their connection, to discover the causes which underlie them, or to give the interpretation of some fact or movement. Sometimes also it is necessary to supplement the brief statement of the text with a fuller narrative.

A knowledge of the mere facts of history apart from their interpretation would have little or no practical value. Hence I seek to induce the student to go beneath the surface and inquire the real significance of any event or movement. I do not put forth my own interpretations, *ex cathedra,* as final, but I direct the student to first sources as far as possible; I mention the more important works in which they may find a subject discussed from the various points of view, and when I give my own opinion, I give the reasons which have led me to adopt it.

My aim is to teach the students how to read history intelligently for themselves. To this end they are required to write essays which shall embody the results of their own inquiry & reflection.

The students are expected to take notes upon the lectures; & I hold periodical examinations during the year both oral and written, in which the students are examined upon the text-book and the lectures. There is also a final review at the end of the year, preliminary to the annual examination.[1]

It has been fashionable to dismiss with disapproval the nineteenth-century "recitation-and-text" method of instruction. Certainly it was feasible only with small classes; and, as Stoddard's recollections indicate, it could be boring enough when the recitations consisted in giving yet another polish to the glossy syllogisms of Pearson or Paley.

---

[1] ETS Archives: "1883" folder.

But no lecturer who has had to slog through material in order to "cover the essential points" for his class day after day can look at the notes written in the margins of the basic textbook (usually Kurtz) by Allen's students without a certain wistfulness. With the main outline of the subject established by preliminary reading and also by a few questions at the beginning of class, the remainder of the hour was free for the comments, observations, and elaborations which did not simply baldly recapitulate, but rather illuminated historical events. With the basic outline of events already before them on the printed page, furthermore, the students had no need to duplicate the narrative hastily in note-form. Instead they were free to think as they listened, jotting down only what particularly caught their interest out of the flow of what Henry Sylvester Nash aptly described not as a "lecture" or an "exposition," but "penetrating talk":

Not Evolution but Development is the right way to contemplate progress in Religion.

As the Protestant deified the Bible, and in every need finds there the oracle of God saying whatever he wishes to find, he makes it an open door to Heaven. Thus works the mind in one way. The Catholic deified the sacrament & finds there the open door. The Lutheran made both means of grace. The Anglican leaves the question open. God immanent reveals himself to all who seek. There is communion wherever there is faith.

The only confessional tolerated today is that of the pulpit.

The Church of the future must come by assimilation of all that is good from whatever source, not by wiping out the past & beginning anew, but in continuity with the old.

Principles for guiding the study of Church History in the 19th century: After the Rationalistic movement of the 18th century had run its course it became evident that a halt must be called. Niebuhr shows how this same spirit was at work in secular as in church history. The 18th century spirit asked, "Is it true?" The question of the 19th century is "What does it mean?" This is the fundamental question of Church History. What if some supposed history be proved a myth? The question remains, "What is its meaning?" Maurice too much inclined to ask "Is it true?" We must know what it means before we can say much as to its truth. Thus the 19th century proceeds in an entirely new spirit. Gieseler & Neander (both died about 1850) are types. They were pupils of Schleiermacher who had begun to work on the same lines to show that all belief, Xian as all else, has always had something to do with universal consciousness.[2]

The Indwelling God

The question "What does it mean?" was one which Allen was constantly posing—not only to his students (as he said in his report to the trustees), but also to himself. He was, in the best sense of the word, a "radical" thinker. "I am always moving, as it seems to me, underground, beneath institutions and customs and formulas of thought, and trying to get at some deeper meaning," he once wrote.[3] And the deepest meaning at which he arrived was theological through and through. In that sense Dean Gray's observation that Allen taught as much theology as church history in classes was profoundly true. What Allen once said about a colleague, Elisha Mulford, applied equally aptly to his own work:

Every position he . . . assumed may be traced back to this fundamental principle. If God indwells in the institutions of common life, then one's conception of revelation is enlarged till it is seen to be a continuous process, which knows no intermission, whose records are to be found in the whole history of humanity, of which the Bible is the eternal symbol, to the interpretation of which it furnishes the key.

[2] Notes taken by F. L. Palmer, '92, in a set of Kurtz's *Church History* (3 vol.) in 1890 (ETS Archives).
[3] Quoted in Slattery, *Allen*, p. 247.

For the same reason, the idea of the redemption of the world is relieved at once and for all, of those limitations and negations which have well nigh nullified its meanings; as for example, that Christ came only to save those known as the elect, that the sacrifice which he offered availed not for all but only for a few. Or that other misconception which has been as a ruling notion in popular theology, that he came to make a redemption possible at the end of life, in some other world and in the distant future.

The world in which God indwells, of whose life he is the constant inspiration, must be already a *redeemed* world. It is an *actual* deliverance which has been accomplished—a deliverance which means that the power of evil has been broken, that the devil and his angels, the unearthly powers of darkness, have *no* dominion, but only God alone. Hence this world becomes the theatre where God works out his revelation of himself, in the purification and elevation of the social order, lifting up humanity and drawing it into closer relations with himself. The kingdom of God is here because it is a redeemed world, capable of the highest realization of the divine. It is a world where the Glory of God is shining in the face of Jesus Christ.

The Incarnation of God in Christ thus becomes the central truth, the all inclusive truth of the divine revelation in history. For it bears witness to and it asserts the relation of the divine to the human. In Christ the human and the divine are united in one personality, showing how the human can be taken up into the Divine, how the Divine can enter the human. Henceforth we cease our attempts to draw the line where the human ceases and the divine begins. It is enough to know that they have entered into the closest relationship in Christ who becomes the central personality for the whole race. The schism and the separation between the divine and the human which marked the consciousness of the old world is overcome. The divine consciousness and the human consciousness are reconciled with each other. . . .

But the incarnation is not an idea only. It stands forth as the greatest objective fact in human history. No language could be too realistic for its narration or description. Its oc-

currence marked as distinct an epoch in history as the creation of man or his first appearance on the Earth. It was as tho'
in Christ God had entered into humanity in order to complete and crown the work of creation.

From henceforth humanity, realizing the fact of its actual
redemption, enters into a higher life—the life of the Spirit.
Mankind through Christ, who is the typical man, has been
lifted up into the mind of the Spirit of God. A continuing incarnation of Christ in humanity, or the indwelling life and
activity of God, the infinite Spirit, is that which is most real
in human history. This is the principle of the supernatural
life. The infinite spirit of God pervades and elevates humanity, bringing to it the increasing consciousness of its divine
endowment. The sense of evil, the consciousness of sin, the
fear of the divine judgments, the desire for perfection, these
are the evidences of the life of the Spirit. In this life of the
Spirit all human institutions, all human endeavors to elevate
the race, all charitable work, all ameliorating influences of
every kind, all manifestations of human sympathy, all educational influences, all scholarship and research guided by the
love of truth in whatever sphere or department of human inquiry, all genuine literature and art,—all these are the manifestations of the life of the Spirit in humanity. They are essentially religious in their aim. They are to be held as vitally
related to the Christian life. They share in the spirit of Christian worship.

And from humanity aware of its redemption, and conscious
of the indwelling life of the spirit of God, there fall away the
burdens, the harrowing depressing fears, all things contradic-
tory to the highest reason—doctrines of devils, purgatories and
intermediate states, physical conceptions of the resurrection—
all the elaborate machinery by which humanity has been separated from its Maker, God.

The Church of God now rises into all the beauty of its
original conception in the mind of Christ. It is preeminently
an institution still, with a visible order and visible sacraments,
but it drops the principle of the old exclusiveness, entering
into a necessary and harmonious relationship with all that
springs from the life of the Spirit of God in humanity. It may

still hold men in its embrace, though they think to renounce it: for they cannot escape from its witnessing power, as it stands to fulfil its divine purpose, testifying to the life of the indwelling God in nature, in humanity, in history, to the union of the Divine with the human in the Incarnation of the Son of God, to the supernatural character of the life of mankind through the presence and operation of a Holy Spirit.[4]

This *credo* explains much. It explains why Phillips Brooks was Allen's warm friend, and through him became more and more closely connected in spirit with the School as the years passed; for Brooks in Boston preached with incomparable vitality and genius the same Incarnational theology which Allen taught in Cambridge. It also explains Elisha Mulford's friendship for Allen, and his willingness to lecture at the School on religion and modern thought in the last two years of his life (he died in 1885). For this was indeed Mulford's creed, as Allen said —a creed surmised at home, worked out in Germany, and refined in conversations with Maurice in England. It had been the foundation of Mulford's first book, *The Nation,* in which he had depicted the nation as the chosen means whereby the freedom of the individual and of society is to be realized—as "not inferior in the slightest degree to the Church, so far as its divine origin, or character, or purpose, are concerned, but rather clothed with the majesty of God on earth: the realization of the redemptive purpose in history, under a political form in which Christ is the only Sovereign."[5] It had been the central theme of his second book, *The Republic of God* (whose title Allen had suggested): a massive interpretation of the Nicene Creed in the trebly-distilled phrases which, like all distillations, were sometimes as colorless as they

[4] A. V. G. Allen, "Elisha Mulford—A Memorial Sermon, Feb. 18, 1886" (MS deposited in ETS Archives).
[5] *Ibid.*

were clear, but which also contained oddly prophetic
notes—describing God in one passage as the "ground of
being," and Christ, in another, as the "man for others."
Allen's *credo* also explains his abiding fondness for Greek
theology and his almost instinctive recoil from its Latin
successor. *The Continuity of Christian Thought,* Allen's
first large-scale published work, in which he traced with
loathing the way by which the Incarnational, immanentist
principle of Greek thought had been overlaid among the
Latins by the contrary principle of "distant Deity, separate
and remote from the world," [6] not to reappear until the
modern era, was a passionate book. It had a hero: Clement
of Alexandria; it had two villains: Augustine and Calvin;
and it dismissed one thousand years of history in one
sweeping phrase: "Latin Christianity is seen as a paren-
thesis in the larger record of the life of Christendom." [7]
In it Allen laid defiantly to rest the Calvinistic bugbear of
his youth, and sang for joy at his new confidence in the
reality of God's indwelling Presence. And not Allen alone.
There is scarcely a page of the book which the modern
historian would not wish to revise radically (and Allen
himself made revisions for later editions); yet in its day
the book had very wide vogue. English bishops assigned
it to their ordinands as required reading; Randall Davidson, among others, never forgot what it had meant to him.
Westcott praised it. Harnack liked it. Even Professor
Richey at the General Seminary commended it warmly
to his classes (somewhat to Allen's astonishment). Whatever its flaws of interpretation, therefore, the *Continuity*
has remained a significant historical document, revealing
by the very heat of the banked fires of resentment that occasionally flare up within its pages, how intolerably heavy
was the pall which Calvinism cast over so much of Protes-

---

[6] Slattery, *Allen,* p. 90. Quoted from a letter to his brother.
[7] A. V. G. Allen, *The Continuity of Christian Thought: A Study of Modern Theology in the Light of Its History,* p. 438.

tant religious thought in the nineteenth century. Allen's *credo*, seen against that background, also helps to explain why students who came to Cambridge from other religious backgrounds and more conservative institutions were so enthusiastic about the atmosphere of freedom and confidence which they discovered there.

The Deeper Unity

Implicit in this attitude of trust was a capacity for broadening sympathies and a deepening respect for even the movements or men of the past which were not naturally congenial to Allen. Over the years, his attitude to Augustine, Calvin, and even Jonathan Edwards become more understanding as he perceived complexities in their thought to which he had earlier been insensitive. Like Wharton, he took delight in detecting patterns of relationships beneath the surface of institutions which connected even the most apparently disparate. This was brought out most clearly in his *Christian Institutions,* in which one of the most interesting features was his suggestion that the bishop and the monastery represent distinct phases of Christianity which have mutually acted on each other over the centuries, and that this distinction between the "secular" and the "religious" can be seen penetrating even the sphere of theology and the creeds. Allen had great interest in the restoration of Christian unity; but he had once said, "It is vain to think that lasting union or organic unity can be reached by ignoring or suppressing theological distinctions. A truer method would compel each denomination to review its origin and career in order to better the knowledge of its work and place in history, and then in the interest of the same purpose to study the history of other Churches." [8] In *Christian Institutions* he

---

[8] Slattery, *Allen,* p. 116. Quoted from an address on Christian Union delivered at Andover Theological Seminary June 17, 1887.

gave hints of the deeper unity which such a study might reveal:

The Protestant world, differing as it does in so many aspects, whether in doctrine or organization or worship, from the Mediaeval world out of which it grew, does yet retain a striking resemblance, in external appearance at least, to the Christendom which it superseded. The larger divisions of Protestantism still perpetuate the various attitudes of monasticism, so far as they were expressions of certain permanent tendencies in religion, each of which needs and seeks the shelter of institutional life, all of which together, and no one of them apart from the rest, are competent to represent the workings of the soul under the tuition of the Spirit. It was the wisdom of the papacy, and its signal service to humanity, that it recognized them all and tolerated them all,—not only the greater orders, but those seemingly countless divisions and subdivisions which we cease to follow, so minute are their ramifications, but each standing nevertheless for some one special doctrine of the faith or historic fact in the life of Christ, some single truth which the world seemed in danger of neglecting. And if a human institution like the papacy could rise to such an expanded view of the demands of the religious life, and conserve their utterance, much more can the Protestant world, always under the headship of Christ and sharing in His life, recognize this unity amid great diversity. From this point of view we may remind ourselves how the divisions of Protestantism still retain reminders of a world which they have outgrown. In the Lutheran Church may be traced the spirit of the Augustinian order, with which its origin was so clearly connected,—the reverence for Augustine and for that theology and type of piety with which his name is forever associated. The Reformed Church has points of affinity with the Dominican order,—in its wide diffusion in every land, in the importance which, like the Lutheran Church, it attaches to doctrine and to preaching, but also to organization, upon which it lays a deeper stress. The Methodist Church is almost a reproduction of the Franciscan order, and Wesley as it were the successor of Francis of Assisi, taking the world for his parish, with his ardent love of souls, differing from the Reformed Church on those points in which the Franciscan differed from the Dominican, and pre-eminently in all that relates to or flows from the doctrine of the freedom of the human will. The Church of England perpetuates more distinctly the secular church of the Middle Ages, but in its capacity as a national church has included more than one variety of monastic attitude. In the High Anglican school may be seen the reproduction of the spirit of Cluny, with its doctrine of church authority, and its love of a rich, elaborate ritual or its devotion to an imposing architecture; or, on the other hand, in the Low Church party, as it is called, we catch the tone of Bernard of Clairvaux, who regarded ritual with indifference and impressed upon the Cistercian order the sin of spending money upon the details of gorgeous rites, or the adornment of the houses for the worship of God with meaningless architectural decoration, who gave the inward experience of religion the highest place, accompanied only with the worship which is in spirit and in truth. The Congregational Church, which has been prolific in offshoots organized on the same principle of the independence of the local church, appears like a reversion to the earlier and simpler organization of the Benedictine order, when each monastery was independent and complete in itself,—an order which has rivalled, if not surpassed, the Dominican in learning and scholarship and in devotion to Christian literature. It would be impossible to enumerate them all, but the Baptist Church may be mentioned with its logical insistence upon what theories imply, with its endeavor to secure a more complete discipline and realization of all that a Protestant church involves, with its recognition in an emphatic way of the significance of the Old Testament in its relation to the New,—in this attitude there is a suggestion of one of the larger but more rigid monastic orders, the Carmelite, which claimed as its founder a great prophet of the older dispensation, Elijah upon Mount Carmel, an order whose extensive membership exhibited a devotion and enthusiasm for their monastic foundation which is not surpassed in monastic annals. And how many other lesser orders there were, who had learned the truth that God speaks to the soul in silence, and that in silent prayer and silent worship the Spirit is active, helping the infirmities of men in those groanings which cannot be uttered. If the monastic orders were one under the headship of the papacy these Protestant orders are quite as surely one under Christ, holding to the Catholic faith also, of which the essence is the God-man, a divine-human leader, Jesus the Son of the living God.[9]

In the end, as in the beginning, Allen always returned to Christ. As he wrote at the end of his little book on *Religious Progress,* in which he had been at pains to point out the weakness of some of the naive and over-confident expectations of "inevitable" progress current at the turn of the century:

Each successive revival of Church life, which has drawn inspiration by reverting to the earlier ages of Christian history, has been forcing us back to Him in whom they took their origin. How many efforts to retell the story of his life have been made in our own generation, while the conviction grows that it has not yet been told, that the "life of Christ" must always remain to be written. In this lies our hope that Christ is beginning to live in the modern Church as He has not yet lived since He first walked the earth in human form. In the power of his life, we may trust that the religious differences which now distinguish will no longer divide or separate us. Our theological differences we may still cherish as an inheritance from the past, or as so many diverse means by which differing personalities grasp and retain the central, common truth. When we discern the true value of our differences, while we shall hold them more firmly, we shall also more easily subordinate them to the higher virtue of Christian charity. In this way the unity of the Church, which has not to be anew created but which really exists already, may find what is also sorely needed, some common mode of manifestation to the world.[10]

---

[9] A. V. G. Allen, *Christian Institutions*, pp. 275-277.
[10] A. V. G. Allen, *Religious Progress*, pp. 136-137.

The "Washburn" Touch

After Dr. Allen's death in 1908, he was succeeded by Henry Bradford Washburn of the class of 1894, who had held an instructorship in 1901-02 while at the same time serving as rector of St. Mark's, Worcester (the parish from which he ultimately came to the School six years later). Washburn served as professor of church history from 1908 to 1940 (when he retired), adding the deanship to his other honors in 1920.

Dean Washburn was as obviously out of the New England mold as Dr. Allen had been: the firm mouth, the determined chin, the aquiline nose were those of Puritan worthies of centuries before. Dr. Allen always looked a little rumpled; Dean Washburn never did. That difference between them is obvious even in photographs. But in other respects no photograph could do Dean Washburn justice. As with Lincoln, there were gleams of the spirit which no camera could capture. Behind the disciplined imperturbability (which in some photographs came out almost as a frown) was a rich vein of humor and compassion, and the true Yankee's wry, chuckling appreciation of the human comedy. The voice, the meticulously articulated speech ("beyond a perrrradventchah," he used to say) crackled with vitality. Dr. Allen's way of talking was fascinatingly meandering; Dean Washburn's sentences were clear, usually short, uncomplicated in structure, with a kind of snap at the end: as bracing as water from a mountain spring.

In his approach to history, Dean Washburn played Neander to Dr. Allen's Mosheim. Where Allen's gaze had roved over centuries, absorbed by the history of ideas embodied in institutions, Dean Washburn's centered sharply, but not unkindly, on individuals. This difference between the two men became gradually accentuated as Washburn found his own footing in teaching. In 1931, he wrote:

Between fifteen and twenty years ago . . . I noticed that a change was almost unconsciously taking place in my methods of teaching. Theretofore my interest had been in events, in movements, in institutions, in doctrines. Thereafter it shifted gradually to a curiosity about the man or the men in whose life the event had taken place, or whose energy had brought the event to pass, to a desire to know those whose inspiration and enthusiasm had brought the institution into existence, and whose contagious conviction had given it momentum. I found myself forgetting Christianity and thinking about Christ; not caring whether the fifteenth chapter of First Corinthians formed an unassailable argument for immortality, but asking myself what it meant to St. Paul. . . . And passing in such a way from the impersonal to the personal, I found myself giving my classes the alternative of reading general Church histories or reading religious biography. Fully persuaded that religious experience is the stuff out of which institutions and doctrines are made, that the experience is eternal while the expression of it is temporal, I have given it the first place in the students' lives and in my own, and in consequence, for me at least, the study of the dead past has become a very vital and contemporary affair.[11]

The effect of this method, both on the dean and on the students in his classes, was to broaden their sympathies in ways that they would hardly have predicted. They discovered that their own comprehension of religion had been widened and deepened—in particular, by the careful study of men with whom they had, or thought they had, no taste or opinion in common. In this they duplicated the experience of Allen a generation before. The students were sometimes amused to hear so forthright a Protestant as Dean Washburn expatiate on the virtues of Hildebrand, Ignatius Loyola, or Pius IX, but they were also impressed. They caught a glimpse of the insight which had been so vividly demonstrated earlier in the School's history in the

---

[11] H. B. Washburn, *Men of Conviction*, pp. 1-2.

teaching both of Wharton and Allen: the insight that the
convictions of men of the past (no matter how antique
their dress) were still vital and present in the world, the
convictions of Athanasius fully as much as those of Pio
Nono. Dean Washburn once said that even to men immersed in contemporary problems, turning to history
brought help: "First, because looking back gives one a
long-range view of any problem, and, second, because
dealing with a matter historically frees one from slavery to
the present." [12] And in biography, he went on, "the lives
of men reveal the motives of conduct more sensitively than
such motives may be found in dates and events and
achievements." [13] True to his own method, when he became interested in the divorce between "philanthropy"
and "religion" which was becoming increasingly obvious
in the 1920's (for example, in the consciously articulated
motives of those engaged in medicine, nursing, or social
work), he studied the problem in and through the lives
of men of the past: Samuel Barnett of Whitechapel, St.
Vincent de Paul, Francis of Assisi, and Jesus himself.
From them he got his compass bearings.

Muller the Meticulous

In 1914, James Arthur Muller of the class of 1910 was
called as instructor to assist Professor Washburn. After an
interlude spent in China, Muller returned in 1923 to become professor of church history and lecturer in liturgics,
the post which he held until his death in 1945.

Of Swiss ancestry, Muller was a professionally trained
historian before he entered the ministry, competent in
political and social, as well as ecclesiastical, history. Indefatigable orderliness was characteristic of his work and
of his life. A keenly humorous (as well as charitable) ap-

[12] H. B. Washburn, *The Religious Motive in Philanthropy: Studies in
Biography*, p. 8.
[13] *Ibid.*

preciation of quirks of inconsistency in others did not
deter him from remaining inflexibly faithful to the standards which he had set for himself. It was he who first
put in order the jumble of papers which constituted the
School archives. It was he who went down into the cellars
of Mission House and discovered for himself the forgotten, dust-covered parcels of letters from the missionary-
bishop Shereschewsky after members of the staff had assured him that no such documents existed. And he was no
less exact in other spheres. No matter how often or how
late at night cars drove the wrong way down St. John's
Road past the Muller residence, an upstairs window
would shoot open, and the professor would be heard vehemently reminding the driver in his unmistakable piccolo
tones that St. John's Road was a one-way street. Students
who cut matters close by delivering course papers to his
house just before midnight on the evening of the day
when they were due were disconcerted to feel the other
end of the essay paper firmly grasped and drawn from
their fingers as they poked it through the letter slot in
Professor Muller's front door. The Professor had come
downstairs in his pajamas to wait out the last five minutes
before midnight in his vestibule to make sure that no one
was unjustly classed among the lucklessly tardy, whose
papers would be gathered up from the vestibule floor the
next morning.

Church history in Dr. Allen's and Dean Washburn's
classes always had an homiletical twist. Under Professor
Muller, however, the tone changed. Like other contemporary historians, Muller was far more conscious than
earlier historians had been of the easy inaccuracies which
can distort the most conscientious reconstruction of past
events. He was consequently so leery of the interpretation
which, unbeknownst to the reader, falsifies even as it attempts to explain, that he eschewed virtually any attempt
to interpret at all. Not for him the large and cloudy can-

vas on the grand scale which had been Dr. Allen's favored
medium, nor the impressionistic "conversation pieces" in
which Dean Washburn had excelled. He made it his responsibility to set forth the historical narrative with as
much care and accuracy as he could muster (and that was a
great deal); but he left all interpretation strictly to his
listeners and readers. In portraiture his choice of detail
was deft, making his subjects come to life: Stephen Gardiner, Trudeau, Philander Chase, Schereschewsky, or the
trustees and faculty of the Episcopal Theological School.
In each instance, however, he scrupulously let them speak
for themselves, even to the extent of preserving crabbed
idiosyncrasies of spelling, punctuation, or syntax, rather
than run the risk of so distorting the original by the in-
trusion of words of his own that a future age might discover in each portrait only James Arthur Muller in different varieties of fancy dress. He exemplified modern historical scholarship at its most thorough, assiduous, cautious, and untiring. And he taught his students to be like
him. It was in keeping with his nature that when he discovered that he was suffering from incurable cancer, he
neither attempted to conceal the extent of his illness nor
permitted it to take on dramatic overtones. Sandwiching
seminars and tutorials in between bouts of fever as long
as he could, he continued to be courageously matter of
fact about his condition, frank, and wryly humorous to
the end.[14]

[14] Professor Muller was succeeded by the Rev. Massey H. Shepherd, Jr.,
who had first joined the faculty in 1940. When Dr. Shepherd resigned in
1954 to accept a professorship at the Church Divinity School of the
Pacific, his place was taken by Professor Raymond W. Albright, who had
first come to the School as a visiting lecturer in 1951, and become a
permanent member of the faculty in 1952. Dr. Albright, who recalled
Professor Muller in his unfailing helpfulness to his students, his meticulous attention to scholarly accuracy, and the courage with which he
faced illness, died of cancer in 1965. The present church history department consists of the Rev. Professor Lloyd George Patterson, Jr., Prof.
Larry Lee Bothell, and the Rev. John Robert Wright. Dr. Patterson first
became a member of the faculty in 1958, Mr. Bothell in 1965, Dr. Wright
in 1966.

✻ 15

The Influence of
Henry Sylvester Nash

THE LINE OF DESCENT in church history—Allen, Washburn, Muller—is easy to draw; and so is the line in Old Testament. The line in New Testament and ethics is more complicated. Over the years it has looped and twisted like a wisteria vine, connecting not only Christian ethics and New Testament, but also theology (in which Stone and Gray, although they were the first professors, did not have a decisive or enduring influence), and the ever-proliferating subjects once casually lumped together under the heading of pastoralia. Where the line begins, however, is easy to discover. It begins with Henry Sylvester Nash. He ranks with Steenstra, Allen, and Wharton as one of the major spiritual and intellectual influences which determined the direction of the School's development and gave it its peculiar character.

The Face of Dr. Nash

Nash is one of the most interesting figures in the School's history, and it is probable that his personal influence has been more persistent in its effect upon successive generations of students than that of any other of his contemporaries. Steenstra, Wharton, even Allen have become in the last thirty years little more than bare names with perhaps one or two amusing stories attached. But at least until ten years ago this was not true of Nash. Although he died in 1912, and his books, with the exception of *The Atoning Life,* have long been out of print, his spirit has continued to live in the School for which he sacrificed so much—financial ease, a wider audience, a wider reputation. Periodically a student will find his interest caught by something about Nash's face as it is depicted in the portrait of him painted for the School in 1907, will be impelled to find out the name of the subject, search out his books and read them, and discover that a profound spiritual influence has been introduced into his life to mold and shape it in unforeseen ways.

The face itself was anything but conventionally handsome. Seen from the front, with his dark hair parted in the middle and curling down over his ears to fall in a fringe over the edge of his collar behind, Nash looked like a homelier version of Sir Henry Irving, the actor (and Irving himself was homely enough). In profile, his face bore a striking resemblance (as the students once pointed out in a Christmas play) to that of the mummified Rameses II: the same overshot jaw and long, receding, pointed chin; the same large nose and ears, the same scrawny neck, the same deep eye-sockets, with the brows sweeping away from the nose in a curving, lifting line. As in the desiccated face of the Egyptian Pharaoh, furthermore, one could detect in Nash's features a hint of fires within: pride, ambition, imperious intellect, a hot temper, and an indomitable will. But there the resemblance ended. In Nash passion had been consecrated to the service of Christ. His was a spirit of intense personal devotion to Christ, fervent patriotism, and deep and abiding concern for social justice. Because of his frail constitution and delicate health, the veil of flesh seemed to have worn thin to a point of translucence, so that the spirit shone through with unusual brightness and power. It could transform his homeliness into beauty even as people watched in amazement. Sometimes it made him seem almost incandescent.

Nash's passionate devotion to Christ, to his country, and to social justice had poignant roots in his own past, for he had been forced to learn the "cost of discipleship" early. In 1862, when he was eight years old, his father, Francis Nash, rector of a Kentucky parish, out of loyalty to his religious and political convictions took steps to free two slaves who had been given to his wife some years before by her father as a wedding present. His parishioners, who were more sympathetic with the Confederacy than with the Union, were so enraged by this action that they drove the Nashes out of town, forcing them to flee for their lives across the river into Illinois. There the Nashes eventually found refuge on a shabby, untenanted farm; but it was too late to sow a crop, and in the ensuing winter the family almost starved to death. Thereafter, wherever Francis Nash went in his ministry—Illinois, Nebraska, Iowa—grinding poverty was the family's constant companion. As a result of this bitter experience, Henry Nash acquired a prejudice against the rich and comfortable which it took all his powers of sympathy and reason to subdue in later life. It was a wound that was scarred over, but always sensitive to the touch.[1]

Resolved to enter Harvard, Nash came to Cambridge from his home in Iowa in June, 1875. Discovering that Latin was among the subjects required, and that his country schooling had placed him behind in other subjects as well, he took a freshman reading list and books to the Vermont farm where his aunts lived. There, perched day after day in the crotch of an apple tree in the orchard, he caught up on the required subjects, taught himself

---

[1] This story, which Henry Sylvester Nash told his children in later life, I owe to the kindness of Mrs. Norman B. Nash.

Latin from scratch, and returned to Harvard in September to take examinations which propelled him not only into Harvard, but into the sophomore class.[2] He graduated in 1878, entered ETS, and graduated from the School in 1881. He carried on the entire work of the middler year *in absentia*, while teaching at De Veaux College, Niagara, in order to earn desperately needed money. He was brought back to the School as an instructor in 1882, made a full professor a year later (at twenty-nine), and taught at the School until he died in 1912. In 1907, looking back over the years, Dr. Allen said that Nash was the most brilliant man who had ever studied at the School.

In the Classroom

Nash's method of teaching was all his own. He lectured at breakneck speed, flipping over the pages of a notebook or pile of cards rapidly as he spoke. Only students who knew shorthand could take down the body of what he said (some learned shorthand especially in order to be able to). This was the opposite of Steenstra or Kellner, who dictated even the punctuation marks. In the classroom he wore what suited him at the moment, heedful of comfort more than of convention. In good weather (and good health) he might appear on the lecture platform garbed with appropriate solemnity in a frock coat, to speak with the supple voice and telling gestures of the Irving he closely resembled. In bad weather (and bad health—in winter he had one cold after another) he would sit on one of the radiators, swathed to the eyebrows in heavy coat and muffler, sometimes even keeping his hat on for warmth, and lecture from there.[3]

The outline of his courses in the Calendar had characteristic personal touches: "The development of Christology—Our Lord in the minds of his chosen; The Synop-

---

[2] The details in this story also were furnished by Mrs. Nash.
[3] Remembered by William E. Gardner of the class of 1898.

tic Gospels—Our Lord in His thought concerning Himself and His Kingdom; Exegesis of the Epistle to the Romans—Pauline doctrine of Justification by Faith as the foundation of genuine Ethics; Exegesis of the Gospel of St. John—The Apostolic thought about our Lord and our Lord's thought about Himself in unison." [4] This form of announcement, with its touch of Evangelical piety, was pedagogically wise. It gave the central theme of the course, as well as its overall subject, at the outset; and it was a testimony to the reality of Nash's own faith which might reassure the junior plunged by Nash's unrelenting scholarship into the midst of "the Critical Problem." For in academic realms Nash expected the best. Charles Slattery, whom both faculty and trustees would have liked to make dean of the School after the death of Dean Hodges, said of his training under Nash:

He was accustomed to have men under him who came with thorough university training. He therefore assumed capacity and willingness to work hard. When I was his pupil, he spent the first year in a rapid reading of the Greek Testament, with introductions to the various books, and special consideration of the Synoptic problem and the sources of the Life of Christ; the second year, we worked over the Epistle to the Romans in minute detail; the third year was devoted to the Fourth Gospel. I remember how in the first year he threw us up against the most difficult critical questions of the age. We wrote nine theses that first year. The first was on the Tübingen Hypothesis—of which till then none of us had ever heard. We then wrote a thesis upon a reading of the New Testament to find every reference and allusion to the Parousia: these references and allusions we tabulated and arranged, that he might have, from first-hand knowledge, the New Testament doctrine. He commanded us to read many "Lives" of Christ—which he designated—and required us to relate in a thesis the point of view and method of each. Some men were frightened

---

[4] *ETS Catalogue,* 1890-91.

by the robustness of his attack. His was no Sunday-school course, shielding our faith. We were given the supreme documents of Christianity and we were set to find their meaning and their truth. If they were filled with hard questions which might later unsettle our faith, we were forced to face the issue at once, while we were yet only candidates for the Ministry. Dr. Nash treated us on the first day of his course as grown men who must know all.

It is only fair to say, however, that in meeting whatever difficulties there were, we had the superb help of Dr. Nash's own faith. He never dodged the perplexities. Some critical questions he felt to be settled. Others he held in solution. Still others he believed insoluble in this world. Once when a pupil asked him what St. Paul meant by a certain phrase, he said with a reverence which was from the heart, "I don't know: that is one of the questions I mean to ask St. Paul when I see him." Nash was at his height in his exposition of the Epistle to the Romans. He struggled to give us all that the commentators in the past had thought of this passage and that; then, with this historic interpretation fused with his own best thought, he gave us his interpretation; and beyond that, he gave us the profound expression of his own faith.[5]

Nash the Prophet

It is obvious even from Nash's brief descriptions of the themes of his various courses that he carried into his New Testament classroom his great interest in theology and ethics. Outside the classroom it had free rein. Like Allen and Wharton, Nash let his mind range widely over history, literature, philosophy, and law (he was especially fond of dipping into Thayer's *Case Book on Constitutional Law*).[6] His mind, like theirs, probed beneath the surface of things to discover patterns that unite the ages. The fruits of this appeared even in the book which, on the surface,

[5] Charles L. Slattery, *Certain American Faces*, pp. 86-89.
[6] Q. M. Wilder, "Henry Sylvester Nash" (ETS Senior Thesis, May 1, 1942).

might appear no more than a chronological treatment of the development of his own special field, *The History of the Higher Criticism*; but they provide both the basic framework and the illustrative ornament of his other books, *Ethics and Revelation, The Genesis of the Social Conscience,* and *The Atoning Life.*

Nash's contemporaries found his books difficult. They said that his style was obscure. But his style, while individual, is not in the least obscure. Nash wrote in short, clear, often epigrammatic sentences. The trouble lay with his thought itself, and with what it presupposed. Nash, like Elisha Mulford, subjected his ideas to a long process of refining before he set them down on paper; and when he finally did so, he would express as it were the perfected thought, but with little reference to the intermediate stages through which it had passed, and almost no mention at all of the informational material which had nourished it on its way. He left that for his readers to supply for themselves out of their own reading and personal experience. No doubt the finished book would have swollen to unwieldy proportions had he done otherwise. But few readers had a store of knowledge like Nash's on which to draw. Furthermore, so much experience and learning and thought had gone into each sentence, that it was, in a sense, under pressure. Even now some of Nash's sentences look to the awestruck reader as if they might easily spring open at a touch and disgorge an entire library. As a result, the books do not provide material for an hour of easy diversion or effortless instruction. Instead, they offer what may serve as the subject of meditation for a lifetime. For Nash was a prophet. In the conditions of his own day he discerned forces at work which have since created the massive problems that beset the modern world. He probed the foundations of the faith which makes attack on these problems possible. In the McKinley era it may have sounded a little odd; but today it makes him read like a contemporary.

In 1899 Nash told a Philadelphia audience:

. . . It is plain that our experience is soon to reach, if it has not already reached, a point where we must lay anew the foundations of the conviction that universal history has a moral end. When we reflect that humanity is rapidly acquiring for the first time a single nervous organism, so that the things which happened yesterday in the remotest quarters of the globe are forced upon our attention to-day; when we consider how the mental map, upon which the average man follows the objects that interest him, has broadened, and when we think of the way in which comparative study is making more or less real to us the things that are or have been real to every branch of our race,—we may say, without conceit, that the extent of experience within the reach of the average man of former days, when put beside the experience possible to the same man in our own time, looks provincial.

But it is not only in point of extent that the experience open to a fairly educated mind is much greater to-day than ever before. Its potential depth and intensity also is greater. Psychology is furnishing the individual with the materials of a completer self-knowledge. Sociology is doing a similar work for society. The organized common consciousness of humanity is beginning to know itself to a degree far beyond the social self-knowledge attained by our forefathers. So, on the one hand, the area of human life that comes within the horizon of average intelligence is broader, and, on the other, knowledge of the facts of our social being and the condition of social well-being is deeper. Therefore history, the recorded experience of the race, as interpreted in the light of our own experience, presses upon our knowledge and our conscience with increasing force. The supreme question for every man and woman of our time who would achieve deep thought and a commanding purpose, the question of the Sphinx, which we must answer if we would not be devoured, is, How must I

interpret the universe, if I am to take history, not as a drama
that has the irony of the universe behind it, but as a real
drama into which the heart of the universe puts itself? How
shall I conceive history to have a moral end? [7]

Nash's prediction was that the effect of the expansion of
the individual's world through the increasing information
pressed upon him would be, not faith, but doubt. Doubt,
he felt, was seldom a purely mental process. He once said:

The bulk of it is due to practical causes. The believer's world
becomes too large for his old convictions. The fixed, clear
lines of belief waver and shift and threaten to disappear.
Dogmatic precision, with its beauty and restfulness, becomes
impossible. Traditional forms of opinion break down. Under
the growing pressure of an increasing body of raw mental
material it is increasingly difficult to correlate the new with
the old. "Experience, like a flood, soaks all-effacing in." [8]

Practical skepticism of this kind cuts the nerve of social action; and in the America of the turn of the century
Nash saw a danger of this: "Our Democracy is entering on
a new phase. Before the war it was a country Democracy.
Now it is becoming more and more a city Democracy.
And this change is closely connected with other changes,
both political and economic. It is far harder to be a thinking believer in Democratic ideals than it was fifty years
ago." [9]

Infected by such skepticism, purposes can be weakened,
and ideals wither unless the roots of faith, which experience has proved to be shallow, are driven deeper. To survive, indeed, faith must go down to the bedrock conviction which was the center of the thought of Hooker and
Coleridge and Maurice, and which—in non-Christian dis-

---

[7] H. S. Nash, *Ethics and Revelation*, pp. 1-3.

[8] H. S. Nash, "The Belief in Democracy and Justification by Faith" in
Slocum Lectures 1903-1904, pp. 80-81.

[9] *Ibid.*, p. 82.

guise—can be the basic assumption of others as well. As Nash said, widening experience must find its center, and achieve unity and coherence, through the revelation of the living unity of God: "John Stuart Mill, when hard pressed by the demands of his own thorough reason, confessed that by his belief in the unity of Nature he meant to publish his conviction that, no matter how great the difficulties and problems besetting and besieging his mind, there is an inherent connection in things which makes it impossible for the honest intelligence to be brought to permanent confusion." [10]

This was the faith which Habakkuk proclaimed, and which enabled him to face the political corruption and moral decadence of Israel in his day honestly, but without despair; for driven deep into himself, "so deep that the knowledge of self becomes the knowledge of God," [11] God revealed himself to Habakkuk in the integrity of his redeeming and creative purpose, giving him an indestructible conviction that his great ideal could not be reduced to "permanent moral confusion." [12]

"Justified by His Faith"

It was in this aspect of his thought that Nash re-expressed in fresh terms the old doctrine of Justification by Faith which had been so emphasized by the Evangelicals—and, indeed, written into the heart of the School's charter. Tracing the development of faith from Habakkuk's day to St. Paul, he asserted that the new element which Paul introduced, drawn partly from his experience within the Roman Empire which, with its world-trade and world-politics and world-sympathy, paralleled the modern world, was the vision of social unity. "Above the horizon came the true society where all men were one." [13]

---

[10] *Ibid.*
[11] *Ibid.*, p. 83.
[12] *Ibid.*
[13] *Ibid.*, p. 86.

The unity of man, social unity, is the supreme mystery. Here
. . . we are dealing with something which, if we handle it
as a phrase, is an easy-going commonplace. Take it, however,
as a reality, and it becomes a supreme difficulty. Put your
Democratic ideal in New York. Do you really believe that it
can be realized? That so vast and heterogeneous a mass of
humanity, so huge a body of alien or indifferent or hostile
interests can be lifted to the level of the true society, where
the interest of each is the aim of all, and where the rich man's
privilege is the best insurance of the poor man's right? Social
unity as a glib phrase, mouthed over by men of loose though
well-meaning tongue, that is an easy thing. But real social
unity,—that is a monstrously hard thing to believe in.[14]

To believe in an ideal so far above the actuality requires
an act of faith:

Faith has multitudinous forms. The essence of them all is the
outreaching will in our breasts that lifts us above things as
they are, to endue us with the authority and power to make
them as they ought to be. Now our forefathers have taught
us to call the ultimate form of the ideal and the ultimate form
of authority by the name of "God." By "God" we mean the
meeting place where the deepest being of things, and the
final purpose of things come together, blend and fuse into an
irresistible object of interest and trust. And this God, so the
Christ teaches us, is not a being who is pent up within his own
infinitude. He could not be himself, unless he went forth from
himself. He is a supreme mental and moral force invading
history and pervading consciousness. And by faith we reach up
to Him, make ourselves one with Him. . . . And by faith
alone can we be saved from fear, from dread, from cowardice
and vanity, from the kind of doubt that does not inspire but
undoes us, from that unbelief in ourselves, in our nation and
our race, which eats into and destroys the very foundations of
society.[15]

---

[14] *Ibid.*, pp. 87-88.
[15] *Ibid.*, p. 89.

We must, that is, be justified by faith:

To be justified by faith in God means to have one's self-respect grounded as deep as His nature, given a base as broad as His being. It means the attainment of a self-respect so fine and strong and high that our petty achievements of riches and culture and fame cannot make us proud, while all our failures and incompetences cannot dishearten us. And when once we are clothed with a self-respect like that, respect for ourselves and reverence for others become inseparable things. . . . To the man or woman intent on perfect righteousness, or entire justice, there is a double abyss confronting the conscience. In our own hearts is the abyss of personal vulgarity, and selfishness and sin. The gulf between what I am and what I long to be is so deep and broad that many and many a time it seems to me that all the powers of God and man together cannot bridge it. And there is a gulf in the heart of society. How terrible it is! Live in the slums. Come to know the awful mass of fallen womanhood, of brutal manhood which our great cities house. Or, not going so far from home as that, realize what business and politics are doing all around you. . . . Then how shall you bridge these two abysses? How lay the foundations of your respect for yourself, your reverence for mankind, so deep and broad that no power on earth can shake it? The answer is justification by faith, faith in God, faith in God's faith in us. This, allowing for inevitable changes in the meanings of words, is what Paul means by his great proposition.[16]

And what of the man who has been "justified by faith"? He becomes, in Nash's phrase, a "strenuous idealist."[17] The redeemed man, because of the ideal rising up in his heart, cannot help but be a "merciless critic of social reality" as well as a merciless critic of his own sins. But he is not simply a critic. Taking Christ as "God's pledge of the unity between the ideal and the real," [18] the expression of

---

[16] *Ibid.*, pp. 91-92.
[17] Nash, *Ethics and Revelation*, p. 261.
[18] *Ibid.*, pp. 263-264.

the creative goodness of God, he becomes himself creatively good. "He finds in Christ the equipment for citizenship in the Free State. He recognizes his political and social relations as sacred." [19] "He is not an atom. Strip him of his connections with his fellows and he is nothing. He must be at home in relationships with an ever-growing number of persons of all sorts and conditions. He must carry the campaign against caste into larger issues. He must face all that is disagreeable and problematic in Democracy, concealing nothing, blinking nothing away." [20]

The Church and the Free State

The Church, in this modern world, "wins new knowledge of herself." [21]

She is the body of Christ, the body of those who have, through trust, laid hold on the creative goodness, who have opened themselves, by a great act of faith and admiration, to the infinite missionary energy of God. She is the society of those who seek a perfect self-knowledge, a perfect self-masterhood. She is the community of those whose creed permits them to acknowledge no good as true good, unless it be eternal good, good that belongs by right to all. Those who seek self-knowledge and self-mastery through her fellowship and sacraments and Word are well assured that, only by imparting themselves to the disinherited and the lowly, can they truly possess themselves in the eternal. They are sure, unless their creed is a plaything, that the central reality of life is the being and beauty of God as they are offered through Christ to all mankind. They themselves, through appropriation of the divine being and beauty, have been delivered from the tyranny of fad and fashion and fate. They are now in league one with

---

[19] *Ibid.*

[20] H. S. Nash, *Genesis of the Social Conscience: The Relation between the Establishment of Christianity in Europe and the Social Question*, p. 304.

[21] Nash, *Ethics and Revelation*, p. 264.

another, and all with God, to impart the selfsame being and
beauty to every child of man, and to bring to the shores of
light the human capacities now hidden in darkness. Unless,
then, they lack the courage to draw a straight conclusion from
simple premises, they must know that the Church is to test
and approve herself by her power to tutor and train a social
conscience that shall steadily put the commonwealth to shame,
so long as some of its members have no inheritance to dwell
in.[22]

.   .   .   .

The supreme, coordinating fact in this new world is the
Free State. The deepest concern of that State, when it once
clearly understands its place and calling in history, is for the
underprivileged and the lowly. The State is now a spiritual
organism, having justice for its inspiration, and the widest
spread of individuality for its good. The Free State of antiquity was content on the whole to insure the well-being of
its existing citizens. But the Free State of modernity must
create citizens, and extend the full privileges of citizenhood.
It is a spiritual organism, manifesting its spirituality in many
ways, but notably in its tightening hold on the means and
methods of education. Within the Free State, the layman's
world has risen to the level of a full suffrage in spiritual
affairs. To minister to that world, giving its views of good
coherence and lasting vitality, is the function of the modern
Church.[23]

.   .   .   .

The framework of history will not easily be changed. The
brute, the satyr, the man who sells his fellow-men for a pair
of shoes, the woman who spends her soul in building ignoble
aristocracies,—these folk will not soon perish from the earth.
Yet this does not daunt the prophet, the freeman, who has
learned to walk in the ways of the Great Companion. The
springs of his interest and reverence lie deep down in his own
nature and in God's being, so deep that no army of hostile
circumstances, besieging his will, can stop their flow. He does
not daydream or deceive himself, when he prophesies of a

---

[22] *Ibid.*, pp. 264-265.
[23] *Ibid.*, p. 269.

time when man's whole being shall be at the call of his highest purpose, and when every detail of human life shall be pregnant with meaning and rich with worth. The sincerity of the universe, the unity of God, the beauty of Christ, teach him that the eternal being and good believe in him. He believes in that belief, and so is saved, enabled to believe in himself. Out of his own nature is given to him the hope that he may become a man of attentive reason and impassioned prayer, with a conscience possessing both the gentleness and the severity of God, toiling gladly to make the earth a fit place for babes to draw their first breath in, and a gladsome place for old folk to look their last upon, making his own life a part of the joyous and refreshing story of the Son of God, who, by living amongst us and dying for us, hath given a new heart and an eternal hope to our race.[24]

The Atoning Life

The cost of such a life would not be light, and Nash knew it. He could see in the frailty of his own body, permanently damaged by the semi-starvation suffered in the Illinois backwoods, part of the price exacted; for his bodily weakness stemmed directly from the disaster which had overtaken the Nash family when his father, in the simple and conscientious performance of his duty, had done no more than give two harmless human beings their freedom. But as he grew older he had learned as well of a different kind of cost: the cost of forgiveness. It seems probable that, proud and sensitive as he was, he realized at some point that he must sacrifice either his love for Christ or his memory of wrongs and injuries done him—justifiably bitter though the memory might be. More than that: he realized that he must forgive those who had wronged him in order to restore a relationship broken by injury, and thereby keep alive the spiritual bond out of which alone healing and redemption could come. To acquiesce in in-

---

[24] *Ibid.*, pp. 276-277.

jury by refusing to take the initiative in forgiveness would be ultimately to shrivel his own spirit and to betray his Lord. It must have been out of self-knowledge as simple and honest as this, that he gained the insight which he embroidered upon in his last book, *The Atoning Life*:

Fellowship, when we enter into it with our whole being, both reveals and conceals the Atonement. Conceals it, because the atoning life that makes good the breaches in the Moral Law works silently, in the deep of life; it is never heard in the streets. Reveals it, because whenever we get down to the foundations of fellowship, we find the fact of the Atonement, the divine and human necessity of it. If we discard for a while all specific theories about the Atonement; and if, going farther in our desire to keep inside our actual knowledge, we even disuse for a time the specific term "atonement" and substitute a general phrase, then our best experience goes into the conviction that the atoning life lies at the roots of good society.

My friend and I—if I sin against him, what shall he do? Stand on his dignity? Shut himself up within his innocence? Nurse his wound until it festers? Leave me to myself to find out my fault in all its grievousness and then come to him confessing my sin? Imprisoned within his goodness, he makes himself an egotist, caring more for his hurts than for the majesty of the Moral Law which shines forth so clearly in friendship. If he stays long within his self-made prison, his goodness will become the goodness of a prig. But he dare not shut himself within his consciousness of innocence. Only by taking the shame of my sin as his own, by gladly bearing the pain it gives him, can he be true to himself. In healing silence he makes atonement to the ideal of friendship in his heart, makes atonement for my sin, and so makes good my breach in the Moral Law.

What shall the father do when his boy transgresses? Let his fatherhood be what it ought to be, the finest form of comradeship? In the fullest sense he lives his life within his boy's life. He uses his vantage-ground of years and experience, not as a judgment-seat on some little Sinai from which to thunder at his boy, but as an interpreter who seeks to lead the boy into clear self-knowledge and self-mastery. With the uttermost reverence he treats his boy's right to be himself. And in proportion to his reverence is his intimacy. The mystery of intimacy is not for those who dominate others, but for those who treat others as their peers. The father, true comrade to his boy, ruling him by reverence and through interpretation of life,—when his boy grievously transgresses, what shall he do? He makes the shame of the sin his own. His grief over it is keener than his boy's can possibly be, because he knows far more of the forces of evil. He knows how sin breeds sin. Looking into the depths of Satan in society and in his own heart, his boy's transgression racks him with pain. But he does not substitute a sermon for sympathy. He takes the shame of the sin as his own shame. He makes atonement for his Son to the Law whose seat is within his will. . . .[25]

.   .   .   .

The Atonement is the price paid by God and man for the right to forgive. . . . It is not an arbitrary action hanging upon His sovereign and inscrutable will. It is an eternal process of His nature. . . . The atoning life of God is an organic process within His creative unity. When we put the question in the right way, the answer to it is as inevitable as the laws of nature. God's place of self-revelation is in the depth of the common life and lot, its glorifying wants and ennobling hopes. Here He speaks His saving words. Standing in this place, the thoughts of the Apostles become our personal thoughts. "God was in Christ, reconciling the world unto Himself, and not imputing their trespasses unto them: and hath committed unto us the word of reconciliation." Without any connection with our merits and deserts God exhibited in our midst the life and death of Christ as a place of atonement, a meeting-place between God and man. Hither comes the sinful, wandering, will of man, doubting human perfection, despairing about the supreme hope. And here in Christ man sees his will taken up into the mystery and unity of the divine will. He appropriates as his own the words of St.

---

[25] H. S. Nash, *The Atoning Life*, pp. 131-134.

John, "We have fellowship one with another, and the blood of Jesus Christ, God's Son, cleanses us from all sin." [26]

.   .   .   .

. . . Then within our hearts the mystery of the divine being is unclosed. Within our prayer we hear the voice of the Holy Spirit. God praying to God! God pledging himself to man! We go forth from our prayers into a hostile or indifferent world, seeking for tasks that the worldling calls impossible. . . .

We look into our own hearts and take full account of our cowardice, our love of ease, our infidelity, our sin. We look out upon history and see rising out of the depths, as the seer in the Book of Daniel saw them, one form after another, half human and half brute, visions of world-empire and world-trade. Man is a wolf to man. The pitiful refuge of the cliff-dwellers is in our view; the battlefields where Christians have slaughtered one another; the slums where humanity reeks and rots; the social evil, the vilest among our manifold disgraces; the numberless private griefs and wrongs; the poignant appeal of human pain. With eyes unveiled we see our world.

But the pain and the sin and the shame we make our own. We live the atoning life. We put our being into the corporate being of the Church of Christ. Our prayers are common prayers. Our wills interknitted constitute a common will. And from that will issues the world's higher law. Here and there it moulds life to its liking. Here and there appear portions of the life that is truly redeemed, where the sting of selfishness is taken from pain and where the corporate will of man gives promise of its power to banish evil. We give ourselves to our fellows in order to know and master ourselves. We do not think of sacrifice as an end in itself. We sacrifice ourselves in order to assert ourselves in the highest way. We rule our neighbors by living in them and bearing their burdens. The atoning life is our last word about ourselves. It is our last, our deepest word about God. Thanks be to Him, it is our most intimate obligation. Through Christ and His fellowship the being and beauty of God speak home to us.

---

[26] *Ibid.*, pp. 135, 136, 138-139.

It is the ministry of beauty to restore and freshen our confidence in our world. So long as the spell is on us, the sincerity of the universe is a thing certain and assured. Even so is it with the creative unity of God in Christ. Through the Saviour we enter upon our heritage. The thrill of possession runs through us. People with no abiding place, who have somehow come into the inheritance of an old estate, know what a joy it is to walk their bounds. The folk whom Christ hath redeemed enjoy this thrill of possession in its sweetest and purest form. They have inherited the earth. Please God, at some far-off day,—whether it be a hundred years or a hundred thousand, it is not theirs to think or say,—righteousness and right shall rule in the affairs of men. The sting shall be drawn from death and pain.[27]

When Nash spoke of the sting of death and pain, he spoke of what he knew. He had learned, while writing *The Atoning Life,* that the sentence of death was upon him. He had Hodgkin's disease. The treatment prescribed by the doctors in an attempt to stem the advance of the disease was frequently acutely painful. He learned at this time also that his second son and namesake, a senior at Harvard, had diabetes. In those days, before the discovery of insulin, diabetes too carried with it the sentence of death. Nash said nothing of this to his friends and colleagues in the School. His classes, traditionally sensitive seismographs of emotional upheavals within a theological school, sensed nothing amiss. It had always been Nash's maxim to "burn your own smoke." [28] But after his death four years later, among his papers, friends found the prayer which he had written on the day when he learned the true nature of the illness that was draining the life from his son. It has had a special place among the prayers used by the alumni of the School ever since:

"O God, Author of the world's joy, Bearer of the world's pain, make us glad that we are men, and that we have in-

---

[27] *Ibid.,* pp. 145-148.
[28] E. S. Drown, *Henry Sylvester Nash—Memorial Sermon.*

herited the world's burden. Deliver us from the luxury of
cheap melancholy; and at the heart of all our trouble and
sorrow let unconquerable gladness dwell."

Nash's Significance

In Henry Sylvester Nash the spirit which has characterized
the Episcopal Theological School received mature and
definitive expression. This is not to minimize the contributions of either his predecessors or his successors. It is
simply to say that in his unusual mind the qualities, the
characteristic interests associated with the various men
who had played a prominent part in the founding, nur-
turing and development of the School were quintessen-
tialized, as it were. For that reason he may be fairly rated
the most significant figure in its history. His thought contains so many strands: Steenstra's unflinching candor and
reverent determination to know the Word of God from
within, asserting by the integrity of his critical approach
the Bible's right to be understood "in its own sense . . .
along the lines of its own meaning and purpose"; Wharton's interest in the stable Life beneath unstable Forms,
and in the Law whereby that Life achieves consistent self-
expression in a changing world; Allen's absorbed preoccupation with continuity: patiently unravelling the web of
history to trace the diverse threads of religious, and in
particular Christian, experience running back to the Early
Church; the fervent Evangelical piety of the School's lay
founders—expressed in those doctrines of the Atonement
and of Justification by Faith which had been central in the
teaching of Bishop Eastburn and of such importance to
Benjamin Tyler Reed; the profound and complex patriotism of Elisha Mulford, his ears attuned to the divine
calling of family and nation to fulfill a spiritual destiny;
the unaffected moral earnestness of men like Amos Adams
Lawrence, humbly and quietly resolved to see high ethical
principles receive unequivocal, practical actualization in
political and social justice. All of these strains were pres-

ent, and carrying them back and back he revealed their ultimate origin in the very being of God.

While bringing into focus the concerns of the past, furthermore, Nash was also a transitional figure whose thought was a prognostication of what was to come. He once wrote that one of the pressing needs for minister and layman alike was "a vital theology that springs from life and, returning quickly to the life out of which it sprang, gives form and clarity to experience." [29] His last book was an attempt to meet that need. Such an approach, however, obviously concentrates attention on experience itself, and on the disciplines which collate and categorize it: sociology, psychology. Nash was aware that it had dangers. In one of his lectures he prophesied that it would tempt the clergy into idolatry—taking idolatry to mean, in his words, "the denial of ultimate reality and a subordination of the invisible to the visible world." [30] Before his death he asserted that theology as such was fast disappearing. Ministers, he said, were attempting to be "practical" and settling questions individually as they arose without reference to any larger framework within which they had a place.[31] Such an helter-skelter approach would give experience neither clarity nor form. But honest, intelligent examination of the phenomena of the visible world was something he welcomed. He welcomed it, furthermore, not only for the added light which it would throw on the individual man, but fully as much for what it would reveal about the nature of the corporate structures which interlock, like so many Chinese puzzles, to constitute human society. Nash was interested in comparative religion and in the sociology which helped to interpret its discoveries. He was interested in socialism, and saw in it (as

---

[29] Nash, *The Atoning Life*, p. vii.

[30] "The Problem of Human Unity" (ETS Archives: notes on H. S. Nash's course in Romans taken by A. H. Kennedy in 1905).

[31] *Ibid.*

he pointed out in *The Genesis of the Social Conscience*) obvious religious connotations despite the movement's open anti-religious bias. The "Social Question" was "in the air" in the 1900's, and Nash was therefore only being in tune with his time when he emphasized it in his books; but not every writer on the subject, in stressing the responsibility of the individual, was as careful as Nash to distinguish between belief in the right to individuality and belief in individualism, or showed Nash's sensitivity to the social role of collective organisms: the Church, the State, Big Business.[32] In his developing interest in these subjects Nash prefigured the progression which has been characteristic of theological education since his day, and which has gathered momentum as it went: the transference to places in the regular curriculum of subjects which used to be outside it. In this, too, he did not anticipate but typified the School of his day.

Nash was followed in the teaching of the New Testament (after an interval of temporary lecturers) by his son Norman Burdett Nash of the class of 1915. Like his father, Norman Nash became more and more interested in the problems of social ethics, and after 1925 he made this his major field. His standard of scholarship was as high as his father's had been, and the ingenuous wholeheartedness with which he threw himself into whatever he had to do— whether teaching or touch football—was also a Nash trait. His unflinching truthfulness in class harked back to the days of Steenstra. In 1939 he resigned to become rector of St. Paul's School, returning to Boston in 1947 to succeed Henry Knox Sherrill as Bishop of Massachusetts.

William Henry Paine Hatch, of the class of 1902, became a member of the faculty in 1917, one year after Norman Nash had joined it, and served as professor of the literature and interpretation of the New Testament until

---

[32] *E.g.*, a book by Nash's neighbor across the Cambridge Common, Francis Greenwood Peabody, *Jesus Christ and the Social Question*.

1946, when he became professor emeritus. Renowned on both sides of the Atlantic for his leadership in textual criticism, he was, throughout his years at the School, its most distinguished scholar. Beside his sometimes volcanic colleague, Dr. Hatch appeared a gentle and limpid spirit; but his students soon learned that he was indefatigable when it came to conducting them on safari through the commentaries. And when the occasion seemed to him to demand it, he could, with his usual air of benevolent innocence, make a remark so penetrating that the subject, pierced to the heart, would be dropped forthwith. Dr. Hatch carried his formidable learning lightly, and does so still; for although he officially retired and left Cambridge twenty years ago, he has ever since continued to spend part of each year in teaching. In his ninety-second year, he has surpassed the record of that Nestor among theological professors, Dr. Packard.[33]

---

[33] After Dr. Hatch retired, his place at the head of the New Testament department was taken by the Rev. Sherman E. Johnson, who had first joined the faculty in 1940, the same year as Dr. Shepherd. He resigned in 1951 to become dean of the Church Divinity School of the Pacific. His colleague, Professor Charles H. Buck, Jr., of the class of 1941, resigned in 1953 to become dean of St. Paul's Cathedral in Boston. The present New Testament department consists of the Rev. Professor Charles William Frederick Smith, who came to the School in 1951, and the Rev. Professor Henry Millis Shires, who came to the School in 1954. The Rev. Professor Eugene Van Ness Goetchius, of the class of 1952, who joined the faculty in 1957, was a member of the New Testament Department until 1963, when he became Professor of Biblical Languages.

ℵ 16

The Branching Vine

Theology

In theology the approach that Henry Sylvester Nash had adopted at the School was further developed by Edward S. Drown, of the class of 1887, who taught at the School from the year of his graduation virtually until he died in 1935; for although he retired in 1933, he continued to live across the street from the School, and taught an elective course on his favorite theologian, J. F. D. Maurice, in 1935. Drown used to say that he only taught what he had learned from Nash; but this, as his affectionately admiring students and colleagues would assert with some asperity, did Drown himself less than justice. Dr. Allen, bearing witness to his own debt to Coleridge, had once said that he found the Englishman's works "endlessly suggestive"; Dr. Drown's debt to Nash was of the same description. He adopted those of Nash's suggestions which particularly fired his imagination, took them apart, put them together again, and built upon them in a way that was his own. An example is his book *The Creative Christ*. The title obviously echoes Nash. Some of the ideas in the book are, as Dr. Drown takes care to state, derived from Maurice;

some, from Dorner. But the book's essential quality is characteristically Drown: clear, thoughtful, kind—never forcing the pace, never forcing his opinion on the reader. Indeed, Dr. Drown's quiet skill in unraveling tangled skeins of thought made him a masterly teacher in the classroom. Because of this, his teaching soaked into his students' minds unobtrusively to become an integral part of their own thinking. Years after they had left the School, they would come across an old theology notebook, leaf through it, and discover to their astonishment, in their notes of Dr. Drown's lectures, the germ of some of their most effective sermons.

Dr. Drown's term of service to the School was longer than that of any other member of the faculty, and it was he who kept the memory of the early faculty of the School fresh by recounting quaint anecdotes about them which he had garnered over the years. In himself he was a symbol, as well as an agent, of continuity in the School community; and after his death, the same role was assumed by his widow, who lived across the street from the School until she died in 1958. Mrs. Drown had been Mrs. A. V. G. Allen before she became Mrs. Drown, and had first come to live at the School in 1907. This might have made little difference had she been a lady of enigmatic or taciturn disposition; but as she was nothing of the kind, it made a great deal. A gifted storyteller in her own right, she had a command of pertinent anecdote which was as unlimited as it was immediate. In her talk, the Boston and Cambridge of the 1890's and the 1900's returned to spirited life. By the strength of her memories of past friendships, she made Henry Sylvester Nash and Phillips Brooks vivid presences in the School as long as she lived.

Dr. Drown did not teach theology by himself throughout his career. Angus Dun of the class of 1917 came to assist him in 1920, became assistant professor in 1922, professor in 1928, and dean in 1940—resigning in 1944 to become Bishop of Washington. He introduced courses in "the psychology of religion" into the curriculum, and pioneered new ways of training the students in pastoral care. The sympathetic breadth of his outlook was succinctly expressed at the conclusion of a paper on the Creeds prepared in 1924 for the Round Table Conference on "The Person of Christ in the Thought of To-day" at the Church Congress: ". . . our task is to practise that most arduous discipline of love whereby we go out of the world in which we live to enter with reverence and understanding into the world where our brother lives, taking Christ with us and finding Christ there." [1] In his ecumenical labors of future years, it was a discipline which he was to be called upon to practice repeatedly.

In addition to Drown and Dun, the School had the services of William Lawrence Wood of the class of 1913 as professor of the philosophy of religion between 1933 and 1936 (when he died as a result of being hit by a car on Brattle Street), and of Richard Stanley Merrill Emrich (who spent one year at the School in the class of 1935 before going on to Union) as instructor in theology from 1937 to 1940, and assistant professor of social ethics from 1940 until 1946, when he resigned to become Suffragan Bishop of Michigan. Through Professor Wood, the Oxford Group made its influence felt in the School for some years, while, through Professor Emrich, the School became sensitive to influences of a rather different kind: Reinhold Niebuhr, Barth, Brunner, William Temple, Kierkegaard, and Baron von Hügel.[2]

---

[1] Angus Dun, *Honest Liberty in the Church*, p. 118.
[2] The Rev. William J. Wolf of the class of 1943 became a member of the theology department in 1945. He was joined in 1947 by the Rev. Frederick William Dillistone. Dr. Dillistone resigned in 1952, returning to his native England, where he became Dean of Liverpool. The present department consists of Professor Wolf, the Rev. Professor Owen C. Thomas, of the class of 1949, and the Rev. Carl Edwards.

Practical Theology Under William Lawrence

The great expansion in these years, however, was in the no-man's-land between theology and practical theology. Signs of increasing interest in a more technical approach to the problems associated with pastoral care appeared first, as might be expected, in the calendar of lecturers at the School, who began to multiply rapidly in the late 1890's. Missionary bishops turned up in growing numbers. The *Catalogue* for 1887-88 reported that thirty-nine bishops had visited the School "so far," and listed addresses (in special services) by the Bishops of Arizona, South Dakotah, Shanghai, and T. S. Tyng of the Japan Mission. (The School had also enjoyed the privilege of hearing the Bishops of Central New York, Albany, and Maine in Lent.) Significantly, however, there had been three other talks. Mr. Robert Treat Paine had spoken on "organizing charitable work." Dr. Shattuck had spoken on hygiene. And Professor J. B. Laughlin of Harvard had spoken on "Political Economy and Christianity." That was the year before Dean Gray died. The following year, Dr. Allen arranged a session in church history for the seniors, which was an "Introduction to Ethnic Religion"—using Maurice's *Religions of the World* as a basic text.

During William Lawrence's tenure of the deanship from 1889 to 1893 the system of addresses was made more orderly, and even greater variety secured. "Imperfect correlation of the subjects" of the regular curriculum had impelled Lawrence to persuade his colleagues to re-arrange the basic courses somewhat, as well as to offer one or two electives[3] (it was at this time that two hardy perennials first made their appearance: a course on Maurice, and a course on "modern religious movements in the Anglican Church"). It was natural, therefore, that a similar policy should be followed with outside lecturers. Most

---

[3] Lawrence, *Seventy-three Years of ETS*, p. 21.

of the addresses were missionary in character, but some
described the opportunities in other fields: work among
the freedmen, in settlement houses, or within charitable
organizations. In 1891-92 three lectures on church music
were given, two on "The Family in National and Social
Life," and three on "Some Relations between the Community and the Criminal" by W. F. Spalding of the Massachusetts Prison Reform Association. The lectures on the
family were given by the Rev. S. W. Dike of the Divorce
Reform League, who had lectured in 1887-88 on (pre-
dictably) "Marriage and Divorce." In 1891-92 there were
twenty-six of these addresses in all. That this was a portent
Lawrence made clear in 1893, in his last annual report.
Speaking for the faculty, he pointed out that in the university the "great teachers in all departments of learning
are revealing the relation of the different truths to each
other." He continued:

We expect of our Church that she will not only be strong in
the development of parishes, in the education of the people,
in worship and in an appreciation of an historic liturgy, but
that she will be a guide in the great ethical, social and political problems which this age and country have to meet; that
she will be a leader in religious thought and that men will
turn to her not only because she is earnest, dignified and
practical, but because she has a large spiritual vision, an eye
intent upon the revelation of new truth, and a heart open to
the reception of truth from whatever source it may come.[4]

Among the practical suggestions which he made, so far
as the School was concerned, were that fellows and junior
teachers should be appointed so that Allen and Steenstra
could be freed to do more writing, and that a foundation
should be established for the study of sociology and social
work and comparative religion.

Because of lack of money, not one of these suggestions

[4] *ETS Catalogue,* 1893-94.

was adopted. But the need was admitted. As one solution, the trustees suggested in 1893-94 that the students should be required to take "certain philosophical, ethical and sociological courses in Harvard" as a part of the required course of study. Henry Sylvester Nash in association with some of the students formed the "My Neighbor" Club, which held weekly meetings for the "Christian study of sociological problems."

The Hodges Era

All this was firmly encouraged by George Hodges when he became dean of the School in 1894. With his background at Calvary Church in Pittsburgh, where, due to his inspiration, his parishioners had taken a leading role in social work and political reform in the city, he had no doubt of the necessity of training clergymen as well as laymen to understand the issues and act intelligently. This had formed the burden of a book of sermons, *The Heresy of Cain,* which he had published just before coming to the School. Preaching on "The Gospel of the Kingdom" in the Chapel on the Sunday after his arrival in Cambridge, he had said of the gospel:

It is for the church, but it is equally for the home and the office. It has to do with society, with politics, with elections, and, in fine, with the exercise of power, be it in whatever form it may. . . .

The Christian minister should feel a personal responsibility for all the unhappiness about him. He should have a lively interest in all that is happening in his immediate surroundings; have a lively interest in politics; in whatever concerns the good of the state and the city; in caring for and helping the unemployed; in short, look into all that comes into the life of man.

He should be instructed in theology, but more in sociology. It is well to be interested in the history of Jerusalem, but it is better to know well the history of one's own state, city, or town.[5]

To make room for such studies in the regular curriculum, however, proved impracticable. In Dean Hodges' first report, where the importance of understanding the political, economic, and social roots of social unrest was again emphasized, there was a telltale sentence: "The introduction, however, of such subjects into a course already full and exacting can be effected only by the application of the elective principle to our entire arrangement of studies." [6] The report suggested that more time was needed to adjust this. (It certainly was—about sixty-five years.)

As Lawrence had done, Hodges made up for the gap in the curriculum by offering a course on sociology as an elective for the seniors in 1895-96. The teacher was the wise Robert Archey Woods of the South End House in Boston, and it was the beginning for him of nineteen years of part-time teaching at the School. The organization of the course as reported in the *Catalogue* indicates how demanding it was. No other Episcopal seminary offered anything like it: "The Organization of Labor. I. Before the Wage System. II. The Industrial Revolution. III. Trade Unions in England. IV. Labor Organizations in the United States. V. Tactics of Organized Labor. VI. The Eight Hour Day. VII. The Living Wage. VIII. The Weak in the Struggle. IX. The Higher Strategy of Labor. X. Educational Bearings of the Labor Movement. XI. Steps toward Co-operation. XII. Labor and Social Progress."

The social evils which a minister was likely to encounter in his work were discussed in another course of lectures which were given apart from the regular or elective course

---

[5] Julia S. Hodges, *George Hodges,* pp. 128-129.
[6] *ETS Catalogue,* 1894-95.

of study. The Rev. Frederick B. Allen, Superintendant of the Boston City Mission, had given a series on "City Charity Work" in 1888-89. He was brought back in 1894-95, while the sociology course was still being planned, to lecture and lead discussion of the following subjects: 1. Church Alms; 2. Private Relief; 3. State Aid, Alms-houses, and Outdoor Relief; 4. Parish Care of the Poor; 5. Church Work for Children; 6. Children in Institutions; 7. Neglected and Dependent Children; 8. Wayward Children; Reformatories; 9. Boys' and Girls' Clubs; 10. Protection of Children from Cruelty; 11. Summer Excursions and Playrooms; 12. Crime and Its Treatment; 13. Prison Reform; 14. Gambling; 15. The Social Evil; 16. Rescue Work for Men and Women; 17. Municipal Reform; 18. The Housing of the Poor.

In 1899 Dean Hodges repeated Lawrence's statement of six years before, asserting the need of lectureships in comparative religion, to prepare men for foreign missions; in social service, to prepare them for work in tenement-house districts in great cities; and also in polity, elocution, church music, and liturgics. And once again lack of money meant that nothing was done. It was not, in fact, until 1907 that the chair in history of religion and missions was established by the efforts of the alumni. Social service, in the new guise of Christian social ethics, did not become established until after the war, with the return of Norman Nash. Liturgics became the stepchild of the church history department under Professor Muller in 1923. But polity, elocution, and church music—like religious education—received only part-time attention for many years to come. In these fields the expedient of temporary instructors continued to be employed much as it had been when formal theological education had begun almost a century before. It was not until 1941 that the School obtained its first professor of religious education with the appointment of Adelaide Teague Case. The first full-time appointment in church music was not made until 1952, when Dr. Peter Waring became instructor.[7]

The chair in history of religion and missions proved to be a happy addition to the School, but unfortunately it collapsed after only thirty-three years of service. It was held by Philip Mercer Rhinelander from 1907 to 1911, when he resigned to become Bishop of Pennsylvania. James Thayer Addison of the class of 1913 became instructor in the history of religion and missions in 1915, and after an interlude during the war, returned as assistant professor in 1919, became professor in 1926, and served until 1940, when he resigned to become first vice-president of the National Council, in charge of foreign missions. Addison's acute sense of perspective and his sympathetic understanding of religious traditions different from his own were notable; and by prearrangement he took great pains to keep his point of view fresh and practical by frequent travel in the mission field. His departure left a vacancy which the School did not fill; and missions once more became a curricular stepchild.

While Dean Hodges had to persuade both the trustees (who had to find the money) and the professors (who had to yield the course time) before he could fit "sociological" courses into the curriculum, he could do precisely what he liked when it came to instruction in homiletics, a field in which he was an acknowledged master. And he did. With his sense of humor, his experience, and his talent in writing books that appealed to children and young people as well as to adults, he was unusually well quali-

---

[7] Professor Case died in 1948. The Rev. Charles Batten joined the faculty as professor of Christian education in 1956, and immediately began to exercise a strong influence among the students because of his irresistible combination of enthusiasm, humor, and common sense. He died of cancer in 1965. Professor Waring resigned in 1966 to accept an appointment at the University of New Hampshire.

fied to teach in this field. How practical his course was may be gathered from the description of it which he wrote himself for inclusion in the School *Catalogue* for 1894-95:

Middler Homiletics. . . . Lectures: I. The Preacher Himself; II. The Bestowal of Time; III. The Preacher's Reading; IV. Studies and Sermons; V. The Preacher's Purpose; VI. Kinds of Sermons; VII. Sermons that Ought to be Preached; VIII. Sermons that Ought Not to be Preached; IX. The Making of a Sermon; X. The Making of a Sermon; XI. With Notes and Without; XII. Preaching to the People.

Senior Homiletics. Sermons every Wednesday Evening Prayer. Criticized the following day. Lectures given on Parish Work: Before Christmas on Parish Instruction, especially as regards the Sunday-School and the confirmation class; before Easter on Parish Organization, touching the purposes, methods and management of parochial societies; and after Easter on Parish Ministration, considering the visitation of the people in health and in sickness, dealing with doubt, comforting the bereaved. 2 hours a week.

In the *Catalogue* for 1897-98, Hodges suggested "the erection of a parish house for the better discipline of the students in the organization of the machinery of the modern parish." Whether this was to be associated with the Chapel congregation—thus giving effect, in a Cambridge setting, to the proposal made so long ago by Milo Mahan at General of having a normal parish attached to the seminary where the students could acquire parish experience—does not appear. Unless the present, weary little gymnasium cowering behind Winthrop Hall is a relic of this plan (for its origin is not made clear in the archives), nothing came of this scheme. When, in Dean Washburn's time, the School tried combining the professorship of pastoral care with the responsibility for ministering to the Chapel congregation, the plan did not work well.

The 1920's and Beyond

In the 1920's the case work system was applied to the training in pastoral care under the leadership of Angus Dun. Dr. Richard Cabot and others provided insights from the point of view of the doctor. In addition, in a return to a tradition as old as Bishop Meade and Bishop Griswold, first Bishop Lawrence, and then Bishop Sherrill were asked to give a course in pastoral care based on their varied experience in the ministry. The effect of this may be judged from the report given by Cornelius Du Bois of the class of 1931:

Really practical courses in Pastoral Theology are not forgotten. Each man in his first and third year must take a half-year course in Pastoral Care, which in the first year ranges all the way from the keeping of parish records to the care of one's personal appearance. The aim is to keep the student thinking continuously about the pastoral relationship all three years. For the middle year an elective course is provided giving special emphasis to the psychological and psychiatric aspects of Pastoral Care, and prominent doctors and psychiatrists are brought in to lecture. Father Burton of the Society of St. John the Evangelist was one of the outstanding visitors while I had the course, giving a splendid account of his work as prison chaplain and strongly appealing for volunteers for that important side of the pastoral ministry.

I shall never forget the course in Pastoral Care given last year for the seniors by Bishop Sherrill of Massachusetts. We met every Wednesday evening in the Dean's home, and sat around the fire in an intimate and informal way listening to the experiences and conclusions of a truly great pastor. He touched upon a wide variety of topics, from parish organization and social service to marriage and divorce and how to deal with panhandling. From time to time he brought in visitors to speak on boys' work, rural work, or the value of the confessional. One evening we met at the Bishop's home and heard a Roman Catholic priest speak on Pastoral Care from his point of view and experience. . . .

The social gospel occupies an important place in the curriculum, though not to the minimizing of the foundation stones of theology or biblical study. Courses are given in such subjects as the Social Teachings of Jesus, the Church and Social Problems, and Christian Social Teachings in History, and there are seminar courses in such topics as the Family. Opportunity is given for practical social-work experience. A large number of students last year gave up one afternoon occasionally to visit a neighboring almshouse, and brought back many interesting tales of their contacts with the sick, the aged, and the feeble-minded. Then there are Friendship Tours which the students are invited to go on, and by means of which they can see the living-quarters of the different races in Boston. Every summer certain men attend the Cincinnati Summer School of Social Service, and come back with glowing accounts of their work among juvenile delinquents, maladjusted families, and the unemployed.[8]

In the experiences of the student in the early 1930's were seeds which, in the 1940's and 1950's, were to burgeon to such an extent that additions to the faculty in the field of practical theology became essential. Joseph F. Fletcher was drawn from the Cincinnati School of Applied Religion in 1944, first as Kellner Lecturer, then as a professor. Rollin J. Fairbanks of the class of 1936, after collaborating with Professor Case in the early development of the clinical training program from his post as chaplain at the Massachusetts General Hospital, was appointed to a professorship in 1948. In under seventy years the once feeble shoots of "pastoralia" had become a forest.[9]

---

[8] Cornelius Du Bois, "The Seminary Today" (talk given to the Buffalo Clericus, Feb. 1, 1932), *ETS Bulletin*, Apr., 1932.

[9] The present department of pastoral theology consists of Dean John Bowen Coburn, who came to the School as professor and dean in 1957; Professor Fairbanks; the Rt. Rev. Professor Arthur Carl Lichtenberger of the class of 1925, who became a member of the faculty in 1965; and Associate Professor Emma Lou Benignus, who came to the School in 1965 as lecturer in Christian Education. Dr. Fletcher is Professor of Christian Social Ethics.

Part IV

ENVOI

✖ 17

Centennial Perspective

It is now almost one hundred years to the day since Benjamin Tyler Reed took stock of his fortune, consulted his conscience, and then went to see his rector, Frederic Dan Huntington, to seek his advice about establishing a theological school. On January 22, 1967, the school which ultimately eventuated from that interview began its second century of existence as a legal entity. On June 1, 1967, it will begin its second century of existence as a chartered corporation of the Commonwealth. On December 15, 1967, it will begin its one hundred and first year as a worshipping community. On January 1, 1968, it will begin its one hundred and first year of teaching. On the threshold of such a season of anniversaries, therefore, it hardly seems fitting to lay aside this consideration of the School's past without pausing for a moment to attempt some assessment, however inadequate, of the significance of that history, and some estimate, however tentative, of the degree to which the School has fulfilled the hopes implicit in Reed's long-considered design.

Cambridge and Harvard

One thing is obvious at a glance. The expectations which led Reed and his associates to place the School in Cambridge have almost all been realized. In that respect their judgment has been repeatedly vindicated.

Whether or not the establishment of the School close to Harvard actually boosted the college's enrollment as Hale, Dana, Reed, and Lawrence hoped it would do is impossible to determine. The School's roster and calendar of courses was certainly incorporated in the Harvard *Catalogue* with canny promptness, making the School appear as constituent a part of the university as the then semi-autonomous Harvard Medical School. Events soon rendered this part of the founder's plan unnecessary, however. In 1869 the college's nervousness over its reputation was relieved in a much more telling way by the appointment of Charles William Eliot to succeed President Hill. In Eliot's presence, doubt of any kind seemed almost blasphemous. Within a week or two of his inauguration, he was informed that two divinity students had cut down a small tree which had interfered with the baseball games which they played regularly on the ground in front of the Divinity School. Summoning the two culprits into his presence, Eliot said with his characteristic combination of firmness and calm, "I understand that you have removed a tree from in front of the Divinity School. *Kindly put it back.* Good morning, gentlemen!" The interview took exactly thirty seconds. The hunt—all over the environs of Boston —for a duplicate of the tree took considerably longer. But before a week was up, a reasonable facsimile stood once again in the middle of the baseball field.[1] A man like Eliot required no additional support from a struggling little seminary across the Common.

[1] ETS Archives: "E. L. Stoddard" folder. Stoddard was one of the students who "removed" the tree.

The hope that the School would minister to Episcopalians at Harvard, however, was fulfilled within a very short time. Although the trustees had been unable to prevail on Phillips Brooks to become the School's first dean, they accomplished part of their original purpose by inducing him to come out to preach in the Chapel regularly for seven years after he came to Boston as rector of Trinity Church. Whenever he preached, the Chapel was filled, as Dean Stone testified in his orientation letter to Dean Gray. During the years that Harvard required the students to attend church, most of the students who were Episcopalians attended the Chapel instead of going to Christ Church. A large proportion of them continued to attend even after attendance ceased to be compulsory (Dean Lawrence estimated that roughly one-third of the Episcopal students went to the Chapel in his day). Harvard professors and their families belonged to the Chapel congregation. And by carefully selecting men with distinguished reputations in the parish ministry like Stone, Gray, Lawrence, and Hodges to fill the deanship, the trustees ensured that the Chapel ministry would enjoy experienced and imaginative leadership.

The professors, however, as Dean Stone's letter to Gray shows, were from the beginning absorbed in their teaching, and were willing to help with the Chapel ministry only out of a sense of duty; so it might have been foreseen that when the trustees and the faculty failed to persuade yet another rector of a large and successful parish, Charles Slattery, to follow in the train of Hodges and his predecessors, and turned to Professor Washburn as their second choice, the days of the Chapel congregation were numbered. The alternative was obvious. Even in 1867, Rand and Lawrence had voiced the hope that it would eventually be possible to replace Nicholas Hoppin at Christ Church with a rector more interested in the university (and more soundly Evangelical); and the logic of the situation required that when the School was no longer able to maintain a ministry to Harvard, some such solution should be found. In 1930, it was. Between 1900 and the mid-1920's Prescott Evarts had successfully built up the parish much as Nicholas Hoppin had done in the first period of his long ministry in the parish nearly a century before; but Evarts was wise enough to retire before advancing years could stultify his powers of leadership. Conversations between the leaders of parish and congregation began in 1926; Evarts resigned in 1929; and the Chapel congregation united with Christ Church parish to call the Rev. Charles Leslie Glenn, secretary for college work for the National Council, to assume the rectorship in 1930. With that, the School's long ministry to Harvard Episcopalians came to an end; although in a curious echo of the past, the crowded schedule of parish services on Sunday mornings at Christ Church impelled the Rev. Ronald Maitland, chaplain on the Rhinelander Foundation, to shift the religious services for the Harvard community back to the Chapel for a time in the early 1960's.

The plans laid by Rand and Reed and Lawrence to minister to Episcopalians at Harvard were thus realized with entire success. Yet Nicholas Hoppin and Christ Church, whose rights they treated so cavalierly, may be said to have had the last word after all. By a delectable rewriting of history, in a recent parish brochure the deans of the Episcopal Theological School from Dean Gray to Dean Washburn are listed as curates of Christ Church.

The third reason for placing the School in Cambridge in 1867 had been the advantages which it was hoped would accrue to it through its proximity to the university libraries, museums, and lecture halls. Over the years these proved, as Reed and his associates had expected, to be of inestimable value. The advantages did not run all one way. The School professors sometimes taught in the university—as Dr. Allen did at President Eliot's request

—and university students took courses at the School. But the advantage to the School was very great; for the relationship was always close, even before official affiliation between the two institutions was worked out by President Lowell and Dean Hodges in 1914. Until the 1950's, when congestion began to clog both systems, the proximity of the Harvard libraries eased the strain on the School library—a strain which, in view of the School's always inadequate financial resources, would otherwise have become intolerable. In similar fashion, in the years when the School had become aware of the need for training in political realities, in sociology, economics, and psychology, and had no money with which to procure more than occasional lecturers in these fields, it was possible for the students to take full courses in all of these subjects in the university—an opportunity of which they took advantage. The proximity of Harvard meant that the professors reaped the benefit of consultation with their peers in the university departments. They formed friendships with William James, Royce, Fiske, George Herbert Palmer (who lived in Dean Gray's house in Dean Lawrence's time), Richard Cabot, Crawford Toy, George Foot Moore, and Henry Cadbury. And there was as well the influence exerted by the university through the reform of its own methods of instruction. It was principally through the collaborative association of Thayer Addison and Professor Edward A. Whitney of Harvard (who became a trustee in 1926) that the School adopted the tutorial and general examination system in 1928. The passage of time has done nothing to diminish these advantages.

Independence of Diocesan Control

If the decision to place the School in Cambridge proved to be justified by its outcome, what of the peculiarities of organization which Reed and Wharton wrote into the School's organization in an effort to avoid in the future the squabbles which had unsettled Gambier and General —independence of the diocesan convention, a Board of Trustees composed traditionally of laymen, guarantees of professorial tenure? By and large, these too have proved their worth. Their purpose was to protect the professors from outside interference, while at the same time keeping the School close to the Church through its link with the bishop of the diocese, who was *ex officio* its chief visitor. For a time both aspects of this purpose were fulfilled. It was intended that the professors should in concert determine the School's educational policy as well as plan its curriculum, and they did. From the minutes of faculty meetings it is clear that throughout the period chiefly alluded to in these pages (ending with the retirement of Dean Washburn in 1940), the faculty ran the School. It played a prominent role in the selection of each new dean after Dean Gray (who appears to have been picked principally by Dean Stone and Edward S. Rand); it nominated visitors—and even trustees; it allocated library funds. This corporate tradition was still strong in Dean Taylor's day, when it was understood that every member of the faculty had an equal voice and an equal vote in all decisions—even to nominations for appointments, and recommendations of tenure. Until at least 1952, the rule requiring unanimity in all recommendations for faculty appointments before they could be forwarded to the trustees (the rule to which Dr. Allen referred in his Notes as dating back to the origin of the School) was unfailingly observed. One "No" meant no appointment. Disapproving bishops—even the bishop of the diocese—might express their distrust by refusing to permit their candidates to attend the School. They might write pastoral letters which, without actually saying so, were aimed at the School. Examining chaplains might refuse to recommend ETS students for ordination—as in the Chambré-manipulated "Massachusetts Case" of 1894. But they could not muzzle the professors, nor could they compel their dismissal.

For many years the relationship with the bishop of the diocese developed just as Reed and Wharton had intended that it should. He was always free to help; he was never free to hinder. Bishop Paddock disapproved in principle of a theological school which was not under the thumb of its diocesan bishop; and he felt so strongly about this that after the first year or two, he remained aloof from the School.[2] He was powerless to interfere where no wrong had occurred. It is true that his courteous, but constant, disapproval made Dean Gray nervous. Gray alone appears to have realized what real power the Board of Visitors possessed, and in moods of depression to which he was by no means immune, used to warn Lawrence that they would "all wake up some day to find that the Visitors had gone to the Courts and taken the School right away from them." But the School came to no harm.

On the other hand, when the bishop basically had confidence in the School, as was the case with Eastburn, Brooks, and Lawrence, the influence of the bishop on the School could be great. William Lawrence's episcopate, in fact, probably represents the ideal which Reed and Wharton had in mind. The son of one of Reed's associates, who vividly remembered the School's early days; a former student himself but familiar with other seminary patterns too; well-versed, as onetime professor, vice-dean, and dean, in every department of the School's affairs; alive, through his close association with Harvard, to changes in educational methods and principles; experienced in the

---

[2] Bishop Paddock's attitude would have been shared by most of his episcopal colleagues. The bishops' extreme reluctance to delegate or share in any way their responsibilities for supervising the theological education of ordinands under their respective jurisdictions held up a revision of the 1804 Course of Study from 1856 until 1889. Even at that date, suggestions for additional reading (the 1804 Course of Study was reverently reprinted untouched) were made only with the most jittery delicacy.

intricacies of parochial and diocesan administration—no one was better qualified than Bishop Lawrence to influence the School for its good. Attention in the past has often been concentrated on the fund-raising campaigns whereby, with the ingenuity of Bishop Meade and the indomitable enterprise of Bishop Chase, but on a scale which far surpassed anything achieved in their day, he brought to the School a power to realize long-cherished visions of increased effectiveness. But his correspondence reveals countless other instances of unobtrusive and efficient preoccupation with the School's welfare: suggestions on policy or for minor improvements in administration, gestures of personal confidence, information about the past as a guide to the present. They are all short, clear, frank, without a trace of grandiloquence or pretense. They relax tension, and take the heat out of controversy. In the sometimes touchy negotiations between Christ Church and the Chapel congregation (with the dean and faculty in the background), it was Bishop Lawrence who dredged up from the depths of his memory of fifty years before the recollection that the original circumstances attending the decision to build and establish the Chapel, with its attendant congregation, had given Christ Church some cause for indignation.[3] Thereafter the Chapel committee was more patient when the parishioners made remarks that reflected lingering animus. Professor Muller was no more than just when he said of Bishop Lawrence that "until his death at the age of ninety-one in 1941, [he] remained the School's wisest counsellor, its most effective helper, and its best friend." [4]

---

[3] Letter of Bishop William Lawrence to R. M. Watson, undated (ETS Archives: envelope "Papers relating to the Proposed Union of St. John's Memorial Chapel Congregation with the Congregation of Christ Church, Cambridge").

[4] Muller, *Episcopal Theological School*, p. 90.

One Unforeseen Lacuna

The single, drastic alteration in the basic organization of the School as originally planned by Reed and Wharton was the change of character suffered by the Board of Visitors, followed by the curtailing of its powers and ultimately by its abolition. It is futile to analyze the merits of an organism which develops a malfunction almost immediately after its creation. But it should be pointed out that by the disappearance of this board, the one official link between the School and the diocese (and beyond it, the Church at large) disappeared. It is easy to see why this happened. In an effort to improve the School's "public relations" there had been over the years a disposition to load the board with members (such as High Churchmen) who might be expected to disapprove of the School on principle—the ingenuous assumption being, one may assume, that once they came to know the School better, they would also come to love it. In similar fashion, there was also a disposition to put critical alumni on the board in the same way that a rector may often put one of his more articulate and critical parishioners "on the committee." The result, however, was naturally to increase those very "smelling" propensities of the board which the faculty found such a nuisance, and to which Henry Sylvester Nash and Henry Washburn referred with some disdain in their report in 1910. Steenstra's gruff reference to the visitors in his farewell address in 1907 may also be remembered. The professors, furthermore, were a coherent, congenial group. They were also sensitive (perhaps *over*-sensitive) to the threat of criticism from outside the School, to which —as their correspondence shows—no amount of continued exposure really inured them. Given such a combination of circumstances, the slow exit of the visitors has about it almost the inevitability of Fate.

The effect of this change was two-fold. Most immediately, by removing a body which always loomed as a potential annoyance, it relaxed tension. (The tension, it should be noted, is clearly revealed in Professor Muller's highly illuminating history.) But the change also removed the School one step farther away from the diocese. With the visitors went the last vestige of an official role for the diocesan clergy and laymen (apart from the trustees themselves) in the affairs of the School. The School became, in other words, an autarchy. This was, of course, far from being what the founders of the School had intended; and it is plain, merely from the School *Bulletins* of the 1940's, that it did not satisfy the faculty or the trustees themselves. In an attempt to solve the difficulty, the officers of the Alumni Association were for a time constituted unofficial "visitors"; and some years later the expedient was adopted of creating three alumni delegates to the Board of Trustees, who could attend meetings and have a voice, but no vote. This remains, however, so far as the School's constitution is concerned, the one problem which no one has really solved. The bishop no longer has any *ex officio* connection with the School (although he may have, of course, unofficially, if he happens to be a graduate). He can no longer be its authoritative champion in the conventions of the Church (as the trustees suggested to Paddock that he should be in 1875, and as Brooks and Lawrence were in later years). And it has weakened his power to help within the School itself in a subtle, but unmistakable fashion. Norman Nash was as experienced in the ways of the School, as sympathetic to its problems, as devoted to its interests, and as good a friend of its members as William Lawrence had been. In his years as bishop a week seldom passed without his visiting the School. But he did not feel that his influence there was great. He said so himself. The same may be said of alumni delegates. They can witness, they can interpret, they may even warn;

but they cannot arbitrate. Yet arbitration (with the unstated but perceptible shadow of authority at its back) is—when the need arises—of the essence of the true visitor's function. Impregnability from without can be attained sometimes at the cost of excessive vulnerability within. The unusual, it may be the unique, relationship of mutual confidence which has obtained through so much of the School's history between trustees and faculty, and between the professors themselves may mercifully have left this weakness relatively unexposed; but the experiences of virtually every other seminary in the country should serve as a warning that fundamental differences of opinion develop *sometime*—especially in an institution where professional concern and religious faith are fused —which discussion cannot resolve. When that happens (as it has in English colleges as well as in American seminaries), judicious arbitration alone staves off dissolution. For that day, despite the devices adopted at various times by Reed and Wharton and their successors, the School is as yet ill-prepared.

True to the English Reformation

In addition to establishing a secure haven for the faculty where the brush fires of external ecclesiastical controversy could not penetrate, Reed hoped to perpetuate the Evangelical spirit and the loyalty to the English Reformation that were so dear to him. It was for this reason that the School's charter included the unalterable provision that every professor must, at the beginning of his service, make a declaration of his adherence to the Thirty-nine Articles and to the doctrine of Justification by Faith. The declaration was carefully worded by Stone so as to permit the sense of the declaration to be interpreted relatively freely, but without nullifying the founder's intent. This Article has been faithfully observed. In the Evangelical party's years of declining strength, its spokesmen occasionally reproached the professors for departing, as it seemed to them, from the standards for which the School had originally stood. Dr. Allen always replied that the professors had certainly dropped many of the negations which had been a part of the Evangelical doctrine, but that they had remained unalterably true to its essential principles. In his Notes (preparing for a section of his history which was to deal with the question at some length) he jotted down the negations which had been dropped: Theories of Inerrant Inspiration; the Calvinistic Doctrine of the Atonement; the Doctrine of Endless Punishment; the attitude to Biblical Criticism; and the attitude toward philosophy and science. He asserted:

Dropping negations, the School swung out as the true representative of the Anglican Church in the Age of the Reformation—and not as a party with a badge. The features then remaining were: 1. Loyalty to Scripture as above Tradition. 2. Justification by Faith. 3. The Articles of Religion as defining the Church and the doctrines—And for the rest, freedom of investigation—consciousness of power—as the true representative of the Anglican Church: testing the Prayer Book and interpreting it by Scriptures. But always *Justification by Faith*.[5]

He went on to repeat that a firm adherence to Scripture and to Justification by Faith still left the School free to appropriate all that was good in the history of Christendom with a sense of the identity and continuity which it enjoyed with the Church in all ages. Always, it put the central emphasis on Christ.

Just as its constitution had portended, therefore, the School's essential spirit reproduced the characteristics of the guiding spirit of the English Reformation. One need not read far in Steenstra or Allen or Mulford or Nash or Wharton to discover the same love of learning; the same

---

[5] ETS Archives: "Allen's Notes" folder.

absorption in the study of the Bible (and in particular of the New Testament); the same judicious mingling of the old with the new; the same crusty suspicion of ritual and cultic richness; the same moral earnestness and emphasis on the responsibility that falls to every Christian, not just clergymen; the same unabashed love of country; the same respectful fellow-feeling for Christians who belong to other churches. And underlying all is the abiding faith in what Nash always called the "sincerity of the universe," the belief in a coherence and consistency to reality which exists, however difficult it may be for man to comprehend it, because it derives that consistency from the nature of its Creator, God himself. God is present in his Creation, not apart from it manipulating it like an illogical and arbitrary despot. The word which sends its shaft of light deepest into the mystery of his Being is therefore not Will, but Law. And here, of course, the professors of the Episcopal Theological School joined hands across the years, not only with Maurice and Robertson and Coleridge, but above all with Hooker himself.

"The Immanent Way of Life"

In this analysis of the significance of the spirit which animated the School, however, it would be wrong to stop with the assessment of the Anglican nature of it, important as that is. For in its emphasis on a God who dwells within his Creation even while transcending his Creation, the School passes beyond the confines of Anglicanism, wide though they are. For it is to be understood, as well, as an institutional expression of the great movement of the spirit in the nineteenth century whereby the central conviction of life became precisely one of God's immanence, rather than of God's transcendence. In his *Genesis of the Social Conscience* Nash portrayed this shift in a way which showed that he was entirely aware of the nature and significance of this movement:

The eighteenth century was the proving-ground of the great conceptions which had been slowly forming through two thousand years and more. The universal individual taking the field in the full armor of theory gained for the moment a complete victory over the concrete or historical individual, and over all the institutions that housed him. The old things were thrown into the shade by the new. Bacon said, "We are the ancients." Chesterfield called Homer's heroes "porters." Volney cried, "Cease to admire these ancients." The men of '89 undertook to create a new calendar. But the victory was short-lived. There came the reaction called Romanticism, the necessary protest against the revolutionary scorn for the old things; for a while men loved the very dirt of the Middle Ages. Finally the torrent of reaction exhausted itself, and then the literary and philosophic consciousness of Europe, having learned from the eighteenth century the worth of the new without accepting its underestimate of the old, and having learned from Romanticism reverence for the past without idealizing its darkness and dirt, joined forces with the rising power of science to shift the centre of human feeling from the transcendent to the immanent way of life.[6]

From this faith stem most of the qualities and emphases which have been characteristic of the School, and of its alumni in the past hundred years. Belief in the reality of the indwelling Spirit carries with it emancipation from fear of the changes which transform that reality's external casing. It does not scorn forms or discard them lightly, for it is through the forms that the Spirit expresses itself. It does not assert that the Letter has no significance, for through the Letter the Spirit speaks. But the Letter is not an isolated, discrete, self-dependent entity to be clung to in frantic desperation lest it crumble—and all meaning with it. It is a symbol, not a talisman. The talisman has only an attributed meaning: it reflects. The symbol points beyond itself: it reveals. The Literalist is the man who

[6] Nash, *Genesis of the Social Conscience*, p. 6.

treats the Letter as a talisman. He *idolizes* it. A poor Humpty Dumpty without the gift of self-knowledge, he masters the word, forgetting that—rightly understood—it is always the Word that reveals the Master. The Literalist (and there is always something of the Literalist in all of us) adores the Letter, but actually treats it most of the time with scant attention; as a talisman, it is important for him to have with him, but his mind is concentrated on other things. The man of faith does not adore the Letter, but he scrutinizes it with reverent attention for what it can convey; and if time and weathering impair it as a medium of communication, he will reshape it to make its meaning clear once again.

Here we penetrate to the root conviction which nourishes what Nash called the "immanent way of life." From it almost everything which has distinguished the School and its graduates has logically and naturally proceeded. It explains, also, why the School—when it has engaged in ecclesiastical controversy or had controversy thrust upon it—has aroused the Literalists on every side.

The Higher Criticism of the Bible, for example, was an inevitable part of the "immanent way of life." For twenty years the School was almost alone in giving it a place in the curriculum, drawing upon itself thereby the contumely of those Literalists who are better known as Fundamentalists. Nash's *History of the Higher Criticism* was an attempt not only to chronicle the development of biblical criticism but also to reveal the inner nature of Literalism (and its twin—Infallibility) by showing how each embodied itself in successive historical forms as the chronicle unfolded.

Furthermore, just as the Higher Critical approach alarmed the Literalist, so did the similar approach to the Creeds. It is equally to be expected, therefore, that among the list of books emanating from the School over the years, a significant number should have been devoted to defending the Creed against Literalists from both wings of Christianity in the same way as Nash and Steenstra had defended the Bible. Dr. Allen wrote his one work of controversy on that subject: *Freedom in the Church*. Dean Hodges, throughout his ministry, preached on both the use of the Creeds and on the proper attitude to the Bible repeatedly, using his accustomed simple, sensible, pointed language to make what he meant sharply clear. Dr. Drown wrote on *The Apostles' Creed for To-day*. In the early years of Dean Washburn's era, as a result of another attack directed against the School from afar by the Literalists, the entire faculty collaborated in a unique venture: the production of *Creeds and Loyalties*, in which the history of the development of the Creed and the significance to be attached to its use were dealt with in a series of articles, each written by a different one of the professors. Angus Dun prepared a paper on the use of the Creeds for a Church Congress.

Often (as in the case of the Crapsey trial in 1906) the controversy was not provoked by the faculty in the first instance, but by extreme statements made by some clergyman with whom the faculty had little sympathy. The faculty only entered the controversy later, after equally extreme action had been taken in reply. But to permit such a man to be pilloried in an unjust fashion would have been to betray their own convictions of what was due every man. This was not understood always, even, as it were, in the School's own dooryard. One lady left the Chapel congregation during one of the periods of unrest, saying that "Dean Hodges was a Unitarian, Dr. Nash an atheist, and Mr. Drown impossible."

Nor has the School's belief in the "immanent way of life" slackened in more recent years. It is expressed in the ecumenical labors of Angus Dun and William J. Wolf. The devout examination of a Letter grown somewhat antique and inscrutable has resulted in the criticisms of

the conventional "suburban parish" by Gibson Winter
and Francis Ayres, the joint founders of Parishfield. A
similar concern has, in another field, produced Paul Van
Buren's *Secular Meaning of the Gospel*. The results of
such encounters with Letter and Spirit will obviously vary
in character, depending on the intellectual acuteness, the
learning, and the personal "style" of each man. What
provides the "continuity" is the essential informing conviction or presupposition that is common to them all.

Reverent attention to the changing forms within which
the Spirit finds expression carries with it a disposition to
widen one's purview continually. What were once considered alien disciplines achieve their citizenship. Hence
the willingness with which the School embraced the social
sciences and psychology in the 1890's. Hence the prolifer-
ating subjects associated with Christian social ethics and
pastoral care. Hence also the strong emphasis on social
justice in the episcopates of men like William Scarlett in
Missouri and Norman Nash in Massachusetts, the ministry
among the blind by men like Gabriel Farrell, and among
prisoners by men like Howard Kellett. The "immanent
way of life" leads also to the reverence for man as the
temple of the Spirit which emboldened Henry Nash to
seek within the simplest and most universal experiences of
family life the revelation of the divine mysteries of the
Atonement and Justification by Faith, which guided the
episcopates of men like William Lawrence and Henry
Hobson and Henry Knox Sherrill, with their strong
pastoral emphasis, which—in a more troubled day—led
ETS alumni to St. Jude's compound in Montgomery, Alabama, in countless numbers from every part of the United
States—and led Jonathan Daniels to Selma.

Changing Forms

There is thus a continuing spirit, a continuing faith
which as recognizably informs the Episcopal Theological

School in our day as it did when the School was young. But while the spirit continues, forms themselves change. The cells of the human body change completely every seven years. In that sense every photograph is also an epitaph. Institutions change more slowly than the human body, no doubt; but even they in time become new institutions bearing old names. And it would be foolish to assume that Cambridge alone escapes the logic of Francis Wharton's vision of the stable life that persists within unstable forms. A comparison of the School as it was throughout much of its history with the descriptions of the School in the early 1950's reveals that in the last twenty years the "School of the Prophets" mold within which the School's corporate life was formed has been broken, and fallen away. Since the end of the Second World War, the increase in the number of students, in the number of professors, in the number of administrators, has, gradually, simply crowded out the small-scale intimacy which had been characteristic of the School in former times. The Sherman Johnsons in 1946 were the only family still to hold a regular weekly "at home" on Wednesday evenings. By 1947 the resulting squash had become so uncomfortable, even the Johnsons were forced to relinquish the old custom. In 1948, between-lecture discussions over a cigarette in the Lawrence Room, with professors like Wolf and Buck arguing over the nature of miracle—the theologian putting pieces together as rapidly as the biblical critic separated them—were still a staple part of the School routine. By 1953 the professors had little time to meet one another except in the Gray Room before and after services and at faculty meetings. In the 1950's the Christmas Play had to move out of the School altogether, along with the School Dance. Indeed, the *Bulletins* from 1946 on, with their constant record of renovations, alterations, enlargements and new construction, read like the diary of a mother whose son has reached the stage where he grows clear out of his clothes every six months. For the theological school, as for the parish, this appears to be an age of transition. Dr. Allen used to say that "every age is an age of transition." The old garment may have warmed the body very satisfactorily for years; but it does so no longer. Here, too, it may be that, in the future, the reverent scrutiny of a half-defaced Letter will reveal ways of reshaping it so as to make it once again the communicative symbol it used to be.

"A Boundless Hope"

As the School pauses on the threshold of a new century, therefore, it may take courage from its past. Thanks to the generosity of many devoted friends (among whom, in a persistent echo of long ago, descendants of William Appleton still figure), it begins its second century as it began its first, unusually well fitted out with buildings in which to carry on its task. It begins it also—thanks to them—very much better off for money. For that reason its leaders need not look forward to a duplication of the anxious and thin years of its first youth in which Amos Adams Lawrence and James Sullivan Amory despaired each year of seeing the poverty-stricken institution survive. Instead they can devote their full energies to giving appropriate expression in the mid-twentieth century to the spirit which Phillips Brooks discerned in the School over fifty years ago:

Full of deep sympathy with present thought, quick with the spirit of inquiry; eager to train its men to think and reason; equipped with teaching power of the highest order; believing in the ever-increasing manifestation of the truth of God; anxious to blend the most earnest piety with the most active intelligence, and so to cultivate a deep, enthusiastic, reasonable faith, the Cambridge School stands very high among the powers which bid us hope great things.[7]

---

[7] *ETS Catalogue*, 1894-95, *et seq.*

For the Episcopal Theological School to think of attempting to live up to those words on its own would be to give way to despair. What school in our harried and restless day can consider itself capable of maintaining such wisdom, such honesty, such nobility, such calm? But a theological school is not "on its own." Benjamin Tyler Reed acted with keen insight when he made the one unchangeable Article in the Charter of the Episcopal Theological School the declaration that the School's teaching and practice shall ever embody the doctrine of Justification by Faith. As Henry Sylvester Nash used to say to his classes:

God's belief in us is like our friend's belief in us: it makes us humble and it makes us strong. We accept God's belief in us, God's estimate of us, just as we accept our mother's, our sweetheart's, our friend's—on faith. We know ourselves to be unworthy of it, but our acceptance of it is a source of strength, enabling us in some small measure to live up to it. Thus when we believe that God believes in us, there comes a new power into our lives making for righteousness; we are justified, made righteous by faith—by our faith in God's faith in us.

Trustees, dean, faculty, students made humble and strong by their mutual belief in one another—knowing themselves to be unworthy of it, but by their acceptance of it as a source of strength, finding themselves enabled in some measure to live up to it—on such a relationship the health of every human institution depends. And that relationship is grounded on no shallow foundation but in the heart of God himself.

Nearly sixty years ago Dr. Allen stood up to speak to the alumni whom he had taught in the course of forty years. He spoke of the School's beginning and of its harsh first years. He spoke of what it had stood for since that time, and of the difficult days through which it had passed when so many in the Church had looked on it askance. The problem for the School and for the Church, he said, was always that of "harmonizing things as they are—the institution—the sacredness of things as they are, with the new Truth that comes down from God himself, God in direct communication with man." That was the way men in Italy had felt at the time of the Renaissance, the way men felt at the time of the Reformation. "It is," he admitted, "of course, a dangerous thing to keep the open mind for the new truth, but everything is dangerous in this world. There will always be fanaticism; there will be perversions of all kinds waiting upon this conviction that God speaks to the world and teaches us today." [8] It was something, he felt, to have kept that faith through all the vicissitudes of the School's forty years. But it was not with pride in what the School had stood for that he ended what was to be his last speech. Like Steenstra, after ranging through all the fields of thought in which the School had won distinction over the years, he turned instead to something much more simple, the root of his learning and of his happiness, his faith in Christ. His words are as apt now as they were then. They closed Dr. Allen's career, and they may equally appropriately close this book:

We are slowly getting nearer to the fountain light of all our being. We are getting back again to Christ as no other age in the history of the world has known him. We begin to see him, and even more clearly than those who walked with him in the flesh, because we can read the influences that acted upon the time in a way in which the actors could not realize them. We only wait for the spark of divine fire. That I live in the hopes of seeing. Christ means to us more than we have hitherto seen. He means to us these two things in particular,— the coming into the world of a love such as the world had never known before, and also a boundless hope.[9]

---

[8] "Fortieth Anniversary Alumni Banquet, June, 1907" (ETS Archives).
[9] Ibid.

Bibliography

In order to make the bibliography as useful as possible on its own, the books, articles, or manuscript sources cited in the footnotes have been included in the works listed below. The arrangement within each section is chronological with reference to the subject under discussion.

A. THEOLOGICAL EDUCATION: GENERAL BACKGROUND

Kelly, Robert L. *Theological Education in America—A Study of 161 Theological Schools in the United States and Canada.* New York, 1924.

Brown, William A., and May, Mark A. *The Education of American Ministers.* 4 vols. New York, 1934.

Niebuhr, H. Richard, Williams, Daniel Day, and Gustafson, James M. *The Advancement of Theological Education.* New York, 1957.

B. THEOLOGICAL EDUCATION: THE SCHOOLS OF THE PROPHETS AND THE EARLY SEMINARIES (NON-EPISCOPAL)

Gambrell, Mary Latimer. *Ministerial Training in Eighteenth-Century New England.* New York, 1937. Contains an interesting discussion of the contents of the personal libraries of Bellamy, Smalley, and Emmons, and a description of "educational procedure in the Schools of the Prophets."

Sweet, William W. "The Rise of Theological Schools in America," *Church History,* VI, No. 3 (Sept., 1937).

Bainton, Roland H. *Yale and the Ministry—A History of Education for the Christian Ministry at Yale from the Founding in 1701.* New York, 1957.

Woods, Leonard. *History of the Andover Theological Seminary*. Boston, 1885. Besides the account of the early years at Andover by one of the seminary's first two professors, the book prints the text of the seminary's constitution, original statutes, bylaws, confession of faith, as well as significant committee reports and personal letters.

Rowe, Henry K. *History of Andover Theological Seminary*. Newton, Mass., 1933.

Williams, George Huntston (ed.). *The Harvard Divinity School —Its Place in Harvard University and in American Culture*. Boston, 1954. Professor Conrad Wright's survey of the development of the school in the nineteenth century contains helpful references to books and methods of instruction employed by the early professors.

C. THEOLOGICAL EDUCATION IN THE EPISCOPAL CHURCH (EX-CEPT AT ETS)

1. *General background*

It is taken for granted that any student will naturally consult the more general historical studies of Addison, Albright, Chorley, De-Mille, and Manross. References to the subject will also be found in almost every clerical memoir or biography. Of the works consulted, the following proved to be especially useful:

Manross, W. W. *The Episcopal Church in the United States, 1800-1840*. New York, 1938.

Brewer, C. H. *History of Religious Education in the Episcopal Church to 1835*. New Haven, 1924.

Wilberforce, S. *A History of the Protestant Episcopal Church*. London, 1856. Wilberforce's lively interest in theological education and in the welfare of the Negro gives this book an unusual slant.

Caswall, Henry. *America and the American Church*. London, 1839. Caswall was at Gambier in Chase's time.

Bullock, F. W. B. *A History of Training for the Ministry of the Church of England in England and Wales from 1800 to 1874*. St. Leonard's-on-Sea, 1955. Contains, as well, "an introduction from 1539 to 1799 and an appendix of notes on training for the ministry of the Anglican Communion outside England and Wales from 1539 to 1874." A very helpful guide, stuffed with snippets of quotations from a wide variety of pertinent sources.

Perry, William S. (ed.). *General Conventions of the Protestant Episcopal Church, Journals of 1785-1835*. 3 vols. Claremont, N.H., 1874.

General Conventions of the Protestant Episcopal Church, Journals of, published triennially. Appendix F in the *Journal* for 1844 contains the report on the visitation of General Theological Seminary. The *Journal* for 1889 contains the bishops' supplement to the Course of Study of 1804.

White, William. *Memoirs of the Protestant Episcopal Church in the United States of America* (ed. by B. F. De Coasta). New York, 1880.

Wilson, Bird. *Memoir of the Life of the Right Reverend William White, D.D., Bishop of the Protestant Episcopal Church in the State of Pennsylvania.* Philadelphia, 1839.

Clark, Thomas March. *Reminiscences.* New York, 1895.

2. *The General Theological Seminary*

The best account of the development of the seminary is in "General Theological Seminary 1821-1936," *Historical Magazine of the Protestant Episcopal Church,* V, No. 3 (Sept., 1936). It includes the following:

Hardy, Edward Roche, Jr. "The Organization and Early Years of the General Theological Seminary."

Chorley, E. Clowes. "The Oxford Movement in the Seminary."

Manross, William Wilson. "Growth and Progress since 1860."

Mampoteng, Charles. "The Library and American Church History."

Gates, Milo H. "Deans and Professors."

An earlier account is that by Dean E. A. Hoffman: "Histori-

cal Sketch of the General Theological Seminary," printed as part of William Stevens Perry's *The History of the American Episcopal Church 1587-1883,* Monograph VII, Vol. II. Boston, 1885.

Documents associated with the establishment and early years of the seminary are contained in *Proceedings relating to the Organization of the General Theological Seminary of the Protestant Episcopal Church in the United States of America from its Inception to its final Establishment in the City of New York, together with the regular Proceedings of the Board of Trustees from its Commencement, A.D. 1821 until 1838.* New York, 1854. Subsequent volumes of the trustees' *Proceedings* are equally full and informative.

Additional material is to be found in the following:

Turner, Samuel. *Introductory Discourse Delivered at New Haven at the Opening of the Theological Seminary of the Protestant Episcopal Church, September 13, 1820.*

———. *Autobiography of the Rev. Samuel H. Turner, D.D., Late Professor of Biblical Learning and the Interpretation of Scripture in the General Theological Seminary of the Protestant Episcopal Church in the United States of America.* New York, 1863.

Hobart, John Henry. *An Introductory Address on the Occa-*

sion of the Opening of the General Theological Seminary, New York, *1822*.

Berrian, William. *Memoir of the Life of the Right Reverend John Henry Hobart, D. D.* (Vol. I of the 3 vol. *Posthumous Works of John Henry Hobart, D.D.*) New York, 1832-33.

Dix, Morgan (ed.). *History of the Parish of Trinity Church in the City of New York.* 4 vols. New York, 1898-1906. Reprints some Hobart letters.

Walworth, Clarence E. *The Oxford Movement in America, or, Glimpses of Life in an Anglican Seminary.* New York, 1895.

Brand, W. F. *Life of William Rollinson Whittingham, Fourth Bishop of Maryland.* 2 vols. New York, 1883. Prints letters relating to Whittingham's mooted return to General as "President."

Crapsey, Algernon Sidney. *The Last of the Heretics.* New York, 1924. Like Walworth (see above), Crapsey grinds ecclesiastical axes with gusto. He presents a vivid portrait of the first Professor Seabury in these reminiscences.

3. *Virginia*

Goodwin, W. A. R. (ed.). *History of the Theological Seminary in Virginia and Its Historical Background.* 2 vols. New York, 1923. In addition to an historical account, these volumes also contain accounts of the Episcopal High School, the Bishop Payne Divinity School, biographical sketches of the Bishops of Virginia, the seminary professors, influential trustees, monographs on the work of seminary graduates in the mission field, reminiscences by a number of graduates, and transcripts of the minutes of the Board of Trustees, 1821-1866, and of the minutes of the Education Society, 1818-1842. A remarkably useful collection which few seminaries nowadays, unfortunately, could hope to afford to duplicate.

Walker, Cornelius. *The Life and Correspondence of Rev. William Sparrow, D. D., Late Professor of Systematic Divinity and Evidences in the Episcopal Theological Seminary of Virginia.* Philadelphia, 1876.

Packard, Thomas J. (ed.). *Recollections of a Long Life by Joseph Packard D. D. 1812-1902.* Washington, D.C., 1902. Edited by Professor Packard's son.

Johns, John. *A Memoir of the Life of the Right Rev. William Meade, D. D., Bishop of the Protestant Episcopal Church in the Diocese of Virginia.* Baltimore, 1867. Contains letters and other Meade papers, Dr. Sparrow's Memorial Sermon on the bishop, and a list of some of Bishop Meade's writings.

A picture of life at Virginia in the 1850's which is less tinted by

Centennial euphoria may be obtained from the letters of Phillips Brooks quoted in the late Professor Raymond W. Albright's carefully annotated *Focus on Infinity: A Life of Phillips Brooks* (New York, 1961). It should be kept in mind, however, that the negative tone of the letters is due less to abnormal inadequacy on the part of Virginia than to Brooks's stage of development at the time. Intellectually vigorous theological students seldom see their seminary through the eyes of little Pippa.

4. *Gambier*
Smythe, George Franklin. *Kenyon College.* New Haven, 1924.
———. *A History of the Diocese of Ohio Until the Year 1918.* Cleveland, 1931.
Chase, Philander. *Reminiscences: An Autobiography Comprising a History of the Principal Events in the Author's Life to A.D. 1847.* 2 vols. Boston, 1848.
Dyer, Heman. *Records of an Active Life.* New York, 1886.
Carus, William. *Memorials of the Right Reverend Charles Pettit McIlvaine, D. D., D. C. L., Late Bishop of Ohio in the Protestant Episcopal Church in the United States.* London and New York, 1882.

5. *Massachusetts to 1847*
Berry, Joseph Breed. *History of the Diocese of Massachusetts 1810-1872.* Boston, 1959. Very fully footnoted, not only with references to sources, but with biographical details about the more obscure figures in the narrative.
Stone, J. S. *Memoir of the Life of the Right Rev. Alexander Viets Griswold, D.D. Bishop of the Protestant Episcopal Church in the Eastern Diocese.* Philadelphia, 1844.
Howe, M. A. DeWolfe. *Memoirs of the Life and Services of the Right Rev. Alonzo Potter, D.D., LL.D., Bishop of the Protestant Episcopal Church in the Diocese of Pennsylvania.* Philadelphia, 1871.
Hopkins, John Henry, Jr. *The Life of the Late Right Reverend John Henry Hopkins, First Bishop of Vermont by One of His Sons.* New York, 1873.
Loring, Susan M. (ed.). *Selections from the Diaries of William Appleton 1786-1862.* Boston, 1922.
The Banner of the Cross. 1831-1832.
Conventions of the Protestant Episcopal Church in the Diocese of Massachusetts, Journals of. Those from 1784 to 1828 were printed in 1849 from extant manuscript records by order of the Convention of 1848. Thereafter they were printed annually. The *Journals* for 1831, 1835, 1836, 1837, 1845, and 1846 contain references to the various abortive attempts to establish a diocesan seminary.
Hopkins, John Henry. *Defence of the Convention of the Protestant Episcopal Church in the*

State of Massachusetts against certain Editorial Statements of the Paper called "The Banner of the Cross." Boston, 1832.

Correspondence relative to the Varney bequest of 1836 is in folders marked "Before 1866" and "1866-67" in the archives of the Episcopal Theological School deposited in the School Library.

D. THE EPISCOPAL THEOLOGICAL SCHOOL

1. *General history—printed sources*

Muller, James Arthur. *The Episcopal Theological School 1867-1943.* Cambridge, Mass., 1943. An accurate and comprehensive history. The book contains lists of trustees, deans, professors, instructors, and lecturers, a list of books written by members of the faculty, and a bibliography describing both manuscript and printed sources. Although the book is virtually without documentation in the footnotes, every statement and quotation (with the exception of quotations from Dr. Drown's talks taken down in note form by Professor Muller himself) has its source in manuscript or printed material still extant at the School. It is, therefore, completely reliable.

Gray, George Zabriskie. "The Episcopal Theological School in Cambridge, Mass.," in *The History of the American Episcopal Church 1587-1883* (ed. by W. S. Perry), Vol. II, Monograph VII. Boston, 1885.

Nash, Henry Sylvester. "The Episcopal Theological School," *The Churchman,* June 26, 1886.

Allen, A. V. G. "The Early Days of the Cambridge School," *The Church Militant,* Apr., 1904.

Lawrence, William. "The Cambridge School—Fifty Years Ago," *The Church Militant,* Nov., 1919.

———. "The Episcopal Theological School," *ibid.,* May, 1920.

———. *Beginnings of the Episcopal Theological School,* a supplement to *The Official Bulletin of the Episcopal Theological School,* June, 1927. This is substantially duplicated in Bishop Lawrence's "Recollections of Early Boston Churchmen," *Boston Evening Transcript,* July 2, 1927.

———. "Cambridge—1884-1893," in *Memories of a Happy Life.* Boston, 1926. A typewritten draft of this chapter, which was read at a clerical club, is in the "Notes by W. Lawrence, E. L. Stoddard, C. J. Palmer" folder in the ETS Archives.

———. *Seventy-Three Years of the Episcopal Theological School, Cambridge: A Narrative.* 1940.

Suter, J. W. "Historical Paper," prepared for the School's Fiftieth Anniversary, and printed in the *ETS Bulletin,* June, 1917. The same issue of the *Bulletin* also prints Bishop

Lawrence's sermon and speech on that occasion, together with the reminiscences of Dean Hodges, John G. Bacchus, and Reuben Kidner.

Dun, Angus. "The Episcopal Theological School—75 Years Old," *The Church Militant*, May, 1942.

2. *Biography—printed sources (listed chronologically according to subject)*

Lawrence, William. "Manton Eastburn," in *Trinity Church in the City of Boston, Massachusetts 1733-1933*. Boston, 1933.

————. "Three Bishops—Eastburn, Paddock, and Brooks," *The Church Militant*, Apr., 1922.

Potter, Henry Codman. *Reminiscences of Bishops and Archbishops*. New York and London, 1906. Chapter on Bishop Eastburn (pp. 49-70).

Day, Gardiner M. *The Biography of a Church; A Brief History of Christ Church, Cambridge, Massachusetts*. Cambridge, 1951. Chapter on Nicholas Hoppin (pp. 42-55).

Brooks, Phillips. *Alexander Hamilton Vinton, A Memorial Sermon*. Boston, 1881.

Moore, J. B. "A Sketch of the Life of Francis Wharton," in Wharton's *The Revolutionary Diplomatic Correspondence of the United States*. Washington, D. C., 1891.

Wharton, Helen A. *Francis Wharton, A Memoir*. Philadelphia, 1891. Contains reminiscences of Wharton at Cambridge by A. V. G. Allen and William Wilberforce Newton.

Huntington, Arria S. *Memoir and Letters of Frederic Dan Huntington, First Bishop of Central New York*. Boston, 1906.

Gray, George Zabriskie. *John S. Stone, D. D. A Memorial Sermon*. 1882.

Smith, W. G., and Smith, H. G. *Fidelis of the Cross: James Kent Stone*. New York, 1926.

Allen, A. V. G. "Elisha Mulford," *Christian Union*, March 11, 1886.

Lawrence, William. "Memoir of Amos Adams Lawrence," *Proceedings of the Massachusetts Historical Society*, Dec., 1897, and Jan., 1898.

————. *Life of Amos A. Lawrence; with Extracts from His Diary and Correspondence*. Cambridge, 1888.

————. *George Zabriskie Gray D.D.—A Memorial Sermon*. 1890.

————. *Life of Phillips Brooks*. New York and London, 1930. The bishop's personal memories of Brooks bring him to life with special vividness.

————. *Phillips Brooks: A Study*. Cambridge, 1903.

Allen, A. V. G. *Life and Letters of Phillips Brooks*. 2 vols. New York, 1900.

Albright, R. W. *Focus on Infinity: A Life of Phillips Brooks*. New York, 1961. Contains references to Brooks's friendship with B. T. Reed and Wharton.

Addison, Charles Morris. "Professor P. H. Steenstra," *The Church Militant*, Apr., 1902.

———. "Peter Henry Steenstra: A Memorial Sermon," in the *ETS Bulletin*, Nov., 1911.

Nash, Henry S. *Alexander Viets Griswold Allen: A Memorial Sermon*. Cambridge, 1910.

Slattery, Charles Lewis. *Alexander Viets Griswold Allen 1841-1908*. Quotes extensively from letters and journals no longer extant elsewhere.

———. *Certain American Faces: Sketches from Life*. New York, 1918. Essays on A. V. G. Allen, H. S. Nash, and Phillips Brooks.

Rogers, Arthur. "Professor Alexander V. G. Allen," *The Church Militant*, Apr., 1902.

Salomon, Richard G. "Laying the Foundations," *Kenyon Alumni Bulletin*, Apr.-June, 1962. On Allen's days at Kenyon.

Allen, A. V. G. "William Lawrence as Dean of the Cambridge School," *The Church Militant*, October, 1903.

Winthrop, Robert C., Jr. *Memoir of Robert M. Mason*. Cambridge, 1881.

———. *Memoir of Robert C. Winthrop*. Boston, 1897.

Winthrop, Robert C. *Reminiscences of Foreign Travel; a Fragment of Autobiography*. Boston, 1894.

Goodwin, Daniel. *In Memory of Robert Winthrop*. Chicago, 1894.

James, Henry. *Charles W. Eliot, President of Harvard University 1869-1909*. 2 vols. Boston, 1930.

Mann, A. *In Memory of Robert Treat Paine. A Sermon*. 1911.

Slattery, Charles Lewis. *Edward Lincoln Atkinson*. New York, 1904.

Nash, H. S. "His Memory is as Music" (a memoir of Augustine Heard Amory), *The Church Militant*, May, 1904.

Moulton, A. W. *A Memoir of Augustine Heard Amory*. Salem, 1909.

Drown, Edward S. *Henry Sylvester Nash: A Memorial Sermon*. 1912.

Drown, Paulina Cony Smith. "Henry Sylvester Nash," *ETS Bulletin*, Apr., 1950.

Hodges, Julia S. *George Hodges*. New York, 1926.

Muller, J. A. "George Hodges, Popularizer of Church History," *Historical Magazine of the Protestant Episcopal Church*, Mar., 1940.

Addison, Daniel Dulany. "George Hodges—Twenty-five Years Dean," *The Church Militant*, Feb., 1919.

Clark, D. W. "One Very Good Dean: George Hodges," *Methodist Review*, Oct., 1920.

Twombly, Clifford G. "The Halo of Dean Hodges: A Memorial Sermon," *ETS Bulletin*, Supplement No. 2, Nov., 1919.

Melish, J. H. *Franklin Spencer Spalding*. New York, 1917.

Robbins, Howard Chandler. *Charles Lewis Slattery*. New York and London, 1931.

Washburn, Henry Bradford. *Philip Mercer Rhinelander, Seventh Bishop of Pennsylvania*. New York, 1950.

———. "Maximilian Kellner: A Memorial Sermon," *ETS Bulletin*, Apr., 1936.

Nash, Norman Burdett. "Edward Staples Drown: A Memorial Sermon," *ETS Bulletin*, July, 1936.

Lawrence, Frederic Cunningham. "William Lawrence Wood: A Memorial Sermon," *ETS Bulletin*, July, 1936.

Sherrill, Henry Knox. *William Lawrence: Later Years of a Happy Life*. Cambridge, 1943.

———. *Among Friends: An Autobiography*. Boston and Toronto, 1962.

Washburn, H. B. "James Arthur Muller: A Memorial Sermon," *ETS Bulletin*, Apr., 1946.

Blackman, G. L. "Acta Paulinae: An Essay in Recollection," *ETS Bulletin*, Sept., 1964. A memoir of Mrs. Drown.

Brief memorial notices have appeared in the *ETS Bulletin* as follows:

"Adelaide Teague Case" (July, 1948)

"James Thayer Addison" (by Charles L. Taylor, Jr. Apr., 1953)

"Paulina Cony Drown" (by David W. Norton, Jr. July, 1959)

"Henry Bradford Washburn" (Memorial Pamphlet edited by Gabriel Farrell. 1962)

"Norman Burdett Nash" (by Henry Knox Sherrill. Jan., 1963)

"Charles Edward Batten" (Sept., 1963)

"Raymond Wolf Albright" (by Lloyd G. Patterson. Sept., 1965)

In addition to the books, articles, or sermons listed above, which are straightforwardly biographical in theme, two volumes of *festschriften* contain significant material. *Munera Studiosa*, edited by Massey Hamilton Shepherd, Jr., and Sherman Elbridge Johnson, and published in Cambridge in 1946 to honor "the Reverend William Henry Paine Hatch, Ph.D., D.Theol., Edmund Swett Rousmaniere Professor of the Literature and Interpretation of the New Testament in the Episcopal Theological School, on the occasion of his seventieth birthday," includes, besides a bibliography of Dr. Hatch's writings up to that time, a brief but very perceptive appreciation of Dr. Hatch by Dean Washburn. "Horizons of Theological Education: Essays in Honor of Charles L. Taylor," edited by John B. Coburn, Walter D. Wagoner, and Jesse H. Ziegler in the Summer, 1966, edition of *Theological Education* (Volume II, No. 4) includes a brief *curriculum vitae*, and three chapters of interest to future historians of the School: "Charles

Taylor as Pastor's Teacher," by Pitt S. Willand, "Charles Taylor as Dean," by James Garfield, and "Curriculum Revision at the Episcopal Theological School and some Dynamics of its Acceptance," by William J. Wolf.

3. *School publications*

Annual *Catalogue,* 1868 to present.

Official Bulletin (and Supplements), 1909 to present.

Annual letters *To the Friends of the Episcopal Theological School* (and Supplements). The first letter issued in 1929.

Indenture (of Benjamin Tyler Reed). 1867.

Indentures (of Benjamin Tyler Reed and Robert Means Mason). 1868.

Consecration of St. John's Memorial Chapel. 1870.

A Statement of the Trustees of the Episcopal Theological School, Cambridge, Mass. to which is appended the Correspondence between them and Mr. Nathan Matthews, of Boston. Cambridge, 1873. The frontispiece is an engraving of the preliminary design of buildings for the Brattle Street site by Ware and Van Brunt. The text includes the 1867 Indenture, the Charter, a synopsis of the Course of Study, a report on the progress of the buildings, the purchase of land, the development of the library, and a list of early benefactors of the School.

Act of Incorporation and By-Laws. Boston, 1874.

Summary of the Records of the Trustees. Boston, 1887. Précis of trustees minutes, Jan. 22, 1867—Mar. 29, 1887, with index.

Charter and By-Laws. 1904.

Fundamental Articles, Charter, By-Laws, and Officers. 1911.

Of the School in Cambridge (Endowment Campaign booklet). 1922.

4. *Books, articles, or printed sermons by members of the faculty which are referred to in the text (printed material already cited is not repeated here):*

Wharton, Francis. *A Willing Reunion Not Impossible.* Boston, 1863.

———. "Church Parties as Apologists," *Bibliotheca Sacra,* July, 1880.

———. "Certain Legal Analogies," *Bibliotheca Sacra,* Apr., 1883.

———. *Involuntary Confession: A Monograph.* Philadelphia, 1860.

———. "Romanticism in its Relations to Rome," *Bibliotheca Sacra,* July, 1871.

Steenstra, Peter Henry. *The Being of God as Unity and Trinity.* Boston and New York, 1896.

Mulford, Elisha. *The Nation: the Foundations of Civil Or-*

der and Political Life in the United States. Boston, 1870. (New ed. 1894.)

——. The Republic of God: An Institute of Theology. Boston, 1881. (5th edition 1882.)

Allen, Alexander Viets Griswold. The Continuity of Christian Thought. Boston, 1884. (New and revised edition, 1884. Another edition, 1930.)

——. Christian Institutions. Edinburgh, 1898.

——. Religious Progress. Boston and New York, 1894.

——. Freedom in the Church, or The Doctrine of Christ as the Lord hath Commanded, and as the Church hath Received the same according to the Commandments of God. New York, 1907.

Washburn, Henry Bradford. Men of Conviction. New York and London, 1931. An earlier draft of the autobiographical first chapter is printed in the ETS Bulletin, Apr., 1927, under the title: "The Practical Value of Religious Biography."

——. The Religious Motive in Philanthropy: Studies in Biography. Philadelphia, 1931.

Nash, Henry Sylvester. Ethics and Revelation. New York, 1899.

——. "The Belief in Democracy and Justification by Faith" in Slocum Lectures 1903-1904.

——. Genesis of the Social Conscience: The Relation between the Establishment of Christianity in Europe and the Social Question. New York, 1902.

——. The History of the Higher Criticism of the New Testament, being the History of the Process whereby the Word of God has won the Right to be Understood. New York, 1900. (New edition, 1906.)

——. The Atoning Life. New York, 1908. (Reprinted, 1950.)

——. Prayers and Meditations, ed. by C. L. Slattery. New York, 1915. (Printed posthumously. Reprinted, 1916. Revised and enlarged edition edited by J. W. Suter and printed 1958.)

Drown, Edward S. The Apostles' Creed To-day. New York, 1917.

——. The Creative Christ: A Study of the Incarnation in Terms of Modern Thought. New York, 1922.

Dun, Angus. "The Person of Christ in the Thought of To-day: The Creeds," Honest Liberty in the Church. New York, 1924.

Hodges, George. The Heresy of Cain. New York, 1914.

The Rev. Drs. Muller, Washburn, Hatch, Dun, McComb, Nash, and Addison. Creeds and Loyalty: Essays on the History, Interpretation, and Use of the Creeds. New York, 1924. The germ of this book was "The Faith and the Creeds," a letter from the faculty to the alumni in the *ETS Bulletin*, Jan., 1924.

5. *Manuscripts, typescripts, and scrapbooks in the School archives*

The basic source is a large collection of letters sorted and filed chronologically by Professor Muller in a series of folders covering the years between 1866 (and before) and 1942. The collection is especially rich in letters for the period between 1866 and 1919. After that the folders become steadily skimpier. The letters are from and to trustees, deans, professors, alumni, and prospective benefactors. Interspersed are reports from the visitors and from the faculty in the mid-1880's. The correspondence stems from the following sources:

1. Files of the president of the Board of Trustees (E. S. Rand was particularly meticulous in preserving significant letters and notes).

2. Files of the dean.

3. Copies of extracts from personal letters written by Benjamin Tyler Reed.

4. Copies or originals of letters from John Seely Stone to Heman Dyer, Charles Wyntrop, and other Stone papers collected by Dr. A. V. G. Allen when he contemplated writing a life of Dean Stone.

5. Personal letters to Dr. Allen from Wharton, Gray, and Steenstra collected by Dr. Allen when gathering material for a history of the School.

6. A few letters to Bishop William Lawrence containing reminiscences of alumni—collected when Bishop Lawrence was preparing a history of the School.

The early files also contain reports and letters referred to in the trustees minutes for 1867.

In addition, there are the following:

Trustees minutes.

Visitors minutes.

Faculty minutes. Reports of faculty committees are pasted into the Faculty Meeting Records until 1920. Thereafter the minutes record *précis* only, and sometimes simply record that "a Report" was presented. After 1935, the minutes become increasingly uninformative.

Minutes of student societies.

Faculty reports to trustees (for the years 1885-96, 1898-1930). These are also in print at the end of the *Catalogue* for the ensuing academic year. The Dean's Annual Report to the Trustees is filed with the trustees minutes.

Treasurers' reports.

A. V. G. Allen's notes on the School's history (special folder).

A. V. G. Allen's "Elisha Mulford: A Memorial Sermon" (MS. bound).

Stenographic report of the Alumni Banquet in honor of the School's Fortieth Anniversary, June 4, 1907. (A full transcript of speeches by H. B. Washburn (toastmaster), Dean Hodges, Bishop Lawrence, P. H. Steenstra, A. V. G. Allen, and others.)

A volume in journal form of Dean Hodges's notes on School affairs, 1901-1909. Candid and humorous.

A volume in journal form of Dean Hodges's notes on "Precedents and Customs"—a reminder to himself of administrative deadlines throughout the academic year. 1904-1914.

Scrapbook of clippings on the election of Bishop Paddock and the Matthews offer of $100,000 to the School in 1873.

Scrapbook of clippings, programs, and notices concerning Dean Gray, Dean Lawrence, and the School, 1884-1893, collected by Bishop Lawrence.

Envelope containing clippings and pamphlets on "the Massachusetts Case" and the Pastoral Letter, 1894, collected by Dean Hodges.

Dean Hodges's journal (a scrapbook with diary entries as well). 33 volumes. 1881-1907.

Bishop Lawrence's notes of lectures in rhetoric, homiletics, and theology at Andover Theological Seminary in 1871-72.

Notes of lectures at the School as follows:

A. V. G. Allen's lectures on the English and German Reformation (by F. L. Palmer in 1891).

A. V. G. Allen's lectures in church history (taken by F. L. Palmer in the margin and flyleaves of a 3 vol. set of Kurtz's *Church History* in 1890).

H. S. Nash's lectures on the Fourth Gospel (taken in semi-shorthand by A. H. Palmer in 1905).

H. S. Nash's lectures on Romans (taken in semi-shorthand by T. R. Ludlow in 1909-10 under the title "The problem of human unity").

E. S. Drown's lectures in apologetics (taken in semi-shorthand by A. H. Kennedy in 1904-05).

G. Hodges's lectures on the Book of Common Prayer (MS. notes and pamphlets by himself).

The following honors theses by ETS seniors are also helpful:

Wilder, Q. M. "Henry Sylvester Nash." Based in part on conversations with friends and relatives now dead.

Goodwin, A. M. "The Social Gospel of George Hodges."

Patterson, D. D. "Richard Henry Dana III and Notes about his 40 Years of Trusteeship at E.T.S."

Selective Index of Names and Topics

Seminary textbooks cited only once in the text are not included here. They may be found in the book lists referred to under the heading "Textbooks."